DEBATES IN
INTERNATIONAL RELATIONS

Bradley A. Thayer
Missouri State University

Nuray V. Ibryamova
Rhodes College

D0162035

Longman
New York   San Francisco   Boston
London   Toronto   Sydney   Tokyo   Singapore   Madrid
Mexico City   Munich   Paris   Cape Town   Hong Kong   Montreal

Acquisitions Editor: Vikram Mukhija
Marketing Manager: Lindsey Prudhomme
Production Manager: Savoula Amanatidis
Project Coordination, Text Design, and Electronic Page Makeup: Electronic
    Publishing Services Inc., NYC
Cover Design Manager: John Callahan
Cover Designer: Base Art Co.
Senior Manufacturing Buyer: Alfred C. Dorsey
Printer and Binder: R. R. Donnelley and Sons Company—Harrisonburg
Cover Printer: R. R. Donnelley and Sons Company—Harrisonburg

For permission to use copyrighted material, grateful acknowledgment is made to the
copyright holders on p. 320, which are hereby made part of this copyright page.

Library of Congress Cataloging-in-Publication Data
Thayer, Bradley A.
    Debates in international relations / Bradley A. Thayer and Nuray V. Ibryamova.
        p.   cm.
    Includes bibliographical references.
    ISBN 978-0-205-56812-3
1. International relations.   I. Ibryamova, Nuray V.   II. Title.
    JZ1242.T42 2010
    327–dc22   2008053877

Longman
is an imprint of

www.pearsonhighered.com
1 2 3 4 5 6 7 8 9 10—DOH—12 11 10 09
ISBN-13: 978-0-205-56812-3
ISBN-10:   0-205-56812-2

For my exceptional undergraduate professors—
Julia Annas, Joel Feinberg, Keith Lehrer,
Stanley Reynolds, Michael Sullivan, Thomas Volgy,
Allen Whiting, and Clifton Wilson—
with heartfelt thanks for your help
along the path of understanding.

—*Bradley A. Thayer*

To my parents,
Bedriye and Vasfi Çatalkaya

—*Nuray V. Ibryamova*

BRIEF CONTENTS

PART IV
INTERNATIONAL ORGANIZATION   224

DETAILED CONTENTS

PREFACE

The United States is at a unique time and place in international politics. It is the world's dominant power and will remain so for the foreseeable future. The United States has the potential to influence global issues and the ability to shape the outcome of international relations. At the same time, its military and economic might does not make it immune to forces around the world that frequently have a direct impact on American foreign and domestic policies. In an age of globalization, when technology and communications have helped collapse time and space, domestic and foreign policies are becoming harder to differentiate, and the international and local are increasingly intertwined. Accordingly, *Debates in International Relations* addresses not only America's choices, but global choices as well.

In the early twenty-first century, we live in a world where traditional international relations concerns must be supplemented by discussions of new forces and issues. The war on terror is the best example of this need. It is unlike any other—the enemy is no longer a state but individuals and organizations. The war on terror involves law enforcement as much as the military, and its end is anything but clearly defined. Changes like this are no less significant in other areas of international relations. For example, the global economic crisis, call centers in Bangalore, the rapid spread of avian flu, and worldwide support for Barack Obama in the 2008 election are but only a few examples of the profound impact of globalization on our daily lives.

These intersections introduce novel complications and problems for all countries, and how we respond to these will have a defining impact on the world in which we live. This debate-style reader helps students understand many of the fundamental issues in international relations that have and will continue to occupy a central place in the years to come. It also presents students with the choices American policymakers frequently face and the potential impact of these policies on world politics as well as on populations throughout the world. Finally, this reader—in some cases and as appropriate—compares these choices to the policy alternatives that other countries have adopted.

FEATURES

The topics of debate selected for *Debates in International Relations* address some of the fundamentals of the discipline of international relations such as anarchy, as well as pressing issues of the day, including Iraq and the war on terror. These are the concepts and topics that students must understand

and examine critically in each of the four major sections of the discipline: international approaches, international security, international political economy, and international organization.

To advance and facilitate learning, the readings in each chapter are framed as a debate. Each of the readings is well-argued, concise, and addresses the key issues on both sides of the argument. This pedagogical format is particularly useful for three reasons. First, it provides the readers with the salient values and principles present on both sides, as well as the costs and rewards the particular choice entails. This reader does not adjudicate issues, but rather, it illuminates the benefits and consequences of each position. Readers are encouraged to choose what they value more and to understand fully what they gain or lose to achieve their desired choice. Students will learn that the iron law of Economics 101—you do not get anything for free, every choice has a cost—applies to international politics as well.

Second, while the readings supply sharply juxtaposed and tightly argued opposing arguments, we also provide a framework of analysis in the introduction of each section—we identify valid points made by each author, and provide additional questions and implications to consider—to help the students develop critical thinking skills by guiding them through the arguments. Additionally, the readings and our introduction will prompt further discussion of the subject and spark student interest. By participating in these debates and discussions, students are better able to understand what is at stake for them as individuals, for their country, and the world.

Finally, by posing these important issues as debates, the study of international relations is made more relevant and thus more exciting. What students learn they can apply immediately to understand in much more detail the news that night, items in the next day's newspaper, their other classes, or in debates with their peers or family. We remember how exciting it was as undergraduates to learn about an important issue and to think through its implications. Most often, we were prompted to do so by a question asked by a professor or in the readings. We could not wait to discuss the issue with our friends and to pontificate about its implications for the world and our lives. We remember that excitement and seek to encourage that spirit in a new generation of students.

The first part, "Perspectives on International Relations," addresses key questions in the discipline, such as the causes of state behavior (Chapter 1), the role of values on foreign policy (Chapter 2), democratic peace (Chapter 3), a broad but critical discussion of America's grand strategy (Chapter 4), and the benefits and risks associated with globalization (Chapter 5).

The second part introduces issues of international security that receive daily media coverage, including whether Western ideas have triumphed or whether we face a clash of civilizations (Chapter 6), the Iraq war (Chapter 7),

President Bush's war on terror (Chapter 8), and Iran's quest for nuclear weapons (Chapter 11). The policies adopted by the government directly impact the lives of ordinary Americans, whether it is through someone's family member or a friend deploying in Iraq, following the screening measures at our nation's airports, or wondering how much gasoline will cost. The section also focuses on two items that are part of policymakers' agenda—how to address the rise of China (Chapter 9) and how to make sure that the world's growing nuclear arsenal does not fall into the wrong hands (Chapter 10).

The third part considers themes of international political economy. The topics include a discussion on the importance and possible solutions to energy security (Chapter 12), a debate on the benefits of free trade (Chapter 13), the growing discontent with international financial institutions (Chapter 14), and strategies for addressing global poverty (Chapter 15).

Finally, the last part on international organization evaluates the role and significance of intergovernmental and non-governmental organizations in international relations. It begins by looking at the functions and growing influence of NGOs in today's political climate and answers questions on the role of the state in the advent of globalization (Chapter 16). The section also looks at the region with the most advanced political and economic integration in the world—the European Union—and discusses one of the most hotly debated challenges it faces: whether to admit Turkey, a large and relatively poor Muslim country, as a member (Chapter 17). It also examines the innovation of the International Criminal Court and U.S. absence from this new international body (Chapter 18), as well as the merits of humanitarian intervention against the cornerstone of international law—state sovereignty (Chapter 19). The section ends with an overview of one of the most pressing global problems—climate change—and looks at the dilemmas posed by it to developed and developing countries alike (Chapter 20).

SUPPLEMENTS

Pearson Longman is pleased to offer several resources to qualified adopters of *Debates in International Relations* and their students that will make teaching and learning from this book even more effective and enjoyable.

For Instructors

MyPoliSciKit Video Case Studies for International Relations and Comparative Politics   Featuring video from major news sources and providing reporting and insight on recent world affairs, this DVD series helps instructors integrate current events into their courses by letting them use the clips as lecture launchers or discussion starters.

For Students

Longman Atlas of World Issues (0-321-22465-5)   Introduced and selected by Robert J. Art of Brandeis University and excerpted from the acclaimed Penguin Atlas Series, the *Longman Atlas of World Issues* is designed to help students understand the geography and major issues facing the world today, such as terrorism, debt, and HIV/AIDS. These thematic, full-color maps examine forces shaping politics today at a global level. Explanatory information accompanies each map to help students better grasp the concepts being shown and how they affect our world today. Available at no additional charge when packaged with this book.

The New Signet World Atlas (0-451-19732-1)   From Penguin USA, this pocket-sized yet detailed reference features 96 pages of full-color maps plus statistics, key data, and much more. Available at a discount when packaged with this book.

The Penguin Dictionary of International Relations (0-140-51397-3)   This indispensable reference by Graham Evans and Jeffrey Newnham includes hundreds of cross-referenced entries on the enduring and emerging theories, concepts, and events that are shaping the academic discipline of international relations and today's world politics. Available at a discount when packaged with this book.

Research and Writing in International Relations (0-321-27766-X)   Written by Laura Roselle and Sharon Spray of Elon University, this brief and affordable guide provides the basic step-by-step process and essential resources that are needed to write political science papers that go beyond simple description and into more systematic and sophisticated inquiry. This text focuses on the key areas in which students need the most help: finding a topic, developing a question, reviewing literature, designing research, analyzing findings, and last, actually writing the paper. Available at a discount when packaged with this book.

Study Cards for International Relations (0-321-29231-6)   Packed with useful information, Allyn & Bacon/Longman's Study Cards make studying easier, more efficient, and more enjoyable. Course information is distilled down to the basics, helping students quickly master the fundamentals, review a subject for understanding, or prepare for an exam. Because they are laminated for durability, students can keep these Study Cards for years to come and pull them out whenever they need a quick review. Available at no additional charge when packaged with this book.

Careers in Political Science (0-321-11337-3)   Offering insider advice and practical tips on how to make the most of a political science degree, this booklet by Joel Clark of George Mason University shows students the tremendous potential such a degree offers and guides them through: deciding whether political science is right for them; the different career options available; job requirements and skill sets; how to apply, interview, and compete for jobs after graduation; and much more. Available at a discount when packaged with this book.

ACKNOWLEDGMENTS

We thank our editor at Pearson Longman, Vikram Mukhija, for his strong support of this project and for guiding it through fair and foul weather. We also thank Elizabeth Daniel, Toni Magyar, Savoula Amanatidis, Nancy Danahy, Lindsey Prudhomme, Jessica Muraviov, and many others at Pearson Longman for their great assistance in all stages of this project. This reader went through several rounds of external reviews and so numerous reviewers have taken the time to comment on this project. We would like to thank them for their insightful observations and suggestions: Ali Alootalebi, University of Wisconsin, Eau Claire; Katherine Barbieri, University of South Carolina; Bethany Barratt, Roosevelt University; Amanda Bigelow, Illinois Valley Community College; Robert Blanton, University of Memphis; Michaelene Cox, Illinois State University; Timothy Lynn Elliot, Brigham Young University; Michael Grossman, Mount Union College; Patrick James, University of South Carolina; David K. Jesuit, Central Michigan University; Seung-Ho Joo, University of Minnesota, Morris; Guoli Liu, College of Charleston; Karl K. Schonberg, St. Lawrence University; Philip Schrodt, University of Kentucky; Stephen Wegren, Southern Methodist University; and Pamela Zeiser, University of North Florida.

Bradley A. Thayer
Nuray V. Ibryamova

PART I
PERSPECTIVES ON INTERNATIONAL RELATIONS

In the examination of cross-border events and phenomena, the discipline of international relations focuses on the importance of key issues that help explain topics under discussion. Different theoretical paradigms frequently place overwhelming emphasis on different key variables and assumptions that play a prominent role in the explanation, predictions, and policy prescriptions they offer. One such key fundamental is the notion of anarchy in the international system as a determining factor of state behavior. Others include security, the role of ideas and values in international relations, grand strategic options that countries face, and the defining characteristic of our age—globalization.

Chapter 1 looks at a fundamental problem of international relations theory: anarchy. Kenneth Waltz, the father of structural realism, argues that anarchy is the ordering principle of the international system and the determining force of international politics. Social constructivist Alexander Wendt, on the other hand, maintains that structure and agency play an equally prominent role. As such, in the course of their interaction with each other, states create their own intersubjective understandings, including of each other, which inform their relationships.

Chapter 2 examines one of the key issues for international relations: the extent to which our values should influence our foreign policies. The discussion departs from the realist notion in international relations theory whereby national interests, rather than morality, should determine a nation's approach to international events. In a true realist fashion, George Kennan insists that foreign policy should be governed by a country's national interests, and enumerates the problems that the introduction of morality would bring to this realm. In contrast, Leslie Gelb and Justine Rosenthal point out that values have always played a role in U.S. foreign policy and argue that the trend has only intensified in the last two decades. Despite some contradictory developments, ultimately, the United States benefits from the presence of moral arguments in the making of foreign policy.

The next chapter (Chapter 3) discusses one of the most prominent theories in the field of international relations: democratic peace. In his seminal piece on liberalism and peace, Michael Doyle argues that liberal states are indeed pacifist and do not fight one another, but they remain in a state of war against non-liberal states. Edward Mansfield and Jack Snyder, on the other hand, while not denying the benefits of democracy, warn that societies that are in the process of democratization are some of the most volatile ones. Hence, they argue, we should encourage democracy-building, but transitions must be carefully managed.

Chapter 4 discusses the choices that practitioners of U.S. foreign policy have in deciding the global grand strategy of the country, which will determine America's position in the world and its relations with the rest of the world. The first reading, by Bradley A. Thayer, advocates a strategy of primacy, where the United States works to maintain its hegemony over world affairs. The practical results of this strategy are said to be increased security for the United States and its allies and continued economic dominance. Christopher Layne, on the other hand, submits that the primacy cannot last very long and in fact weakens the country. The United States should consider a strategy of retrenchment from its position of global hegemony and instead should focus on strengthening itself.

Chapter 5 discusses the benefits and problems created by globalization. Specifically, it looks at counterarguments by Guy Sorman and Joseph Stiglitz on the impact of globalization on economic growth, democracy, global equity, local culture, and state sovereignty. While Sorman ardently believes in the positive contributions of globalization, Stiglitz argues that more can be done to harness the forces of globalization for a greater number of people.

CHAPTER 1 ANARCHY *v.* ORDER

Anarchy as the Cause of Permanent Insecurity in International Relations

Advocate: Kenneth N. Waltz

Source: "The Anarchic Structure of World Politics," *Theory of International Politics* (New York: McGraw-Hill, 1979), excerpt.

Anarchy Does Not Have to Cause Insecurity in International Relations

Advocate: Alexander Wendt

Source: "Anarchy Is What States Make of It: The Social Construction of Power Politics," *International Organization*, vol. 46, no. 2 (1992), pp. 391–425, excerpt.

Anarchy is a fundamental concept in the discipline of international relations. It literally means "no government," or the "absence of government," so it denotes the lack of an overarching authority in the international system of states. In other words, contrary to the hierarchy of power that exists in domestic politics, such as local (for example, Chicago), state (Illinois), and federal (United States) governments, in international politics there is no government, no higher power than the sovereign state. There is no world government. This central fact defines the discipline of international politics—the study of politics where there is no government. Contrast that with the study of domestic politics, such as American politics, which is the study of politics in hierarchy. Anarchy is a concept that has been widely accepted by the majority of theoretical approaches in the discipline, such as neorealism and neoliberalism. The assumption that the state system is anarchical has very important implications for the behavior of the states: it impacts their propensity to wage war as well as to cooperate.

THE NEOREALIST VIEW

The concept of anarchy is a defining feature of the neorealist view of the world. According to Kenneth Waltz, the father of structural realism, also called *neorealism,* the anarchical structure of the international system of states makes it one of self-help, where each state's primary concern is security and where states must provide for their own security through their own means—their military power and their alliances. The consequences of the anarchical self-help system are a high degree of uncertainty and mistrust among states. They cannot fully

4

rely on each other for protection, and there is no higher governing authority, so states can wholly depend on themselves only for their own defense.

States that have the best chances of providing for their security, and achieving their national interests, are the most powerful ones. That means that states must accumulate power, both military and economic, if they are to survive. The efforts of one state to increase its power—even if it is done for defensive purposes—make its neighbors fearful. The neighboring states then also work to enhance their security, thereby increasing the level of insecurity in the system as a whole. This phenomenon is known as the *security dilemma*—as a result of one state arming, all arm, and so tragically they are better armed, but no more secure.

The effects of anarchy are also evident in the ability of states to cooperate in international regimes or organizations. As Waltz and other neorealists point out, states are interested not only in how much they gain from a given cooperative endeavor, but also how much other states—maybe even their rivals—will gain. Because gains contribute to increasing each state's power, the relative gains that each state would receive make cooperation difficult to achieve because states will fear that other states are gaining more in relative terms through cooperation.

In sum, Waltz and his fellow neorealists argue that the anarchical structure of the international system determines how states behave in international politics.

THE CONSTRUCTIVIST VIEW

A core concept of constructivism is the social construction of reality. Although there are different variants of this social theory, most believe that agency and structure co-constitute each other. In plain language, this means that the structure of the international system and states shape each other. In contrast to Waltz's view, then, constructivists do not give precedence to anarchy over the agency of the states.

Wendt's central claim is that anarchy in the international system does not automatically lead to self-help and power politics; the security dilemma does not have to be the *sine qua non* of anarchy. Instead, what defines the structures that organize our actions are collective meanings. Actors—whether states or humans—acquire their identity and interests by participating in such collective meanings. However, identities and interests are relational and subject to change.

Continued interaction between two states leads to both of them having intersubjective knowledge: each state has a certain perception of the other. This knowledge influences how these two states behave toward each other. Depending on the shared meaning these two states have of each other, the security dilemma is not the predetermined outcome of their relationship. For example, both Iran and Great Britain have missiles, but the United States is concerned about Iranian missiles and not about British missiles due to the intersubjective knowledge shared by the United States and Great Britain. Hence, the intersubjective knowledge that actors gain in their interaction creates collective meanings that inform their identities and interests. This is a path to the creation of order in international politics.

POINTS TO PONDER

1. According to Waltz, how does structure influence the nature of international politics?
2. According to Waltz, what are the causes of war?
3. What does Wendt mean by "Anarchy is what states make of it"?
4. According to constructivists, how do identities and interests inform the behavior of states?

Kenneth N. Waltz
The Anarchic Structure of World Politics

Political Structures

To mark international-political systems off from other international systems, and to distinguish systems-level from unit-level forces, requires showing how political structures are generated and how they affect, and are affected by, the units of the system. How can we conceive of international politics as a distinct system? What is it that intervenes between interacting units and the results that their acts and interactions produce? To answer these questions, this chapter first examines the concept of social structure and then defines structure as a concept appropriate for national and for international politics.

A system is composed of a structure and of interacting units. The structure is the system-wide component that makes it possible to think of the system as a whole. The problem is . . . to contrive a definition of structure free of the attributes and the interactions of units. Definitions of structure must leave aside, or abstract from, the characteristics of units, their behavior, and their interactions. Why must those obviously important matters be omitted? They must be omitted so that we can distinguish between variables at the level of the units and variables at the level of the system. The problem is to develop theoretically useful concepts to replace the vague and varying systemic notions that are customarily employed—notions such as environment, situation, context, and milieu. Structure is a useful concept if it gives clear and fixed meaning to such vague and varying terms. . . .

The concept of structure is based on the fact that units differently juxtaposed and combined behave differently and in interacting produce different outcomes. I first want to show how internal political structure can be defined. In a book on international-political theory, domestic political structure has to be examined in order to draw a distinction between expectations about behavior and outcomes in the internal and external realms. Moreover, considering domestic political structure now will make the elusive international-political structure easier to catch later on.

Structure defines the arrangement, or the ordering, of the parts of a system. Structure is not a collection of political institutions but rather the arrangement of them. How is the arrangement defined? The constitution of a state describes some parts of the arrangement, but political structures as they develop are not identical with formal constitutions. In defining structures, the first question to answer is this: What is the principle by which the parts are arranged?

Domestic politics is hierarchically ordered. The units—institutions and agencies—stand vis-à-vis each other in relations of super- and subordination. The ordering principle of a system gives the first, and basic, bit of information about how the parts of a realm are related to each other. In a polity the hierarchy of offices is by no means completely articulated, nor are all ambiguities about relations of super- and subordination removed. Nevertheless, political actors are formally differentiated according to the degrees of their authority, and their distinct functions are specified. By "specified" I do not mean that the law of the land fully describes the duties that different agencies perform, but only that broad agreement prevails on the tasks that various parts of a government are to undertake and on the extent of the power they legitimately wield. Thus Congress supplies the military forces; the President commands them. Congress makes the laws; the executive branch enforces them; agencies administer laws; judges interpret them. Such specification of roles and differentiation of functions is found in any state, the more fully so as the state is more highly developed. The specification of functions of formally differentiated parts gives the second bit of structural information. This second part of the definition adds some content to the structure, but only enough to say more fully how the units stand in relation to one another. The roles and the functions of the British Prime Minister and Parliament, for example, differ from those of the American President and Congress. When offices are juxtaposed and functions are combined in different ways, different behaviors and outcomes result, as I shall shortly show.

A domestic political structure is thus defined: first, according to the principle by which it is ordered; second, by specification of the functions of formally differentiated units; and third, by the distribution of capabilities across those units. Structure is a highly abstract notion, but the definition of structure does not abstract from everything. To do so would be to leave everything aside and to include nothing at all. The three-part definition of structure includes only what is required to show how the units of the system are positioned or arranged. Everything else is omitted. Concern for tradition and culture, analysis of the character and personality of political actors, consideration of the conflictive and accommodative processes of politics, description of the making and execution of policy—all such matters are left aside. Their omission does not imply their unimportance. They are omitted because we want to figure out the expected effects of structure on process and of process on structure. That can be done only if structure and process are distinctly defined.

I defined domestic political structures first by the principle according to which they are organized or ordered, second by the differentiation of units and the specification of their functions, and third by the distribution of capabilities across units. Let us see how the three terms of the definition apply to international politics.

1. Ordering Principles

Structural questions are questions about the arrangement of the parts of a system. The parts of domestic political systems stand in relations of super- and subordination. Some are entitled to command; others are required to obey. Domestic systems are centralized and hierarchic. The parts of international-political systems stand in relations of coordination. Formally, each is the equal of all the others. None is entitled to command; none is required to obey. International systems are decentralized and anarchic. The ordering principles of the two structures are distinctly different, indeed, contrary to each other. Domestic political structures have governmental institutions and offices as their concrete counterparts. International politics, in contrast, has been called "politics in the absence of government."[1] International organizations do exist, and in ever-growing numbers. Supranational agents able to act effectively, however, either themselves acquire some of the attributes and capabilities of states, as did the medieval papacy in the era of Innocent III, or they soon reveal their inability to act in important ways except with the support, or at least the acquiescence, of the principal states concerned with the matters at hand. Whatever elements of authority emerge internationally are barely once removed from the capability that provides the foundation for the appearance of those elements. Authority quickly reduces to a particular expression of capability. In the absence of agents with system-wide authority, formal relations of super- and subordination fail to develop.

The first term of a structural definition states the principle by which the system is ordered. Structure is an organizational concept. The prominent characteristic of international politics, however, seems to be the lack of order and of organization. How can one think of international politics as being any kind of an order at all? The anarchy of politics internationally is often referred to. If structure is an organizational concept, the terms "structure" and "anarchy" seem to be in contradiction. If international politics is "politics in the absence of government," what are we in the presence of? In looking for international structure, one is brought face to face with the invisible, an uncomfortable position to be in. . . .

International-political systems, like economic markets, are formed by the co-action of self-regarding units. International structures are defined in terms of the primary political units of an era, be they city states, empires, or nations. Structures emerge from the coexistence of states. No state intends to participate in the formation of a structure by which it and others will be constrained. International-political systems, like economic markets, are individualist in origin, spontaneously generated, and unintended. In both systems, structures are formed by the coaction of their units. Whether those units live, prosper, or die depends on their own efforts. Both systems are formed and maintained on a principle of self-help that applies to the units. . . .

Actors may perceive the structure that constrains them and understand how it serves to reward some kinds of behavior and to penalize others. But then again they either may not see it or, seeing it, may for any of many reasons fail to conform their actions to the patterns that are most often rewarded and least often punished. To say that "the structure selects" means simply that those who conform to accepted and successful practices more often rise to the top and are likelier to stay there. The game one has to win is defined by the structure that determines the kind of player who is likely to prosper. . . .

2. The Character of the Units

The second term in the definition of domestic political structure specifies the functions performed by differentiated units. Hierarchy entails relations of super- and subordination among a system's parts, and that implies their differentiation. In defining domestic political structure the second term, like the first and third, is needed because each term points to a possible source of structural variation. The states that are the units of international-political systems are not formally differentiated by the functions they perform. Anarchy entails relations of coordination among a system's units, and that implies their sameness. The second term is not needed in defining international-political structure, because, so long as anarchy endures, states remain like units. International structures vary only through a change of organizing principle or, failing that, through variations in the capabilities of units. . . .

States vary widely in size, wealth, power, and form. And yet variations in these and in other respects are variations among like units. In what way are they like units? How can they be placed in a single category? States are alike in the tasks that they face, though not in their abilities to perform them. The differences are of capability, not of function. States perform or try to perform tasks, most of which are common to all of them; the ends they aspire to are similar. Each state duplicates the activities of other states at least to a considerable extent. Each state has its agencies for making, executing, and interpreting laws and regulations, for raising revenues, and for defending itself. Each state supplies out of its own resources and by its own means most of the food, clothing, housing, transportation, and amenities consumed and used by its citizens. All states, except the smallest ones, do much more of their business at home than abroad. One has to be impressed with the functional similarity of states and, now more than ever before, with the similar lines their development follows. From the rich to the poor states, from the old to the new ones, nearly all of them take a larger hand in matters of economic regulation, of education, health, and housing, of culture and the arts, and so on almost endlessly. The increase of the activities of states is a strong and strikingly uniform international trend. The functions of states are similar, and distinctions among them arise principally from their varied capabilities. International politics consists of like units duplicating one another's activities.

3. The Distribution of Capabilities

The parts of a hierarchic system are related to one another in ways that are determined both by their functional differentiation and by the extent of their capabilities. The units of an anarchic system are functionally undifferentiated. The units of such an order are then distinguished primarily by their greater or lesser capabilities for performing similar tasks. This states formally what students of international politics have long noticed. The great powers of an era have always been marked off from others by practitioners and theorists alike. Students of national government make such distinctions as that between parliamentary and presidential systems; governmental systems differ in form. Students of international politics make distinctions between international-political systems only according to the number of their great powers. The structure of a system changes with changes in the distribution of capabilities across the system's units. And changes in structure change expectations about how the units of the system will behave and about the outcomes their interactions will produce. Domestically, the differentiated parts of a system may perform similar tasks. We know from observing the American government that executives sometimes legislate and legislatures sometimes execute. Internationally, like units sometimes perform different tasks. . . .

In defining international-political structures we take states with whatever traditions, habits, objectives, desires, and forms of government they may have. We do not ask whether states are revolutionary or legitimate, authoritarian or democratic, ideological or pragmatic. We abstract from every attribute of states except their capabilities. Nor in thinking about structure do we ask about the relations of states—their feelings of friendship and hostility, their diplomatic exchanges, the alliances they form, and the extent of the contacts and exchanges among them. We ask what range of expectations arises merely from looking at the type of order that prevails among them and at the distribution of capabilities within that order. We abstract from any particular qualities of states and from all of their concrete connections. What emerges is a positional picture, a general description of the ordered overall arrangement of a society written in terms of the placement of units rather than in terms of their qualities. . . .

NOTE

1. William T. R. Fox, "The Uses of International Relations Theory," in William T. R. Fox, ed., *Theoretical Aspects of International Relations* (Notre Dame, Ind.: University of Notre Dame Press, 1959), p. 35.

––––––––––

Alexander Wendt
Anarchy Is What States Make of It

Anarchy and power politics

Classical realists such as Thomas Hobbes, Reinhold Niebuhr, and Hans Morgenthau attributed egoism and power politics primarily to human nature, whereas structural realists or neorealists emphasize anarchy. The difference stems in part from different interpretations of anarchy's causal powers. Kenneth Waltz's work is important for both. In *Man, the State, and War*, he defines anarchy as a condition of possibility for or "permissive" cause of war, arguing that "wars occur because there is nothing to prevent them."[1] It is the human nature or domestic politics of predator states, however, that provide the initial impetus or "efficient" cause of conflict which forces other states to respond in kind.[2]. . . Waltz's *Theory of International Politics*, the logic of anarchy seems by itself to constitute self-help and power politics as necessary features of world politics.[3]. . .

Anarchy, self-help, and intersubjective knowledge

Waltz defines political structure on three dimensions: ordering principles (in this case, anarchy), principles of differentiation (which here drop out), and the distribution of capabilities.[4] By itself, this definition predicts little about state behavior. It does not predict whether two states will be friends or foes, will recognize each other's sovereignty, will have dynastic ties, will be revisionist or status quo powers, and so on. These factors, which are fundamentally intersubjective, affect states' security interests and thus the character of their interaction under anarchy. . . . Put more generally, without assumptions about the structure of identities and interests in the system, Waltz's definition of structure cannot predict the content or dynamics of anarchy. Self-help is one such intersubjective structure and, as such, does the decisive explanatory work in the theory. The question is whether self-help is a logical or contingent feature of anarchy. In this section, I develop the concept of a "structure of identity and interest" and show that no particular one follows logically from anarchy.

A fundamental principle of constructivist social theory is that people act toward objects, including other actors, on the basis of the meanings that the objects have for them.[5] States act differently toward enemies than they do toward friends because enemies are threatening and friends are not. Anarchy and the distribution of power are insufficient to tell us which is which. U.S. military power has a different significance for Canada than for Cuba, despite their similar "structural" positions, just as British missiles have a different significance for the United States than do Soviet missiles. The distribution of power may always affect states' calculations, but how it does so depends on the intersubjective understandings and expectations, on the "distribution of knowledge," that constitute their conceptions of self and other.[6] If society "forgets" what a university is, the powers and practices of professor and student cease to exist; if the United States and Soviet Union decide that they are no longer enemies, "the cold war is over." It is collective meanings that constitute the structures which organize our actions.

Actors acquire identities—relatively stable, role-specific understandings and expectations about self—by participating in such collective meanings.[7] Identities are inherently relational: "Identity, with its appropriate attachments of psychological reality, is always identity within a specific, socially constructed world," Peter Berger argues.[8] Each person has many identities linked to institutional roles, such as brother, son, teacher, and citizen.

Similarly, a state may have multiple identities as "sovereign," "leader of the free world," "imperial power," and so on.[9] The commitment to and the salience of particular identities vary, but each identity is an inherently social definition of the actor grounded in the theories which actors collectively hold about themselves and one another and which constitute the structure of the social world.

Identities are the basis of interests. Actors do not have a "portfolio" of interests that they carry around independent of social context; instead, they define their interests in the process of defining situations.[10] . . . Sometimes situations are unprecedented in our experience, and in these cases we have to construct their meaning, and thus our interests, by analogy or invent them de novo. More often they have routine qualities in which we assign meanings on the basis of institutionally defined roles. When we say that professors have an "interest" in teaching, research, or going on leave, we are saying that to function in the role identity of "professor," they have to define certain situations as calling for certain actions. This does not mean that they will necessarily do so (expectations and competence do not equal performance), but if they do not, they will not get tenure. The absence or failure of roles makes defining situations and interests more difficult, and identity confusion may result. This seems to be happening today in the United States and the former Soviet Union: without the cold war's mutual attributions of threat and hostility to define their identities, these states seem unsure of what their "interests" should be.

An institution is a relatively stable set or "structure" of identities and interests. Such structures are often codified in formal rules and norms, but these have motivational force only in virtue of actors' socialization to and participation in collective knowledge. Institutions are fundamentally cognitive entities that do not exist apart from actors' ideas about how the world works.[11] This does not mean that institutions are not real or objective, that they are "nothing but" beliefs. As collective knowledge, they are experienced as having an existence "over and above the individuals who happen to embody them at the moment."[12] In this way, institutions come to confront individuals as more or less coercive social facts, but they are still a function of what actors collectively "know." Identities and such collective cognitions do not exist apart from each other; they are "mutually constitutive."[13] On this view, institutionalization is a process of internalizing new identities and interests, not something occurring outside them and affecting only behavior; socialization is a cognitive process, not just a behavioral one. Conceived in this way, institutions may be cooperative or conflictual, a point sometimes lost in scholarship on international regimes, which tends to equate institutions with cooperation. There are important differences between conflictual and cooperative institutions to be sure, but all relatively stable self-other relations—even those of "enemies"—are defined intersubjectively.

Self-help is an institution, one of various structures of identity and interest that may exist under anarchy. Processes of identity-formation under anarchy are concerned first and foremost with preservation or "security" of the self. Concepts of security therefore differ in the extent to which and the manner in which the self is identified cognitively with the other,[14] and, I want to suggest, it is upon this cognitive variation that the meaning of anarchy and the distribution of power depends. Let me illustrate with a standard continuum of security systems.[15]

At one end is the "competitive" security system, in which states identify negatively with each other's security so that ego's gain is seen as alter's loss. Negative identification under anarchy constitutes systems of "realist" power politics: risk-averse actors that infer intentions from capabilities and worry about relative gains and losses. At the limit—in the Hobbesian war of all against all—collective action is nearly impossible in such a system because each actor must constantly fear being stabbed in the back.

In the middle is the "individualistic" security system, in which states are indifferent to the relationship between their own and others' security. This constitutes "neoliberal" systems: states are still self-regarding about their security but are concerned primarily with absolute gains rather than relative gains. One's position in the distribution of power is less important, and collective action is more possible (though still subject to free riding because states continue to be "egoists").

Competitive and individualistic systems are both "self-help" forms of anarchy in the sense that states do not positively identify the security of self with that of others but instead treat security as the individual responsibility of each. Given the lack of a positive cognitive identification on the basis of which to build security regimes, power politics within such systems will necessarily consist of efforts to manipulate others to satisfy self-regarding interests.

This contrasts with the "cooperative" security system, in which states identify positively with one another so that the security of each is perceived as the responsibility of all. This is not self-help in any interesting sense, since the "self" in terms of which interests are defined is the community; national interests are international interests.[16] In practice, of course, the extent to which states' identification with the community varies, from the limited form found in "concerts" to the full-blown form seen in "collective security" arrangements.[17] Depending on how well developed the collective self is, it will produce security practices that are in varying degrees altruistic or prosocial. This makes collective action less dependent on the presence of active threats and less prone to free riding.[18] Moreover, it restructures efforts to advance one's objectives, or "power politics," in terms of shared norms rather than relative power.[19]

On this view, the tendency in international relations scholarship to view power and institutions as two opposing explanations of foreign policy is therefore misleading, since anarchy and the distribution of power only have meaning for state action in virtue of the understandings and expectations that constitute institutional identities and interests. Self-help is one such institution, constituting one kind of anarchy but not the only kind. Waltz's three-part definition of structure therefore seems underspecified. In order to go from structure to action, we need to add a fourth: the intersubjectively constituted structure of identities and interests in the system.

This has an important implication for the way in which we conceive of states in the state of nature before their first encounter with each other. Because states do not have conceptions of self and other, and thus security interests, apart from or prior to interaction, we assume too much about the state of nature if we concur with Waltz that, in virtue of anarchy, "international political systems, like economic markets, are formed by the coaction of self-regarding units."[20] We also assume too much if we argue that, in virtue of anarchy, states in the state of nature necessarily face a "stag hunt" or "security dilemma."[21] These claims presuppose a history of interaction in which actors have acquired "selfish" identities and interests; before interaction (and still in abstraction from first- and second-image factors) they would have no experience upon which to base such definitions of self and other. To assume otherwise is to attribute to states in the state of nature qualities that they can only possess in society.[22] Self-help is an institution, not a constitutive feature of anarchy.

What, then, *is* a constitutive feature of the state of nature before interaction? Two things are left if we strip away those properties of the self which presuppose interaction with others. The first is the material substrate of agency, including its intrinsic capabilities. For human beings, this is the body; for states, it is an organizational apparatus of governance. In effect, I am suggesting for rhetorical purposes that the raw material out of which members of the state system are constituted is created by domestic society before states enter the constitutive process of international society,[23] although this process implies neither stable territoriality nor sovereignty, which are internationally negotiated terms of individuality (as discussed further below). The second is a desire to preserve this material substrate, to survive. This does not entail "self-regardingness," however, since actors do not have a self prior to interaction with an other; how they view the meaning and requirements of this survival therefore depends on the processes by which conceptions of self evolve.

This may all seem very arcane, but there is an important issue at stake: are the foreign policy identities and interests of states exogenous or endogenous to the state system? The former is the answer of an individualistic or undersocialized systemic theory for which rationalism is appropriate; the latter is the answer of a fully socialized systemic theory. Waltz seems to offer the latter and proposes two mechanisms, competition and socialization, by which structure conditions state action.[24] The content of his argument about this conditioning, however, presupposes a self-help system that is not itself a constitutive feature of anarchy. As James Morrow points out, Waltz's two mechanisms condition behavior, not identity and interest.[25]. . .

Anarchy and the social construction of power politics

If self-help is not a constitutive feature of anarchy, it must emerge causally from processes in which anarchy plays only a permissive role.[26] This reflects a second principle of constructivism: that the meanings in terms of which action is organized arise out of interaction.[27]. . .

Consider two actors—ego and alter—encountering each other for the first time.[28] Each wants to survive and has certain material capabilities, but neither actor has biological or domestic imperatives for power, glory, or conquest (still bracketed), and there is no history of security or insecurity between the two. What should they do? Realists would probably argue that each should act on the basis of worst-case assumptions about the other's intentions, justifying such an attitude as prudent in view of the possibility of death from making a mistake. Such a possibility always exists, even in civil society; however, society would be impossible if people made decisions purely on the basis of worst-case possibilities. Instead, most decisions are and should be made on the basis of probabilities, and these are produced by interaction, by what actors *do*.

In the beginning is ego's gesture, which may consist, for example, of an advance, a retreat, a brandishing of arms, a laying down of arms, or an attack.[29] For ego, this gesture represents the basis on which it is prepared to respond to alter. This basis is unknown to alter, however, and so it must make an inference or "attribution" about ego's intentions and, in particular, given that this is anarchy, about whether ego is a threat.[30] The content of this inference will largely depend on two considerations. The first is the gesture's and ego's physical qualities, which are in part contrived by ego and which include the direction of movement, noise, numbers, and immediate consequences of the gesture.[31] The second consideration concerns what alter would intend by such qualities were it to make such a gesture itself. Alter may make an attributional "error" in its inference about ego's intent, but there is also no reason for it to assume a priori—before the gesture—that ego is threatening, since it is only through a process of signaling and interpreting that the costs and probabilities of being wrong can be determined.[32] Social threats are constructed, not natural.

Consider an example. Would we assume, a priori, that we were about to be attacked if we are ever contacted by members of an alien civilization? I think not. We would be highly alert, of course, but whether we placed our military forces on alert or launched an attack would depend on how we interpreted the import of their first gesture for our security—if only to avoid making an immediate enemy out of what may be a dangerous adversary. The possibility of error, in other words, does not force us to act on the assumption that the aliens are threatening: action depends on the probabilities we assign, and these are in key part a function of what the aliens do; prior to their gesture, we have no systemic basis for assigning probabilities. If their first gesture is to appear with a thousand spaceships and destroy New York, we will define the situation as threatening and respond accordingly. But if they appear with one spaceship, saying what seems to be "we come in peace," we will feel "reassured" and will probably respond with a gesture intended to reassure them, even if this gesture is not necessarily interpreted by them as such.[33]

This process of signaling, interpreting, and responding completes a "social act" and begins the process of creating intersubjective meanings. It advances the same way. The first social act creates expectations on both sides about each other's future behavior: potentially mistaken and certainly tentative, but expectations nonetheless. Based on this tentative knowledge, ego makes a new gesture, again signifying the basis on which it will respond to alter, and again alter responds, adding to the pool of knowledge each has about the other, and so on over time. The mechanism here is reinforcement; interaction rewards actors for holding certain ideas about each other and discourages them from holding others. If repeated long enough, these "reciprocal typifications" will create relatively stable concepts of self and other regarding the issue at stake in the interaction.[34]

It is through reciprocal interaction, in other words, that we create and instantiate the relatively enduring social structures in terms of which we define our identities and interests. . . .

Competitive systems of interaction are prone to security "dilemmas," in which the efforts of actors to enhance their security unilaterally threaten the security of the others, perpetuating distrust and alienation. The forms of identity and interest that constitute such dilemmas, however, are themselves ongoing effects of, not exogenous to, the interaction; identities are produced in and through "situated activity."[35] We do not *begin* our relationship with the aliens in a security dilemma; security dilemmas are not given by anarchy or nature. . . .

The mirror theory of identity-formation is a crude account of how the process of creating identities and interests might work, but it does not tell us why a system of states—such as, arguably, our own—would have ended up with self-regarding and not collective identities. In this section, I examine an efficient cause, predation, which, in conjunction with anarchy as a permissive cause, may generate a self-help system. In so doing, however, I show the key role that the structure of identities and interests plays in mediating anarchy's explanatory role.

The predator argument is straightforward and compelling. For whatever reasons—biology, domestic politics, or systemic victimization—some states may become predisposed toward aggression. The aggressive behavior of these predators or "bad apples" forces other states to engage in competitive power politics, to meet fire with fire, since failure to do so may degrade or destroy them. One predator will best a hundred pacifists because anarchy provides no guarantees. This argument is powerful in part because it is so weak: rather than making the strong assumption that all states are inherently power-seeking (a purely reductionist theory of power politics), it assumes that just one is power-seeking and that the others have to follow suit because anarchy permits the one to exploit them.

In making this argument, it is important to reiterate that the possibility of predation does not in itself force states to anticipate it a priori with competitive power politics of their own. The possibility of predation does not mean that "war may at any moment occur"; it may in fact be extremely unlikely. Once a predator emerges, however, it may condition identity- and interest-formation in the following manner.

In an anarchy of two, if ego is predatory, alter must either define its security in self-help terms or pay the price. . . .

The timing of the emergence of predation relative to the history of identity-formation in the community is therefore crucial to anarchy's explanatory role as a permissive cause. Predation will always lead victims to defend themselves, but whether defense will be collective or not depends on the history of interaction within the potential collective as much as on the ambitions of the predator. Will the disappearance of the Soviet threat renew old insecurities among the members of the North Atlantic Treaty Organization? Perhaps, but not if they have reasons independent of that threat for identifying their security with one another. Identities and interests are relationship-specific, not intrinsic attributes of a "portfolio"; states may be competitive in some relationships and solidary in others. . . .

The source of predation also matters. If it stems from unit-level causes that are immune to systemic impacts (causes such as human nature or domestic politics taken in isolation), then it functions in a manner analogous to a "genetic trait" in the constructed world of the state system. Even if successful, this trait does not select for other predators in an evolutionary sense so much as it teaches other states to respond in kind, but since traits cannot be unlearned, the other states will continue competitive behavior until the predator is either destroyed or transformed from within. However, in the more likely event that predation stems at least in part from prior systemic interaction—perhaps as a result of being victimized in the past (one thinks here of Nazi Germany or the Soviet Union)—then it is more a response to a learned identity and, as such, might be transformed by future social interaction in the form of appeasement, reassurances that security needs will be met, systemic effects on domestic politics, and so on. In this case, in other words, there is more hope that process can transform a bad apple into a good one. . . .

This raises anew the question of exactly how much and what kind of role human nature and domestic politics play in world politics. The greater and more destructive this role, the more significant predation will be, and the less amenable anarchy will be to formation of collective identities. Classical realists, of course, assumed that human nature was possessed by an inherent lust for power or glory. My argument suggests that assumptions such as this were made for a reason: an unchanging Hobbesian man provides the powerful efficient cause necessary for a relentless pessimism about world politics that anarchic structure alone, or even structure plus intermittent predation, cannot supply. . . .

Assuming for now that systemic theories of identity-formation in world politics are worth pursuing, let me conclude by suggesting that the realist-rationalist alliance "reifies" self-help in the sense of treating it as something separate from the practices by which it is produced and sustained. Peter Berger and Thomas Luckmann define reification as follows: "[It] is the apprehension of the products of human activity *as if* they were something else than human products—such as facts of nature, results of cosmic laws, or manifestations of divine will. Reification implies that man is capable of forgetting his own authorship of the human world, and further, that the dialectic between man, the producer, and his products is lost to consciousness. The reified world is . . . experienced by man as a strange facticity, an *opus alienum* over which he has no control rather than as the *opus proprium* of his own productive activity."[36] By denying or bracketing states' collective authorship of their identities and interests, in other words, the realist-rationalist alliance denies or brackets the fact that competitive power politics help create the very "problem of order" they are supposed to solve—that realism is a self-fulfilling prophecy. Far from being exogenously given, the intersubjective knowledge that constitutes competitive identities and interests is constructed every day by processes of "social will formation."[37] It is what states have made of themselves.

NOTES

1. Kenneth Waltz, *Man, the State, and War* (New York: Columbia University Press, 1959), p. 232.
2. Ibid., pp. 169–70.
3. Kenneth Waltz, *Theory of International Politics* (Boston: Addison-Wesley, 1979). *Interests: The Foreign Aid Regime, 1949–1989* (Princeton, N.J.: Princeton).
4. Waltz, *Theory of International Politics*, pp. 79–101.
5. See, for example, Herbert Blumer, "The Methodological Position of Symbolic Interactionism," in his *Symbolic Interactionism: Perspective and Method* (Englewood Cliffs, N.J.: Prentice-Hall, 1969), p. 2. Throughout this article, I assume that a theoretically productive analogy can be made between individuals and states. There are at least two justifications for this anthropomorphism. Rhetorically, the analogy is an accepted practice in mainstream international relations discourse, and since this article is an immanent rather than external critique,

it should follow the practice. Substantively, states are collectivities of individuals that through their practices constitute each other as "persons" having interests, fears, and so on. A full theory of state identity- and interest-formation would nevertheless need to draw insights from the social psychology of groups and organizational theory, and for that reason my anthropomorphism is merely suggestive.

6. The phrase "distribution of knowledge" is Barry Barnes's, as discussed in his work *The Nature of Power* (Cambridge: Polity Press, 1988); see also Peter Berger and Thomas Luckmann, *The Social Construction of Reality* (New York: Anchor Books, 1966). The concern of recent international relations scholarship on "epistemic communities" with the cause-and-effect understandings of the world held by scientists, experts, and policymakers is an important aspect of the role of knowledge in world politics; see Peter Haas, "Do Regimes Matter? Epistemic Communities and Mediterranean Pollution Control," *International Organization* 43 (Summer 1989), pp. 377–404; and Ernst Haas, *When Knowledge Is Power.* My constructivist approach would merely add to this an equal emphasis on how such knowledge also *constitutes* the structures and subjects of social life.

7. For an excellent statement of how collective meanings constitute identities, see Peter Berger, "Identity as a Problem in the Sociology of Knowledge, "*European Journal of Sociology*, vol. 7, no. 1, 1966, pp. 32–40. See also David Morgan and Michael Schwalbe, "Mind and Self in Society: Linking Social Structure and Social Cognition," *Social Psychology Quarterly* 53 (June 1990), pp. 148–64. In my discussion, I draw on the following interactionist texts: George Herbert Mead, *Mind, Self, and Society* (Chicago: University of Chicago Press, 1934); Berger and Luckmann, *The Social Construction of Reality;* Sheldon Stryker, *Symbolic Interactionism: A Social Structural Version* (Menlo Park, Calif.: Benjamin/Cummings, 1980); R. S. Perinbanayagam, *Signifying Acts: Structure and Meaning in Everyday Life* (Carbondale: Southern Illinois University Press, 1985); John Hewitt, *Self and Society: A Symbolic Interactionist Social Psychology* (Boston: Allyn & Bacon, 1988); and Turner, *A Theory of Social Interaction.* Despite some differences, much the same points are made by structurationists such as Bhaskar and Giddens. See Roy Bhaskar, *The Possibility of Naturalism* (Atlantic Highlands, N.J.: Humanities Press, 1979); and Anthony Giddens, *Central Problems in Social Theory* (Berkeley: University of California Press, 1979).

8. Berger, "Identity as a Problem in the Sociology of Knowledge," p. 111.

9. While not normally cast in such terms, foreign policy scholarship on national role conceptions could be adapted to such identity language. See Kal Holsti, "National Role Conceptions in the Study of Foreign Policy," *International Studies Quarterly* 14 (September 1970), pp. 233–309; and Stephen Walker, ed., *Role Theory and Foreign Policy Analysis* (Durham, N.C.: Duke University Press, 1987). For an important effort to do so, see Stephen Walker, "Symbolic Interactionism and International Politics: Role Theory's Contribution to International Organization," in C. Shih and Martha Cottam, eds., *Contending Dramas: A Cognitive Approach to Post-War International Organizational Processes* (New York: Praeger, forthcoming).

10. On the "portfolio" conception of interests, see Barry Hindess, *Political Choice and Social Structure* (Aldershot, U.K.: Edward Elgar, 1989), pp. 2–3. The "definition of the situation" is a central concept in interactionist theory.

11. In neo-Durkheimian parlance, institutions are "social representations." See Serge Moscovici, "The Phenomenon of Social Representations," in Rob Farr and Serge Moscovici, eds., *Social Representations* (Cambridge: Cambridge University Press, 1984), pp. 3–69. See also Barnes, *The Nature of Power*. Note that this is a considerably more socialized cognitivism than that found in much of the recent scholarship on the role of "ideas" in world politics, which tends to treat ideas as commodities that are held by individuals and intervene between the distribution of power and outcomes. For a form of cognitivism closer to my own, see Emanuel Adler, "Cognitive Evolution: A Dynamic Approach for the Study of International Relations and Their Progress," in Emanuel Adler and Beverly Crawford, eds., *Progress in Postwar International Relations* (New York: Columbia University Press, 1991), pp. 43–88.

12. Berger and Luckmann, *The Social Construction of Reality*, p. 58.

13. See Giddens, *Central Problems in Social Theory*; and Alexander Wendt and Raymond Duvall, "Institutions and International Order," in Ernst-Otto Czempiel and James Rosenau, eds., *Global Changes and Theoretical Challenges* (Lexington, Mass.: Lexington Books, 1989), pp. 51–74.

14. Proponents of choice theory might put this in terms of "interdependent utilities." For a useful overview of relevant choice-theoretic discourse, most of which has focused on the specific case of altruism, see Harold Hochman and Shmuel Nitzan, "Concepts of Extended Preference," *Journal of Economic Behavior and Organization* 6 (June 1985), pp. 161–76. The literature on choice theory usually does not link behavior to issues of identity. For an exception, see Amartya Sen, "Goals, Commitment, and Identity," *Journal of Law, Economics, and Organization* 1 (Fall 1985), pp. 341–55; and Robert Higgs, "Identity and Cooperation: A Comment on Sen's Alternative Program," *Journal of Law, Economics, and Organization* 3 (Spring 1987), pp. 140–42.

15. Security systems might also vary in the extent to which there is a functional differentiation or a hierarchical relationship between patron and client, with the patron playing a hegemonic role within its sphere of influence in defining the security interests of its clients. I do not examine this dimension here; for preliminary discussion, see Alexander Wendt, "The States System and Global Militarization," Ph.D. diss., University of Minnesota, Minneapolis, 1989; and Alexander Wendt and Michael Barnett, "The International System and Third World Militarization," unpublished manuscript, 1991.

16. This amounts to an "internationalization of the state." For a discussion of this subject, see Raymond Duvall and Alexander Wendt, "The International Capital Regime and the Internationalization of the State," unpublished manuscript, 1987. See also R. B. J. Walker, "Sovereignty, Identity, Community: Reflections on the Horizons of Contemporary Political Practice," in R. B. J. Walker and Saul Mendlovitz, eds., *Contending Sovereignties* (Boulder, Colo.: Lynne Rienner, 1990), pp. 159–85.

17. On the spectrum of cooperative security arrangements, see Charles Kupchan and Clifford Kupchan, "Concerts, Collective Security, and the Future of Europe," *International Security* 16 (Summer 1991), pp. 114–61; and Richard Smoke, "A Theory of Mutual Security," in Richard Smoke and Andrei Kortunov, eds., *Mutual Security* (New York: St. Martin's Press, 1991), pp. 59–111. These may be usefully set alongside Christopher Jencks' "Varieties of Altruism," in Jane Mansbridge, ed., *Beyond Self-Interest* (Chicago: University of Chicago Press, 1990), pp. 53–67.

18. On the role of collective identity in reducing collective action problems, see Bruce Fireman and William Gamson, "Utilitarian Logic in the Resource Mobilization Perspective," in Mayer Zald and John McCarthy, eds., *The Dynamics of Social Movements* (Cambridge, Mass.: Winthrop, 1979), pp. 8–44; Robyn Dawes et al., "Cooperation for the Benefit of Us—Not Me, or My Conscience," in Mansbridge, *Beyond Self-Interest*, pp. 97–110; and Craig Calhoun, "The Problem of Identity in Collective Action," in Joan Huber, ed., *Macro-Micro Linkages in Sociology* (Beverly Hills, Calif.: Sage, 1991), pp. 51–75.

19. See Thomas Risse-Kappen, "Are Democratic Alliances Special?" unpublished manuscript, Yale University, New Haven, Conn., 1991. This line of argument could be expanded usefully in feminist terms. For a useful overview of the relational nature of feminist conceptions of self, see Paula England and Barbara Stanek Kilbourne, "Feminist Critiques of the Separative Model of Self: Implications for Rational Choice Theory," *Rationality and Society* 2 (April 1990), pp. 156–71. On feminist conceptualizations of power, see Ann Tickner, "Hans Morgenthau's Principles of Political Realism: A Feminist Reformulation," *Millennium* 17 (Winter 1988), pp. 429–40; and Thomas Wartenberg, "The Concept of Power in Feminist Theory," *Praxis International* 8 (October 1988), pp. 301–16.

20. Waltz, *Theory of International Politics*, p. 91.

21. See Waltz, *Man, the State, and War*; and Robert Jervis, "Cooperation Under the Security Dilemma," *World Politics* 30 (January 1978), pp. 167–214.

22. My argument here parallels Rousseau's critique of Hobbes. For an excellent critique of realist appropriations of Rousseau, see Michael Williams, "Rousseau, Realism, and Realpolitik," *Millennium* 18 (Summer 1989), pp. 188–204. Williams argues that far from being a fundamental starting point in the state of nature, for Rousseau the stag hunt represented a stage in man's fall. On p. 190, Williams cites Rousseau's description of man prior to leaving the state of nature: "Man only knows himself; he does not see his own well-being to be identified with or contrary to that of anyone else; he neither hates anything nor loves anything; but limited to no more than physical instinct, he is no one, he is an animal." For another critique of Hobbes on the state of nature that parallels my constructivist reading of anarchy, see Charles Landesman, "Reflections on Hobbes: Anarchy and Human Nature," in Peter Caws, ed., *The Causes of Quarrel* (Boston: Beacon, 1989), pp. 139–48.

23. Empirically, this suggestion is problematic, since the process of decolonization and the subsequent support of many Third World states by international society point to ways in which even the raw material of "empirical statehood" is constituted by the society of states. See Robert Jackson and Carl Rosberg, "Why

Africa's Weak States Persist: The Empirical and the Juridical in Statehood," *World Politics* 35 (October 1982), pp. 1–24.

24. Waltz, *Theory of International Politics*, pp. 74–77.

25. See James Morrow, "Social Choice and System Structure in World Politics," *World Politics* 41 (October 1988), p. 89. Waltz's behavioral treatment of socialization may be usefully contrasted with the more cognitive approach taken by Ikenberry and the Kupchans in the following articles: G. John Ikenberry and Charles Kupchan, "Socialization and Hegemonic Power," *International Organization* 44 (Summer 1989), pp. 283–316; and Kupchan and Kupchan, "Concerts, Collective Security, and the Future of Europe." Their approach is close to my own, but they define socialization as an elite strategy to induce value change in others, rather than as a ubiquitous feature of interaction in terms of which all identities and interests get produced and reproduced.

26. The importance of the distinction between constitutive and causal explanations is not sufficiently appreciated in constructivist discourse. See Wendt, "The Agent-Structure Problem in International Relations Theory," pp. 362–65; Wendt, "The States System and Global Militarization," pp. 110–13; and Wendt, "Bridging the Theory/Meta-Theory Gap in International Relations," *Review of International Studies* 17 (October 1991), p. 390.

27. See Blumer, "The Methodological Position of Symbolic Interactionism," pp. 2–4.

28. This situation is not entirely metaphorical in world politics, since throughout history states have "discovered" each other, generating an instant anarchy as it were. A systematic empirical study of first contacts would be interesting.

29. Mead's analysis of gestures remains definitive. See Mead's *Mind, Self, and Society*. See also the discussion of the role of signaling in the "mechanics of interaction" in Turner's *A Theory of Social Interaction*, pp. 74–79 and 92–115.

30. On the role of attribution processes in the interactionist account of identity-formation, see Sheldon Stryker and Avi Gottlieb, "Attribution Theory and Symbolic Inter–actionism," in John Harvey et al., eds., *New Directions in Attribution Research*, vol. 3 (Hillsdale, N.J.: Lawrence Erlbaum, 1981), pp. 425–58; and Kathleen Crittenden, "Sociological Aspects of Attribution," *Annual Review of Sociology*, vol. 9, 1983, pp. 425–46. On attributional processes in international relations, see Shawn Rosenberg and Gary Wolfsfeld, "International Conflict and the Problem of Attribution," *Journal of Conflict Resolution* 21 (March 1977), pp. 75–103.

31. On the "stagecraft" involved in "presentations of self," see Erving Goffman, *The Presentation of Self in Everyday Life* (New York: Doubleday, 1959). On the role of appearance in definitions of the situation, see Gregory Stone, "Appearance and the Self," in Arnold Rose, ed., *Human Behavior and Social Processes* (Boston: Houghton Mifflin, 1962), pp. 86–118.

32. This discussion of the role of possibilities and probabilities in threat perception owes much to Stewart Johnson's comments on an earlier draft of my article.

33. On the role of "reassurance" in threat situations, see Richard Ned Lebow and Janice Gross Stein, "Beyond Deterrence," *Journal of Social Issues*, vol. 43, no. 4, 1987, pp. 5–72.

34. On "reciprocal typifications," see Berger and Luckmann, *The Social Construction of Reality*, pp. 54–58.
35. See C. Norman Alexander and Mary Glenn Wiley, "Situated Activity and Identity Formation," in Morris Rosenberg and Ralph Turner, eds., *Social Psychology: Sociological Perspectives* (New York: Basic Books, 1981), pp. 269–89.
36. See Berger and Luckmann, *The Social Construction of Reality*, p. 89. See also Douglas Maynard and Thomas Wilson, "On the Reification of Social Structure," in Scott McNall and Gary Howe, eds., *Current Perspectives in Social Theory*, vol. 1 (Greenwich, Conn.: JAI Press, 1980), pp. 287–322.
37. See Richard Ashley, "Social Will and International Anarchy," in Hayward Alker and Richard Ashley, eds., *After Realism*, work in progress, Massachusetts Institute of Technology, Cambridge, and Arizona State University, Tempe, 1992.

CHAPTER 2 REALISM v. MORALITY IN FOREIGN POLICY

Realism in Foreign Policy

Advocate: George Kennan

Source: "Morality and Foreign Policy," *Foreign Affairs*, vol. 64, no. 2 (Winter 1985/1986), pp. 205–218, excerpt.

Morality in Foreign Policy

Advocates: Leslie H. Gelb and Justine A. Rosenthal

Source: "The Rise of Ethics in Foreign Policy: Reaching a Values Consensus," *Foreign Affairs*, vol. 82, no. 3 (May/June 2003), pp. 2–7, excerpt.

The end of the Cold War ushered in an era of democracy to many parts of the globe and brought individual political and civil liberties to millions of people. In the new age of globalization, issues such as human rights and environmental safety, rose in significance. The United States undertook humanitarian intervention in Kosovo, committing thousands of troops and tax dollars. In the post-9/11 era, the expansion of democracy and freedom have become bywords of the Bush Administration's policies in the Middle East.

The debate on values and ethics in international relations is steeped in a long historical and philosophical tradition. The extent to which the national interest should reflect moral values has drawn significant interest and diverging opinions. In the era defined by the fight against terrorism, the issue becomes even more important because many of the measures implemented may require the restriction of civil liberties.

IN FAVOR OF REALISM IN FOREIGN POLICY

A long-standing feature of realist international relations has been the separation of ethics and morality from the conduct of foreign policy. The notions of "right" and "wrong" were seen as incompatible with the pursuit of the national interest, whether that was ensuring a country's security, expanding its power, or improving the welfare of its citizens. This line of reasoning played a prominent part in the political discourse, where humanitarian interventions or peacekeeping missions intended to prevent ethnic cleansing or genocide have been severely criticized on the basis that they would spend American blood and treasure on conflicts in which the United States had no evident interest.

In a similar line, George Kennan argues that foreign policy should be based on the national interest, which the government should be prepared to pursue without moral pretension or apology. The existence of a national state and its sovereignty negates the necessity of moral justification for the actions of its government. Kennan maintains that if moral behavior is to be observed, then it should be done in a country's own conduct, rather than in judging other countries' strategies. Because there are no international standards on values and morality, the United States should not seek to reform others, but instead focus on its national interests.

IN FAVOR OF MORALITY IN FOREIGN POLICY

In a dramatic reversal since the days when Woodrow Wilson's ideas of self-determination, democracy, and collective security were considered utopian, values and moral principles have taken a central role in U.S. foreign policy in recent years. Specifically, the Bush Administration embraced "democracy promotion," particularly in the Middle East, as one of the main thrusts of its global strategy. As Leslie Gelb and Justine Rosenthal persuasively argue, the emphasis on values and morality has achieved new importance in the post-9/11 era, when they influence many foreign policy decisions.

Gelb and Rosenthal also caution, however, that humanitarian intervention as well as democracy promotion and counterterrorism carry contradictions and considerable costs. Inconsistencies in the application remain and, frequently, the United States finds itself on a different moral track from the rest of the world. Gelb and Rosenthal suggest that, although values may never come to dominate foreign policy, they play a bigger role now than ever before.

POINTS **TO PONDER**

1. Was the invasion of Iraq a morally justifiable war?
2. How did the United States reconcile its support for dictatorships with appeals for human rights during the Cold War?
3. Are national interests compatible with considerations of morality?

George F. Kennan
Morality and Foreign Policy

Certain distinctions should be made before one wanders farther into this thicket of problems.

First of all, the conduct of diplomacy is the responsibility of governments. For purely practical reasons, this is unavoidable and inalterable. This responsibility is not diminished by the fact that government, in formulating foreign policy, may choose to be influenced by private opinion. What we are talking about, therefore, when we attempt to relate moral considerations to foreign policy, is the behavior of governments, not of individuals or entire peoples.

Second, let us recognize that the functions, commitments and moral obligations of governments are not the same as those of the individual. Government is an agent, not a principal. Its primary obligation is to the interests of the national society it represents, not to the moral impulses that individual elements of that society may experience. No more than the attorney vis-à-vis the client, nor the doctor vis-à-vis the patient, can government attempt to insert itself into the consciences of those whose interests it represents.

Let me explain. The interests of the national society for which government has to concern itself are basically those of its military security, the integrity of its political life and the well-being of its people. These needs have no moral quality. They arise from the very existence of the national state in question and from the status of national sovereignty it enjoys. They are the unavoidable necessities of a national existence and therefore not subject to classification as either "good" or "bad." They may be questioned from a detached philosophic point of view. But the government of the sovereign state cannot make such judgments. When it accepts the responsibilities of governing, implicit in that acceptance is the assumption that it is right that the state should be sovereign, that the integrity of its political life should be assured, that its people should enjoy the blessings of military security, material prosperity and a reasonable opportunity for, as the Declaration of Independence put it, the pursuit of happiness. For these assumptions the government needs no moral justification, nor need it accept any moral reproach for acting on the basis of them.

This assertion assumes, however, that the concept of national security taken as the basis for governmental concern is one reasonably, not extravagantly, conceived. In an age of nuclear striking power, national security can never be more than relative; and to the extent that it can be assured at all, it must find its sanction in the intentions of rival powers as well as in their capabilities. A concept of national security that ignores this reality and, above all, one that fails to concede the same legitimacy to the security needs of others that it claims for its own, lays itself open to the same moral reproach from which, in normal circumstances, it would be immune.

Whoever looks thoughtfully at the present situation of the United States in particular will have to agree that to assure these blessings to the American people is a task of such dimensions that the government attempting to meet it successfully will have very little, if any, energy and attention left to devote to other undertakings, including those suggested by the moral impulses of these or those of its citizens.

Finally, let us note that there are no internationally accepted standards of morality to which the U.S. government could appeal if it wished to act in the name of moral principles. It is true that there are certain words and phrases sufficiently high-sounding the world over so that most governments, when asked to declare themselves for or against, will cheerfully subscribe to them, considering that such is their vagueness that the mere act of subscribing to them carries with it no danger of having one's freedom of action significantly impaired. To this category of pronouncements belong such documents as the Kellogg-Briand Pact, the Atlantic Charter, the Yalta Declaration on Liberated Europe, and the prologues of innumerable other international agreements.

Ever since Secretary of State John Hay staged a political coup in 1899 by summoning the supposedly wicked European powers to sign up to the lofty principles of his Open Door notes (principles which neither they nor we had any awkward intention of observing), American statesmen have had a fondness for hurling just such semantic challenges at their foreign counterparts, thereby placing themselves in a graceful posture before domestic American opinion and reaping whatever political fruits are to be derived from the somewhat grudging and embarrassed responses these challenges evoke.

To say these things, I know, is to invite the question: how about the Helsinki accords of 1975? These, of course, were numerous and varied. There is no disposition here to question the value of many of them as refinements of the norms of international intercourse. But there were some, particularly those related to human rights, which it is hard to relegate to any category other than that of the high-minded but innocuous professions just referred to. These accords were declaratory in nature, not contractual. The very general terms in which they were drawn up, involving the use of words and phrases that had different meanings for different people, deprived them of the character of specific obligations to which signatory governments could usefully be held. The Western statesmen who pressed for Soviet adherence to these pronouncements must have been aware that some of them could not be implemented on the Soviet side, within the meanings we would normally attach to their workings, without fundamental changes in the Soviet system of power—changes we had no reason to expect would, or could, be introduced by the men then in power. Whether it is morally commendable to induce others to sign up to declarations, however high-minded in resonance, which one knows will not and cannot be implemented, is a reasonable question. The Western negotiators, in any case, had no reason to plead naïveté as their excuse for doing so.

When we talk about the application of moral standards to foreign policy, therefore, we are not talking about compliance with some clear and generally accepted international code of behavior. If the policies and actions of the U.S. government are to be made to conform to moral standards, those standards are going to have to be America's own, founded on traditional American principles of justice and propriety. When others fail to conform to those principles, and when their failure to conform has an adverse effect on American interests, as distinct from political tastes, we have every right to complain and, if necessary, to take retaliatory action. What we cannot do is to assume that our moral standards are theirs as well, and to appeal to those standards as the source of our grievances.

So much for basic principles. Let us now consider some categories of action that the U.S. government is frequently asked to take, and sometimes does take, in the name of moral principle.

These actions fall into two broad general categories: those that relate to the behavior of other governments that we find morally unacceptable, and those that relate to the behavior of our own government. Let us take them in that order.

There have been many instances, particularly in recent years, when the U.S. government has taken umbrage at the behavior of other governments on grounds that at least implied moral criteria for judgment, and in some of these instances the verbal protests have been reinforced by more tangible means of pressure. These various interventions have marched, so to speak, under a number of banners: democracy, human rights, majority rule, fidelity to treaties, fidelity to the U.N. Charter, and so on. Their targets have sometimes been the external policies and actions of the offending states, more often the internal practices. The interventions have served, in the eyes of their American inspirers, as demonstrations not only of the moral deficiencies of others but of the positive morality of ourselves; for it was seen as our moral duty to detect these lapses on the part of others, to denounce them before the world, and to assure—as far as we could with measures short of military action—that they were corrected.

Those who have inspired or initiated efforts of this nature would certainly have claimed to be acting in the name of moral principle, and in many instances they would no doubt have been sincere in doing so. But whether the results of this inspiration, like those of so many other good intentions, would justify this claim is questionable from a number of standpoints.

Let us take first those of our interventions that relate to internal practices of the offending governments. Let us reflect for a moment on how these interventions appear in the eyes of the governments in question and of many outsiders.

The situations that arouse our discontent are ones existing, as a rule, far from our own shores. Few of us can profess to be perfect judges of their rights and their wrongs. These are, for the governments in question, matters of internal affairs. It is customary for governments to resent interference by outside powers in affairs of this nature, and if our diplomatic history is any indication, we ourselves are not above resenting and resisting it when we find ourselves its object.

Interventions of this nature can be formally defensible only if the practices against which they are directed are seriously injurious to our interests, rather than just our sensibilities. There will, of course, be those readers who will argue that the encouragement and promotion of democracy elsewhere is always in the interests of the security, political integrity and prosperity of the United States. If this can be demonstrated in a given instance, well and good. But it is not invariably the case. Democracy is a loose term. Many varieties of folly and injustice contrive to masquerade under this designation. The mere fact that a country acquires the trappings of self-government does not automatically mean that the interests of the United States are thereby furthered. There are forms of plebiscitary "democracy" that may well prove less favorable to American interests than a wise and benevolent authoritarianism. There can be tyrannies of a majority as well as tyrannies of a minority, with the one hardly less odious than the other. Hitler came into power (albeit under highly unusual circumstances) with an electoral mandate, and there is scarcely a dictatorship of this age that would not claim the legitimacy of mass support.

There are parts of the world where the main requirement of American security is not an unnatural imitation of the American model but sheer stability, and this last is not always assured by a government of what appears to be popular acclaim. In approaching this question, Americans must overcome their tendency toward generalization and learn to examine each case on its own merits. The best measure of these merits is not the attractiveness of certain general semantic symbols but the effect of the given situation on the tangible and demonstrable interests of the United States.

Furthermore, while we are quick to allege that this or that practice in a foreign country is bad and deserves correction, seldom if ever do we seem to occupy ourselves seriously or realistically with the conceivable alternatives. It seems seldom to occur to us that even if a given situation is bad, the alternatives to it might be worse—even though history provides plenty of examples of just this phenomenon. In the eyes of many Americans it is enough for us to indicate the changes that ought, as we see it, to be made. We assume, of course, that the consequences will be benign and happy ones. But this is not always assured. It is, in any case, not we who are going to have to live with those consequences: it is the offending government and its people. We are demanding, in effect, a species of veto power over those of their practices that we dislike, while denying responsibility for whatever may flow from the acceptance of our demands.

Finally, we might note that our government, in raising such demands, is frequently responding not to its own moral impulses or to any wide general movements of American opinion but rather to pressures generated by politically influential minority elements among us that have some special interest—ethnic, racial, religious, ideological or several of these together—in the foreign situation in question. Sometimes it is the sympathies of these minorities that are most prominently aroused, sometimes their antipathies. But in view of this diversity of motive, the U.S. government, in responding to such pressures and making itself their spokesman, seldom acts consistently. Practices or policies that arouse our official displeasure in one country are cheerfully condoned or ignored in another. What is bad in the behavior of our opponents is good, or at least acceptable, in the case of our friends. What is unobjectionable to us at one period of our history is seen as offensive in another.

This is unfortunate, for a lack of consistency implies a lack of principle in the eyes of much of the world; whereas morality, if not principled, is not really morality. Foreigners, observing these anomalies, may be forgiven for suspecting that what passes as the product of moral inspiration in the rhetoric of our government is more likely to be a fair reflection of the mosaic of residual ethnic loyalties and passions that make themselves felt in the rough and tumble of our political life.

Similar things could be said when it is not the internal practices of the offending government but its actions on the international scene that are at issue. There is, here, the same reluctance to occupy one's self with the conceivable alternatives to the procedures one complains about or with the consequences likely to flow from the acceptance of one's demands. And there is frequently the same lack of consistency in the reaction. The Soviet action in Afghanistan, for example, is condemned, resented and responded to by sanctions. One recalls little of such reaction in the case of the somewhat similar, and apparently no less drastic, action taken by China in Tibet some years ago. The question inevitably arises: is it principle that determines our reaction? Or are there other motives?

Where measures taken by foreign governments affect adversely American interests rather than just American moral sensibilities, protests and retaliation are obviously in order; but then they should be carried forward frankly for what they are, and not allowed to masquerade under the mantle of moral principle.

Leslie H. Gelb and Justine A. Rosenthal

The Rise of Ethics in Foreign Policy

Something quite important has happened in American foreign policymaking with little notice or digestion of its meaning. Morality, values, ethics, universal principles—the whole panoply of ideals in international affairs that were once almost the exclusive domain of preachers and scholars—have taken root in the hearts, or at least the minds, of the American foreign policy community. A new vocabulary has emerged in the rhetoric of senior government officials, Republicans and Democrats alike. It is laced with concepts dismissed for almost 100 years as "Wilsonian." The rhetoric comes in many forms, used to advocate regime change or humanitarian intervention or promote democracy and human rights, but almost always the ethical agenda has at its core the rights of the individual.

This development of morality cannot be seen simply as a postmodern version of the "white man's burden," although it has that tenor in some hands. These values are now widely shared around the world by different religions and cultures. Movements for democracy or justice for war crimes are no longer merely American or Western idiosyncrasies. And although some in America's foreign-policy community may still be using moral language to cloak a traditional national security agenda, one gets the sense that the trend is more than that. In the past, tyrants supported by Washington did not have to worry a lot about interference in their domestic affairs. Now, even if Washington needs their help, some price has to be exacted, if only sharp public criticism. Moral matters are now part of American politics and the politics of many other nations. They are rarely, even in this new age, the driving forces behind foreign policy, but they are now a constant force that cannot be overlooked when it comes to policy effectiveness abroad or political support at home.

The Evolution of an Idea

The moral phenomenon we are now witnessing did not materialize out of whole cloth. It evolved over time, in fits and starts, solidifying only in the last 30 years.

From the dawn of human history, there have been laws about the initiation and conduct of war. The ancient Egyptians and the fourth century BC Chinese military strategist Sun Tzu set out rules on how and why to begin wars and how those wars should be fought. Saint Augustine argued that an act of war needs a just cause, and Saint Thomas Aquinas believed that battle requires the authority of a sovereign power and should be acted out with good intention. The sixteenth-century French jurist Jean Bodin held that war was a necessary evil and largely the domain of the sovereign. And the seventeenth-century legalist Hugo Grotius, after witnessing the atrocities of the Thirty Years' War, wrote on the protection of noncombatants and methods to promote and ensure peace.

These and many other figures played a role in creating the system of international law and a related kind of international morality that we witness today. But the debates often occurred on the periphery of international practice and related more to the rights of the aristocracy and the sovereign state than to a universal set of values.

The Hague Conventions of the late nineteenth and early twentieth centuries, the precursors of the Geneva Conventions, set out "laws of war" with the aim of protecting combatants and noncombatants alike and outlining rules for the treatment of prisoners and the wounded. These guidelines helped make war somewhat more humane but did not address the ethics of larger foreign policy questions. And some of these issues were taken up on a targeted basis by transnational organizations in the nineteenth century. Thus Quakers in the United Kingdom and the United States joined hands in an antislavery movement, and women from around the world united to champion women's suffrage. But not until Woodrow Wilson did a modern world leader step forward to put ethics and universal values at the heart of a nation's foreign policy.

Wilson called for making matters such as national self-determination and democracy equal to the rights of man. Yet the perceived failure of his efforts made his successors less bold. Franklin Roosevelt's Four Freedoms speech and his subsequent stewardship of the creation of the United Nations fell short of Wilson's lofty ideals. The UN at its core was based far more on great-power politics than on universal principles.

Perhaps the boldest single effort to enshrine human rights as a universal value came with the Nuremberg trials, which charged Nazi rulers and followers alike with war crimes and "crimes against humanity." But although the tribunals astonished, the precedents they set were soon put aside, viewed more as victor's justice than as a universal and shared symbol of morality.

The Cold War did not get high marks for morality either. It pitted an evil system against a far better one, but on both sides the moral gloves came off when it came time to fight. The left in the United States challenged what it saw as U.S. moral misdeeds: supporting dictators and the like. But none of these challenges struck home and prevailed in American politics until the presidencies of Richard Nixon and Jimmy Carter.

The realpolitik policies of Nixon and Henry Kissinger generated a backlash among both Republicans and Democrats on grounds of immorality.

The Republican right attacked detente as acceptance of the evil Soviet empire. The Democrats, and soon their presidential standard-bearer Jimmy Carter, attacked Kissinger's approach as contrary to "American values." And Carter made morality in U.S. foreign policy a core issue in his presidential campaign.

Although as president Carter did alter policies toward numerous dictatorships—such as those of Argentina, Uruguay, and Ethiopia—he also hedged his moral bets in places such as the Philippines, Iran, and Saudi Arabia. These contradictions served as examples of the almost inevitable policy inconsistencies that result when leaders try to balance security priorities with an ethical agenda.

His successor, Ronald Reagan, maintained Carter's ethical rhetoric but changed the focus to address communist dictatorships. He aided indigenous foes of the Soviet Union in Afghanistan, Angola, Cambodia, and Nicaragua. Again, however, the impossibility of consistently applying morality became clear. Even as Reagan made moves to defeat communism, he was criticized for supporting right-wing death squads in El Salvador, mining the harbors of the "democratically" elected government in Nicaragua, and trading arms and Bibles for hostages with Iranian zealots.

Carter used ethical rhetoric to pummel dictatorships on the right, whereas Reagan pummeled those on the left. But both made agile use of ethics and values in their foreign policies.

They left behind something approaching a consensus among Democrats and Republicans that morality and values should play a bigger role in U.S. actions abroad. With the passing of the Cold War and America's emergence as the sole superpower, moreover, the tradeoffs between security and ethics became less stark, and a moral foreign policy seemed more affordable.

What Now?

Debates over right and wrong are now embedded both in the international arena and in domestic deliberations. Protecting individual rights, advancing the rule of law, preventing genocide, and the like have become an inescapable part of arguments over policy. This is so not only in the public circus, where what is said rightly sparks a modicum of cynicism, but in private counsels in and out of government, where such arguments used to be dismissed as "unrealistic" or simply ignored.

Just how much ethical rhetoric has permeated policymaking is almost nowhere more clearly evident than in the lead up to war with Iraq. The debate about whether and why to go to war has featured a value-laden rhetoric: freedom for the Iraqi people, democracy for Iraq if not for the whole region, and the use of the United Nations (even if grudgingly) to help justify invasion. And this language is often proffered even more by the traditional realists than by the traditional liberals. Even if, in the end, a U.S.-led war effort serves to strengthen American power in the region more than anything else, the use of ethical rhetoric will have been a necessary ingredient in furthering that national security agenda.

Values now count in virtually every foreign policy discussion, at times for good, at times for ill, and always as a complicating factor. The cases where ethics must be factored in these days are startling in number and complexity.

For the longest time, Americans engaged in a sterile debate over human rights. It was a debate between those who believed the United States had to fight the bad guys no matter what the security tradeoffs, and those who believed the United States had no business interfering with the internal affairs of other states. Dictators used this split to neutralize U.S. pressure. Now that left and right have largely joined forces on the issue, however, dictators have to bend their precious local values and pay more heed to American entreaties—all the more so when those entreaties are inextricably bound to military and financial inducements. Human rights probably never will be effective as a public battering ram. Countries are complicated beasts most resistant when directly challenged. But leaders around the world understand today that they cannot take American money, beg American protection, and consistently escape the acknowledgment of American values.

Humanitarian intervention, meanwhile, is perhaps the most dramatic example of the new power of morality in international affairs. The notion that states could invade the sovereign territory of other states to stop massive bloodshed (call it genocide or ethnic cleansing or whatever) was inconceivable until the 1990s. The right of states or groups within states to mutilate and kill fellow citizens on a mass scale seemed to have assumed God-given proportions. But in the space of a few years, this pillar of international politics was badly shaken. The UN approved interventions in Bosnia and Somalia. NATO took military action in Kosovo. And the Organization of American States blessed the U.S.-led intervention in Haiti. What is more, the international community was quite prepared to intervene militarily in Rwanda had the Clinton administration not prevented it. Just think of it: states endorsing the principle that morality trumps sovereignty.

Even the historic triumph of this trumping, however, does not eliminate the moral problems raised by doing good through humanitarian intervention. Who is to be saved? The ethics of choice here remain cloudy indeed. Not everyone will be saved, particularly not minorities within major powers. And who is to assume the burdens of repairing and bettering societies that intervention pulverizes? The costs are staggering and the list of funders is wanting.

Other checks on crimes against humanity exist now as well. The UN has established war crimes tribunals to prosecute those who committed atrocities in Yugoslavia and Rwanda, and British authorities arrested former Chilean dictator Augusto Pinochet on charges of mass executions, torture, and other crimes against humanity. Even though these prosecutions may not deter all would-be killers, some justice is better than no justice at all.

As for the promotion of democracy, who could imagine how far America's commitment to it would go after Wilson's flop on the international and domestic stages? Just look at the odd soulmates who have found common ground on this issue in recent years: Morton Halperin and Paul Wolfowitz, George Soros and George W. Bush, even "realists" such as Richard Haass.

To be sure, some who ridiculed Presidents Clinton and Carter and their clans for advocating democracy now adopt this ideal whole, without so much as a blush, and perhaps may revert to their original positions under international duress. Whether or not they do so, the realists' warnings about democracy as a double-edged sword are worth remembering. It can be used to justify actions that otherwise would require better explanations; in this way democracy protects weak arguments. And its advocacy could compel excesses, such as rushing to elections before the development of a liberal society to underpin those elections.

We may be better off now that so many leaders, good ones and bad ones, feel they must protest their yearning for democracy. These protestations might actually entrap them, forcing them to do more good than they had ever considered desirable for their own ends. Still, this democratic ideal contains so much power that some prudence about rushing its implementation seems wise. Even if done cautiously, however, implementing democratic ideals carries its own contradictions. The Clinton and Bush administrations have promoted democracy around the world yet said little or nothing about the need for it in places such as China, Egypt, and Saudi Arabia.

The counterterrorism agenda only heightens these inconsistencies. It further divides Americans and Muslims around the world, many of whom see terrorists as freedom fighters. And many now in the Bush administration condemned President Clinton's decision not to make major issues of Russia's treatment of the Chechens or China's treatment of Muslim Uighurs, but have more or less abandoned that brief in the name of a common front against al Qaeda and like organizations.

Then there is the fact that the United States is often on a different ethical and moral track from others. Most nations have approved of the genocide convention, the International Criminal Court, the treaty banning land mines, and the Kyoto Protocol on climate change, all of which they consider part of their moral stance. But the United States rejects these and other such agreements on grounds that it suffers disproportionately under their terms. Such conflicts between the ethical and the practical will not be sorted out easily and so will remain a source of tension. But it is better to dispute matters such as land mines and global warming than to go to war over traditional power issues.

Yes, it will remain very rare for ethical and moral concerns to dominate foreign policy, particularly when it comes to national security issues. Yes, nations will continue to dispute the merits of their respective ethical and moral systems. Yes, within nations, there will be battles over whether moral or practical concerns should come first and over which moral concerns should take precedence. Even as universal values become more a part of the foreign policies of nations, those policies will still be ridden with contradictions and hypocrisies. And yes, the morality of the strong will generally still prevail over that of the weak, and considerations of value almost inevitably will have to take second place. But they used to have no place. Second place means that leaders now have to be mindful of ignoring or abusing what are increasingly seen as universal values.

We have passed from an era in which ideals were always flatly opposed to self-interests into an era in which tension remains between the two, but the stark juxtaposition of the past has largely subsided. Now, ideals and self-interests are both generally considered necessary ingredients of the national interest. For all the old and new policy problems this entails, Americans and most of the world are better off.

CHAPTER 3

DEMOCRATIC PEACE *v.* THE DANGERS OF DEMOCRATIZATION

In Favor of Democratic Peace

Advocate: Michael W. Doyle

Source: "Liberalism and World Politics," *The American Political Science Review*, vol. 80, no. 4 (1986), pp. 1155–1169, excerpt.

Democratic Peace and War

Advocates: Edward D. Mansfield and Jack Snyder

Source: "Democratization and War," *Foreign Affairs*, vol. 74, no. 3 (May 1995), pp. 35–42, excerpt.

The Democratic Peace theory is one of the mainstays of the liberal paradigm in international relations theory. Its main premise is that democracies do not fight one another. The same does not apply to non-democratic states, however: democracies do fight non-democracies, especially weak ones. The theory has both its strident adherents as well as vociferous critics. Research suggests that some of the most conflict-prone countries are the ones that experience transitions to democracy.

The implications of the Democratic Peace theory are significant, particularly with respect to policies of democracy promotion. If true, it would suggest that as the number of democratic countries in the world grows, interstate conflict will continue to decrease as democracies do not fight one another. Hence, there is an incentive to encourage democratization processes around the world, including in troubled spots such as the Middle East.

IN SUPPORT OF DEMOCRATIC PEACE

For many students who study international relations, the Democratic Peace theory is one of the most empirically grounded theories. It is also a key component of the liberal paradigm. Drawing on liberal states' domestic constitutional arrangements and international political and economic interdependence, proponents of the Democratic Peace theory attempt to explain the liberal states' disinclination to wage war on one another. In addition, through looking at the relative lack of violence among democratic states, the theory provides a foundation for policies of democracy promotion.

Michael Doyle is one of the most prominent scholars to be linked to the Democratic Peace theory. He argues that peace tends to prevail among liberal states, although not in their relations with non-liberal states. Looking at historical evidence and tracing his argument back to the writings of philosopher Immanuel Kant, Doyle argues that because of their democratic constitutions, internationalism and cosmopolitanism, liberal states exercise restraint and are more pacifist. This tendency of liberal states to be more peaceful with one another forms the basis for the United States' alliances with other countries, such as the North Atlantic Treaty Organization (NATO).

IN SUPPORT OF MANAGING TRANSITIONS

Although democratic states may not fight one another, empirical evidence suggests that the most conflict-prone countries are the ones undergoing a process of democratization. As Edward Mansfield and Jack Snyder point out, several factors make such societies especially volatile and susceptible to violence.

Transformational processes always create winners and losers, threaten the position of elites, and ignite nationalist feelings, which all may lead to conflict. Although the masses may not be supportive of such inclinations, propaganda waged by interested elites contributes to violence. Mansfield and Snyder suggest that more should be done to help countries undergoing democratic transitions.

POINTS **TO PONDER**

1. Why do democracies not fight one another?
2. Should we promote democracy if transitions lead to an increase in violence?
3. Is the United States justified in promoting democracy around the world, particularly in key areas such as the Middle East?

Michael W. Doyle

Liberalism and World Politics

Liberal Internationalism

Modern liberalism carries with it two legacies. They do not affect liberal states separately, according to whether they are pacifistic or imperialistic, but simultaneously.

The first of these legacies is the pacification of foreign relations among liberal states.[1] During the nineteenth century, the United States and Great Britain engaged in nearly continual strife; however, after the Reform Act of 1832 defined actual representation as the formal source of the sovereignty of the British parliament, Britain and the United States negotiated their disputes. They negotiated despite, for example, British grievances during the Civil War against the North's blockade of the South, with which Britain had close economic ties. Despite severe Anglo-French colonial rivalry, liberal France and liberal Britain formed an entente against illiberal Germany before World War I. And from 1914 to 1915, Italy, the liberal member of the Triple Alliance with Germany and Austria, chose not to fulfill its obligations under that treaty to support its allies. Instead, Italy joined in an alliance with Britain and France, which prevented it from having to fight other liberal states and then declared war on Germany and Austria. Despite generations of Anglo-American tension and Britain's wartime restrictions on American trade with Germany, the United States leaned toward Britain and France from 1914 to 1917 before entering World War I on their side.

Beginning in the eighteenth century and slowly growing since then, a zone of peace, which Kant called the "pacific federation" or "pacific union," has begun to be established among liberal societies. More than 40 liberal states currently make up the union. Most are in Europe and North America, but they can be found on every continent, as Appendix 1 indicates.

Here the predictions of liberal pacifists (and President Reagan) are borne out: liberal states do exercise peaceful restraint, and a separate peace exists among them. This separate peace provides a solid foundation for the United States' crucial alliances with the liberal powers, e.g., the North Atlantic Treaty Organization and our Japanese alliance. This foundation appears to be impervious to the quarrels with our allies that bedeviled the Carter and Reagan administrations. It also offers the promise of a continuing peace among liberal states, and as the number of liberal states increases, it announces the possibility of global peace this side of the grave or world conquest.

Of course, the probability of the outbreak of war in any given year between any two given states is low. The occurrence of a war between any two adjacent states, considered over a long period of time, would be more probable. The apparent absence of war between liberal states, whether adjacent or not, for almost 200 years thus may have significance. Similar claims cannot be made for feudal, fascist, communist, authoritarian, or totalitarian forms of rule (Doyle, 1983a, pp. 222), nor for pluralistic or merely similar societies. More significant perhaps is that when states are forced to decide on which side of an impending world war they will fight, liberal states all wind up on the same side despite the complexity of the paths that take them there. These characteristics do not prove that the peace among liberals is statistically significant nor that liberalism is the sole valid explanation for the peace.[2] They do suggest that we consider the possibility that liberals have indeed established a separate peace—but only among themselves.

Liberalism also carries with it a second legacy: international "imprudence" (Hume, 1963, pp. 346–47). Peaceful restraint only seems to work in liberals' relations with other liberals. Liberal states have fought numerous wars with nonliberal states. (For a list of international wars since 1816 see Appendix 2.)

Many of these wars have been defensive and thus prudent by necessity. Liberal states have been attacked and threatened by nonliberal states that do not exercise any special restraint in their dealings with the liberal states. Authoritarian rulers both stimulate and respond to an international political environment in which conflicts of prestige, interest, and pure fear of what other states might do all lead states toward war. War and conquest have thus characterized the careers of many authoritarian rulers and ruling parties, from Louis XIV and Napoleon to Mussolini's fascists, Hitler's Nazis, and Stalin's communists.

Yet we cannot simply blame warfare on the authoritarians or totalitarians, as many of our more enthusiastic politicians would have us do.[3] Most wars arise out of calculations and miscalculations of interest, misunderstandings, and mutual suspicions, such as those that characterized the origins of World War I. However, aggression by the liberal state has also characterized a large number of wars. Both France and Britain fought expansionist colonial wars throughout the nineteenth century. The United States fought a similar war with Mexico from 1846 to 1848, waged a war of annihilation against the American Indians, and intervened militarily against sovereign states many times before and after World War II. Liberal states invade weak nonliberal states and display striking distrust in dealings with powerful nonliberal states (Doyle, 1983b).

Neither realist (statist) nor Marxist theory accounts well for these two legacies. While they can account for aspects of certain periods of international stability (Aron, 1968, pp. 151–54; Russett, 1985), neither the logic of the balance of power nor the logic of international hegemony explains the separate peace maintained for more than 150 years among states sharing one particular form of governance—liberal principles and institutions. Balance-of-power theory expects—indeed is premised upon—flexible arrangements of geostrategic rivalry that include preventive war. Hegemonies wax and wane, but the liberal peace holds. Marxist "ultra-imperialists" expect a form of peaceful rivalry among capitalists, but only liberal capitalists maintain peace. Leninists expect liberal capitalists to be aggressive toward nonliberal states, but they also (and especially) expect them to be imperialistic toward fellow liberal capitalists.

Kant's theory of liberal internationalism helps us understand these two legacies. . . .

The First Definitive Article requires the civil constitution of the state to be republican. By *republican* Kant means a political society that has solved the problem of combining moral autonomy, individualism, and social order. A private property and market-oriented economy partially addressed that dilemma in the private sphere. The public, or political, sphere was more troubling. His answer was a republic that preserved juridical freedom—the legal equality of citizens as subjects—on the basis of a representative government with a separation of powers. Juridical freedom is preserved because the morally autonomous individual is by means of representation a self-legislator making laws that apply to all citizens equally, including himself or herself. Tyranny is avoided because the individual is subject to laws he or she does not also administer (Kant, *PP*, pp. 99–102; Riley, 1985, chap. 5).[4]

Liberal republics will progressively establish peace among themselves by means of the pacific federation, or union (*foedus pacificum*), described in Kant's Second Definitive Article. The pacific union will establish peace within a federation of free states and securely maintain the rights of each state. The world will not have achieved the "perpetual peace" that provides the ultimate guarantor of republican freedom until "a late stage and after many unsuccessful attempts" (Kant, *UH*, p. 47). At that time, all nations will have learned the lessons of peace through right conceptions of the appropriate constitution, great and sad experience, and good will. Only then will individuals enjoy perfect republican rights or the full guarantee of a global and just peace. In the meantime, the "pacific federation" of liberal republics—"an enduring and gradually expanding federation likely to prevent war"—brings within it more and more republics—despite republican collapses, backsliding, and disastrous wars—creating an ever-expanding separate peace (Kant, *PP*, p. 105).[5] . . .

The pacific union is not a single peace treaty ending one war, a world state, nor a state of nations. Kant finds the first insufficient. The second and third are impossible or potentially tyrannical. National sovereignty precludes reliable subservience to a state of nations; a world state destroys the civic freedom on which the development of human capacities rests (Kant, *UH*, p. 50). Although Kant obliquely refers to various classical interstate confederations and modern diplomatic congresses, he develops no systematic organizational embodiment of this treaty and presumably does not find institutionalization necessary (Riley, 1983, chap. 5; Schwarz, 1962, p. 77). He appears to have in mind a mutual nonaggression pact, perhaps a collective security agreement, and the cosmopolitan law set forth in the Third Definitive Article.[6] . . .

Kant shows how republics, once established, lead to peaceful relations. He argues that once the aggressive interests of absolutist monarchies are tamed and the habit of respect for individual rights engrained by republican government, wars would appear as the disaster to the people's welfare that he and the other liberals thought them to be. The fundamental reason is this:

> If, as is inevitability the case under this constitution, the consent of the citizens is required to decide whether or not war should be declared, it is very natural that they will have a great hesitation in embarking on so dangerous an enterprise. For this would mean calling down on themselves all the miseries of war, such as doing the fighting themselves, supplying the costs of the war from their own resources, painfully making good the ensuing devastation, and, as the crowning evil, having to take upon themselves a burden of debts which will embitter peace itself and which can never be paid off on account of the constant threat of new wars. But under a constitution where the subject is not a citizen, and which is therefore not republican, it is the simplest thing in the world to go to war. For the head of state is not a fellow citizen, but the owner of the state, and war will not force him to make the slightest sacrifice so far as his banquets, hunts, pleasure palaces and court festivals are concerned. He can thus decide on war, without any significant reason, as a kind of amusement, and unconcernedly leave it to the diplomatic corps (who are always ready for such purposes) to justify the war for the sake of propriety. (Kant, *PP*, p. 100)

Yet these domestic republican restraints do not end war. If they did, liberal states would not be warlike, which is far from the case. They do introduce republican caution—Kant's "hesitation"—in place of monarchical caprice. Liberal wars are only fought for popular, liberal purposes. The historical liberal legacy is laden with popular wars fought to promote freedom, to protect private property, or to support liberal allies against nonliberal enemies. Kant's position is ambiguous. He regards these wars as unjust and warns liberals of their susceptibility to them (Kant, *PP*, p. 106). At the same time, Kant argues that each nation "can and ought to" demand that its neighboring nations enter into the pacific union of liberal states (*PP*, p. 102). Thus to see how the pacific union removes the occasion of wars among liberal states and not wars between liberal and nonliberal states, we need to shift our attention from constitutional law to international law, Kant's second source.

Complementing the constitutional guarantee of caution, international law adds a second source for the definitive articles: a guarantee of respect. The separation of nations that asocial sociability encourages is reinforced by the development of separate languages and religions. These further guarantee a world of separate states—an essential condition needed to avoid a "global, soul-less despotism." Yet, at the same time, they also morally integrate liberal states: "as culture grows and men gradually move towards greater agreement over their principles, they lead to mutual understanding and peace" (Kant, *PP*, p. 114). As republics emerge (the first source) and as culture progresses, an understanding of the legitimate rights of all citizens and of all republics comes into play; and this, now that caution characterizes policy, sets up the moral foundations for the liberal peace. Correspondingly, international law highlights the importance of Kantian publicity. Domestically, publicity helps ensure that the officials of republics act according to the principles they profess to hold just and according to the interests of the electors they claim to represent. Internationally, free speech and the effective communication of accurate conceptions of the political life of foreign peoples is essential to establishing and preserving the understanding on which the guarantee of respect depends. Domestically just republics, which rest on consent, then presume foreign republics also to be consensual, just, and therefore deserving of accommodation. The experience of cooperation helps engender further cooperative behavior when the consequences of state policy are unclear but (potentially) mutually beneficial. At the same time, liberal states assume that nonliberal states, which do not rest on free consent, are not just. Because nonliberal governments are in a state of aggression with their own people, their foreign relations become for liberal governments deeply suspect. In short, fellow liberals benefit from a presumption of amity; nonliberals suffer from a presumption of enmity. Both presumptions may be accurate; each, however, may also be self-confirming.

Lastly, cosmopolitan law adds material incentives to moral commitments. The cosmopolitan right to hospitality permits the "spirit of commerce" sooner or later to take hold of every nation, thus impelling states to promote peace and to try to avert war. Liberal economic theory holds that these cosmopolitan ties derive from a cooperative international division of labor and free trade according to comparative advantage. Each economy is said to be better off than it would have been under autarky; each thus acquires an incentive to avoid policies that would lead the other to break these economic ties. Because keeping open markets rests upon the assumption that the next set of transactions will also be determined by prices rather than coercion, a sense of mutual security is vital to avoid security-motivated searches for economic autarky. Thus, avoiding a challenge to another liberal state's security or even enhancing each other's security by means of alliance naturally follows economic interdependence.

A further cosmopolitan source of liberal peace is the international market's removal of difficult decisions of production and distribution from the direct sphere of state policy. A foreign state thus does not appear directly responsible for these outcomes, and states can stand aside from, and to some degree above, these contentious market rivalries and be ready to step in to resolve crises. The interdependence of commerce and the international contacts of state officials help create crosscutting transnational ties that serve as lobbies for mutual accommodation. According to modern liberal scholars, international financiers and transnational and transgovernmental organizations create interests in favor of accommodation. Moreover, their variety has ensured that no single conflict sours an entire relationship by setting off a spiral of reciprocated retaliation. Conversely, a sense of suspicion, such as that characterizing relations between liberal and nonliberal governments, can lead to restrictions on the range of contacts between societies, and this can increase the prospect that a single conflict will determine an entire relationship.

No single constitutional, international, or cosmopolitan source is alone sufficient, but together (and only together) they plausibly connect the characteristics of liberal polities and economies with sustained liberal peace. Alliances founded on mutual strategic interest among liberal and nonliberal states have been broken; economic ties between liberal and nonliberal states have proven fragile; but the political bonds of liberal rights and interests have proven a remarkably firm foundation for mutual nonaggression. A separate peace exists among liberal states.

In their relations with nonliberal states, however, liberal states have not escaped from the insecurity caused by anarchy in the world political system considered as a whole. Moreover, the very constitutional restraint, international respect for individual rights, and shared commercial interests that establish grounds for peace among liberal states establish grounds for additional conflict in relations between liberal and nonliberal societies.

Conclusion

Kant's citizens, too, are diverse in their goals and individualized and rationalized, but most importantly, they are capable of appreciating the moral equality of all individuals and of treating other individuals as ends rather than as means. The Kantian state thus is governed publicly according to law, as a republic. Kant's is the state that solves the problem of governing individualized equals, whether they are the "rational devils" he says we often find ourselves to be or the ethical agents we can and should become. Republics tell us that

> in order to organize a group of rational beings who together require universal laws for their survival, but of whom each separate individual is secretly inclined to exempt himself from them, the constitution must be so designed so that, although the citizens are opposed to one another in their private attitudes, these opposing views may inhibit one another in such a way that the

public conduct of the citizens will be the same as if they did not
have such evil attitudes. (Kant, *PP*, p. 113)

Unlike Machiavelli's republics, Kant's republics are capable of achieving peace among themselves because they exercise democratic caution and
are capable of appreciating the international rights of foreign republics.
These international rights of republics derive from the representation of
foreign individuals, who are our moral equals. Unlike Schumpeter's capitalist
democracies, Kant's republics—including our own—remain in a state of war
with nonrepublics. Liberal republics see themselves as threatened by aggression from nonrepublics that are not constrained by representation. Even
though wars often cost more than the economic return they generate, liberal
republics also are prepared to protect and promote—sometimes forcibly—
democracy, private property, and the rights of individuals overseas against
nonrepublics, which, because they do not authentically represent the rights
of individuals, have no rights to noninterference. These wars may liberate
oppressed individuals overseas; they also can generate enormous suffering.

Preserving the legacy of the liberal peace without succumbing to the
legacy of liberal imprudence is both a moral and a strategic challenge. The
bipolar stability of the international system, and the near certainty of mutual
devastation resulting from a nuclear war between the superpowers, have
created a "crystal ball effect" that has helped to constrain the tendency
toward miscalculation present at the outbreak of so many wars in the past
(Carnesale, Doty, Hoffmann, Huntington, Nye, and Sagan, 1983, p. 44;
Waltz, 1964). However, this "nuclear peace" appears to be limited to the
superpowers. It has not curbed military interventions in the Third World.
Moreover, it is subject to a desperate technological race designed to overcome its constraints and to crises that have pushed even the superpowers to
the brink of war. We must still reckon with the war fevers and moods of
appeasement that have almost alternately swept liberal democracies.

Yet restraining liberal imprudence, whether aggressive or passive, may
not be possible without threatening liberal pacification. Improving the
strategic acumen of our foreign policy calls for introducing steadier strategic
calculations of the national interest in the long run and more flexible
responses to changes in the international political environment. Constraining
the indiscriminate meddling of our foreign interventions calls for a deeper
appreciation of the "particularism of history, culture, and membership"
(Walzer, 1983, p. 5), but both the improvement in strategy and the constraint on intervention seem, in turn, to require an executive freed from the
restraints of a representative legislature in the management of foreign policy
and a political culture indifferent to the universal rights of individuals. These
conditions, in their turn, could break the chain of constitutional guarantees,

the respect for representative government, and the web of transnational contact that have sustained the pacific union of liberal states.

Perpetual peace, Kant says, is the end point of the hard journey his republics will take. The promise of perpetual peace, the violent lessons of war, and the experience of a partial peace are proof of the need for and the possibility of world peace. They are also the grounds for moral citizens and statesmen to assume the duty of striving for peace.

Appendix 1. Liberal Regimes and the Pacific Union, 1700–1982

Period	Period	Period
18th Century	1900–1945	1945–[b]
Swiss Cantons[a]	Switzerland	Switzerland
French Republic,	United States	United States
1790–1795	Great Britain	Great Britain
United States,[a]	Sweden	Sweden
1776–	Canada	Canada
Total = 3	Greece, –1911;	Australia
	1928–1936	New Zealand
1800–1850	Italy, –1922	Finland
Swiss Confederation	Belgium, –1940	Ireland
United States	Netherlands, –1940	Mexico
France, 1830–1849	Argentina, –1943	Uruguay, –1973
Belgium, 1830–	France, –1940	Chile, –1973
Great Britain, 1832–	Chile, –1924, 1932–	Lebanon, –1975
Netherlands, 1848–	Australia, 1901	Costa Rica, –1948;
Piedmont, 1848–	Norway, 1905–1940	1953–
Denmark, 1849–	New Zealand, 1907–	Iceland, 1944–
Total = 8	Colombia,	France, 1945–
	1910–1949	Denmark, 1945
1850–1900	Denmark, 1914–1940	Norway, 1945
Switzerland	Poland, 1917–1935	Austria, 1945–
United States	Latvia, 1922–1934	Brazil, 1945–1954;
Belgium	Germany, 1918–1932	1955–1964
Great Britain	Austria,	Belgium, 1946–
Netherlands	1918–1934	Luxemburg, 1946–
Piedmont, –1861	Estonia, 1919–1934	Netherlands, 1946–
Italy, 1861–	Finland, 1919–	Italy, 1946–
Denmark, –1866	Uruguay, 1919–	Philippines, 1946–1972
Sweden, 1864–	Costa Rica, 1919–	India, 1947–1975, 1977–
Greece, 1864–	Czechoslovakia,	Sri Lanka, 1948–1961;
Canada, 1867–	1920–1939	1963–1971; 1978–
France, 1871–	Ireland, 1920–	Ecuador, 1948–1963;
Argentina, 1880–	Mexico, 1928–	1979–
Chile, 1891–	Lebanon, 1944–	Israel, 1949–
Total = 13	Total = 29	West Germany, 1949–

(*continued*)

Appendix 1. Liberal Regimes and the Pacific Union (*continued*)

Period	Period	Period
1945– (cont.)	1945– (cont.)	1945– (cont.)
Greece, 1950–1967;	Colombia, 1958–	Botswana, 1966–
1975–	Venezuela, 1959–	Singapore, 1965–
Peru, 1950–1962;	Nigeria, 1961–1964;	Portugal, 1976–
1963–1968; 1980–	1979–1984	Spain, 1978–
El Salvador, 1950–1961	Jamaica, 1962–	Dominican Republic,
Turkey, 1950–1960;	Trinidad and Tobago,	1978–
1966–1971	1962–	Honduras, 1981–
Japan, 1951–	Senegal, 1963–	Papua New Guinea, 1982–
Bolivia, 1956–1969; 1982–	Malaysia, 1963–	Total = 50

Note: I have drawn up this approximate list of "Liberal Regimes" according to the four institutions Kant described as essential: market and private property economies; polities that are externally sovereign; citizens who possess juridical rights; and "republican" (whether republican or parliamentary monarchy), representative government. This latter includes the requirement that the legislative branch have an effective role in public policy and be formally and competitively (either inter- or intra-party) elected. Furthermore, I have taken into account whether male suffrage is wide (i.e., 30%) or, as Kant (*MM*, p. 139) would have had it, open by "achievement" to inhabitants of the national or metropolitan territory (e.g., to poll-tax payers or house-holders). This list of liberal regimes is thus more inclusive than a list of democratic regimes, or polyarchies (Powell, 1982, p. 5). Other conditions taken into account here are that female suffrage is granted within a generation of its being demanded by an extensive female suffrage movement and that representative government is internally sovereign (e.g., including, and especially over military and foreign affairs) as well as stable (in existence for at least three years). Sources for these data are Banks and Overstreet (1983), Gastil (1985), *The Europa Yearbook, 1985* (1985), Langer (1968), U.K. Foreign and Commonwealth Office (1980), and U.S. Department of State (1981). Finally, these lists exclude ancient and medieval "republics," since none appears to fit Kant's commitment to liberal individualism (Holmes, 1979).
[a]There are domestic variations within these liberal regimes: Switzerland was liberal only in certain cantons; the United States was liberal only north of the Mason-Dixon line until 1865, when it became liberal throughout.
[b]Selected list, excludes liberal regimes with populations less than one million. These include all states categorized as "free" by Gastil and those "partly free" (four-fifths or more free) states with a more pronounced capitalist orientation.

Appendix 2. International Wars Listed Chronologically

British-Maharattan (1817–1818)
Greek (1821–1828)
Franco-Spanish (1823)
First Anglo-Burmese (1823–1826)
Javanese (1825–1830)
Russo-Persian (1826–1828)
Russo-Turkish (1828–1829)
First Polish (1831)
First Syrian (1831–1832)
Texas (1835–1836)
First British-Afghan (1838–1842)
Second Syrian (1839–1940)

Franco-Algerian (1839–1847)
Peruvian-Bolivian (1841)
First British-Sikh (1845–1846)
Mexican-American (1846–1848)
Austro-Sardinian (1848–1849)
First Schleswig-Holstein (1848–1849)
Hungarian (1848–1849)
Second British-Sikh (1848–1849)
Roman Republic (1849)
La Plata (1851–1852)
First Turco-Montenegran
   (1852–1853)

Appendix 2. International Wars Listed Chronologically (*continued*)

Crimean (1853–1856)
Anglo-Persian (1856–1857)
Sepoy (1857–1859)
Second Turco-Montenegran
 (1858–1859)
Italian Unification (1859)
Spanish-Moroccan (1859–1860)
Italo-Roman (1860)
Italo-Sicilian (1860–1861)
Franco-Mexican (1862–1867)
Ecuadorian-Colombian (1863)
Second Polish (1863–1864)
Spanish-Santo Dominican (1863–1865)
Second Schleswig-Holstein (1864)
Lopez (1864–1870)
Spanish-Chilean (1865–1866)
Seven Weeks (1866)
Ten Years (1868–1878)
Franco-Prussian (1870–1871)
Dutch-Achinese (1873–1878)
Balkan (1875–1877)
Russo-Turkish (1877–1878)
Bosnian (1878)
Second British-Afghan (1878–1880)
Pacific (1879–1883)
British-Zulu (1879)
Franco-Indochinese (1882–1884)
Mahdist (1882–1885)
Sino-French (1884–1885)
Central American (1885)
Serbo-Bulgarian (1885)
Sino-Japanese (1894–1895)
Franco-Madagascan (1894–1895)
Cuban (1895–1898)
Italo-Ethipian (1895–1896)
First Philippine (1896–1898)
Greco-Turkish (1897)
Spanish-American (1898)
Second Phlippine (1899–1902)
Boer (1899–1902)
Boxer Rebellion (1900)
Ilinden (1903)
Russo-Japanese (1904–1905)
Central American (1906)
Central American (1907)
Spanish-Moroccan (1909–1910)
Italo-Turkish (1911–1912)
First Balkan (1912–1913)

Second Balkan (1913)
World War I (1914–1918)
Russian Nationalities (1917–1921)
Russo-Polish (1919–1920)
Hungarian-Allies (1919).
Greco-Turkish (1919–1922)
Riffian (1921–1926)
Druze (1925–1927)
Sino-Soviet (1929)
Manchurian (1931–1933)
Chaco (1932–1935)
Italo-Ethiopian (1935–1936)
Sino-Japanese (1937–1941)
Russo-Hungarian (1956)
Sinai (1956)
Tibetan (1956–1959)
Sino-Indian (1962)
Vietnamese (1965–1975)
Second Kashmir (1965)
Six Day (1967)
Israeli-Egyptian (1969–1970)
Football (1969)
Changkufeng (1938)
Nomohan (1939)
World War II (1939–1945)
Russo-Finnish (1939–1940)
Franco-Thai (1940–1941)
Indonesian (1945–1946)
Indochinese (1945–1954)
Madagascan (1947–1948)
First Kashmir (1947–1949)
Palestine (1948–1949)
Hyderabad (1948)
Korean (1950–1953)
Algerian (1954–1962)
Bangladesh (1971)
Philippine-MNLF (1972–)
Yom Kippur (1973)
Turco-Cypriot (1974)
Ethiopian-Eritrean (1974–)
Vietnamese-Cambodian (1975–)
Timor (1975–)
Saharan (1975–)
Ogaden (1976–)
Ugandan-Tanzanian (1978–1979)
Sino-Vietnamese (1979)
Russo-Afghan (1979–)
Iran-Iraqi (1980–)

Note: This table is taken from Melvin Small and J. David Singer (1982, pp. 79–80). This is a partial list of international wars fought between 1816 and 1980. In Appendices A and B, Small and Singer identify a total of 575 wars during this period, but approximately 159 of them appear to be largely domestic, or civil wars.

This list excludes covert interventions, some of which have been directed by liberal regimes against other liberal regimes—for example, the United States' effort to destabilize the Chilean election and Allende's government. Nonetheless, it is significant that such interventions are not pursued publicly as acknowledged policy. The covert destabilization campaign against Chile is recounted by the Senate Select Committee to Study Governmental Operations with Respect to Intelligence Activities (1975, *Covert Action in Chile, 1963–73*).

Following the argument of this article, this list also excludes civil wars. Civil wars differ from international wars, not in the ferocity of combat, but in the issues that engender them. Two nations that could abide one another as independent neighbors separated by a border might well be the fiercest of enemies if forced to live together in one state, jointly deciding how to raise and spend taxes, choose leaders, and legislate fundamental questions of value. Notwithstanding these differences, no civil wars that I recall upset the argument of liberal pacification.

NOTES

1. Clarence Streit (1938, pp. 88, 90–92) seems to have been the first to point out (in contemporary foreign relations) the empirical tendency of democracies to maintain peace among themselves, and he made this the foundation of his proposal for a (non-Kantian) federal union of the 15 leading democracies of the 1930s. In a very interesting book, Ferdinand Hermens (1944) explored some of the policy implications of Streit's analysis. D. V. Babst (1972, pp. 55–58) performed a quantitative study of this phenomenon of "democratic peace," and R. J. Rummel (1983) did a similar study of "libertarianism" (in the sense of laissez faire) focusing on the postwar period that drew on an unpublished study (Project No. 48) noted in Appendix 1 of his *Understanding Conflict and War* (1979, p. 386). I use the term *liberal* in a wider, Kantian sense in my discussion of this issue (Doyle, 1983a). In that essay, I survey the period from 1790 to the present and find no war among liberal states.

2. Babst (1972) did make a preliminary test of the significance of the distribution of alliance partners in World War I. He found that the possibility that the actual distribution of alliance partners could have occurred by chance was less than 1% (Babst, 1972, p. 56). However, this assumes that there was an equal possibility that any two nations could have gone to war with each other, and this is a strong assumption. Rummel (1983) has a further discussion of the issue of statistical significance as it applies to his libertarian thesis.

3. There are serious studies showing that Marxist regimes have higher military spending per capita than non-Marxist regimes (Payne, n.d.), but this should not be interpreted as a sign of the inherent aggressiveness of authoritarian or totalitarian governments or of the inherent and global peacefulness of liberal regimes. Marxist regimes, in particular, represent a minority in the current international system; they are strategically encircled, and due to their lack of domestic legitimacy, they might be said to "suffer" the twin burden of needing defenses against both external and internal enemies. Andreski (1980), moreover, argues that (purely) military

dictatorships, due to their domestic fragility, have little incentive to engage in foreign military adventures. According to Walter Clemens (1982, pp. 117–18), the United States intervened in the Third World more than twice as often during the period 1946–1976 as the Soviet Union did in 1946–79. Relatedly, Posen and VanEvera (1980, p. 105; 1983, pp. 86–89) found that the United States devoted one quarter and the Soviet Union one tenth of their defense budgets to forces designed for Third World interventions (where responding to perceived threats would presumably have a less than purely defensive character).

4. All citations from Kant are from *Kant's Political Writings* (Kant, 1970), the H. B. Nisbet translation edited by Hans Reiss. The works discussed and the abbreviations by which they are identified in the text are as follows:

PP   *Perpetual Peace* (1795)
UH   *The Idea for a Universal History with a Cosmopolitan Purpose* (1784)
CF   *The Contest of Faculties* (1798)
MM   *The Metaphysics of Morals* (1797)

5. I think Kant meant that the peace would be established among liberal regimes and would expand by ordinary political and legal means as new liberal regimes appeared. By a process of gradual extension the peace would become global and then perpetual; the occasion for wars with nonliberals would disappear as nonliberal regimes disappeared.

6. Kant's *foedus pacificum* is thus neither a *pactum pacis* (a single peace treaty) nor a *civitas gentium* (a world state). He appears to have anticipated something like a less formally Institutionalized League of Nations or United Nations. One could argue that in practice, these two institutions worked for liberal states and only for liberal states, but no specifically liberal "pacific union" was institutionalized. Instead, liberal states have behaved for the past 180 years as if such a Kantian pacific union and treaty of perpetual peace had been signed.

REFERENCES

Andreski, Stanislav. 1980. On the Peaceful Disposition of Military Dictatorships. *Journal of Strategic Studies*, 3:3–10.

Armstrong, A. C. 1931. Kant's Philosophy of Peace and War. *The Journal of Philosophy*, 28:197–204.

Aron, Raymond. 1966. *Peace and War: A Theory of International Relations*. Richard Howard and Annette Baker Fox, trans. Garden City, NY: Doubleday.

Aron, Raymond. 1974. *The Imperial Republic*. Frank Jellinek, trans. Englewood Cliffs, NJ: Prentice Hall.

Babst, Dean V. 1972. A Force for Peace. *Industrial Research*. 14 (April): 55–58.

Banks, Arthur, and William Overstreet, eds. 1983. *A Political Handbook of the World; 1982–1983*. New York: McGraw Hill.

Barnet, Richard. 1968. *Intervention and Revolution*. Cleveland: World Publishing Co.

Brzezinski, Zbigniew, and Samuel Huntington. 1963. *Political Power: USA/USSR*. New York: Viking Press.

Carnesale, Albert, Paul Doty, Stanley Hoffmann, Samuel Huntington, Joseph Nye, and Scott Sagan. 1983. *Living With Nuclear Weapons.* New York. Bantam.

Chan, Steve. 1984. Mirror, Mirror on the Wall . . .: Are Freer Countries More Pacific? *Journal of Conflict Resolution,* 28:617–48.

Clemens, Walter C. 1982. The Superpowers and the Third World. In Charles Kegley and Pat McGowan, eds., *Foreign Policy; USA/USSR.* Beverly Hills: Sage. pp. 111–35.

Doyle, Michael W. 1983a. Kant, Liberal Legacies, and Foreign Affairs: Part 1. *Philosophy and Public Affairs,* 12:205–35.

Doyle, Michael W. 1983b. Kant, Liberal Legacies, and Foreign Affairs: Part 2. *Philosophy and Public Affairs,* 12:323–53.

Doyle, Michael W. 1986. *Empires.* Ithaca: Cornell University Press.

The Europa Yearbook for 1985. 1985. 2 vols. London. Europa Publications.

Friedrich, Karl. 1948. *Inevitable Peace.* Cambridge, MA: Harvard University Press.

Gallie, W. B. 1978. *Philosophers of Peace and War.* Cambridge: Cambridge University Press.

Galston, William. 1975. *Kant and the Problem of History.* Chicago: Chicago University Press.

Gastil, Raymond. 1985. The Comparative Survey of Freedom 1985. *Freedom at Issue,* 82:3–16.

Haas, Michael. 1974. *International Conflict.* New York: Bobbs-Merrill.

Hassner, Pierre. 1972. Immanuel Kant. In Leo Strauss and Joseph Cropsey, eds., *History of Political Philosophy.* Chicago: Rand McNally. pp. 554–93.

Hermens, Ferdinand A. 1944. *The Tyrants' War and the People's Peace.* Chicago: University of Chicago Press.

Hinsley, F. H. 1967. *Power and the Pursuit of Peace.* Cambridge: Cambridge University Press.

Hoffmann, Stanley. 1965. Rousseau on War and Peace. In Stanley Hoffmann, ed. *The State of War.* New York: Praeger. pp. 45–87.

Holmes, Stephen. 1979. Aristippus in and out of Athens. *American Political Science Review,* 73:113–28.

Huliung, Mark. 1983. *Citizen Machiavelli.* Princeton: Princeton University Press.

Hume, David. 1963. Of the Balance of Power. *Essays: Moral, Political, and Literary.* Oxford: Oxford University Press.

Kant, Immanuel. 1970. *Kant's Political Writings.* Hans Reiss, ed. H. B. Nisbet, trans. Cambridge: Cambridge University Press.

Kelly, George A. 1969. *Idealism, Politics, and History.* Cambridge: Cambridge University Press.

Keohane, Robert, and Joseph Nye. 1977. *Power and Interdependence.* Boston: Little Brown.

Langer, William L., ed. 1968. *The Encyclopedia of World History.* Boston: Houghton Mifflin.

Machiavelli, Niccolo. 1950. *The Prince and the Discourses.* Max Lerner, ed. Luigi Ricci and Christian Detmold, trans. New York: Modern Library.

Mansfield, Harvey C. 1970. Machiavelli's New Regime. *Italian Quarterly*, 13:63–95.

Montesquieu, Charles de. 1949 *Spirit of the Laws*. New York: Hafner. (Originally published in 1748.)

Murphy, Jeffrie. 1970. *Kant: The Philosophy of Right*. New York: St. Martins.

Neustadt, Richard. 1970. *Alliance Politics*. New York: Columbia University Press.

Payne, James L. n.d. Marxism and Militarism. *Polity*. Forthcoming.

Pocock, J. G. A. 1975. *The Machiavellian Moment*. Princeton: Princeton University Press.

Polanyi, Karl. 1944. *The Great Transformation*. Boston: Beacon Press.

Posen, Barry, and Stephen VanEvera. 1980. Overarming and Underwhelming. *Foreign Policy*, 40:99–118.

Posen, Barry, and Stephen VanEvera. 1983. Reagan Administration Defense Policy. In Kenneth Oye, Robert Lieber, and Donald Rothchild, eds., *Eagle Defiant*. Boston: Little Brown. pp. 67–104.

Powell, G. Bingham. 1982. *Contemporary Democracies*. Cambridge, MA: Harvard University Press.

Reagan, Ronald. June 9, 1982. Address to Parliament. *New York Times*.

Riley, Patrick. 1983. *Kant's Political Philosophy*. Totowa, NJ: Rowman and Littlefield.

Rummel, Rudolph J. 1979. *Understanding Conflict and War*, 5 vols. Beverly Hills: Sage Publications.

Rummel, Rudolph J. 1983. Libertarianism and International Violence. *Journal of Conflict Resolution*, 27:27–71.

Russett, Bruce. 1985. The Mysterious Case of Vanishing Hegemony. *International Organization*, 39:207–31.

Schumpeter, Joseph. 1950. *Capitalism, Socialism, and Democracy*. New York: Harper Torchbooks.

Schumpeter, Joseph. 1955. The Sociology of Imperialism. In *Imperialism and Social Classes*. Cleveland: World Publishing Co. (Essay originally published in 1919.)

Schwarz, Wolfgang. 1962. Kant's Philosophy of Law and International Peace. *Philosophy and Phenomenological Research*, 23:71–80.

Shell, Susan. 1980. *The Rights of Reason*. Toronto: University of Toronto Press.

Shklar, Judith. 1984. *Ordinary Vices*. Cambridge, MA: Harvard University Press.

Skinner, Quentin. 1981. *Machiavelli*. New York: Hill and Wang.

Small, Melvin, and J. David Singer. 1976. The War-Proneness of Democratic Regimes. *The Jerusalem Journal of International Relations*, 1(4):50–69.

Small, Melvin, and J. David Singer, 1982. *Resort to Arms*. Beverly Hills: Sage Publications.

Streit, Clarence. 1938. *Union Now: A Proposal for a Federal Union of the Leading Democracies*. New York: Harpers.

Thucydides. 1954. *The Peloponnesian War*. Rex Warner, ed. and trans. Baltimore: Penguin.

U.K. Foreign and Commonwealth Office. 1980. *A Yearbook of the Commonwealth 1980*. London: HMSO.

U.S. Congress. Senate. Select Committee to Study Governmental Operations with
    Respect to Intelligence Activities. 1975. *Covert Action in Chile, 1963–74.*
    94th Cong., 1st sess., Washington, D.C.: U.S. Government Printing Office.
U.S. Department of State. 1981. *Country Reports on Human Rights Practices.*
    Washington, D.C.: U.S. Government Printing Office.
Waltz, Kenneth. 1962. Kant, Liberalism, and War. *American Political Science Review,*
    56:331–40.
Waltz, Kenneth. 1964. The Stability of a Bipolar World. *Daedalus,* 93:881–909.
Walzer, Michael. 1983. *Spheres of Justice.* New York: Basic Books.
Weede, Erich. 1984. Democracy and War Involvement. *Journal of Conflict
    Resolution,* 28:649–64.
Wilkenfeld, Jonathan. 1968. Domestic and Foreign Conflict Behavior of Nations.
    Journal of Peace Research, 5:56–69.
Williams, Howard. 1983. *Kant's Political Philosophy.* Oxford: Basil Blackwell.
Wright, Quincy. 1942. *A Study of History.* Chicago: Chicago University Press.
Yovel, Yirmiahu. 1980. *Kant and the Philosophy of History.* Princeton: Princeton
    University Press.

Edward D. Mansfield and Jack Snyder

Democratization and War

Dangers of Transition

The idea that democracies never fight wars against each other has become
an axiom for many scholars. It is, as one scholar puts it, "as close as anything
we have to an empirical law in international relations." This "law" is
invoked by American statesmen to justify a foreign policy that encourages
democratization abroad. In his 1994 State of the Union address, President
Clinton asserted that no two democracies had ever gone to war with each
other, thus explaining why promoting democracy abroad was a pillar of his
foreign policy.

It is probably true that a world in which more countries were mature, stable democracies would be safer and preferable for the United States. But countries do not become mature democracies overnight. They usually go through a
rocky transition, where mass politics mixes with authoritarian elite politics in a
volatile way. Statistical evidence covering the past two centuries shows that in
this transitional phase of democratization, countries become more aggressive
and war-prone, not less, and they do fight wars with democratic states. In fact,
formerly authoritarian states where democratic participation is on the rise are

more likely to fight wars than are stable democracies or autocracies. States that make the biggest leap, from total autocracy to extensive mass democracy—like contemporary Russia—are about twice as likely to fight wars in the decade after democratization as are states that remain autocracies.

This historical pattern of democratization, belligerent nationalism, and war is already emerging in some of today's new or partial democracies, especially some formerly communist states. Two pairs of states—Serbia and Croatia, and Armenia and Azerbaijan—have found themselves at war while experimenting with varying degrees of electoral democracy. The electorate of Russia's partial democracy cast nearly a quarter of its votes for the party of radical nationalist Vladimir Zhirinovsky. Even mainstream Russian politicians have adopted an imperial tone in their dealings with neighboring former Soviet republics, and military force has been used ruthlessly in Chechnya.

The following evidence should raise questions about the Clinton administration's policy of promoting peace by promoting democratization. The expectation that the spread of democracy will probably contribute to peace in the long run, once new democracies mature, provides little comfort to those who might face a heightened risk of war in the short run. Pushing nuclear-armed great powers like Russia or China toward democratization is like spinning a roulette wheel: many of the outcomes are undesirable. Of course, in most cases the initial steps on the road to democratization will not be produced by any conscious policy of the United States. The roulette wheel is already spinning for Russia and perhaps will be soon for China. Washington and the international community need to think not so much about encouraging or discouraging democratization as about helping to smooth the transition in ways that minimize its risks.

The Evidence

Our statistical analysis relies on the classifications of regimes and wars from 1811 to 1980 used by most scholars studying the peace among democracies. Starting with these standard data, we classify each state as a democracy, an autocracy, or a mixed regime—that is, a state with features of both democracies and autocracies. This classification is based on several criteria, including the constitutional constraints on the chief executive, the competitiveness of domestic politics, the openness of the process for selecting the chief executive, and the strength of the rules governing participation in politics. Democratizing states are those that made any regime change in a democratic direction—that is, from autocracy to democracy, from a mixed regime to democracy, or from autocracy to a mixed regime. We analyze wars between states as well as wars between a state and a non-state group, such as liberation movements in colonies, but we do not include civil wars.[1]

Because we view democratization as a gradual process, rather than a sudden change, we test whether a transition toward democracy occurring over one, five, and ten years is associated with the subsequent onset of war. To assess the strength of the relationship between democratization and war, we construct a series of contingency tables. Based on those tables, we compare the probability that a democratizing state subsequently goes to war with the probabilities of war for states in transition toward autocracy and for states undergoing no regime change. The results of all of these tests show that *democratizing states were more likely to fight wars than were states that had undergone no change in regime.* This relationship is weakest one year into democratization and strongest at ten years. During any given ten-year period, a state experiencing no regime change had about one chance in six of fighting a war in the following decade. In the decade following democratization, a state's chance of fighting a war was about one in four. When we analyze the components of our measure of democratization separately, the results are similar. On average, an increase in the openness of the selection process for the chief executive doubled the likelihood of war. Increasing the competitiveness of political participation or increasing the constraints on a country's chief executive (both aspects of democratization) also made war more likely. On average, these changes increased the likelihood of war by about 90 percent and 35 percent respectively.

The statistical results are even more dramatic when we analyze cases in which the process of democratization culminated in very high levels of mass participation in politics. States changing from a mixed regime to democracy were on average about 50 percent more likely to become engaged in war (and about two-thirds more likely to go to war with another nation-state) than states that remained mixed regimes.

The effect was greater still for those states making the largest leap, from full autocracy to high levels of democracy. Such states were on average about two-thirds more likely to become involved in any type of war (and about twice as likely to become involved in an interstate war) than states that remained autocracies. Though this evidence shows that democratization is dangerous, its reversal offers no easy solutions. On average, changes toward autocracy also yielded an increase in the probability of war, though a smaller one than changes toward democracy, compared to states experiencing no regime change.

Nationalism and Democratization

The connection between democratization and nationalism is striking in both the historical record and today's headlines. We did not measure nationalism directly in our statistical tests. Nonetheless, historical and contemporary evidence strongly suggests that rising nationalism often goes hand in hand with rising democracy. It is no accident that the end of the Cold War brought both a wave of democratization and a revival of nationalist sentiment in the former communist states.

In eighteenth-century Britain and France, when nationalism first emerged as an explicit political doctrine, it meant self-rule by the people. It was the rallying cry of commoners and rising commercial classes against rule by aristocratic elites, who were charged with the sin of ruling in their own interests, rather than those of the nation. Indeed, dynastic rulers and imperial courts had hardly been interested in promoting nationalism as a banner of solidarity in their realms. They typically ruled over a linguistically and culturally diverse conglomeration of subjects and claimed to govern by divine right, not in the interest of the nation. Often, these rulers were more closely tied by kinship, language, or culture to elites in other states than to their own subjects. The position of the communist ruling class was strikingly similar: a transnational elite that ruled over an amalgamation of peoples and claimed legitimacy from the communist party's role as the vanguard of history, not from the consent of the governed. Popular forces challenging either traditional dynastic rulers or communist elites naturally tended to combine demands for national self-determination and democratic rule.

This concoction of nationalism and incipient democratization has been an intoxicating brew, leading in case after case to ill-conceived wars of expansion. The earliest instance remains one of the most dramatic. In the French Revolution, the radical Brissotin parliamentary faction polarized politics by harping on the king's slow response to the threat of war with other dynastic states. In the ensuing wars of the French Revolution, citizens flocked to join the revolutionary armies to defend popular self-rule and the French nation. Even after the revolution turned profoundly antidemocratic, Napoleon was able to harness this popular nationalism to the task of conquering Europe, substituting the popularity of empire for the substance of democratic rule. . . .

The Sorcerer's Apprentice

Although democratization in many cases leads to war, that does not mean that the average voter wants war. Public opinion in democratizing states often starts off highly averse to the costs and risks of war. In that sense, the public opinion polls taken in Russia in early 1994 were typical. Respondents said, for example, that Russian policy should make sure the rights of Russians in neighboring states were not infringed, but not at the cost of military intervention. Public opinion often becomes more belligerent, however, as a result of propaganda and military action presented as faits accomplis by elites. This mass opinion, once aroused, may no longer be controllable. . . .

Much the same has happened in contemporary Serbia. Despite the memories of Ustashe atrocities in World War II, intermarriage rates between Croats and Serbs living in Croatia were as high as one in three during the 1980s. Opinion has been bellicized by propaganda campaigns in state-controlled media that, for example, carried purely invented reports of rapes of Serbian women in Kosovo, and even more so by the fait accompli of launching the war itself.

In short, democratizing states are war-prone not because war is popular with the mass public, but because domestic pressures create incentives for elites to drum up nationalist sentiment.

The Causes of Democratic Wars

Democratization typically creates a syndrome of weak central authority, unstable domestic coalitions, and high-energy mass politics. It brings new social groups and classes onto the political stage. Political leaders, finding no way to reconcile incompatible interests, resort to shortsighted bargains or reckless gambles in order to maintain their governing coalitions. Elites need to gain mass allies to defend their weakened positions. Both the newly ambitious elites and the embattled old ruling groups often use appeals to nationalism to stay astride their unmanageable political coalitions.

Needing public support, they rouse the masses with nationalist propaganda but find that their mass allies, once mobilized by passionate appeals, are difficult to control. So are the powerful remnants of the old order—the military, for example—which promote militarism because it strengthens them institutionally. This is particularly true because democratization weakens the central government's ability to keep policy coherent and consistent. Governing a society that is democratizing is like driving a car while throwing away the steering wheel, stepping on the gas, and fighting over which passenger will be in the driver's seat. The result, often, is war. . . .

Managing the Dangers

Though mature democratic states have virtually never fought wars against each other, promoting democracy may not promote peace because states are especially war-prone during the transition toward democracy. This does not mean, however, that democratization should be squelched in the interests of peace. Many states are now democratizing or on the verge of it, and stemming that turbulent tide, even if it were desirable, may not be possible. Our statistical tests show that movements toward autocracy, including reversals of democratization, are only somewhat less likely to result in war than democratization itself. Consequently, the task is to draw on an understanding of the process of democratization to keep its unwanted side effects to a minimum.

Of course, democratization does not always lead to extreme forms of aggressive nationalism, just as it does not always lead to war. But it makes those outcomes more likely. Cases where states democratized without triggering a nationalist mobilization are particularly interesting, since they may hold clues about how to prevent such unwanted side effects. Among the great powers, the obvious successes were the democratization of Germany and Japan after 1945, due to occupation by liberal democracies and the favorable international setting provided by the Marshall Plan, the Bretton Woods economic system, and the democratic military alliance against the Soviet threat. More recently, numerous Latin American states have democratized without nationalism or war. The recent border skirmishes between Peru and Ecuador, however, coincide with democratizing trends in both states and a nationalist turn in Ecuadorian political discourse. Moreover, all three previous wars between that pair over the past two centuries occurred in periods of partial democratization.

In such cases, however, the cure is probably more democracy, not less. In "Wilhelmine Argentina," the Falkland Islands/Malvinas War came when the military junta needed a nationalist victory to stave off pressure for the return of democracy; the arrival of full democracy has produced more pacific policies. Among the East European states, nationalist politics has been unsuccessful in the most fully democratic ones—Poland, the Czech Republic, and Hungary—as protest votes have gone to former communists. Nationalism has figured more prominently in the politics of the less democratic formerly communist states that are nonetheless partially democratizing. States like Turkmenistan that remain outright autocracies have no nationalist mobilization—indeed no political mobilization of any kind. In those recent cases, in contrast to some of our statistical results, the rule seems to be: go fully democratic, or don't go at all.

In any given case, other factors may override the relative bellicosity of democratizing states. These might include the power of the democratizing state, the strength of the potential deterrent coalition of states constraining it, the attractiveness of more peaceful options available to the democratizing state, and the nature of the groups making up its ruling coalition. What is needed is to identify the conditions that lead to relatively peaceful democratization and try to create those circumstances.

One of the major findings of scholarship on democratization in Latin America is that the process goes most smoothly when elites threatened by the transition—especially the military—are given a golden parachute. Above all, they need a guarantee that they will not wind up in jail if they relinquish power. The history of the democratizing great powers broadens this insight. Democratization was least likely to lead to war when the old elites saw a reasonably bright future for themselves in the new social order. British aristocrats, for example, had more of their wealth invested in commerce and industry than in agriculture, so they had many interests in common with the rising middle classes. They could face democratization with relative equanimity. In contrast, Prussia's capital-starved, small-scale Junker landholders had no choice but to rely on agricultural protection and military careers.

In today's context, finding benign, productive employment for the erstwhile communist nomenklatura, military officer corps, nuclear scientists, and smokestack industrialists ought to rank high on the list of priorities. Policies aimed at giving them a stake in the privatization process and subsidizing the conversion of their skills to new, peaceful tasks in a market economy seem like a step in the right direction. According to some interpretations, Russian Defense Minister Pavel Grachev was eager to use force to solve the Chechen confrontation in order to show that Russian military power was still useful and that increased investment in the Russian army would pay big dividends. Instead of pursuing this reckless path, the Russian military elite needs to be convinced that its prestige, housing, pensions, and technical competence will improve if and only if it transforms itself into a Western-style military, subordinate to civilian authority and resorting to force only in accordance with prevailing international norms. Not only do old elites need to be kept happy, they also need to be kept weak. Pacts should not prop up the remnants of the authoritarian system, but rather create a niche for them in the new system.

Another top priority must be creating a free, competitive, and responsible marketplace of ideas in the newly democratizing states. Most of the war-prone democratizing great powers had pluralistic public debates, but the debates were skewed to favor groups with money, privileged access to the media, and proprietary control over information ranging from archives to intelligence about the military balance. Pluralism is not enough. Without a level playing field, pluralism simply creates the incentive and opportunity for privileged groups to propound self-serving myths, which historically have often taken a nationalist turn. One of the rays of hope in the Chechen affair was the alacrity with which Russian journalists exposed the costs of the fighting and the lies of the government and the military. Though elites should get a golden parachute regarding their pecuniary interests, they should be given no quarter on the battlefield of ideas. Mythmaking should be held up to the utmost scrutiny by aggressive journalists who maintain their credibility by scrupulously distinguishing fact from opinion and tirelessly verifying their sources. Promoting this kind of journalistic infrastructure is probably the most highly leveraged investment the West can make in a peaceful democratic transition.

Finally, the kind of ruling coalition that emerges in the course of democratization depends a great deal on the incentives created by the international environment. Both Germany and Japan started on the path toward liberal, stable democratization in the mid-1920s, encouraged by abundant opportunities for trade with and investment by the advanced democracies and by credible security treaties that defused nationalist scaremongering in domestic politics. When the international supports for free trade and democracy were yanked out in the late 1920s, their liberal coalitions collapsed. For China, whose democratization may occur in the context of expanding economic ties with the West, a steady Western commercial partnership and security presence is likely to play a major role in shaping the incentives of proto-democratic coalition politics.

In the long run, the enlargement of the zone of stable democracy will probably enhance prospects for peace. In the short run, much work remains to be done to minimize the dangers of the turbulent transition.

NOTE

1. On the definition of war and the data on war used in this analysis, see Melvin Small and J. David Singer, *Resort to Arms: International and Civil Wars, 1816–1980,* Beverly Hills: Sage, 1982.

CHAPTER 4 AMERICAN PRIMACY v. AMERICAN RETRENCHMENT

Primacy as American Grand Strategy

Advocate: Bradley A. Thayer

Source: "In Defense of Primacy," *The National Interest*, no. 86 (November/December 2006), pp. 32–38, excerpt.

Retrenchment as American Grand Strategy

Advocate: Christopher Layne

Source: "Impotent Power," *The National Interest*, no. 85 (September/October 2006), pp. 42–48, excerpt.

The United States is the most powerful country in the world. In fact, the United States is more powerful than all of the great powers in the world combined, making it the most dominant country in the history of humankind. There is also an agreement that its predominance will end and another hegemon will rise. There is, however, a significant debate over the costs and benefits of U.S. primacy, and whether Washington D.C. should continue to promote actively its hegemony. Because of its overwhelming hard power and considerable soft power, the United States has achieved global dominance in international politics. This condition is known as primacy.

The debate over American primacy is a debate over American grand strategy—how it defines its national interests, the threats to them, and its degree of engagement with the rest of the world. U.S. grand strategy is important because of its implications for the security of the American people, the standing of the country in the world, and its ability to defend its interests while remaining true to the principles enshrined in its founding documents.

IN DEFENSE OF PRIMACY

Proponents of primacy argue that the benefits of this grand strategy outweigh its costs. Some of the benefits of primacy, as Bradley Thayer argues, include increased security for the American people, tremendous influence over international politics, and a global financial and economic system that best suits America's businesses. Acknowledging that the American hegemony will end within a few decades, primacists nonetheless maintain that prolonging it as long as possible is well worth the expense and sacrifices.

Thayer argues that primacy also allows Washington D.C. to exercise great influence in international politics. It has numerous means at its disposal to get other countries to do its bidding, ranging from coercive sanctions to positive incentives. These include democracy promotion, dominance of the international economic and financial systems, and perhaps, most importantly, the enormous "soft power" of the United States: the worldwide attraction of its values, institutions, and traditions.

The prodigious power of the United States is employed in numerous humanitarian missions and in providing a great amount of aid to countries around the world, as in tsunami-hit Indonesia or earthquake-struck Pakistan. As Thayer explains, winning people's hearts and minds through such generosity may be the single most important contribution to the fight against terrorism. Giving up the American empire would jeopardize all of those benefits and would put the American people at greater risks than ever before.

IN DEFENSE OF RETRENCHMENT

Proponents of retrenchment, such as Christopher Layne, argue that the United States simply lacks the resources to maintain its empire. Its imperial ambitions are economically unsustainable in the long term, particularly in the face of competition from rising superpowers, such as China.

First, Layne argues that the excessive military commitments of the United States abroad are eroding its economic foundations. Since the end of the Cold War, the United States has willingly intervened in many places around the world, the quagmire in Iraq being the costliest example of all. The costs of maintaining this military presence will only increase in the future, while depriving the American people from improvements in education, health, and social services.

Second, the persistent trade and budget deficits have led the United States to an untenable economic position. As a result, the United States will not be able to maintain the same military superiority as it has enjoyed since the end of World War II. In the long term, Layne claims, America's over-extension combined with the rise of new powers will likely lead to the end of unipolarity and a new era of multipolarity.

Layne's position is that primacy is a costly and, ultimately, unsustainable grand strategy. Being a hegemon, the United States is frequently tempted to overreach and assert its power heavy handedly, thereby provoking opposition. Even if not a hegemon, the United States will still remain a very powerful country, blessed by its geography. Hence, the American people should be mindful of the costs of hegemony and opt for a more prudent grand strategy.

1. Both Bradley Thayer and Christopher Layne agree that expansionism was in the spirit of the United States' Founding Fathers but disagree on whether they advocated expansionism beyond North America.
2. Does the American empire make Americans more secure? What has been the impact of the wars in Afghanistan and Iraq and attempts to promote democracy in this region on U.S. security?
3. Is retrenchment the same as isolationism?
4. If the United States gave up its position as a hegemon, would it be more or less secure in a multipolar world?

Bradley A. Thayer

In Defense of Primacy

A grand strategy based on American primacy means ensuring the United States stays the world's number one power—the diplomatic, economic and military leader. Those arguing against primacy claim that the United States should retrench, either because the United States lacks the power to maintain its primacy and should withdraw from its global commitments, or because the maintenance of primacy will lead the United States into the trap of "imperial overstretch.". . .

But retrenchment, in any of its guises, must be avoided. If the United States adopted such a strategy, it would be a profound strategic mistake that would lead to far greater instability and war in the world, imperil American security and deny the United States and its allies the benefits of primacy.

There are two critical issues in any discussion of America's grand strategy: *Can* America remain the dominant state? *Should* it strive to do this? America can remain dominant due to its prodigious military, economic and soft power capabilities. The totality of that equation of power answers the first issue. The United States has overwhelming military capabilities and wealth in comparison to other states or likely potential alliances. Barring some disaster or tremendous folly, that will remain the case for the foreseeable future. With few exceptions, even those who advocate retrenchment acknowledge this.

So the debate revolves around the desirability of maintaining American primacy. Proponents of retrenchment focus a great deal on the costs of U.S.

action—but they fail to realize what is good about American primacy. The price and risks of primacy are reported in newspapers every day; the benefits that stem from it are not.

A grand strategy of ensuring American primacy takes as its starting point the protection of the U.S. homeland and American global interests. These interests include ensuring that critical resources like oil flow around the world, that the global trade and monetary regimes flourish and that Washington's worldwide network of allies is reassured and protected. Allies are a great asset to the United States, in part because they shoulder some of its burdens. Thus, it is no surprise to see NATO in Afghanistan or the Australians in East Timor.

In contrast, . . . retrenchment will make the United States less secure than the present grand strategy of primacy. This is because threats will exist no matter what role America chooses to play in international politics. Washington cannot call a "time out", and it cannot hide from threats. Whether they are terrorists, rogue states or rising powers, history shows that threats must be confronted. Simply by declaring that the United States is "going home", thus abandoning its commitments or making unconvincing half-pledges to defend its interests and allies, does not mean that others will respect American wishes to retreat. To make such a declaration implies weakness and emboldens aggression. In the anarchic world of the animal kingdom, predators prefer to eat the weak rather than confront the strong. The same is true of the anarchic world of international politics. If there is no diplomatic solution to the threats that confront the United States, then the conventional and strategic military power of the United States is what protects the country from such threats.

And when enemies must be confronted, a strategy based on primacy focuses on engaging enemies overseas, away from American soil. Indeed, a key tenet of the Bush Doctrine is to attack terrorists far from America's shores and not to wait while they use bases in other countries to plan and train for attacks against the United States itself. This requires a physical, on-the-ground presence that cannot be achieved by offshore balancing. . . .

A remarkable fact about international politics today—in a world where American primacy is clearly and unambiguously on display—is that countries want to align themselves with the United States. Of course, this is not out of any sense of altruism, in most cases, but because doing so allows them to use the power of the United States for their own purposes—their own protection, or to gain greater influence.

Of 192 countries, 84 are allied with America—their security is tied to the United States through treaties and other informal arrangements—and they include almost all of the major economic and military powers. That is a ratio of almost 17 to one (85 to five), and a big change from the Cold War when the ratio was about 1.8 to one of states aligned with the United States versus the Soviet Union. Never before in its history has this country, or any country, had so many allies.

U.S. primacy—and the bandwagoning effect—has also given us extensive influence in international politics, allowing the United States to shape the behavior of states and international institutions. Such influence comes in many forms, one of which is America's ability to create coalitions of like-minded states to free Kosovo, stabilize Afghanistan, invade Iraq or to stop proliferation through the Proliferation Security Initiative (PSI). Doing so allows the United States to operate with allies outside of the UN, where it can be stymied by opponents. American-led wars in Kosovo, Afghanistan, and Iraq stand in contrast to the UN's inability to save the people of Darfur or even to conduct any military campaign to realize the goals of its charter. . . .

You can count with one hand countries opposed to the United States. They are the "Gang of Five": China, Cuba, Iran, North Korea and Venezuela. Of course, countries like India, for example, do not agree with all policy choices made by the United States, such as toward Iran, but New Delhi is friendly to Washington. Only the "Gang of Five" may be expected to consistently resist the agenda and actions of the United States.

China is clearly the most important of these states because it is a rising great power. But even Beijing is intimidated by the United States and refrains from openly challenging U.S. power. China proclaims that it will, if necessary, resort to other mechanisms of challenging the United States, including asymmetric strategies such as targeting communication and intelligence satellites upon which the United States depends. But China may not be confident those strategies would work, and so it is likely to refrain from testing the United States directly for the foreseeable future because China's power benefits, as we shall see, from the international order U.S. primacy creates. . . .

Throughout history, peace and stability have been great benefits of an era where there was a dominant power—Rome, Britain or the United States today. Scholars and statesmen have long recognized the irenic effect of power on the anarchic world of international politics.

Everything we think of when we consider the current international order—free trade, a robust monetary regime, increasing respect for human rights, growing democratization—is directly linked to U.S. power. . . . Without U.S. power, the liberal order created by the United States will end just as assuredly. . . .

Consequently, it is important to note what those good things are. In addition to ensuring the security of the United States and its allies, American primacy within the international system causes many positive outcomes for Washington and the world. The first has been a more peaceful world. During the Cold War, U.S. leadership reduced friction among many states that were historical antagonists, most notably France and West Germany. Today, American primacy helps keep a number of complicated relationships aligned— between Greece and Turkey, Israel and Egypt, South Korea and Japan, India and Pakistan, Indonesia and Australia. This is not to say it fulfills Woodrow Wilson's vision of ending all war. Wars still occur where Washington's interests are not seriously threatened, such as in Darfur, but a Pax Americana does reduce war's likelihood, particularly war's worst form: great power wars.

Second, American power gives the United States the ability to spread democracy and other elements of its ideology of liberalism. Doing so is a source of much good for the countries concerned as well as the United States because . . . liberal democracies are more likely to align with the United States and be sympathetic to the American worldview. So, spreading democracy helps maintain U.S. primacy. In addition, once states are governed democratically, the likelihood of any type of conflict is significantly reduced. This is not because democracies do not have clashing interests. Indeed they do. Rather, it is because they are more open, more transparent and more likely to want to resolve things amicably in concurrence with U.S. leadership. And so, in general, democratic states are good for their citizens as well as for advancing the interests of the United States.

. . . Washington fostered democratic governments in Europe, Latin America, Asia and the Caucasus. Now even the Middle East is increasingly democratic. They may not yet look like Western-style democracies, but democratic progress has been made in Algeria, Morocco, Lebanon, Iraq, Kuwait, the Palestinian Authority and Egypt. By all accounts, the march of democracy has been impressive.

Third, along with the growth in the number of democratic states around the world has been the growth of the global economy. With its allies, the United States has labored to create an economically liberal worldwide network characterized by free trade and commerce, respect for international property rights, and mobility of capital and labor markets. The economic stability and prosperity that stems from this economic order is a global public good from which all states benefit, particularly the poorest states in the Third World. The United States created this network not out of altruism but for the benefit and the economic well-being of America. This economic order forces American industries to be competitive, maximizes efficiencies and growth, and benefits defense as well because the size of the economy makes the defense burden manageable. Economic spin-offs foster the development of military technology, helping to ensure military prowess. . . .

Fourth and finally, the United States, in seeking primacy, has been willing to use its power not only to advance its interests but to promote the welfare of people all over the globe. The United States is the earth's leading source of positive externalities for the world. The U.S. military has participated in over fifty operations since the end of the Cold War—and most of those missions have been humanitarian in nature. Indeed, the U.S. military is the earth's "911 force"—it serves, *de facto*, as the world's police, the global paramedic and the planet's fire department. Whenever there is a natural disaster, earthquake, flood, drought, volcanic eruption, typhoon or tsunami, the United States assists the countries in need. On the day after Christmas in 2004, a tremendous earthquake and tsunami occurred in the Indian Ocean near Sumatra, killing some 300,000 people. The United States was the first to respond with aid. Washington followed up with a large contribution of aid and deployed the U.S. military to South and Southeast Asia for many months to help with the aftermath of the disaster. About 20,000 U.S. soldiers, sailors, airmen and marines responded by providing water, food, medical aid, disease treatment and prevention as well as forensic assistance to help identify the bodies of those killed. Only the U.S. military could have accomplished this Herculean effort. No other force possesses the communications capabilities or global logistical reach of the U.S. military. In fact, UN peacekeeping operations depend on the United States to supply UN forces.

American generosity has done more to help the United States fight the War on Terror than almost any other measure. Before the tsunami, 80 percent of Indonesian public opinion was opposed to the United States; after it, 80 percent had a favorable opinion of America. Two years after the disaster, and in poll after poll, Indonesians still have overwhelmingly positive views of the United States. In October 2005, an enormous earthquake struck Kashmir, killing about 74,000 people and leaving three million homeless. The U.S. military responded immediately, diverting helicopters fighting the War on Terror in nearby Afghanistan to bring relief as soon as possible. To help those in need, the United States also provided financial aid to Pakistan; and, as one might expect from those witnessing the munificence of the United States, it left a lasting impression about America. For the first time since 9/11, polls of Pakistani opinion have found that more people are favorable toward the United States than unfavorable, while support for Al-Qaeda dropped to its lowest level. Whether in Indonesia or Kashmir, the money was well-spent because it helped people in the wake of disasters, but it also had a real impact on the War on Terror. When people in the Muslim world witness the U.S. military conducting a humanitarian mission, there is a clearly positive impact on Muslim opinion of the United States. As the War on Terror is a war of ideas and opinion as much as military action, for the United States humanitarian missions are the equivalent of a blitzkrieg.

There is no other state, group of states or international organization that can provide these global benefits. None even comes close. The United Nations cannot because it is riven with conflicts and major cleavages that divide the international body time and again on matters great and trivial. Thus it lacks the ability to speak with one voice on salient issues and to act as a unified force once a decision is reached. The EU has similar problems. Does anyone expect Russia or China to take up these responsibilities? They may have the desire, but they do not have the capabilities. Let's face it: for the time being, American primacy remains humanity's only practical hope of solving the world's ills. . . .

NOTE

1. John M. Owen IV, "Democracy, Realistically", *The National Interest*, No. 83 (Spring 2006).

Christopher Layne

Impotent Power

• • •

There is a paradox between the magnitude of American power and Washington's inability to use that power to always get what it wants in international politics. There are many factors that limit the exercise of U.S. power. Some of these are obvious, others less so. . . .

The United States, indeed, is a global hegemon and has formidable tools at its disposal, and it can wield its power effectively to attain important policy objectives. For example, the sheer magnitude of America's lead in military power over its closest would-be rivals has a potent effect in dissuading them from trying to emerge as great powers and to challenge the United States's dominant role in a unipolar world. Events since 9/11 have illuminated other ways in which the United States has been able to utilize its hegemonic power. Thus, American military prowess was showcased by the quick collapse of the Taliban and Saddam's Iraq. Moreover, the economic incentives the United States could proffer were vitally important in persuading a reluctant Pakistan to allow itself to ally with the United States in the battle against Al-Qaeda. Central Asian states offered the United States the opportunity to establish military bases—and Putin's Russia acquiesced to this. And the very fact that the United States could defy the United Nations (and major powers such as France, Germany, Russia and China) and carry out the invasion of Iraq (essentially) unilaterally proved—if proof is needed—that the rest of the world could not do much to constrain the United States. . . .

Iraq and Afghanistan are illustrative of an important reason that America's hegemonic power appears illusory: because it is often employed in the pursuit of objectives that are unattainable, such as nation-building and democracy promotion. Both neoconservatives and so-called liberal imperialists seem to believe that the world is like a piece of clay and that the United States can remake other nations—and cultures—in its own image. Although the United States has a long list of failure in such efforts, it keeps trying—most recently in Afghanistan and, of course, Iraq. Before the invasion, administration officials pretty much believed that the processes of democratization and nation-building in Iraq would be a piece of cake. They frequently invoked the examples of post-1945 Germany and Japan as "proof" that the United States could export democracy to Iraq without undue difficulty. For at least three reasons, they should have known better: the use of military force by outside powers to impose democracy rarely works; military occupations seldom are successful; and the preconditions for a successful democratic transformation did not exist in Iraq.

Those who have studied military occupations know that the odds of success are stacked against occupying powers. . . .

The United States has long been addicted to Wilsonian crusading to remake the world, but as realists long—and rightly—have argued, it lacks the material, psychological and spiritual resources to succeed in this effort. . . .

There already are indications that things are changing: American hegemony is beginning to wane and new great powers already are in the process of emerging. This is what the current debate about the implications of China's rise is all about in the United States. But China isn't the only factor in play, and transition from U.S. primacy to multipolarity may be much closer than primacists want to admit. . . .

The European Union will come close to matching the United States in terms of their respective shares of world power. . . . But if the ongoing shift in the distribution of relative power continues, new poles of power in the international system are likely to emerge during the next decade or two. The real issue is not if American primacy will end, but how soon it will end.

In answering this question the key factor may well be whether the United States can afford economically to maintain the overwhelming military superiority necessary to dissuade other states from emerging as peer competitors.

Paul Kennedy's 1987 book, *The Rise and Fall of the Great Powers,* ignited an important debate about the sustainability of American primacy. In a nutshell, Kennedy argued that the United States was doomed to repeat a familiar pattern of imperial decline, because the excessive costs of military commitments abroad were eroding the economic foundations of American power. An important backdrop to Kennedy's book was the so-called "twin deficits": endless federal-budget deficits and a persistent balance-of-trade deficit.

The late 1980s debate about possible American decline was terminated abruptly, however: first, by the Soviet Union's collapse, and then by U.S. economic revival during the Clinton Administration, which also saw the yearly federal budget deficits give way to annual budget surpluses. This had led many of the proponents of American hegemony to assert that the American economy is fairly robust and that, as a result, the United States can afford this grand strategy.

These claims might come as news to most Americans, however. When a company like General Motors—historically one of the flagship corporations of the U.S. economy—teeters on the edge of bankruptcy and sheds some 126,000 jobs, rosy descriptions about the strength of the U.S. economy ring hollow. Similarly, the notion that the U.S. economy is healthy certainly would not be shared by the hundreds of thousands of U.S. workers who have lost their jobs in America's ever-contracting manufacturing sector—often because their jobs have been outsourced to China or India. Even more worrisome, future outsourcing of American jobs is not likely to be confined just to blue collar workers. Rather, an increasing number of high skill and high education jobs will flow from the United States to other countries. Another warning sign that all is not well with the U.S. economy is the "middle class squeeze"—the fact that middle class incomes in the United States have been stagnant since the early 1970s. The hollowing out of America's manufacturing industrial base, the outsourcing of American jobs, and stagnant middle class incomes are flashing red lights, warning that all is far from well with the U.S. economy.

Indeed, the economic vulnerabilities that Kennedy pinpointed in the late 1980s may have receded into the background during the 1990s, but they did not disappear. Once again, the United States is running endless federal budget deficits, and the trade deficit has grown worse and worse. The United States still depends on capital inflows from abroad—with China fast replacing Japan as America's most important creditor—to: finance its deficit spending; finance private consumption; and maintain the dollar's position as the international economic system's reserve currency. Because of the twin deficits, the underlying fundamentals of the U.S. economy are out of alignment. The United States cannot continue to live beyond its means indefinitely. Sooner or later, the bill will come due in the form of sharply higher taxes and interest rates—and, consequently, economic slowdown. . . . In a word (or two), the United States is suffering from "fiscal overstretch."[2]

During the Cold War, Japan (and, during the 1970s, West Germany) subsidized U.S. budget and trade deficits as a quid pro quo for American security guarantees. It will be interesting to see if an emerging geopolitical rival like China—or, for that matter, the European Union—will be as willing to underwrite American primacy in coming decades. Second, there have been big changes on the economic side of the ledger that cast a long shadow over America's long-term economic prospects. For one thing, the willingness of other states to cover America's debts no longer can be taken for granted. Already, key central banks are signaling their lack of confidence in the dollar by diversifying their currency holdings. There are rumblings, too, that OPEC may start pricing oil in euros, and that the dollar could be supplanted by the euro as the international economy's reserve currency. Should this happen, the United States no longer could afford to maintain its primacy.

The domestic economic picture is not so promising, either. The annual federal budget deficits are just the tip of the iceberg. The real problems are the federal government's huge unfunded liabilities for entitlement programs that will begin to come due about a decade hence. Moreover, defense spending and entitlement expenditures are squeezing out discretionary spending on domestic programs. Just down the road, the United States is facing stark "warfare" or "welfare" choices between, on the one hand, maintaining the overwhelming military capabilities upon which its primacy rests, or, on the other hand, discretionary spending on domestic needs, and funding Medicare, Medicaid and Social Security. Here, the proponents of U.S. hegemony overlook a huge change in the U.S. fiscal picture. They assert that the United States can afford to maintain its hegemony because defense spending now accounts only for about 4 percent of U.S. GDP. This is true, but very misleading.

Why? Because under the Bush II Administration, the norm in the allocation of federal discretionary spending that prevailed throughout most of the Clinton Administration has been reversed: the Pentagon's share of discretionary spending in the federal budget once again exceeds domestic spending. What really matters is not the percentage of GNP absorbed by defense spending, but the Defense Department's share of discretionary federal spending. Coupled with mandatory spending on entitlements (and debt service), defense spending is squeezing discretionary federal spending on domestic programs. Given the long-term unsustainability of federal budget deficits, coming years will see strong pressures to reduce federal spending. However, because defense, entitlements and debt service together account for 80 percent of federal spending, it is obvious that—as long as U.S. defense spending continues at the high levels mandated by the need to preserve U.S. hegemony—the burden of federal deficit reduction will fall primarily on the remaining 20 percent of the budget—that is, on discretionary domestic spending. In plain English, that means that the United States will be spending more on guns and less and less on butter—"butter" in this case meaning, among other things, federal government investments in education, infrastructure and research, which all are crucial to keeping the United States competitive in the international economy. Sooner rather than later, Americans will be compelled to ask whether spending to maintain the United

State's hegemonic role in international politics is more important than spending on domestic needs here at home.

In fact, if anything, the costs of the American hegemony are likely to increase in coming years. There are two reasons for this. First, there is the spiraling cost of the Iraq quagmire. Some estimate that the direct and indirect costs of the war to the U.S. economy will end up between $1,026 billion and $1,854 billion.[3]

The second reason that defense spending is likely to increase is that simple fact that the U.S. military is not large enough to meet all of America's commitments. Since the Cold War's end, the United States has shown every sign of succumbing to the "hegemon's temptation"—the temptation to use its military power promiscuously—and Iraq, along with the simultaneous crises with Iran and North Korea, have highlighted the mismatch between America's hegemonic ambitions and the military resources available to support them. To maintain its dominance, the American military will have to be expanded in size, because it is too small to meet present—and likely future—commitments. No one can say for certain how long significant U.S. forces will need to remain in Iraq (and Afghanistan), but its safe to say that substantial numbers of troops will be there for a long time. At the same time, in addition to the ongoing War on Terror (and the concomitant requirements of homeland defense), the United States faces possible future conflicts with North Korea, Iran and China.

During the past 15 years or so since the Soviet Union's collapse, the United States was able to postpone the need to grapple with the painful issues Kennedy raised in 1987. However, the chickens are coming home to roost, and those questions soon will have to be faced. At some point, the relative decline of U.S. economic power that is in the offing will bring American primacy to an end. In the shorter term, however, the United States can prolong its primacy if Americans are willing to pay the price in terms of higher taxes, reduced consumption, and curtailment of domestic programs. But, of course, there is a treadmill-like aspect to preserving American hegemony because perpetuating it will hasten the weakening of the economic base upon which it rests.

The United States is a very powerful state, and will remain so even if it no longer is a hegemon. Hegemony is not only a costly grand strategy, but also one that ultimately is unsustainable. America's real realists—George F. Kennan, Hans Morgenthau, Walter Lippmann and Kenneth Waltz—always warned of the dangers that a hegemonic United States would over-reach itself and, by asserting its power heavy-handedly, provoke opposition to it. They understood that the world is not malleable and will not respond to American-imposed social engineering. They not only recognized that a wise grand strategy must balance ends and means, but also that it must differentiate between desirable objectives and attainable ones. Most of all, the real realists have understood the true paradox of American power: Precisely because of its power and geography, there is very little the United States needs to do in the world in order to be secure; yet the very fact of its overwhelming capabilities has been a constant temptation for American policymakers to intervene abroad unwisely in the pursuit of unattainable goals (nation building or democracy promotion). Real realists like Lippmann, Kennan, Morgenthau and Waltz have highlighted the dangers that await if the United States gives in to the temptations of hegemonic power and have counseled instead that the United States pursue a grand strategy based on prudence and self-restraint. Americans would do well to pay heed to these admonitions as they debate how the United States should alter its grand strategy as the unipolar era inexorably draws to a close.

NOTES

1. The Strategic Assessment Group's analysis of current and projected world power shares was based on the International Futures Model developed by Barry Hughes. For a discussion of methodology and summary of the Strategic Assessment Group's findings, see Gregory F. Treverton and Seth G. Jones, *Measuring National Power* (Santa Monica: Rand Corporation, 2005), pp. iii, ix–x.
2. See Niall Ferguson and Laurence J. Kotlikoff, "Going Critical: American Power and the Consequences of Fiscal Overstretch", *The National Interest*, No. 73 (Fall 2003).
3. See Martin Wolff, "America Failed to Calculate the Enormous Costs of War", *Financial Times*, January 11, 2006, pp. 15.

CHAPTER 5 GLOBALIZATION v. BACKLASH

Globalization and Its Benefits

Advocate: Guy Sorman

Source: "Globalization Is Making the World a Better Place," *2008 Index of Economic Freedom*, The Heritage Foundation, pp. 35–38, excerpt.

Globalization and Its Risks

Advocate: Joseph Stiglitz

Source: "The Overselling of Globalization," *Globalization: What's New*, edited by Michael M. Weinstein, Columbia University Press, 2005, pp. 228–261, excerpt.

Globalization has been a defining feature of our lives since the end of the Cold War. Definitions of globalization vary in their scope, but they reflect increased economic interdependence as well as political and social interconnectedness across the globe. Globalization has been made possible by the advancement of information technology and communications, which have helped collapse time and space in our interconnected world.

Debates on globalization focus on the extent to which the world is truly globalized, the benefits and risks associated with it, and the impact it has had on state sovereignty. The forces of globalization are said to weaken government control over the flow of goods, people, and information, while creating more opportunities for the public.

IN FAVOR OF GLOBALIZATION

The benefits of globalization include increased trade and wealth, advancement of democracy, and spread of the values we cherish. Most frequently associated with growing trade and financial integration, globalization is credited with creating more global wealth and therefore improving the lives of millions of people worldwide. Globalization is also a driving force behind the transformation of our world into a "global village."

Based upon his discussion of the benefits that globalization has brought in six areas, Guy Sorman argues that it is bringing nothing short of a civilizational change. Crediting globalization with lifting hundreds of millions of people out of poverty, Sorman claims that it has also helped spread the ideals of democracy around the globe, including the increased importance of human rights and rule of law. Globalization is also inextricably linked to the ever-growing flow of information and exchange of ideas. For Sorman, as a supporter of globalization, this phenomenon is a recipe for welfare, progress, and happiness, which requires us to safeguard its achievements.

AGAINST GLOBALIZATION

Critics of globalization focus on the lopsided effects of neoliberal economic policies, the sporadic revolt against the homogenization of local cultures and traditions, and the erosion of democracy and state sovereignty. Much of the criticism is focused on the failures of the Washington consensus, which have benefitted few in both developed and developing countries, but have left many more behind.

Prominent economist Joseph Stiglitz argues that globalization has contributed to increasing global inequity. Economically, the spread of globalization's benefits has been uneven, contributing to the growing number of people living in poverty. Democracy has become more vulnerable to economic forces even in developed countries with stable institutions, whereas the polities as well as economies of the developing countries are more than ever susceptible to pressures from corporations and international financial institutions. The countries of the Global South also lack a strong voice in international institutions, which would allow them to have more say in the global economy. Finally, Stiglitz points out that local cultures, social cohesiveness, and even the nation-state itself have been challenged by globalization. For these reasons, he argues that improvements must be made in the international institutions that govern the international economic system that underpins globalization.

POINTS TO PONDER

1. Does globalization improve peoples' lives by improving their standard of living?
2. Does globalization promote democracy?
3. Does globalization promote the right norms and values?
4. What are the threats to globalization?
5. Is globalization democratic?
6. Are the benefits of globalization worth its costs?

Guy Sorman

Globalization Is Making the World a Better Place

What we call "globalization," one of the most powerful and positive forces ever to have arisen in the history of mankind, is redefining civilization as we know it. This is one of my hypotheses. To be more specific, I will try to describe what globalization is, its impact on world peace, and the freedom it brings from want, fear, and misery.

Globalization has six major characteristics: economic development, democracy, cultural enrichment, political and cultural norms, information, and internationalization of the rule of law.

Economic Development

Usually, globalization is described in terms of intensified commercial and trade exchanges, but it is about more than just trade, stock exchanges, and currencies. It is about people. What is significant today is that through globalization many nations are converging toward enhanced welfare.

This convergence is exemplified by the 800 million people who, in the past 30 years, have left poverty and misery behind. They have greater access to health care, schooling, and information. They have more choices, and their children will have even more choices. The absolutely remarkable part is that it happened not by accident but through a combination of good economic policy, technology, and management.

Of course, not all nations are following this path, but since the fall of the Berlin Wall, more and more are coming closer. Only Africa's nations have yet to join, but who would have hoped and predicted 30 years ago that China and India, with such rapidity and efficiency, would pull their people out of misery? There is no reason why Africa, when its turn comes, will not do the same. Convergence should be a source of hope for us all.

Democracy

In general, since 1989, the best system to improve the welfare of all people—not only economically, but also in terms of access to equality and freedom—appears to be democracy, the new international norm. As more and more countries turn democratic or converge toward democratic norms, respect for other cultures increases.

Democracy has guaranteed welfare far better than any dictatorship ever could. Even enlightened despots cannot bring the kind of safety democracy is bringing. Sometimes a trade-off between economic allotment and democracy occurs. Sometimes the economy grows more slowly because of democracy. Let it be that way. Democracy brings values that are as important for the welfare of the human being as economy is.

After all, as history shows, the chance of international war diminishes step by step any time a country moves from tyranny to democracy, as democracies do not war against one other. That more and more nations are turning democratic improves everyone's way of life.

Cultural Enrichment

Critics of globalization frequently charge that it results in an "Americanization of culture" and concomitant loss of identity and local cultural values. I would propose a more optimistic view, and that is that globalization leads to never-ending exchange of ideas, especially through popular culture, since it affects the greatest number of people.

Through popular culture, people from different backgrounds and nations discover one another, and their "otherness" suddenly disappears. For example, a popular Korean television sitcom now popular in Japan has shown its Japanese viewers that, like them, Koreans fall in love, feel despair, and harbor the same hopes and fears for themselves and for their children. This sitcom has transformed the image Japanese have of the Korean nation more profoundly than any number of diplomatic efforts and demonstrates that globalization can erode prejudices that have existed between neighboring countries for centuries.

Furthermore, this process of better understanding allows us to keep our identity and add new identities. The Koreans absorb a bit of the American culture, a bit of the French, a bit of other European societies. Perhaps they have become a different sort of Korean, but they remain Korean nonetheless. It is quite the illusion to think you can lose your identity. And it goes both ways. When you look at the success of cultural exports out of Korea—this so-called new wave through music, television, movies, and art—Korea becomes part of the identity of other people.

Now, as a Frenchman, I am a bit Korean myself. This is how globalization works. We do not lose our identity. We enter into the world that I call the world of multi-identity, and that is progress, not loss.

Political and Cultural Norms

One of the most significant transformations in terms of welfare for the people in the globalized world is the increased respect given to the rights of women and minorities. In many nations, to be a woman or to belong to a minority has not been easy. In the past 30 years, however, women and minorities everywhere have become better informed and have learned that the repression they suffered until very recently is not typical in a modern democracy.

Let us consider India, where a strong caste system historically has subjugated women and untouchables. Thanks to the globalization of democratic norms, these minorities are better protected; through various affirmative action policies, they can access the better jobs that traditionally were forbidden to them. This transformation has positive consequences for them, of course, and also creates better outcomes for their children's welfare and education. We are entering into a better world because of their improved status, thanks to the cultural and democratic exchanges generated by globalization.

Information

Through legacy media and, more and more, through the Internet and cellular phones, everyone today, even in authoritarian countries, is better informed. For one year, I lived in the poorest part of China, and I remember well how a farmer, in the most remote village, knew exactly what was happening not only in the next village, but also in Beijing and New York because of the Internet and his cellular phone. No government can stop information now. People know today that, as they say, "knowledge is power."

Now let us imagine if the genocide in Darfur had happened 20 or 30 years ago. The Darfur population would have been annihilated by the Sudanese government, and no one would have known. Today we all know about the genocide. The reason why the international community has been forced to intervene is because of the flood of information. Knowledge is proving to be the best protection for oppressed minorities and, thus, one of the most vital aspects of globalization.

Internationalization of the Rule of Law

Internationalization of rule of law, of course, has limitations. The institutions in charge of this emerging rule of law, whether the United Nations or the World Trade Organization, are criticized. They are not completely legitimate. They are certainly not perfectly democratic, but you cannot build a democratic organization with non-democratic governments. It becomes a trade-off.

In spite of all the weaknesses of international organizations, the emergence of a real international rule of law replaces the pure barbarism that existed before, which had consisted of the most powerful against the weak. Even though globalization cannot suppress war, it is remarkably efficient at containing war. If you examine the kinds of wars we have today, compared to the history of mankind, the number of victims and number of nations involved are very few. We are all safer because of both this emerging rule of law and the flow of information provided by globalization.

Invented by Entrepreneurs

We also need to remember that globalization is not some historical accident but has been devised and built by those who wanted it. Diplomats did not invent it. Entrepreneurs did.

Let us look at Europe. After World War II, the Europeans discovered that they had been their own worst enemies. For 1,000 years, we were fighting each other. Why? We do not remember very well. Every 30 years, we went to war. The French killed the Germans. The Germans killed the French. When you try to explain this history to your children, they cannot understand. Diplomats and politicians from the 18th century onward unsuccessfully made plans to avoid this kind of civil war within Europe.

Then, in the 1940s, a businessman came along named Jean Monnet. His business was to sell cognac in the United States, and he was very good at it. The idea Jean Monnet had was that perhaps the unification process of Europe should not be started by diplomats. Maybe it should be started by business people. He proceeded to build the European Union on a foundation of commerce. He started with coal and steel in 1950, and it was through the liberation of that trade that he conceived the unification of Europe, which has played a crucial role in the globalization process.

Monnet's guiding principle was that commercial and financial ties would lead to political unification. The true basis of European solidarity has come through trade. Through this method, all of the benefits of globalization have been made possible, because free trade has been at the root level. An attack on free trade is an attack on both globalization and the welfare of the peoples of the world, so we must be very cautious when we discuss trade, as it is the essential key allowing the rest to happen.

None of this is to imply that trade is easy. In the case of Europe, it was made easier because all of the governments were democratic. It is much more complicated to build free trade with non-democratic governments, but because globalization starts with the construction of this materialistic solidarity, ideals must come afterwards.

Two Threats to Globalization

Perhaps what I have presented so far is too optimistic a picture of globalization, but I believe we have good reason to be upbeat. However, there are two threats to globalization that may be taken too lightly today.

Global epidemics

In terms of health care, we are more and more able to cope with the current illnesses of the world. Though Africa still poses a problem, through global efforts it will be possible in the years to come to reduce the major epidemics there: AIDS and malaria.

But new epidemics are threatening the world. If we remember what happened in China some years ago with the SARS epidemic, which was very short, and then the avian flu threat in 2005, you understand that there are new threats somewhere out there and that the modern world is not really prepared. One of the consequences of globalization is that people travel more, which means that viruses travel more and adapt.

Therefore, I think globalization should require the international community to develop ever more sophisticated systems to detect and cure the new epidemics that have been a negative consequence of globalization.

Terrorism

Although wars these days are more limited, new forms of warfare have emerged, which we call terrorism. Terrorism today can seem like a distant menace somewhere between the United States and the Middle East. Because of the global progress of the rule of law, however, violent groups know that it is no longer possible to wage war in the traditional way; therefore, people driven by ideological passions are increasingly tempted by terrorist methods as a way of implementing their agenda.

Those are the true negative aspects of globalization: epidemics and terrorism. Regretfully, we are too focused on the traditional problems like free trade. We are not focused enough on the future threats.

I wish globalization were more popular, but it is our fault if it is not. Perhaps we should use different words. "Globalization" is ugly. We should find a better word, and we should try to explain to the media and students that we are entering into a new civilization of welfare, progress, and happiness, because if they do not understand the beauty of globalization, they will not stand up for it when it is threatened.

Joseph E. Stiglitz

The Overselling of Globalization

Globalization has been sold as bringing unprecedented prosperity to the billions of people who have remained mired in poverty for centuries. Yet, globalization faces enormous resistance especially in the Third World. Why so?

I argue that globalization today has been oversold. I use the term to refer not only to closer integration of the countries and peoples of the world that has resulted from the lowering of transportation and communication costs and manmade barriers but also to the particular policies, the so-called "Washington Consensus," that have been commonly associated with globalization and pushed on developing countries by the international economic institutions. The Washington Consensus emphasizes deregulated markets over government provision, balanced budgets and open borders across which goods and capital freely flow and flexible exchange rates. Many critics of globalization, like myself, are opposed not so much to globalization per se but to the particular set of policies that the International Monetary Fund (IMF) and the United States have imposed on developing countries in recent decades. During this period, many countries have suffered rising poverty, a degraded environment, and destroyed indigenous culture. Right or wrong, critics blame globalization. Moreover, there is widespread feeling that globalization, as practiced, has undermined democratic processes.

Managing globalization well, so that its potential benefits emerge, will not be easy. But unless we understand how globalization came to be misshapen we will not succeed in reforming globalization. In the discussion below (and in my recent book *Globalization and Its Discontents*), I argue that the failures are related to governance of globalization. By and large, the rules of globalization have been determined by the advanced industrial countries, for their interests, or more precisely for the interests of special interests, often to the marked disadvantage of the developing world. Within the democracies of the advanced industrial countries, there is a natural set of checks and balances. Financial and commercial interests loom large, but other groups—like labor and consumers and environmentalists—have a seat at the table. In the international arena this is not so. At the IMF, it is only finance ministers and central bankers whose voices are heard; in trade negotiations, it is the trade ministers, often with close links to commercial and financial interests, who set the agenda. . . .

Reconsidering the Economic Theory of Globalization

The economist's case for globalization is straightforward: it increases a country's economic well-being because it increases the country's opportunities. Countries have more markets in which to sell their goods, more sources of funds with which to finance their development, and access to new technologies to enhance productivity. Increasing opportunities, almost by definition, enhance well-being.

But there are serious flaws in this textbook conclusion. For starters, even if globalization improved average living standards, it would hurt some sectors badly. Second, the notion that free trade and investment promote growth relies on the assumption that private markets are competitive and well functioning. When that is not the case—a circumstance rampant in the world—then, as my work and that of other economists makes clear, trade can actually make an economy worse-off. Economists have recently explored the consequences of imperfect markets. Take the issue of imperfect contracting—so-called agency problems, when one person (a manager) acts on behalf of another person (an owner) though their incentives are not perfectly aligned.

Take as a second example reputation problems—for example when buyers must rely on the reputation of the seller to gauge the quality of products. In both cases, the fact that buyers and sellers do not share the same information may worsen as the size of the market increases, and the ability of mechanisms, like reputation, to control markets may be weakened. Because globalization increases the size of markets it can, under circumstances of imperfect markets, devastate innocent economies.[1] Take Latin America. When the United States Federal Reserve Bank hiked interest rates to unprecedented levels in the early 1980s, it threw Latin America into a decade-long tailspin.

Third, with globalization comes new rules, often imposed by industrialized countries, that can strip countries of the economic tools they could previously use to manage economic crises.

Fourth, globalization, as implemented, has driven down the price of products that poor countries export relative to the price of goods they import. Agricultural subsidies in the North increase production, thereby lowering the price of products grown in the South.

As shown below, globalization has been hijacked by the special interests in the North, often at the expense of the poor in developing countries. For example, the 1994 international trade accord, known as the Uruguay Round, has been hailed in the North as a major achievement. But a recent report says it made the poorest region of the world, Sub-Saharan Africa, worse off (by some 2 percent), largely as a result of the worldwide effects cited earlier.

Cultural and Other Noneconomic Matters

The critics of globalization do not limit themselves to purely economic benefits and costs. While my main focus is on those economic costs and benefits, I want to say a few words about the democracy and culture.

Democratization

Advocates claim that globalization has led to an increased number of democracies. And certainly, the globalization of ideas has been an important impetus. But critics argue that globalization, as practiced, has undermined effective and stable democracy. The economic instability associated with globalization (which I describe more fully below) has brought with it political instability: democratically elected governments have been toppled in Ecuador and Argentina.

A key component of the Washington Consensus has been to open developing countries to short-term speculative capital flows. But that hands foreign investors enormous sway over political processes within these countries. If foreign investors dislike a political candidate, for example, they can withhold loans, driving up interest rates and toppling the economy into depression. In other words, foreign investors can increase the cost of electing someone they dislike.[2] While the recent election of Lula in Brazil shows that capital markets do not yet have a full veto, the episode nonetheless demonstrates that capital markets enter into the political process in an important way. Advocates of globalization say that this is all to the good—foreign investors provide a check against populism and help push good economic policies. But critics point out that the financial markets are myopic; they are not concerned with long-term economic growth, let alone broader social values. They feel happier if an economy has a smaller fiscal deficit, even if that leaves larger unmet education or infrastructure needs.

While the virtues of democracy have been lauded, countries have been told to cede the most important economic decisions, those concerning monetary policy, to independent central banks, focusing exclusively on inflation.

International trade agreements have ceded further authority, e.g. about a wide range of issues, the full impact of which remains uncertain.

For countries that have to turn to the international financial institutions in times of crisis there has been an even greater derogation of economic sovereignty. The conditions imposed go well beyond those which an ordinary bank would impose to ensure repayment. The internationally imposed settlements go deep into areas which, in countries like the United States, would be viewed as quintessentially political. Even when countries might have undertaken policies on their own, there is something unseemly in today's world of having those policies forced on a country, particularly given yesteryear's colonialism. To those in the developing world, the image of the cross-armed Michel Camdessus, the IMF's managing director, standing over Indonesia's Suharto, as he put his signature on a piece of paper, seemingly signing away that country's economic sovereignty, will never be forgotten.[3]

Issues which are of intense political debate in the United States and Europe—whether to privatize Social Security or whether the central bank should worry about unemployment and growth along with inflation—are taken off the political agenda. The IMF tells the country what to do. I thought it was wrong for the IMF to tell crisis-stricken countries in Asia what to do in 1997 and 1998. The role of the economic adviser is to describe the consequences of alternatives, including the risks, and who benefits and who loses. The political process—not some international bureaucrat lacking any political accountability—should make the decision. But another reason I reacted so strongly to what the IMF and Washington told Asian countries to do is that the advice was not, in many cases, based on economic science. . . .

Ceding Sovereignty

Thus, democratic processes even in countries with strong democracies, like the United States, have been undermined by globalization, in the manner in which it has proceeded. Of course, any international agreement can be thought of as ceding some sovereignty. There are gains from global collective action, and these gains may well exceed the costs, including the costs associated with ceding sovereignty. But when international agreements are more designed to advance particular interests, and are not motivated at all by considerations of global public goods or externalities, it is more likely that the costs exceed the benefits. . . .

Weakening of the Nation State

For the past two centuries or so, the center of political power in most of the successful countries has been at the level of the nation state. Globalization has entailed a loss of national sovereignty. International organizations, imposing international agreements, have seized power. So have international capital markets as they have been deregulated. And there are a variety of indirect ways in which globalization has impaired the effectiveness of the nation state, including the erosion of national cultures (to be discussed shortly). In early stages of development, the United States and most other countries relied heavily on tariffs, because they were easy to collect. But under the World Trade Organization (WTO) and especially under pressure from the IMF, countries are restricted in their ability to raise revenues through tariffs, and without good sources of revenue, the state is weakened. Some claim that this may be one of the purposes of these restrictions.

So though globalization may not be the cause of the failed states, it has in some instances contributed to them.

Lack of Democracy at the Global Level

One of the arguments for devolution and decentralization is that real democracy is more effective at the local level. More voices can be heard. There are greater incentives for democratic participation. The converse argument presumably also holds: democratic processes would be expected to be weaker at the global level, and there is ample evidence supporting this conclusion. The international economic organizations are organized, and behave, in ways which are troubling. Voting at the IMF is not based on one-person-one-vote, or one-country-one vote, or even one dollar-one-vote. Voting power is partly related to historical accident, mostly the size of the economy fifty years ago, with some adjustments since. China enjoys less voting power than its economic and political size deserve. The United States, in effect, wields a veto. And while the IMF makes decisions which affect every aspect of society, only the voices of finance ministers and central bank governors are heard.

Other protections that we have come to expect of democratic institutions are missing. The organizations are not transparent—there is no freedom of information act. Some of the critical protections against conflicts of interest are missing.

Similarly, dispute-resolution mechanisms at the WTO lack the openness that we have come to expect in judicial processes in the United States and the United Kingdom. And there is a fear that the judges, while they might be experts in trade law, may not give enough weight to other concerns, whether they are good corporate governance, health and safety, or the environment.

Of course, none of this would make a difference if there were technocratic solutions to the problems confronting globalization; that is, if there were a set of international rules of the game such that everyone were better off with that set of rules than any other. But that is not the case. The lack of democracy means that the rules that get promulgated are not necessarily those that would have emerged had there been a more open, democratic process.

Weakening Social Cohesion and Weakening Local Culture

Finally, the critics of globalization worry about the impact on social cohesion, on traditional values, on culture. But advocates of globalization either pay little attention to these concerns, or see this as another attempt to intrude on consumer sovereignty: just as there should be competition for goods, there should be competition for "cultures"; and if McDonald's triumphs, so be it. Critics see society from a more holistic perspective: contrary to Adam Smith's claims, especially in this arena, individual choices may not lead to socially desirable outcomes. Globalization's critics claim that, in focusing on economics, advocates have too narrow a vision of society, and of individual welfare. . . .

Unbalanced Globalization

Within the narrow realm of economics, critics of globalization have charged that globalization reflects an unbalanced political agenda. I largely agree.

Global Inequities

The inequities are highlighted by the international trade regime. The North has insisted that the South eliminate subsidies and open up their markets, yet the North has maintained protectionist measures and huge agriculture subsides: the United States recently increased these subsidies with a $190 billion farm bill. Agriculture subsidies in the North are so large that they exceed the entire incomes of sub-Saharan Africa. The question naturally arises: how can these poor countries compete?

One of the alleged achievements of the Uruguay Round was the application of free-trade principles to services. But what services? Opening up markets to financial services, to the comparative advantage of the United States, was included. But opening markets to maritime and construction services, of interest to developing countries, was excluded.

The intellectual property regime embedded in the Uruguay Round (the so-called TRIPS agreement) reflected the interests of the pharmaceutical industry and other producers of intellectual property. In pushing for the interests of the drug companies, the 1994 accord might slow the overall pace of innovation. Knowledge itself is one of the most important inputs to the production of knowledge, and the intellectual property regime put into place makes access to knowledge by researchers more difficult. Even at the time the agreement was being negotiated, I and others at the Council of Economic Advisers worried about access to drugs by the very poor in the least developed countries—a concern that subsequent events showed was well justified, as the world watched in horror as AIDS patients in the poorest countries found their access to life-preserving drugs cut off and as the American government rallied behind the drug companies. . . .

The Economic Failures of Globalization

While East Asia benefited greatly by taking advantage of globalization, elsewhere globalization has fallen far short of the promise. In developing countries, in the race between population growth and improving living standards, population won. Though the percentage of people in poverty fell, the absolute number of poor people rose. And poverty reduction occurred almost entirely in China and India, both of which deviated in central ways from the market fundamentalism of the Washington Consensus.

In Latin America, the statistics for the first full decade under reform and globalization are in. Growth rates during the 1990s were little more than half of what they were in the pre-reform decades of the 1950s, 60s, and 70s, let alone the so-called lost decade of the 1980s.[4] The rapid growth that occurred in the early part of the 1990s was not sustained. Critics of globalization might dismiss the fast growth of the early 1990s as unsustainable—just as advocates of globalization dismiss the high-flying growth during the pre-reform decades after World War II as unsustainable. And even in countries which have succeeded in growing strongly, such as Mexico, much of the gains went to the richest 30 percent of the population, and especially the top 10 percent, with many in the bottom worse off.[5]

Increased Global Instability

Meanwhile, globalization has been accompanied by increased instability: close to a hundred countries have had crises in the past three decades.[6] Globalization created economic volatility, and those at the bottom of the income distribution in poor countries often suffer the most. They have no reserves to shield them from economic shocks, and the social safety nets in most developing countries are anemic.[7] With inadequate safety nets, the suffering in these crises of those who lose their jobs is enormous. As the roster of seemingly well managed countries experiencing crises, including those who were given A+'s by the IMF, grows, everyone asks, who will we be next? Among the major emerging markets, only those which have not fully deregulated their capital accounts, like India and China, have been spared. I argue that this is no accident. . . .

NOTES

1. See, e.g. World Bank (1993), Stiglitz (1996), Wade (1992), Amsden (1989).
2. See, in particular, Dixit (2003) and Stiglitz (2000a).
3. Cf. recent experiences in Brazil.
4. See Sen (2000), Rao and Walton (2004).
5. The growth rate averaged 3.2% between 1990 and 1999 versus the 5.5% recorded between 1950 and 1980 (see Cardoso and Fishlow [1992], Ocampo and Martin [2003].) As always, there is some controversy concerning how to interpret such numbers. Critics of globalization point out that frequently, a period of stagnation is followed by a catch; the high growth thus gives an exaggerated picture of the economy's sustainable performance. A better picture is provided by averaging the period of stagnation with the subsequent period. . . .
   On the other hand, many critics of the growth in the earlier decades suggest it was not sustainable—it certainly wasn't sustained, but whether it was because of intrinsic weaknesses in the system, or because the countries were induced, by this earlier period of capital market globalization, to borrow more than was prudent,

remains a subject of debate. In any case, in this perspective, one should include the lost decade of the 80s in the calculations of the earlier period—it was part of the price that had to be paid; even in this perspective, the decade of reform/globalization does not shine well.

6. Bouillon et al. (1998); Inter-American Development Bank (1999), Ros and Bouillon (2000).
7. See Caprio and Klingebiel (1997, 1999) and Caprio et al. (2003).

REFERENCES

Amsden, Alice H. 1989. *Asia's Next Giant: South Korea and Late Industrialization.* New York: Oxford University Press.

Bouillon, Cesar, Arianna Legovini, and Nora Lustig. 1998. "Rising Inequality in Mexico: Returns to Household Characteristics." Prepared for the Latin American and Caribbean Economic Association (LACEA)/Inter-American Development Bank (IADB)/World Bank (WB) Network on Inequality and Poverty's First Meeting on October 21, 1998 in Buenos Aires.

Caprio, G., Jr., and D. Klingebiel. 1999. "Episodes of Systemic and Borderline Financial Crises." World Bank, photocopy.

Caprio, G., Jr., D. Klingebiel, L. Laeven, and G. Noguera. 2003. "Banking Crises Database." World Bank, photocopy.

Cardoso, Eliana and Albert Fishlow. 1992. "Latin American Economic Development: 1950–1980." *Journal of Latin American Studies,* 24, Quincentenary Supplement, pp. 197–218.

Dixit, Avinash. 2003. "Trade Expansion and Contract Enforcement." Journal of Political Economy 111, no. 6, pp. 1293–1317.

Inter-American Development Bank. 1999. "Facing Up to Inequality in Latin America." Economic and Social Progress in Latin America: 1998/1999 Report, IADB, Washington D.C.

Ocampo, Jose Antonio and Juan Martin. 2003. *A Decade of Light and Shadow: Latin America and the Caribbean in the 1990s.* Santiago, Chile: ECLAC.

Rao, Vijavendra and Michael Walton, eds. 2004. *Culture and Public Action.* Stanford University Press.

Ros, Jaime and Cesar Bouillon. 2000. "Mexico: Trade Liberalization, Growth, Inequality and Poverty." In Enrique Ganuza, Ricardo Paes de Barros, Lance Taylor, Rob Vos, eds. *Liberalizacion, Desigualdad y Pobreza: America Latina y el Caribe en los 90,* UNDP.

Sen, Amartya. 2000. "Culture and Development." Paper presented at the World Bank Tokyo Meeting, December 13.

Stiglitz, Joseph E. 1996. "Some Lessons from the East Asian Miracle." *World Bank Research Observer* 11, no. 2 (August): 151–177.

_____. 2000a. "Formal and Informal Institutions." In Dasgupta and Serageldin, eds. *Social Capital: A Multifaceted Perspective,* Washington: World Bank, pp. 59–68.

Wade, Robert. 1992. *Governing the Market: Economic Theory and the Role of Government in East Asian Industrialization.* Princeton University Press.

World Bank. 1993. *The East Asian Miracle: Economic Growth and Public Policy.* New York: Oxford University Press.

PART II

INTERNATIONAL SECURITY

The notion of security underwent a significant transformation in the post-Cold War years. There was a shift from a focus on traditional military security, to a broader understanding of the concept encompassing economic, environmental, societal, and human security. The object of security was no longer just the survival of the state, but also the environment, societal identity, and the individual, among others. With the devastating impact of 9/11, terrorism and the proliferation of weapons of mass destruction rose to the top of the security agenda. This section examines some of the key international security issues confronting states and societies in the international system today.

Chapter 6 discusses the important debate over the triumph of Western ideas or their demise. Francis Fukuyama argues that ideas of liberalism as a political ideology and capitalism as an economic system have triumphed. Accordingly, the world is at the end of history. This means that debates about which political or economic system is best are resolved. Samuel Huntington posits that Western ideas have not triumphed. He argues that there is a growth of civilizational identity among non-Western civilizations, such as the Islamic and Confucian, due to the decline of Western civilization, as well as the rise of other civilizations. This decline of Western civilization and rise of others is leading to increased conflict between civilizations.

Chapter 7 discusses the policy decisions the United States faces in the war in Iraq. With strong opposition at home, the United States can withdraw its troops from Iraq and focus on fighting terrorism elsewhere, or it can continue to maintain its presence and seek a stable, self-governing Iraq. Michael O'Hanlon argues that the surge in Iraq has been a success and advocates its continuation. Untimely U.S. withdrawal may lead to instability and compromise the progress that has been achieved in reducing violence and initiating political reconciliation. Andrew Bacevich, on the other hand, maintains that the war has done more harm than good: it has exposed the limits of American power, served as a breeding ground for jihadists, and has served the interests of the United States' adversaries.

Chapter 8 looks at arguments on whether the United States is winning or losing the war on terror. William Kristol makes the case that the Iraq war is a key and necessary component of the war against terrorism, and the removal of other terrorist-sponsoring regimes may be necessary if we are to achieve victory. David Cole and Jules Lobel, on the other hand, argue that the strategy employed by the Bush Administration, which they call "the preventive paradigm," has backfired and has actually made the country less safe. Cole and Lobel argue that the United States should try and address the fight against terrorism by utilizing the rule of law.

Chapter 9 addresses the rise of China as the next superpower. Utilizing China's interest in continued economic growth, the United States can engage China in the premier international institutions and in the management of the global economy. Alternatively, the United States may choose to confront China and seek to slow its growth and diminish its power. Zbigniew Brzezinski posits that China's rise can take place peacefully. He argues that confrontational foreign policy would disrupt its economic growth, which is the primary goal of the Chinese leadership. John Mearsheimer maintains that China's rise cannot take place peacefully. It would try to dominate Asia and push the United States out of the continent.

Chapter 10 centers on the usefulness of nuclear weapons in view of the security challenges states face in the post-Cold War era. It looks at whether nuclear deterrence or nuclear disarmament is more likely to keep us safe. Robert McNamara argues that all nuclear weapons should be eliminated; otherwise, all nations would be placed at grave danger. Kenneth Waltz looks at why countries seek to acquire nuclear weapons. He argues that their hugely destructive potential is effective in preventing their use. For Waltz, limited nuclear proliferation contributes to stability due to the defensive nature of nuclear weapons.

Chapter 11 asks whether nuclear Iran would pose a threat to the world. S. Enders Wimbush argues that the United States should not compromise with Iran. If Iran were to possess nuclear weapons, it would have the ability to deter U.S. threats, establish itself as a military hegemon in the region, trigger nuclear proliferation among its neighbors, and be able to achieve military victory. Barry Posen takes the opposite stance, arguing that a nuclear Iran would not pose an additional threat because of the overwhelming superiority of the U.S. nuclear arsenal and the regional balance of power.

CHAPTER 6 END OF HISTORY
v. CLASH OF CIVILIZATIONS

The End of History: The Triumph of the West

Advocate: Francis Fukuyama

Source: "The End of History?" *The National Interest*, no. 16 (Summer 1989), pp. 3–18.

The Clash of Civilizations: The West versus the Rest

Advocate: Samuel P. Huntington

Source: "The Clash of Civilizations?" *Foreign Affairs*, vol. 72, no. 3 (Summer 1993), pp. 22–49, excerpt.

The decade following the end of the Cold War was a time of optimism and confidence. The communist regimes of the former Soviet bloc had crumbled and the Soviet Union had disintegrated into fifteen successor states. The liberal West had triumphed and the spread of democracy and capitalism seemed inevitable.

This buoyancy ended with the terrorist attacks on 9/11. The concept of "clash of civilizations" filled the airwaves and entered the public lexicon, becoming an easy answer for many who sought to explain the complex reasons behind the violent attacks. It denotes incompatibility of worldviews and struggles for power on global scale.

END OF HISTORY

The "End of History" thesis as put forward by Francis Fukuyama, argues that humankind had reached the end of an ideological struggle. Liberalism, in both its economic and political versions, had won out over all other ideologies, including fascism and communism. Liberalism, then, was the one ideology that would allow individuals and societies the best opportunities for the development of their potential to the fullest. With the triumph of liberalism, ideological conflict on a grand scale was over; peace was to prevail with the spread of democracy and market capitalism.

The events that have unfolded in the twenty-first century have largely discredited Fukuyama's "End of History" thesis. Political and economic liberalism—although as popular as ever—have not covered the globe, and peace has not prevailed. In fact, the spread of liberal democracy and market economies as championed by the West have been resisted in many localities as counterpoints to local cultures and traditions.

CLASH OF CIVILIZATIONS

Coined in 1993 by Samuel Huntington, the "Clash of Civilizations" thesis highlights the role of culture in international relations. Civilizations, being the largest expressions of cultural identity, were to be the source of major conflict. For Huntington, the clash was inevitable because of the intractable nature of differences among civilizations, their increasing contact with one another as a result of globalization, the growing diminution of local identities, and the role of the West. Although the West is at the height of its power, its ubiquity gives rise to a backlash against its cultural, economic, and political dominance.

Huntington believes that the most hostile response to the power of the West will come from the Islamic and Confucian civilizations. He urges cooperation between the Western civilization and those that are closest to it: the Latin American and Eastern Orthodox. Huntington's prediction for epochal conflict between civilizations thus became a useful explanation for fundamentalist terrorism, whereby culture and religion replaced ideology as the driving forces of violent conflict in the twenty-first century.

The "clash of civilizations," however, ignores the fact that there are struggles within civilizations: for instance, it is difficult to group more than a billion Muslims and argue that they all want the destruction of the United States. Groups are diverse, continually evolve, often as a result of internal struggles. This diversity of prevalent discourses, political evolution, and economic development inevitably affects the outlook of individuals and societies, and their continual evolution.

POINTS **TO PONDER**

1. Why is liberalism considered to be the ideology that best provides for the fulfillment of individuals?
2. Have civilizations replaced the state as the most important unit in international relations?
3. Was the "War on Terrorism" caused by a clash of civilizations? Or did the "War on Terrorism" cause a clash of civilizations?
4. What determines a state's foreign policy: culture, ideology, or national interests?

Francis Fukuyama
The End of History?

In watching the flow of events over the past decade or so, it is hard to avoid
the feeling that something very fundamental has happened in world history.
The past year has seen a flood of articles commemorating the end of the
Cold War, and the fact that "peace" seems to be breaking out in many
regions of the world. Most of these analyses lack any larger conceptual framework for distinguishing between what is essential and what is contingent or
accidental in world history, and are predictably superficial. If Mr. Gorbachev
were ousted from the Kremlin or a new Ayatollah proclaimed the millennium from a desolate Middle Eastern capital, these same commentators
would scramble to announce the rebirth of a new era of conflict.

And yet, all of these people sense dimly that there is some larger process
at work, a process that gives coherence and order to the daily headlines. The
twentieth century saw the developed world descend into a paroxysm of ideological violence, as liberalism contended first with the remnants of abso-
lutism, then bolshevism and fascism, and finally an updated Marxism that
threatened to lead to the ultimate apocalypse of nuclear war. But the century that began full of self-confidence in the ultimate triumph of Western
liberal democracy seems at its close to be returning full circle to where it
started: not to an "end of ideology" or a convergence between capitalism
and socialism, as earlier predicted, but to an unabashed victory of economic
and political liberalism.

The triumph of the West, of the Western *idea,* is evident first of all in the
total exhaustion of viable systematic alternatives to Western liberalism. In the
past decade, there have been unmistakable changes in the intellectual climate
of the world's two largest communist countries, and the beginnings of
significant reform movements in both. But this phenomenon extends
beyond high politics and it can be seen also in the ineluctable spread of consumerist Western culture in such diverse contexts as the peasants' markets
and color television sets now omnipresent throughout China, the cooperative restaurants and clothing stores opened in the past year in Moscow, the

Francis Fukuyama is deputy director of the State Department's policy planning staff and former
analyst at the RAND Corporation. This article is based on a lecture presented at the University
of Chicago's John M. Olin Center for Inquiry Into the Theory and Practice of Democracy. The
author would like to pay special thanks to the Olin Center and to Nathan Tarcov and Allan
Bloom for their support in this and many earlier endeavors. The opinions expressed in this article do not reflect those of the RAND Corporation or of any agency of the U.S. government.

Beethoven piped into Japanese department stores, and the rock music enjoyed alike in Prague, Rangoon, and Tehran.

What we may be witnessing is not just the end of the Cold War, or the passing of a particular period of postwar history, but the end of history as such: that is, the end point of mankind's ideological evolution and the universalization of Western liberal democracy as the final form of human government. This is not to say that there will no longer be events to fill the pages of *Foreign Affairs*'s yearly summaries of international relations, for the victory of liberalism has occurred primarily in the realm of ideas or consciousness and is as yet incomplete in the real or material world. But there are powerful reasons for believing that it is the ideal that will govern the material world *in the long run*. To understand how this is so, we must first consider some theoretical issues concerning the nature of historical change.

I

The notion of the end of history is not an original one. Its best known propagator was Karl Marx, who believed that the direction of historical development was a purposeful one determined by the interplay of material forces, and would come to an end only with the achievement of a communist utopia that would finally resolve all prior contradictions. But the concept of history as a dialectical process with a beginning, a middle, and an end was borrowed by Marx from his great German predecessor, Georg Wilhelm Friedrich Hegel.

For better or worse, much of Hegel's historicism has become part of our contemporary intellectual baggage. The notion that mankind has progressed through a series of primitive stages of consciousness on his path to the present, and that these stages corresponded to concrete forms of social organization, such as tribal, slave-owning, theocratic, and finally democratic-egalitarian societies, has become inseparable from the modern understanding of man. Hegel was the first philosopher to speak the language of modern social science, insofar as man for him was the product of his concrete historical and social environment and not, as earlier natural right theorists would have it, a collection of more or less fixed "natural" attributes. The mastery and transformation of man's natural environment through the application of science and technology was originally not a Marxist concept, but a Hegelian one. Unlike later historicists whose historical relativism degenerated into relativism *tout court,* however, Hegel believed that history culminated in an absolute moment—a moment in which a final, rational form of society and state became victorious.

It is Hegel's misfortune to be known now primarily as Marx's precursor, and it is our misfortune that few of us are familiar with Hegel's work from direct study, but only as it has been filtered through the distorting lens of Marxism. In France, however, there has been an effort to save Hegel from his Marxist interpreters and to resurrect him as the philosopher who most correctly speaks to our time. Among those modern French interpreters of Hegel, the greatest was certainly Alexandre Kojève, a brilliant Russian emigre who taught a highly influential series of seminars in Paris in the 1930s at the *Ecole Practique des Hautes Etudes*.[1] While largely unknown in the United States, Kojève had a major impact on the intellectual life of the continent. Among his students ranged such future luminaries as Jean-Paul Sartre on the Left and Raymond Aron on the Right; postwar existentialism borrowed many of its basic categories from Hegel via Kojève.

Kojève sought to resurrect the Hegel of the *Phenomenology of Mind,* the Hegel who proclaimed history to be at an end in 1806. For as early as this Hegel saw in Napoleon's defeat of the Prussian monarchy at the Battle of Jena the victory of the ideals of the French Revolution, and the imminent universalization of the state incorporating the principles of liberty and equality. Kojève, far from rejecting Hegel in light of the turbulent events of the next century and a half, insisted that the latter had been essentially correct.[2] The Battle of Jena marked the end of history because it was at that point that the *vanguard* of humanity (a term quite familiar to Marxists) actualized the principles of the French Revolution. While there was considerable work to be done after 1806—abolishing slavery and the slave trade, extending the franchise to workers, women, blacks, and other racial minorities, etc.—the basic *principles* of the liberal democratic state could not be improved upon. The two world wars in this century and their attendant revolutions and upheavals simply had the effect of extending those principles spatially, such that the various provinces of human civilization were brought up to the level of its most advanced outposts, and of forcing those societies in Europe and North America at the vanguard of civilization to implement their liberalism more fully.

The state that emerges at the end of history is liberal insofar as it recognizes and protects through a system of law man's universal right to freedom, and democratic insofar as it exists only with the consent of the governed. For Kojève, this so-called "universal homogenous state" found real-life embodiment in the countries of postwar Western Europe—precisely those flabby, prosperous, self-satisfied, inward-looking, weak-willed states whose grandest project was nothing more heroic than the creation of the Common Market.[3] But this was only to be expected. For human history and the conflict that characterized it was based on the existence of "contradictions": primitive man's quest for mutual recognition, the dialectic of the master and slave, the transformation and mastery of nature, the struggle for the universal recognition of rights, and the dichotomy between proletarian and capitalist. But in the universal homogenous state, all prior contradictions are resolved and all human needs are satisfied. There is no struggle or conflict over "large" issues, and consequently no need for generals or statesmen; what remains is primarily economic activity. And indeed, Kojève's life was consistent with his teaching. Believing that there was no more work for philosophers as well, since Hegel (correctly understood) had already achieved absolute knowledge, Kojève left teaching after the war and spent the remainder of his life working as a bureaucrat in the European Economic Community, until his death in 1968.

To his contemporaries at mid-century, Kojève's proclamation of the end of history must have seemed like the typical eccentric solipsism of a French intellectual, coming as it did on the heels of World War II and at the very height of the Cold War. To comprehend how Kojève could have been so audacious as to assert that history has ended, we must first of all understand the meaning of Hegelian idealism.

II

For Hegel, the contradictions that drive history exist first of all in the realm of human consciousness, i.e. on the level of ideas[4]—not the trivial election year proposals of American politicians, but ideas in the sense of large unifying world views that might best be understood under the rubric of ideology. Ideology in this sense is not restricted to the secular and explicit political doctrines we usually associate with the term, but can include religion, culture, and the complex of moral values underlying any society as well.

Hegel's view of the relationship between the ideal and the real or material worlds was an extremely complicated one, beginning with the fact that for him the distinction between the two was only apparent.[5] He did not believe that the real world conformed or could be made to conform to ideological preconceptions of philosophy professors in any simple-minded way, or that the "material" world could not impinge on the ideal. Indeed, Hegel the professor was temporarily thrown out of work as a result of a very material event, the Battle of Jena. But while Hegel's writing and thinking could be stopped by a bullet from the material world, the hand on the trigger of the gun was motivated in turn by the ideas of liberty and equality that had driven the French Revolution.

For Hegel, all human behavior in the material world, and hence all human history, is rooted in a prior state of consciousness—an idea similar to the one expressed by John Maynard Keynes when he said that the views of men of affairs were usually derived from defunct economists and academic scribblers of earlier generations. This consciousness may not be explicit and self-aware, as are modern political doctrines, but may rather take the form of religion or simple cultural or moral habits. And yet this realm of consciousness *in the long run* necessarily becomes manifest in the material world, indeed creates the material world in its own image. Consciousness is cause and not effect, and can develop autonomously from the material world; hence the real subtext underlying the apparent jumble of current events is the history of ideology.

Hegel's idealism has fared poorly at the hands of later thinkers. Marx reversed the priority of the real and the ideal completely, relegating the entire realm of consciousness—religion, art, culture, philosophy itself—to a "super-structure" that was determined entirely by the prevailing material mode of production. Yet another unfortunate legacy of Marxism is our tendency to retreat into materialist or utilitarian explanations of political or historical phenomena, and our disinclination to believe in the autonomous power of ideas. A recent example of this is Paul Kennedy's hugely successful *The Rise and Fall of the Great Powers,* which ascribes the decline of great powers to simple economic overextension. Obviously, this is true on some level: an empire whose economy is barely above the level of subsistence cannot bankrupt its treasury indefinitely. But whether a highly productive modern industrial society chooses to spend 3 or 7 percent of its GNP on defense rather than consumption is entirely a matter of that society's political priorities, which are in turn determined in the realm of consciousness.

The materialist bias of modern thought is characteristic not only of people on the Left who may be sympathetic to Marxism, but of many passionate anti-Marxists as well. Indeed, there is on the Right what one might label the *Wall Street Journal* school of deterministic materialism that discounts the importance of ideology and culture and sees man as essentially a rational, profit-maximizing individual. It is precisely this kind of individual and his pursuit of material incentives that is posited as the basis for economic life as such in economic textbooks.[6] One small example will illustrate the problematic character of such materialist views.

Max Weber begins his famous book, *The Protestant Ethic and the Spirit of Capitalism,* by noting the different economic performance of Protestant and Catholic communities throughout Europe and America, summed up in the proverb that Protestants eat well while Catholics sleep well. Weber notes that according to any economic theory that posited man as a rational profit-maximizer, raising the piece-work rate should increase labor productivity. But in fact, in many traditional peasant communities, raising the piece-work rate actually had the opposite effect of *lowering* labor productivity: at the higher rate, a peasant accustomed to earning two and one-half marks per day found he could earn the same amount by working less, and did so because he valued leisure more than income. The choices of leisure over income, or of the militaristic life of the Spartan hoplite over the wealth of the Athenian trader, or even the ascetic life of the early capitalist entrepreneur over that of a traditional leisured aristocrat, cannot possibly be explained by the impersonal working of material forces, but come preeminently out of the sphere of consciousness—what we have labeled here broadly as ideology. And indeed, a central theme of Weber's work was to prove that contrary to Marx, the material mode of production, far from being the "base," was itself a "superstructure" with roots in religion and culture, and that to understand the emergence of modern capitalism and the profit motive one had to study their antecedents in the realm of the spirit.

As we look around the contemporary world, the poverty of materialist theories of economic development is all too apparent. *The Wall Street Journal* school of deterministic materialism habitually points to the stunning economic success of Asia in the past few decades as evidence of the viability of free market economics, with the implication that all societies would see similar development were they simply to allow their populations to pursue their material self-interest freely. Surely free markets and stable political systems are a necessary precondition to capitalist economic growth. But just as surely the cultural heritage of those Far Eastern societies, the ethic of work and saving and family, a religious heritage that does not, like Islam, place restrictions on certain forms of economic behavior, and other deeply ingrained moral qualities, are equally important in explaining their economic performance.[7] And yet the intellectual weight of materialism is such that not a single respectable contemporary theory of economic development addresses consciousness and culture seriously as the matrix within which economic behavior is formed.

Failure to understand that the roots of economic behavior lie in the realm of consciousness and culture leads to the common mistake of attributing material causes to phenomena that are essentially ideal in nature. For example, it is commonplace in the West to interpret the reform movements first in China and most recently in the Soviet Union as the victory of the material over the ideal—that is, a recognition that ideological incentives could not replace material ones in stimulating a highly productive modern economy, and that if one wanted to prosper one had to appeal to baser forms of self-interest. But the deep defects of socialist economies were evident thirty or forty years ago to anyone who chose to look. Why was it that these countries moved away from central planning only in the 1980s? The answer must be found in the consciousness of the elites and leaders ruling them, who decided to opt for the "Protestant" life of wealth and risk over the "Catholic" path of poverty and security.[8] That change was in no way made inevitable by the material conditions in which either country found itself on the eve of the reform, but instead came about as the result of the victory of one idea over another.[9]

For Kojève, as for all good Hegelians, understanding the underlying processes of history requires understanding developments in the realm of consciousness or ideas, since consciousness will ultimately remake the material world in its own image. To say that history ended in 1806 meant that mankind's ideological evolution ended in the ideals of the French or American Revolutions: while particular regimes in the real world might not implement these ideals fully, their theoretical truth is absolute and could not be improved upon. Hence it did not matter to Kojève that the consciousness of the postwar generation of Europeans had not been universalized throughout the world; if ideological development had in fact ended, the homogenous state would eventually become victorious throughout the material world.

I have neither the space nor, frankly, the ability to defend in depth Hegel's radical idealist perspective. The issue is not whether Hegel's system was right, but whether his perspective might uncover the problematic nature of many materialist explanations we often take for granted. This is not to deny the role of material factors as such. To a literal-minded idealist, human society can be built around any arbitrary set of principles regardless of their relationship to the material world. And in fact men have proven themselves able to endure the most extreme material hardships in the name of ideas that exist in the realm of the spirit alone, be it the divinity of cows or the nature of the Holy Trinity.[10]

But while man's very perception of the material world is shaped by his historical consciousness of it, the material world can clearly affect in return the viability of a particular state of consciousness. In particular, the spectacular abundance of advanced liberal economies and the infinitely diverse consumer culture made possible by them seem to both foster and preserve liberalism in the political sphere. I want to avoid the materialist determinism that says that liberal economics inevitably produces liberal politics, because I believe that both economics and politics presuppose an autonomous prior state of consciousness that makes them possible. But that state of consciousness that permits the growth of liberalism seems to stabilize in the way one would expect at the end of history if it is underwritten by the abundance of a modern free market economy. We might summarize the content of the universal homogenous state as liberal democracy in the political sphere combined with easy access to VCRs and stereos in the economic.

III

Have we in fact reached the end of history? Are there, in other words, any fundamental "contradictions" in human life that cannot be resolved in the context of modern liberalism, that would be resolvable by an alternative political-economic structure? If we accept the idealist premises laid out above, we must seek an answer to this question in the realm of ideology and consciousness. Our task is not to answer exhaustively the challenges to liberalism promoted by every crackpot messiah around the world, but only those that are embodied in important social or political forces and movements, and which are therefore part of world history. For our purposes, it matters very little what strange thoughts occur to people in Albania or Burkina Faso, for we are interested in what one could in some sense call the common ideological heritage of mankind.

In the past century, there have been two major challenges to liberalism, those of fascism and of communism. The former[11] saw the political weakness, materialism, anomie, and lack of community of the West as fundamental contradictions in liberal societies that could only be resolved by a strong state that forged a new "people" on the basis of national exclusiveness. Fascism was destroyed as a living ideology by World War II. This was a defeat, of course, on a very material level, but it amounted to a defeat of the idea as well. What destroyed fascism as an idea was not universal moral revulsion against it, since plenty of people were willing to endorse the idea as long as it seemed the wave of the future, but its lack of success. After the war, it seemed to most people that German fascism as well as its other European and Asian variants were bound to self-destruct. There was no material reason why new fascist movements could not have sprung up again after the war in other locales, but for the fact that expansionist ultranationalism, with its promise of unending conflict leading to disastrous military defeat, had completely lost its appeal. The ruins of the Reich chancellory as well as the atomic bombs dropped on Hiroshima and Nagasaki killed this ideology on the level of consciousness as well as materially, and all of the proto-fascist movements spawned by the German and Japanese examples like the Peronist movement in Argentina or Subhas Chandra Bose's Indian National Army withered after the war.

The ideological challenge mounted by the other great alternative to liberalism, communism, was far more serious. Marx, speaking Hegel's language, asserted that liberal society contained a fundamental contradiction that could not be resolved within its context, that between capital and labor, and this contradiction has constituted the chief accusation against liberalism ever since. But surely, the class issue has actually been successfully resolved in the West. As Kojève (among others) noted, the egalitarianism of modern America represents the essential achievement of the classless society envisioned by Marx. This is not to say that there are not rich people and poor people in the United States, or that the gap between them has not grown in recent years. But the root causes of economic inequality do not have to do with the underlying legal and social structure of our society, which remains fundamentally egalitarian and moderately redistributionist, so much as with the cultural and social characteristics of the groups that make it up, which are in turn the historical legacy of premodern conditions. Thus black poverty in the United States is not the inherent product of liberalism, but is rather the "legacy of slavery and racism" which persisted long after the formal abolition of slavery.

As a result of the receding of the class issue, the appeal of communism in the developed Western world, it is safe to say, is lower today than any time since the end of the First World War. This can be measured in any number of ways: in the declining membership and electoral pull of the major European communist parties, and their overtly revisionist programs; in the corresponding electoral success of conservative parties from Britain and Germany to the United States and Japan, which are unabashedly pro-market and anti-statist; and in an intellectual climate whose most "advanced" members no longer believe that bourgeois society is something that ultimately needs to be overcome. This is not to say that the opinions of progressive intellectuals in Western countries are not deeply pathological in any number of ways. But those who believe that the future must inevitably be socialist tend to be very old, or very marginal to the real political discourse of their societies.

One may argue that the socialist alternative was never terribly plausible for the North Atlantic world, and was sustained for the last several decades primarily by its success outside of this region. But it is precisely in the non-European world that one is most struck by the occurrence of major ideological transformations. Surely the most remarkable changes have occurred in Asia. Due to the strength and adaptability of the indigenous cultures there, Asia became a battleground for a variety of imported Western ideologies early in this century. Liberalism in Asia was a very weak reed in the period after World War I; it is easy today to forget how gloomy Asia's political future looked as recently as ten or fifteen years ago. It is easy to forget as well how momentous the outcome of Asian ideological struggles seemed for world political development as a whole.

The first Asian alternative to liberalism to be decisively defeated was the fascist one represented by Imperial Japan. Japanese fascism (like its German version) was defeated by the force of American arms in the Pacific war, and liberal democracy was imposed on Japan by a victorious United States. Western capitalism and political liberalism when transplanted to Japan were adapted and transformed by the Japanese in such a way as to be scarcely recognizable.[12] Many Americans are now aware that Japanese industrial organization is very different from that prevailing in the United States or Europe, and it is questionable what relationship the factional maneuvering that takes place with the governing Liberal Democratic Party bears to democracy. Nonetheless, the very fact that the essential elements of economic and political liberalism have been so successfully grafted onto uniquely Japanese traditions and institutions guarantees their survival in the long run. More important is the contribution that Japan has made in turn to world history by following in the footsteps of the United States to create a truly universal consumer culture that has become both a symbol and an underpinning of the universal homogenous state. V.S. Naipaul travelling in Khomeini's Iran shortly after the revolution noted the omnipresent signs advertising the products of Sony, Hitachi, and JVC, whose appeal remained virtually irresistible and gave the lie to the regime's pretensions of restoring a state based on the rule of the *Shariah*. Desire for access to the consumer culture, created in large measure by Japan, has played a crucial role in fostering the spread of economic liberalism throughout Asia, and hence in promoting political liberalism as well.

The economic success of the other newly industrializing countries (NICs) in Asia following on the example of Japan is by now a familiar story. What is important from a Hegelian standpoint is that political liberalism has been following economic liberalism, more slowly than many had hoped but with seeming inevitability. Here again we see the victory of the idea of the universal homogenous state. South Korea had developed into a modern, urbanized society with an increasingly large and well-educated middle class that could not possibly be isolated from the larger democratic trends around them. Under these circumstances it seemed intolerable to a large part of this population that it should be ruled by an anachronistic military regime while Japan, only a decade or so ahead in economic terms, had parliamentary institutions for over forty years. Even the former socialist regime in Burma, which for so many decades existed in dismal isolation from the larger trends dominating Asia, was buffeted in the past year by pressures to liberalize both its economy and political system. It is said that unhappiness with strongman Ne Win began when a senior Burmese officer went to Singapore for medical treatment and broke down crying when he saw how far socialist Burma had been left behind by its ASEAN neighbors.

But the power of the liberal idea would seem much less impressive if it had not infected the largest and oldest culture in Asia, China. The simple existence of communist China created an alternative pole of ideological attraction, and as such constituted a threat to liberalism. But the past fifteen years have seen an almost total discrediting of Marxism-Leninism as an economic system. Beginning with the famous third plenum of the Tenth Central Committee in 1978, the Chinese Communist party set about decollectivizing agriculture for the 800 million Chinese who still lived in the countryside. The role of the state in agriculture was reduced to that of a tax collector, while production of consumer goods was sharply increased in order to give peasants a taste of the universal homogenous state and thereby an incentive to work. The reform doubled Chinese grain output in only five years, and in the process created for Deng Xiao-ping a solid political base from which he was able to extend the reform to other parts of the economy. Economic statistics do not begin to describe the dynamism, initiative, and openness evident in China since the reform began.

China could not now be described in any way as a liberal democracy. At present, no more than 20 percent of its economy has been marketized, and most importantly it continues to be ruled by a self-appointed Communist party which has given no hint of wanting to devolve power. Deng has made none of Gorbachev's promises regarding democratization of the political system and there is no Chinese equivalent of *glasnost*. The Chinese leadership has in fact been much more circumspect in criticizing Mao and Maoism than Gorbachev with respect to Brezhnev and Stalin, and the regime continues to pay lip service to Marxism-Leninism as its ideological underpinning. But anyone familiar with the outlook and behavior of the new technocratic elite now governing China knows that Marxism and ideological principle have become virtually irrelevant as guides to policy, and that bourgeois consumerism has a real meaning in that country for the first time since the revolution. The various slowdowns in the pace of reform, the campaigns against "spiritual pollution" and crackdowns on political dissent are more properly seen as tactical adjustments made in the process of managing what is an extraordinarily difficult political transition. By ducking the question of political reform while putting the economy on a new footing, Deng has managed to avoid the breakdown of authority that has accompanied Gorbachev's *perestroika*. Yet the pull of the liberal idea continues to be very strong as economic power devolves and the economy becomes more open to the outside world. There are currently over 20,000 Chinese students studying in the U.S. and other Western countries, almost all of them the children of the Chinese elite. It is hard to believe that when they return home to run the country they will be content for China to be the only country in Asia unaffected by the larger democratizing trend. The student demonstrations in Beijing that broke out first in December 1986 and recurred recently on the occasion of Hu Yao-bang's death were only the beginning of what will inevitably be mounting pressure for change in the political system as well.

What is important about China from the standpoint of world history is not the present state of the reform or even its future prospects. The central issue is the fact that the People's Republic of China can no longer act as a beacon for illiberal forces around the world, whether they be guerrillas in some Asian jungle or middle class students in Paris. Maoism, rather than being the pattern for Asia's future, became an anachronism, and it was the mainland Chinese who in fact were decisively influenced by the prosperity and dynamism of their overseas co-ethnics—the ironic ultimate victory of Taiwan.

Important as these changes in China have been, however, it is developments in the Soviet Union—the original "homeland of the world proletariat"—that have put the final nail in the coffin of the Marxist-Leninist alternative to liberal democracy. It should be clear that in terms of formal institutions, not much has changed in the four years since Gorbachev has come to power: free markets and the cooperative movement represent only a small part of the Soviet economy, which remains centrally planned; the political system is still dominated by the Communist party, which has only begun to democratize internally and to share power with other groups; the regime continues to assert that it is seeking only to modernize socialism and that its ideological basis remains Marxism-Leninism; and, finally, Gorbachev faces a potentially powerful conservative opposition that could undo many of the changes that have taken place to date. Moreover, it is hard to be too sanguine about the chances for success of Gorbachev's proposed reforms, either in the sphere of economics or politics. But my purpose here is not to analyze events in the short-term, or to make predictions for policy purposes, but to look at underlying trends in the sphere of ideology and consciousness. And in that respect, it is clear that an astounding transformation has occurred.

Emigres from the Soviet Union have been reporting for at least the last generation now that virtually nobody in that country truly believed in Marxism-Leninism any longer, and that this was nowhere more true than in the Soviet elite, which continued to mouth Marxist slogans out of sheer cynicism. The corruption and decadence of the late Brezhnev-era Soviet state seemed to matter little, however, for as long as the state itself refused to throw into question any of the fundamental principles underlying Soviet society, the system was capable of functioning adequately out of sheer inertia and could even muster some dynamism in the realm of foreign and defense policy. Marxism-Leninism was like a magical incantation which, however absurd and devoid of meaning, was the only common basis on which the elite could agree to rule Soviet society.

What has happened in the four years since Gorbachev's coming to power is a revolutionary assault on the most fundamental institutions and principles of Stalinism, and their replacement by other principles which do not amount to liberalism *per se* but whose only connecting thread is liberalism. This is most evident in the economic sphere, where the reform economists around Gorbachev have become steadily more radical in their support for free markets, to the point where some like Nikolai Shmelev do not mind being compared in public to Milton Friedman. There is a virtual consensus among the currently dominant school of Soviet economists now that central planning and the command system of allocation are the root cause of economic inefficiency, and that if the Soviet system is ever to heal itself, it must permit free and decentralized decision-making with respect to investment, labor, and prices. After a couple of initial years of ideological confusion, these principles have finally been incorporated into policy with the promulgation of new laws on enterprise autonomy, cooperatives, and finally in 1988 on lease arrangements and family farming. There are, of course, a number of fatal flaws in the current implementation of the reform, most notably the absence of a thoroughgoing price reform. But the problem is no longer a *conceptual* one: Gorbachev and his lieutenants seem to understand the economic logic of marketization well enough, but like the leaders of a Third World country facing the IMF, are afraid of the social consequences of ending consumer subsidies and other forms of dependence on the state sector.

In the political sphere, the proposed changes to the Soviet constitution, legal system, and party rules amount to much less than the establishment of a liberal state. Gorbachev has spoken of democratization primarily in the sphere of internal party affairs, and has shown little intention of ending the Communist party's monopoly of power; indeed, the political reform seeks to legitimize and therefore strengthen the CPSU's rule.[13] Nonetheless, the general principles underlying many of the reforms—that the "people" should be truly responsible for their own affairs, that higher political bodies should be answerable to lower ones, and not vice versa, that the rule of law should prevail over arbitrary police actions, with separation of powers and an independent judiciary, that there should be legal protection for property rights, the need for open discussion of public issues and the right of public dissent, the empowering of the Soviets as a forum in which the whole Soviet people can participate, and of a political culture that is more tolerant and pluralistic—come from a source fundamentally alien to the USSR's Marxist-Leninist tradition, even if they are incompletely articulated and poorly implemented in practice.

Gorbachev's repeated assertions that he is doing no more than trying to restore the original meaning of Leninism are themselves a kind of Orwellian doublespeak. Gorbachev and his allies have consistently maintained that intraparty democracy was somehow the essence of Leninism, and that the various liberal practices of open debate, secret ballot elections, and rule of law were all part of the Leninist heritage, corrupted only later by Stalin. While almost anyone would look good compared to Stalin, drawing so sharp a line between Lenin and his successor is questionable. The essence of Lenin's democratic centralism was centralism, not democracy; that is, the absolutely rigid, monolithic, and disciplined dictatorship of a hierarchically organized vanguard Communist party, speaking in the name of the *demos*. All of Lenin's vicious polemics against Karl Kautsky, Rosa Luxemburg, and various other Menshevik and Social Democratic rivals, not to mention his contempt for "bourgeois legality" and freedoms, centered around his profound conviction that a revolution could not be successfully made by a democratically run organization.

Gorbachev's claim that he is seeking to return to the true Lenin is perfectly easy to understand: having fostered a thorough denunciation of Stalinism and Brezhnevism as the root of the USSR's present predicament, he needs some point in Soviet history on which to anchor the legitimacy of the CPSU's continued rule. But Gorbachev's tactical requirements should not blind us to the fact that the democratizing and decentralizing principles which he has enunciated in both the economic and political spheres are highly subversive of some of the most fundamental precepts of both Marxism and Leninism. Indeed, if the bulk of the present economic reform proposals were put into effect, it is hard to know how the Soviet economy would be more socialist than those of other Western countries with large public sectors.

The Soviet Union could in no way be described as a liberal or democratic country now, nor do I think that it is terribly likely that *perestroika* will succeed such that the label will be thinkable any time in the near future. But at the end of history it is not necessary that all societies become successful liberal societies, merely that they end their ideological pretensions of representing different and higher forms of human society. And in this respect I believe that something very important has happened in the Soviet Union in the past few years: the criticisms of the Soviet system sanctioned by Gorbachev have been so thorough and devastating that there is very little chance of going back to either Stalinism or Brezhnevism in any simple way. Gorbachev has finally permitted people to say what they had privately understood for many years, namely, that the magical incantations of Marxism-Leninism were nonsense, that Soviet socialism was not superior to the West in any respect but was in fact a monumental failure. The conservative opposition in the USSR, consisting both of simple workers afraid of unemployment and inflation and of party officials fearful of losing their jobs and privileges, is outspoken and may be strong enough to force Gorbachev's ouster in the next few years. But what both groups desire is tradition, order, and authority; they manifest no deep commitment to Marxism-Leninism, except insofar as they have invested much of their own lives in it.[14] For authority to be restored in the Soviet Union after Gorbachev's demolition work, it must be on the basis of some new and vigorous ideology which has not yet appeared on the horizon.

If we admit for the moment that the fascist and communist challenges to liberalism are dead, are there any other ideological competitors left? Or put another way, are there contradictions in liberal society beyond that of class that are not resolvable? Two possibilities suggest themselves, those of religion and nationalism.

The rise of religious fundamentalism in recent years within the Christian, Jewish, and Muslim traditions has been widely noted. One is inclined to say that the revival of religion in some way attests to a broad unhappiness with the impersonality and spiritual vacuity of liberal consumerist societies. Yet while the emptiness at the core of liberalism is most certainly a defect in the ideology— indeed, a flaw that one does not need the perspective of religion to recognize[15]—it is not at all clear that it is remediable through politics. Modern liberalism itself was historically a consequence of the weakness of religiously- based societies which, failing to agree on the nature of the good life, could not provide even the minimal preconditions of peace and stability. In the contem- porary world only Islam has offered a theocratic state as a political alternative to both liberalism and communism. But the doctrine has little appeal for non- Muslims, and it is hard to believe that the movement will take on any universal significance. Other less organized religious impulses have been successfully sat- isfied within the sphere of personal life that is permitted in liberal societies.

The other major "contradiction" potentially unresolvable by liber- alism is the one posed by nationalism and other forms of racial and ethnic consciousness. It is certainly true that a very large degree of conflict since the Battle of Jena has had its roots in nationalism. Two cataclysmic world wars in this century have been spawned by the nationalism of the developed world in various guises, and if those passions have been muted to a certain extent in postwar Europe, they are still extremely powerful in the Third World. Nationalism has been a threat to liberalism historically in Germany, and continues to be one in isolated parts of "post-historical" Europe like Northern Ireland.

But it is not clear that nationalism represents an irreconcilable contradic- tion in the heart of liberalism. In the first place, nationalism is not one single phenomenon but several, ranging from mild cultural nostalgia to the highly organized and elaborately articulated doctrine of National Socialism. Only systematic nationalisms of the latter sort can qualify as a formal ideology on the level of liberalism or communism. The vast majority of the world's nationalist movements do not have a political program beyond the negative desire of independence *from* some other group or people, and do not offer anything like a comprehensive agenda for socio-economic organization. As such, they are compatible with doctrines and ideologies that do offer such agendas. While they may constitute a source of conflict for liberal societies, this conflict does not arise from liberalism itself so much as from the fact that the liberalism in question is incomplete. Certainly a great deal of the world's ethnic and nationalist tension can be explained in terms of peoples who are forced to live in unrepresentative political systems that they have not chosen.

While it is impossible to rule out the sudden appearance of new ideologies or previously unrecognized contradictions in liberal societies, then, the present world seems to confirm that the fundamental principles of socio-political organization have not advanced terribly far since 1806. Many of the wars and revolutions fought since that time have been undertaken in the name of ideologies which claimed to be more advanced than liberalism, but whose pretensions were ultimately unmasked by history. In the meantime, they have helped to spread the universal homogenous state to the point where it could have a significant effect on the overall character of international relations.

IV

What are the implications of the end of history for international relations? Clearly, the vast bulk of the Third World remains very much mired in history, and will be a terrain of conflict for many years to come. But let us focus for the time being on the larger and more developed states of the world who after all account for the greater part of world politics. Russia and China are not likely to join the developed nations of the West as liberal societies any time in the foreseeable future, but suppose for a moment that Marxism-Leninism ceases to be a factor driving the foreign policies of these states—a prospect which, if not yet here, the last few years have made a real possibility. How will the overall characteristics of a de-ideologized world differ from those of the one with which we are familiar at such a hypothetical juncture?

The most common answer is—not very much. For there is a very widespread belief among many observers of international relations that underneath the skin of ideology is a hard core of great power national interest that guarantees a fairly high level of competition and conflict between nations. Indeed, according to one academically popular school of international relations theory, conflict inheres in the international system as such, and to understand the prospects for conflict one must look at the shape of the system—for example, whether it is bipolar or multipolar—rather than at the specific character of the nations and regimes that constitute it. This school in effect applies a Hobbesian view of politics to international relations, and assumes that aggression and insecurity are universal characteristics of human societies rather than the product of specific historical circumstances.

Believers in this line of thought take the relations that existed between the participants in the classical nineteenth century European balance of power as a model for what a de-ideologized contemporary world would look like. Charles Krauthammer, for example, recently explained that if as a result of Gorbachev's reforms the USSR is shorn of Marxist-Leninist ideology, its behavior will revert to that of nineteenth century imperial Russia.[16] While he finds this more reassuring than the threat posed by a communist Russia, he implies that there will still be a substantial degree of competition and conflict in the international system, just as there was say between Russia and Britain or Wilhelmine Germany in the last century. This is, of course, a convenient point of view for people who want to admit that something major is changing in the Soviet Union, but do not want to accept responsibility for recommending the radical policy redirection implicit in such a view. But is it true?

In fact, the notion that ideology is a superstructure imposed on a substratum of permanent great power interest is a highly questionable proposition. For the way in which any state defines its national interest is not universal but rests on some kind of prior ideological basis, just as we saw that economic behavior is determined by a prior state of consciousness. In this century, states have adopted highly articulated doctrines with explicit foreign policy agendas legitimizing expansionism, like Marxism-Leninism or National Socialism.

The expansionist and competitive behavior of nineteenth-century European states rested on no less ideal a basis; it just so happened that the ideology driving it was less explicit than the doctrines of the twentieth century. For one thing, most "liberal" European societies were illiberal insofar as they believed in the legitimacy of imperialism, that is, the right of one nation to rule over other nations without regard for the wishes of the ruled. The justifications for imperialism varied from nation to nation, from a crude belief in the legitimacy of force, particularly when applied to non-Europeans, to the White Man's Burden and Europe's Christianizing mission, to the desire to give people of color access to the culture of Rabelais and Molière. But whatever the particular ideological basis, every "developed" country believed in the acceptability of higher civilizations ruling lower ones—including, incidentally, the United States with regard to the Philippines. This led to a drive for pure territorial aggrandizement in the latter half of the century and played no small role in causing the Great War.

The radical and deformed outgrowth of nineteenth-century imperialism was German fascism, an ideology which justified Germany's right not only to rule over non-European peoples, but over *all* non-German ones. But in retrospect it seems that Hitler represented a diseased bypath in the general course of European development, and since his fiery defeat, the legitimacy of any kind of territorial aggrandizement has been thoroughly discredited.[17] Since the Second World War, European nationalism has been defanged and shorn of any real relevance to foreign policy, with the consequence that the nineteenth-century model of great power behavior has become a serious anachronism. The most extreme form of nationalism that any Western European state has mustered since 1945 has been Gaullism, whose self-assertion has been confined largely to the realm of nuisance politics and culture. International life for the part of the world that has reached the end of history is far more preoccupied with economics than with politics or strategy.

The developed states of the West do maintain defense establishments and in the post-war period have competed vigorously for influence to meet a worldwide communist threat. This behavior has been driven, however, by an external threat from states that possess overtly expansionist ideologies, and would not exist in their absence. To take the "neo-realist" theory seriously, one would have to believe that "natural" competitive behavior would reassert itself among the OECD states were Russia and China to disappear from the face of the earth. That is, West Germany and France would arm themselves against each other as they did in the 1930s, Australia and New Zealand would send military advisers to block each others' advances in Africa, and the U.S.-Canadian border would become fortified. Such a prospect is, of course, ludicrous: minus Marxist-Leninist ideology, we are far more likely to see the "Common Marketization" of world politics than the disintegration of the EEC into nineteenth-century competitiveness. Indeed, as our experience in dealing with Europe on matters such as terrorism or Libya prove, they are much further gone than we down the road that denies the legitimacy of the use of force in international politics, even in self-defense.

The automatic assumption that Russia shorn of its expansionist communist ideology should pick up where the czars left off just prior to the Bolshevik Revolution is therefore a curious one. It assumes that the evolution of human consciousness has stood still in the meantime, and that the Soviets, while picking up currently fashionable ideas in the realm of economics, will return to foreign policy views a century out of date in the rest of Europe. This is certainly not what happened to China after it began its reform process. Chinese competitiveness and expansionism on the world scene have virtually disappeared: Beijing no longer sponsors Maoist insurgencies or tries to cultivate influence in distant African countries as it did in the 1960s. This is not to say that there are not troublesome aspects to contemporary Chinese foreign policy, such as the reckless sale of ballistic missile technology in the Middle East; and the PRC continues to manifest traditional great power behavior in its sponsorship of the Khmer Rouge against Vietnam. But the former is explained by commercial motives and the latter is a vestige of earlier ideologically-based rivalries. The new China far more resembles Gaullist France than pre-World War I Germany.

The real question for the future, however, is the degree to which Soviet elites have assimilated the consciousness of the universal homogenous state that is post-Hitler Europe. From their writings and from my own personal contacts with them, there is no question in my mind that the liberal Soviet intelligentsia rallying around Gorbachev has arrived at the end-of-history view in a remarkably short time, due in no small measure to the contacts they have had since the Brezhnev era with the larger European civilization around them. "New political thinking," the general rubric for their views, describes a world dominated by economic concerns, in which there are no ideological grounds for major conflict between nations, and in which, consequently, the use of military force becomes less legitimate. As Foreign Minister Shevardnadze put it in mid-1988:

> The struggle between two opposing systems is no longer a deter-
> mining tendency of the present-day era. At the modern stage, the
> ability to build up material wealth at an accelerated rate on the
> basis of front-ranking science and high-level techniques and
> technology, and to distribute it fairly, and through joint efforts
> to restore and protect the resources necessary for mankind's sur-
> vival acquires decisive importance.[18]

The post-historical consciousness represented by "new thinking" is only one possible future for the Soviet Union, however. There has always been a very strong current of great Russian chauvinism in the Soviet Union, which has found freer expression since the advent of *glasnost*. It may be possible to return to traditional Marxism-Leninism for a while as a simple rallying point for those who want to restore the authority that Gorbachev has dissipated. But as in Poland, Marxism-Leninism is dead as a mobilizing ideology: under its banner people cannot be made to work harder, and its adherents have lost confidence in themselves. Unlike the propagators of traditional Marxism-Leninism, however, ultranationalists in the USSR believe in their Slavophile cause passionately, and one gets the sense that the fascist alternative is not one that has played itself out entirely there.

The Soviet Union, then, is at a fork in the road: it can start down the path that was staked out by Western Europe forty-five years ago, a path that most of Asia has followed, or it can realize its own uniqueness and remain stuck in history. The choice it makes will be highly important for us, given the Soviet Union's size and military strength, for that power will continue to preoccupy us and slow our realization that we have already emerged on the other side of history.

V

The passing of Marxism-Leninism first from China and then from the Soviet Union will mean its death as a living ideology of world historical signifi-cance. For while there may be some isolated true believers left in places like Managua, Pyongyang, or Cambridge, Massachusetts, the fact that there is not a single large state in which it is a going concern undermines completely its pretensions to being in the vanguard of human history. And the death of this ideology means the growing "Common Marketization" of international relations, and the diminution of the likelihood of large-scale conflict between states.

This does not by any means imply the end of international conflict *per se*. For the world at that point would be divided between a part that was historical and a part that was post-historical. Conflict between states still in history, and between those states and those at the end of history, would still be possible. There would still be a high and perhaps rising level of ethnic and nationalist violence, since those are impulses incompletely played out, even in parts of the post-historical world. Palestinians and Kurds, Sikhs and Tamils, Irish Catholics and Walloons, Armenians and Azeris, will continue to have their unresolved grievances. This implies that terrorism and wars of national liberation will continue to be an important item on the international agenda. But large-scale conflict must involve large states still caught in the grip of history, and they are what appear to be passing from the scene.

The end of history will be a very sad time. The struggle for recognition, the willingness to risk one's life for a purely abstract goal, the worldwide ideological struggle that called forth daring, courage, imagination, and idealism, will be replaced by economic calculation, the endless solving of technical problems, environmental concerns, and the satisfaction of sophisticated consumer demands. In the post-historical period there will be neither art nor philosophy, just the perpetual caretaking of the museum of human history. I can feel in myself, and see in others around me, a powerful nostalgia for the time when history existed. Such nostalgia, in fact, will continue to fuel competition and conflict even in the post-historical world for some time to come. Even though I recognize its inevitability, I have the most ambivalent feelings for the civilization that has been created in Europe since 1945, with its north Atlantic and Asian offshoots. Perhaps this very prospect of centuries of boredom at the end of history will serve to get history started once again.

NOTES

1. Kojève's best-known work is his *Introduction à la lecture de Hegel* (Paris: Editions Gallimard, 1947), which is a transcript of the *Ecole Practique* lectures from the 1930s. This book is available in English entitled *Introduction to the Reading of Hegel* arranged by Raymond Queneau, edited by Allan Bloom, and translated by James Nichols (New York: Basic Books, 1969).

2. In this respect Kojève stands in sharp contrast to contemporary German interpreters of Hegel like Herbert Marcuse who, being more sympathetic to Marx, regarded Hegel ultimately as an historically bound and incomplete philosopher.

3. Kojève alternatively identified the end of history with the postwar "American way of life," toward which he thought the Soviet Union was moving as well.

4. This notion was expressed in the famous aphorism from the preface to the *Philosophy of History* to the effect that "everything that is rational is real, and everything that is real is rational."

5. Indeed, for Hegel the very dichotomy between the ideal and material worlds was itself only an apparent one that was ultimately overcome by the self-conscious subject; in his system, the material world is itself only an aspect of mind.

6. In fact, modern economists, recognizing that man does not always behave as a *profit*-maximizer, posit a "utility" function, utility being either income or some other good that can be maximized: leisure, sexual satisfaction, or the pleasure of philosophizing. That profit must be replaced with a value like utility indicates the cogency of the idealist perspective.

7. One need look no further than the recent performance of Vietnamese immigrants in the U.S. school system when compared to their black or Hispanic classmates to realize that culture and consciousness are absolutely crucial to explain not only economic behavior but virtually every other important aspect of life as well.

8. I understand that a full explanation of the origins of the reform movements in China and Russia is a good deal more complicated than this simple formula would suggest. The Soviet reform, for example, was motivated in good measure by Moscow's sense of *insecurity* in the technological-military realm. Nonetheless, neither country on the eve of its reforms was in such a state of *material* crisis that one could have predicted the surprising reform paths ultimately taken.

9. It is still not clear whether the Soviet peoples are as "Protestant" as Gorbachev and will follow him down that path.

10. The internal politics of the Byzantine Empire at the time of Justinian revolved around a conflict between the so-called monophysites and monothelites, who believed that the unity of the Holy Trinity was alternatively one of nature or of will. This conflict corresponded to some extent to one between proponents of different racing teams in the Hippodrome in Byzantium and led to a not insignificant level of political violence. Modern historians would tend to seek the roots of such conflicts in antagonisms between social classes or some other modern economic category, being unwilling to believe that men would kill each other over the nature of the Trinity.

11. I am not using the term "fascism" here in its most precise sense, fully aware of the frequent misuse of this term to denounce anyone to the right of the user. "Fascism" here denotes any organized ultra-nationalist movement with universalistic pretensions—not universalistic with regard to its nationalism, of course, since the latter is exclusive by definition, but with regard to the movement's belief in its right to rule other people. Hence Imperial Japan would qualify as fascist while former strongman Stoessner's Paraguay or Pinochet's Chile would not. Obviously fascist ideologies cannot be universalistic in the sense of Marxism or liberalism, but the structure of the doctrine can be transferred from country to country.

12. I use the example of Japan with some caution, since Kojève late in his life came to conclude that Japan, with its culture based on purely formal arts, proved that the universal homogenous state was not victorious and that history had perhaps not ended. See the long note at the end of the second edition of *Introduction à la Lecture de Hegel*, 462–3.

13. This is not true in Poland and Hungary, however, whose Communist parties have taken moves toward true power-sharing and pluralism.
14. This is particularly true of the leading Soviet conservative, former Second Secretary Yegor Ligachev, who has publicly recognized many of the deep defects of the Brezhnev period.
15. I am thinking particularly of Rousseau and the Western philosophical tradition that flows from him that was highly critical of Lockean or Hobbesian liberalism, though one could criticize liberalism from the standpoint of classical political philosophy as well.
16. See his article, "Beyond the Cold War," *New Republic*, December 19, 1988.
17. It took European colonial powers like France several years after the war to admit the illegitimacy of their empires, but decolonialization was an inevitable consequence of the Allied victory which had been based on the promise of a restoration of democratic freedoms.
18. *Vestnik Ministerstva Inostrannikh Del SSSR* no. 15 (August 1988), 27–46. "New thinking" does of course serve a propagandistic purpose in persuading Western audiences of Soviet good intentions. But the fact that it is good propaganda does not mean that its formulators do not take many of its ideas seriously.

Samuel P. Huntington

The Clash of Civilizations?

The Next Pattern of Conflict

World politics is entering a new phase, and intellectuals have not hesitated to proliferate visions of what it will be—the end of history, the return of traditional rivalries between nation states, and the decline of the nation state from the conflicting pulls of tribalism and globalism, among others. Each of these visions catches aspects of the emerging reality. Yet they all miss a crucial, indeed a central, aspect of what global politics is likely to be in the coming years.

It is my hypothesis that the fundamental source of conflict in this new world will not be primarily ideological or primarily economic. The great divisions among humankind and the dominating source of conflict will be cultural. Nation states will remain the most powerful actors in world affairs, but the principal conflicts of global politics will occur between nations and groups of different civilizations. The clash of civilizations will dominate global politics. The fault lines between civilizations will be the battle lines of the future.

Conflict between civilizations will be the latest phase in the evolution of conflict in the modern world. For a century and a half after the emergence of the modern international system with the Peace of Westphalia, the conflicts of the Western world were largely among princes—emperors, absolute monarchs and constitutional monarchs attempting to expand their bureaucracies, their armies, their mercantilist economic strength and, most important, the territory they ruled. In the process they created nation states, and beginning with the French Revolution the principal lines of conflict were between nations rather than princes. In 1793, as R. R. Palmer put it, "The wars of kings were over; the wars of peoples had begun." This nineteenth-century pattern lasted until the end of World War I. Then, as a result of the Russian Revolution and the reaction against it, the conflict of nations yielded to the conflict of ideologies, first among communism, fascism-Nazism and liberal democracy, and then between communism and liberal democracy. During the Cold War, this latter conflict became embodied in the struggle between the two superpowers, neither of which was a nation state in the classical European sense and each of which defined its identity in terms of its ideology.

These conflicts between princes, nation states and ideologies were primarily conflicts within Western civilization, "Western civil wars," as William Lind has labeled them. This was as true of the Cold War as it was of the world wars and the earlier wars of the seventeenth, eighteenth and nineteenth centuries. With the end of the Cold War, international politics moves out of its Western phase, and its centerpiece becomes the interaction between the West and non-Western civilizations and among non-Western civilizations. In the politics of civilizations, the peoples and governments of non-Western civilizations no longer remain the objects of history as targets of Western colonialism but join the West as movers and shapers of history.

The Nature of Civilizations

. . . . What do we mean when we talk of a civilization? A civilization is a cultural entity. Villages, regions, ethnic groups, nationalities, religious groups, all have distinct cultures at different levels of cultural heterogeneity. . . . A civilization is thus the highest cultural grouping of people and the broadest level of cultural identity people have short of that which distinguishes humans from other species. It is defined both by common objective elements, such as language, history, religion, customs, institutions, and by the subjective self-identification of people. People have levels of identity: a resident of Rome may define himself with varying degrees of intensity as a Roman, an Italian, a Catholic, a Christian, a European, a Westerner. The civilization to which he belongs is the broadest level of identification with which he intensely identifies. People can and do redefine their identities and, as a result, the composition and boundaries of civilizations change. . . .

Why Civilizations Will Clash

Civilization identity will be increasingly important in the future, and the world will be shaped in large measure by the interactions among seven or eight major civilizations. These include Western, Confucian, Japanese, Islamic, Hindu, Slavic-Orthodox, Latin American and possibly African civilization. The most important conflicts of the future will occur along the cultural fault lines separating these civilizations from one another.

Why will this be the case?

First, differences among civilizations are not only real; they are basic. Civilizations are differentiated from each other by history, language, culture, tradition and, most important, religion. The people of different civilizations have different views on the relations between God and man, the individual and the group, the citizen and the state, parents and children, husband and wife, as well as differing views of the relative importance of rights and responsibilities, liberty and authority, equality and hierarchy. These differences are the product of centuries. They will not soon disappear. They are far more fundamental than differences among political ideologies and political regimes. Differences do not necessarily mean conflict, and conflict does not necessarily mean violence. Over the centuries, however, differences among civilizations have generated the most prolonged and the most violent conflicts.

Second, the world is becoming a smaller place. The interactions between peoples of different civilizations are increasing; these increasing interactions intensify civilization consciousness and awareness of differences between civilizations and commonalities within civilizations. North African immigration to France generates hostility among Frenchmen and at the same time increases receptivity to immigration by "good" European Catholic Poles. Americans react far more negatively to Japanese investment than to larger investments from Canada and European countries. . . . The interactions among peoples of different civilizations enhance the civilization-consciousness of people that, in turn, invigorates differences and animosities stretching or thought to stretch back deep into history.

Third, the processes of economic modernization and social change throughout the world are separating people from longstanding local identities. They also weaken the nation state as a source of identity. In much of the world religion has moved in to fill this gap, often in the form of movements that are labeled "fundamentalist." Such movements are found in Western Christianity, Judaism, Buddhism and Hinduism, as well as in Islam. In most countries and most religions the people active in fundamentalist movements are young, college-educated, middle-class technicians, professionals and business persons. . . . The revival of religion, "la revanche de Dieu," as Gilles Kepel labeled it, provides a basis for identity and commitment that transcends national boundaries and unites civilizations.

Fourth, the growth of civilization-consciousness is enhanced by the dual role of the West. On the one hand, the West is at a peak of power. At the same time, however, and perhaps as a result, a return to the roots phenomenon is occurring among non-Western civilizations. Increasingly one hears references to trends toward a turning inward and "Asianization" in Japan, the end of the Nehru legacy and the "Hinduization" of India, the failure of Western ideas of socialism and nationalism and hence "re-Islamization" of the Middle East, and now a debate over Westernization versus Russianization in Boris Yeltsin's country. A West at the peak of its power confronts non-Wests that increasingly have the desire, the will and the resources to shape the world in non-Western ways.

In the past, the elites of non-Western societies were usually the people who were most involved with the West, had been educated at Oxford, the Sorbonne or Sandhurst, and had absorbed Western attitudes and values. At the same time, the populace in non-Western countries often remained deeply imbued with the indigenous culture. Now, however, these relationships are being reversed. A de-Westernization and indigenization of elites is occurring in many non-Western countries at the same time that Western, usually American, cultures, styles and habits become more popular among the mass of the people.

Fifth, cultural characteristics and differences are less mutable and hence less easily compromised and resolved than political and economic ones. In the former Soviet Union, communists can become democrats, the rich can become poor and the poor rich, but Russians cannot become Estonians and Azeris cannot become Armenians. In class and ideological conflicts, the key question was "Which side are you on?" and people could and did choose sides and change sides. In conflicts between civilizations, the question is "What are you?" That is a given that cannot be changed. And as we know, from Bosnia to the Caucasus to the Sudan, the wrong answer to that question can mean a bullet in the head. Even more than ethnicity, religion discriminates sharply and exclusively among people. A person can be half-French and half-Arab and simultaneously even a citizen of two countries. It is more difficult to be half-Catholic and half-Muslim.

Finally, economic regionalism is increasing. . . . The importance of regional economic blocs is likely to continue to increase in the future. On the one hand, successful economic regionalism will reinforce civilization-consciousness. On the other hand, economic regionalism may succeed only when it is rooted in a common civilization. The European Community rests on the shared foundation of European culture and Western Christianity. The success of the North American Free Trade Area depends on the convergence now underway of Mexican, Canadian and American cultures. Japan, in contrast, faces difficulties in creating a comparable economic entity in East Asia because Japan is a society and civilization unique to itself. However strong the trade and investment links Japan may develop with other East Asian countries, its cultural differences with those countries inhibit and perhaps preclude its promoting regional economic integration like that in Europe and North America.

Common culture, in contrast, is clearly facilitating the rapid expansion of the economic relations between the People's Republic of China and Hong Kong, Taiwan, Singapore and the overseas Chinese communities in other Asian countries. With the Cold War over, cultural commonalities increasingly overcome ideological differences, and mainland China and Taiwan move closer together. If cultural commonality is a prerequisite for economic integration, the principal East Asian economic bloc of the future is likely to be centered on China. This bloc is, in fact, already coming into existence. . . .

As people define their identity in ethnic and religious terms, they are likely to see an "us" versus "them" relation existing between themselves and people of different ethnicity or religion. The end of ideologically defined states in Eastern Europe and the former Soviet Union permits traditional ethnic identities and animosities to come to the fore. Differences in culture and religion create differences over policy issues, ranging from human rights to immigration to trade and commerce to the environment. Geographical propinquity gives rise to conflicting territorial claims from Bosnia to Mindanao. Most important, the efforts of the West to promote its values of democracy and liberalism as universal values, to maintain its military predominance and to advance its economic interests engender countering responses from other civilizations. Decreasingly able to mobilize support and form coalitions on the basis of ideology, governments and groups will increasingly attempt to mobilize support by appealing to common religion and civilization identity.

The clash of civilizations thus occurs at two levels. At the micro-level, adjacent groups along the fault lines between civilizations struggle, often violently, over the control of territory and each other. At the macro-level, states from different civilizations compete for relative military and economic power, struggle over the control of international institutions and third parties, and competitively promote their particular political and religious values. . . .

The West versus the Rest

The West is now at an extraordinary peak of power in relation to other civilizations. Its superpower opponent has disappeared from the map. Military conflict among Western states is unthinkable, and Western military power is unrivaled. Apart from Japan, the West faces no economic challenge. It dominates international political and security institutions and with Japan international economic institutions. Global political and security issues are effectively settled by a directorate of the United States, Britain and France, world economic issues by a directorate of the United States, Germany and Japan, all of which maintain extraordinarily close relations with each other to the exclusion of lesser and largely non-Western countries. Decisions made at the U.N. Security Council or in the International Monetary Fund that reflect the interests of the West are presented to the world as reflecting the desires of the world community. . . .

Western domination of the U.N. Security Council and its decisions, tempered only by occasional abstention by China, produced U.N. legitimation of the West's use of force to drive Iraq out of Kuwait and its elimination of Iraq's sophisticated weapons and capacity to produce such weapons. . . . The West in effect is using international institutions, military power and economic resources to run the world in ways that will maintain Western predominance, protect Western interests and promote Western political and economic values.

That at least is the way in which non-Westerners see the new world, and there is a significant element of truth in their view. Differences in power and struggles for military, economic and institutional power are thus one source of conflict between the West and other civilizations. Differences in culture, that is basic values and beliefs, are a second source of conflict. . . . At a superficial level much of Western culture has indeed permeated the rest of the world. At a more basic level, however, Western concepts differ fundamentally from those prevalent in other civilizations. Western ideas of individualism, liberalism, constitutionalism, human rights, equality, liberty, the rule of law, democracy, free markets, the separation of church and state, often have little resonance in Islamic, Confucian, Japanese, Hindu, Buddhist or Orthodox cultures. Western efforts to propagate such ideas produce instead a reaction against "human rights imperialism" and a reaffirmation of indigenous values, as can be seen in the support for religious fundamentalism by the younger generation in non-Western cultures. The very notion that there could be a "universal civilization" is a Western idea, directly at odds with the particularism of most Asian societies and their emphasis on what distinguishes one people from another. . . . In the political realm, of course, these differences are most manifest in the efforts of the United States and other Western powers to induce other peoples to adopt Western ideas concerning democracy and human rights. Modern democratic government originated in the West. When it has developed in non-Western societies it has usually been the product of Western colonialism or imposition.

The central axis of world politics in the future is likely to be, in Kishore Mahbubani's phrase, the conflict between "the West and the Rest" and the responses of non-Western civilizations to Western power and values.[1] Those responses generally take one or a combination of three forms. At one extreme, non-Western states can, like Burma and North Korea, attempt to pursue a course of isolation, to insulate their societies from penetration or "corruption" by the West, and, in effect, to opt out of participation in the Western-dominated global community. The costs of this course, however, are high, and few states have pursued it exclusively. A second alternative, the equivalent of "band-wagoning" in international relations theory, is to attempt to join the West and accept its values and institutions. The third alternative is to attempt to "balance" the West by developing economic and military power and cooperating with other non-Western societies against the West, while preserving indigenous values and institutions; in short, to modernize but not to Westernize.

NOTE

1. Kishore Mahbubani, "The West and the Rest," *The National Interest*, Summer 1992, pp. 3–13.

CHAPTER 7 IRAQ: WITHDRAW v. STAY THE COURSE

Staying the Course as U.S. Strategy in Iraq

Advocate: Michael O'Hanlon

Source: "Lessons of the Surge," *The Washington Times*, November 4, 2008.

Withdrawal as U.S. Strategy in Iraq

Advocate: Andrew J. Bacevich

Source: "Surge to Nowhere," *The Washington Post*, January 20, 2008.

The invasion of Iraq in 2003 is arguably one of the most controversial U.S. foreign policy decisions in the country's history. The purported goals of the war were to prevent further cooperation between the Iraqi government and the terrorist organization al-Qaeda, and to ensure that no weapons of mass destruction fall into terrorist hands where they could threaten the security of the United States and its allies. Later on, helping Iraq become democratic and the Middle East more stable were also added as objectives.

As the expectations for quick and successful finish of the operation went awry, the voices of discontent in the United States became louder. The key question in the debate is whether the United States will ever be able to win the "peace" in Iraq, so that a stable, self-governing, and reasonably democratic country can emerge. The uncertainty of this development requires a discussion of the costs of this conflict to the United States in terms of the lives of its troops, opportunity costs, and security benefits as a result of the altered regional balance in the Middle East.

IN FAVOR OF THE IRAQ WAR

Support for the Iraq war focuses on the progress that has been made recently and the risks U.S. withdrawal will pose. Acknowledging the mistakes of the past few years, supporters of continued U.S. military deployment in the country argue that the gains of the past year can be solidified and the United States can bring the war to a successful conclusion. Untimely reduction or full withdrawal of U.S. troops, on the other hand, will interrupt the political process and plunge Iraq in chaos.

In a similar vein, Michael O'Hanlon argues that the strategy adopted in the war in Iraq in 2007 has been successful in providing more security for the civilian population. This has been accomplished through a remarkable reduction in the level of violence and increasing trust in the government, creating the foundation for political reconciliation in the country. Advising the Iraqi leadership to accept a new agreement on the status of U.S. troops in the country, O'Hanlon warns that their premature withdrawal from Iraq will jeopardize these recent successes and lead to more instability.

AGAINST THE IRAQ WAR

With the war in Iraq continuing to claim American lives and requiring billions of additional tax-payer dollars every year, critics of the Bush Administration's policy have become more vocal. Claiming that the war is unwinnable, they call for immediate reduction of troop levels or full withdrawal. They have sought to mobilize public opinion, thereby making the war a key electoral issue.

Andrew Bacevich summarizes many of the arguments held by opponents of the war. He makes the case that the "surge" has accomplished very little in terms of political reconciliation, but has ensured that the United States will continue to spend money and risk the lives of its young men and women indefinitely. Iraq is in a state of turmoil, unable to control its own borders or provide services to its citizens. Bacevich argues that the Iraq war has demonstrated to the world the limits of U.S. power, has served as a recruiting tool for jihadists, helped raise anti-Americanism to record levels, and benefited Iran to the detriment of U.S. national interests.

POINTS **TO PONDER**

1. What were the reasons for the U.S. invasion of Iraq?
2. Why have key allies of the United States not joined in this effort?
3. Does the situation in Iraq mean that democracy in the Middle East is doomed to failure?

Michael O'Hanlon
Lessons of the Surge

Many Americans and Iraqis think of the recent surge in Iraq as simply the temporary addition of more U.S. troops to the war effort in 2007 and the first half of 2008. This is incorrect. It is also dangerous.

Partly because they misunderstand the true nature of the surge, many American and Iraqi political leaders now seem to want American forces out of Iraq as fast as possible. Iraqi leaders also now seem unwilling to accept a reasonable Status of Forces Agreement (SOFA) to govern the actions of U.S. troops in their country after the current U.N. Security Council mandate expires at the end of the year.

In fact, the basic logic of the surge continues—and must continue—even now that the increases in U.S. combat formations in Iraq has come to an end. At its core, the surge has been about cooperatively protecting the Iraqi civilian population. This is the central point policymakers in Baghdad, Washington and other capitals around the world need to appreciate.

At the risk of falling victim to Pentagonese, I would propose we broaden our understanding of the surge by thinking of that word as an acronym. Gen. David Petraeus' strategy has been a remarkable success, reducing the rate of violence by more than 80 percent in Iraq over the last two years while also helping spark the beginnings of a process of political reconciliation. It took far more than the simple addition of 30,000 American troops, on top of the 140,000 already there when the surge began, to make this happen. So instead of surge, think SURGE:

The "S" in surge should be understood as an emphasis on security. This is, as noted, the centerpiece of the strategy. Protecting the Iraqi civilian population has been essential to restore trust in government and trust across sectarian lines, to rekindle hopefulness about the country's future, and restore some degree of normalcy in daily life. In practical terms, among other things it has meant setting up joint security stations across Iraq in the country's urban centers to live and work near vulnerable populations. Increased troop totals have been just part of the story.

"U" stands for unity of effort (as an assistant of Gen. Petraeus' suggested to me). It means Iraqis, Americans and others working collaboratively toward a common purpose. It has led to Americans and Iraqis living together in the joint security stations and patrolling and when necessary fighting together in Iraq's toughest neighborhoods. It has also led to development of a campaign plan that is gradually passing more and more responsibility to Iraqis for all aspects of their country's governance.

"R" must stand for reconciliation. This has been an absolutely crucial aspect of the progress in Iraq since 2007. Prime Minister Nouri al-Maliki has purged many Shia extremist leaders that he considered irreconcilable, and replaced them in many cases with former Ba'athists (most Sunni) with whom he thought he could work. Iraqi and American leaders convinced Muqtada al-Sadr to agree to a cease-fire; the United States also launched the so-called Sons of Iraq program, paying some of the very same tribesmen (generally Sunni) who has been part of the insurgency a couple years ago to cooperate with us in providing security.

More progress in needed here, given Mr. al-Maliki's concerns about the loyalties of some Sons of Iraq and various key pieces of key legislation not yet agreed to. But the trends have been good.

"G" stands for government capacity in Iraq. As a key example, while American forces surged by 30,000 in 2007, Iraqi security forces have grown by some 200,000 over the last two years. They now total more than half a million personnel. This year's remarkable additional progress in improving security, even as U.S. forces have declined in country, has been possible only because indigenous forces have performed so well—a track record of which all Iraqis can be proud.

"E" stands for excellence in execution. Doing counterinsurgency and stabilization missions correctly is very hard, requiring excellent troop training and leadership at all levels of command.

Not only Americans, but Iraqis need to bear in mind the true logic of the surge. Having been offered a SOFA deal that grants them legal jurisdiction over foreign contractors, that increases advance consultations on sensitive military operations, that provides more jurisdiction over certain types of crimes committed by American GIs than developing-country governments usually obtain, they continue to insist on better terms even at the risk of sending U.S. forces home prematurely.

In so doing, they are failing to remember the importance of several of the above precepts, starting with the fact that the "U" in surge stands for unity of effort, "R" stands for a reconciliation process they have hardly yet completed among themselves, and "E" stands for excellence that U.S. troops themselves arguably did not fully attain in Iraq until 2007–08.

Whatever the SOFA ultimately says, Iraqis can always ask us to leave at any point, and we will leave—just as the United States has done in the Philippines, Saudi Arabia and elsewhere in modern times. But they should think twice before doing so.

Once gone, it is unlikely we would be willing to come back. Iraqi brinkmanship over the SOFA is no longer just a nettlesome worry for Washington; it is becoming a risky and irresponsible gamble that could soon jeopardize their nation's future stability.

Andrew J. Bacevich

Surge to Nowhere

As the fifth anniversary of Operation Iraqi Freedom nears, the fabulists are again trying to weave their own version of the war. The latest myth is that the "surge" is working.

In President Bush's pithy formulation, the United States is now "kicking ass" in Iraq. The gallant Gen. David Petraeus, having been given the right tools, has performed miracles, redeeming a situation that once appeared hopeless. Sen. John McCain has gone so far as to declare that "we are winning in Iraq." While few others express themselves quite so categorically, McCain's remark captures the essence of the emerging story line: Events have (yet again) reached a turning point. There, at the far end of the tunnel, light flickers. Despite the hand-wringing of the defeatists and naysayers, victory beckons.

From the hallowed halls of the American Enterprise Institute waft facile assurances that all will come out well. AEI's Reuel Marc Gerecht assures us that the moment to acknowledge "democracy's success in Iraq" has arrived. To his colleague Michael Ledeen, the explanation for the turnaround couldn't be clearer: "We were the stronger horse, and the Iraqis recognized it." In an essay entitled "Mission Accomplished" that is being touted by the AEI crowd, Bartle Bull, the foreign editor of the British magazine Prospect, instructs us that "Iraq's biggest questions have been resolved." Violence there "has ceased being political." As a result, whatever mayhem still lingers is "no longer nearly as important as it was." Meanwhile, Frederick W. Kagan, an AEI resident scholar and the arch-advocate of the surge, announces that the "credibility of the prophets of doom" has reached "a low ebb."

Presumably Kagan and his comrades would have us believe that recent events vindicate the prophets who in 2002—03 were promoting preventive war as a key instrument of U.S. policy. By shifting the conversation to tactics, they seek to divert attention from flagrant failures of basic strategy. Yet what exactly has the surge wrought? In substantive terms, the answer is: not much.

As the violence in Baghdad and Anbar province abates, the political and economic dysfunction enveloping Iraq has become all the more apparent. The recent agreement to rehabilitate some former Baathists notwithstanding, signs of lasting Sunni-Shiite reconciliation are scant. The United States has acquired a ramshackle, ungovernable and unresponsive dependency that is incapable of securing its own borders or managing its own affairs. More than three years after then-national security adviser Condoleezza Rice handed President Bush a note announcing that "Iraq is sovereign," that sovereignty remains a fiction.

A nation-building project launched in the confident expectation that the United States would repeat in Iraq the successes it had achieved in Germany and Japan after 1945 instead compares unfavorably with the U.S. response to Hurricane Katrina. Even today, Iraqi electrical generation meets barely half the daily national requirements. Baghdad households now receive power an average of 12 hours each day—six hours fewer than when Saddam Hussein ruled. Oil production still has not returned to pre-invasion levels. Reports of widespread fraud, waste and sheer ineptitude in the administration of U.S.

aid have become so commonplace that they barely last a news cycle. (Recall, for example, the 110,000 AK-47s, 80,000 pistols, 135,000 items of body armor and 115,000 helmets intended for Iraqi security forces that, according to the Government Accountability Office, the Pentagon cannot account for.) U.S. officials repeatedly complain, to little avail, about the paralyzing squabbling inside the Iraqi parliament and the rampant corruption within Iraqi ministries. If a primary function of government is to provide services, then the government of Iraq can hardly be said to exist.

Moreover, recent evidence suggests that the United States is tacitly abandoning its efforts to create a truly functional government in Baghdad. By offering arms and bribes to Sunni insurgents—an initiative that has been far more important to the temporary reduction in the level of violence than the influx of additional American troops—U.S. forces have affirmed the fundamental irrelevance of the political apparatus bunkered inside the Green Zone.

Rather than fostering political reconciliation, accommodating Sunni tribal leaders ratifies the ethnic cleansing that resulted from the civil war touched off by the February 2006 bombing of the Golden Mosque in Samarra, a Shiite shrine. That conflict has shredded the fragile connective tissue linking the various elements of Iraqi society; the deals being cut with insurgent factions serve only to ratify that dismal outcome. First Sgt. Richard Meiers of the Army's 3rd Infantry Division got it exactly right: "We're paying them not to blow us up. It looks good right now, but what happens when the money stops?"

In short, the surge has done nothing to overturn former secretary of state Colin Powell's now-famous "Pottery Barn" rule: Iraq is irretrievably broken, and we own it. To say that any amount of "kicking ass" will make Iraq whole once again is pure fantasy. The U.S. dilemma remains unchanged: continue to pour lives and money into Iraq with no end in sight, or cut our losses and deal with the consequences of failure.

In only one respect has the surge achieved undeniable success: It has ensured that U.S. troops won't be coming home anytime soon. This was one of the main points of the exercise in the first place. As AEI military analyst Thomas Donnelly has acknowledged with admirable candor, "part of the purpose of the surge was to redefine the Washington narrative," thereby deflecting calls for a complete withdrawal of U.S. combat forces. Hawks who had pooh-poohed the risks of invasion now portrayed the risks of withdrawal as too awful to contemplate. But a prerequisite to perpetuating the war—and leaving it to the next president—was to get Iraq off the front pages and out of the nightly news. At least in this context, the surge qualifies as a masterstroke. From his new perch as a New York Times columnist, William Kristol has worried that feckless politicians just might "snatch defeat out of the jaws of victory." Not to worry: The "victory" gained in recent months all but guarantees that the United States will remain caught in the jaws of Iraq for the foreseeable future.

Such success comes at a cost. U.S. casualties in Iraq have recently declined. Yet since Petraeus famously testified before Congress last September, Iraqi insurgents have still managed to kill more than 100 Americans. Meanwhile, to fund the war, the Pentagon is burning through somewhere between $2 billion and $3 billion per week. Given that further changes in U.S. policy are unlikely between now and the time that the next administration can take office and get its bearings, the lavish expenditure of American lives and treasure is almost certain to continue indefinitely.

But how exactly do these sacrifices serve the national interest? What has the loss of nearly 4,000 U.S. troops and the commitment of about $1 trillion—with more to come—actually gained the United States?

Bush had once counted on the U.S. invasion of Iraq to pay massive dividends. Iraq was central to his administration's game plan for eliminating jihadist terrorism. It would demonstrate how U.S. power and beneficence could transform the Muslim world. Just months after the fall of Baghdad, the president declared, "The establishment of a free Iraq at the heart of the Middle East will be a watershed event in the global democratic revolution." Democracy's triumph in Baghdad, he announced, "will send forth the news, from Damascus to Tehran—that freedom can be the future of every nation." In short, the administration saw Baghdad not as a final destination but as a way station en route to even greater successes.

In reality, the war's effects are precisely the inverse of those that Bush and his lieutenants expected. Baghdad has become a strategic cul-de-sac. Only the truly blinkered will imagine at this late date that Iraq has shown the United States to be the "stronger horse." In fact, the war has revealed the very real *limits* of U.S. power. And for good measure, it has boosted anti-Americanism to record levels, recruited untold numbers of new jihadists, enhanced the standing of adversaries such as Iran and diverted resources and attention from Afghanistan, a theater of war far more directly relevant to the threat posed by al-Qaeda. Instead of draining the jihadist swamp, the Iraq war is continuously replenishing it.

Look beyond the spin, the wishful thinking, the intellectual bullying and the myth-making. The real legacy of the surge is that it will enable Bush to bequeath the Iraq war to his successor—no doubt cause for celebration at AEI, although perhaps less so for the families of U.S. troops. Yet the stubborn insistence that the war must continue also ensures that Bush's successor will, upon taking office, discover that the post-9/11 United States is strategically adrift. Washington no longer has a coherent approach to dealing with

Islamic radicalism. Certainly, the next president will not find in Iraq a useful template to be applied in Iran or Syria or Pakistan.

According to the war's most fervent proponents, Bush's critics have become so "invested in defeat" that they cannot see the progress being made on the ground. Yet something similar might be said of those who remain so passionately invested in a futile war's perpetuation. They are unable to see that, surge or no surge, the Iraq war remains an egregious strategic blunder that persistence will only compound.

CHAPTER 8

THE UNITED STATES IS WINNING THE WAR ON TERROR *v.* THE UNITED STATES IS LOSING THE WAR ON TERROR

The United States Is Winning the War on Terror

Advocate: William Kristol

Source: "Victory in Spite of All Terror," *The Weekly Standard*, vol. 10, no. 41, July 18, 2005.

The United States Is Losing the War on Terror

Advocates: David Cole and Jules Lobel

Source: "Why We're Losing the War on Terror," *The Nation*, September 24, 2007, excerpt.

The events of September 11, 2001 irreversibly changed the course of modern U.S. history. The attacks placed the country on a course that has had an impact all around the world. The steps that the United States took to prevent another assault of similar nature were both domestic and international; the "war on terror" became the overarching leitmotif for the next several years.

Domestically, the United States focused its efforts on coordinating surveillance and intelligence gathering and sharing. Internationally, the most visible results of U.S. policy were the wars in Afghanistan and Iraq. In Afghanistan, the United States sought to annihilate the group behind the 9/11 attacks, al-Qaeda, and punish the Taliban for sheltering and collaborating with it. In Iraq, the United States sought to remove Saddam Hussein from power and help democratize the country.

In the years since 9/11, there has not been another terrorist attack on U.S. territory. The administration and its supporters attribute this to the success of its policies as part of the "war on terror." However, many critics argue that the United States has neglected its fight. They say that the most significant distraction has been the war in Iraq, which has become a rallying cause for terrorists from around the world.

THE UNITED STATES IS WINNING THE WAR ON TERROR

By looking at the terrorist attacks perpetrated around the globe, William Kristol asserts that the Bush Administration is indeed waging a "global war on terror." There have been attacks from Bali to London, and Casablanca to New York; these attacks have been deadly and violent, aimed at terrorizing people in the West with the aim of achieving concrete political goals in the Middle East.

Kristol also posits that the war in Iraq is inextricably part of the global war on terror. Had Saddam been left in power, he argues, anti-Americanism, terrorism, and extremism in the Middle East would have only grown worse. Establishing a modern and vibrant democracy in Iraq would be the beginning of the end for jihadists around the world. If our world is to remain civilized, then, according to Kristol, victory in the global war on terror is indispensible. To achieve victory is to insist on removing regimes that cooperate with and provide shelter to terrorist groups, and to bring about change in states that provide breeding grounds for terror.

THE UNITED STATES IS LOSING THE WAR ON TERROR

Echoing the sentiments of many critics, Cole and Lobel argue that the strategy of prevention that the Bush Administration adopted after 9/11 has largely failed to make us safer. The domestic measures employed have eroded the rule of law through the impingement of civil liberties, focus on ethnic profiling of people of Middle Eastern origin, and the practice of torture. The number of terrorist attacks around the world has increased dramatically. The Iraq war has made us much more vulnerable to terrorism because it has diverted precious resources from the fight against al-Qaeda and has served as a recruiting ground and inspiration for would-be terrorists.

Cole and Lobel posit that the Bush Administration's policies have instead exacerbated the dangers Americans face. They blame the administration for failing to effectively implement preventive measures, including the recommendations of the bipartisan 9/11 Commission, which gave the administration failing grades. Moreover, the tactics used by the administration have actually made it more difficult to bring terrorist suspects to justice. Guantanamo, secret CIA jails, and the war in Iraq have all contributed to the loss of credibility by the United States around the globe, and the further alienation of the Arab world. Cole and Lobel claim that following the rule of law—with judicial processes and international accountability—can be an asset, not an obstacle, in the war against terror.

POINTS TO PONDER

1. What is the "Global War on Terror"?
2. What constitutes a victory in the "war on terror"?
3. How does the "war on terror" differ from other wars?

4. How much global support does the United States have for its war on terror?

5. How have U.S. policies helped or hurt the war on terror?

William Kristol

Victory in Spite of All Terror

> You ask, What is our policy? I will say; It is to wage war, by sea, land and air, with all our might and with all the strength that God can give us. . . . That is our policy. You ask, What is our aim? I can answer with one word: Victory—victory at all costs, victory in spite of all terror, victory, however long and hard the road may be; for without victory there is no survival.
> —*Winston Churchill, first speech as prime*
> *minister to the House of Commons May 13, 1940*

The armed forces designate the struggle in which we are currently engaged as the GWOT—the Global War on Terror. The term encompasses everything from the military battles in Afghanistan and Iraq, to covert operations, intelligence gathering, and diplomatic efforts all around the world.

The term "global war on terror" has come in for considerable ridicule from sophisticates on the left, and for some disparagement from Bush supporters on the right.

Much of the left believes that the various struggles against different forms of terrorism are better understood as local challenges, and are not part of one "global" struggle; that in any case the effort shouldn't be thought of as a "war"; that "terror" is far too broad a term to use to categorize the deeds of the very different opponents we face. Meanwhile some on the right are made nervous by the "Wilsonianism" of "global," the militarism of "war," and the rhetorical imprecision of "terror." Of this last point in particular, some conservatives have made intellectual sport, pointing out that "terror" is a tactic or a method, that you can't fight a war against a tactic, and that we should more bluntly acknowledge that what we are at war against is radical Islam.

But President Bush and the U.S. military are more right than their critics. Over the last decade, the attacks have ranged from Nairobi to New York, from Bali to Madrid, and from Casablanca to London. This suggests that it is reasonable to consider the struggle a global one. The bloodiness of the attacks suggests it is reasonable to call this a war. And the fact that the attackers' strategy depends entirely on creating terror among civilized people—and the fact that terror in the West is necessary for the jihadists to accomplish their more concrete political aims in the Middle East—suggest it is by no means unreasonable to speak of a war against "terror." After all, we shun and condemn acts of terror. Our enemies embrace and glorify such acts.

Last Thursday's attack on London is the latest in the global war on terror. But it was not the only attack that day. On the same day, "the insurgent group al Qaeda in Iraq," as the *Washington Post* put it, announced it had killed Egypt's top diplomat in Baghdad, Ihab Sherif. Yet how is this "insurgent" group different from the "terrorist" group "the Secret Organization of al Qaeda in Europe"? It isn't.

The insurgents in Iraq are terrorists. They are killing innocent civilians just as surely and just as ruthlessly as their allies in London. Could the war on terror have been successfully prosecuted without removing Saddam? We at *The Weekly Standard* do not believe so. Given the terrorist ties between al Qaeda and Saddam, given what a victorious Saddam, freed of sanctions and inspectors, would have meant to the cause of extremism and anti-Americanism and, yes, terrorism in the Middle East—we cannot imagine leaving Saddam in power. Yet, however one comes down on that judgment, it cannot be denied that the current war in Iraq is part of the global war on terror. Indeed, it is that war's central front. Not only because there are so many terrorists in Iraq, but because, as Abu Zarqawi has acknowledged, creating a successful democracy in Iraq will be the beginning of the end for jihadist terrorists worldwide.

The terrorists who attacked London demanded that Britain pull out of Iraq, as well as out of Afghanistan. It could well be that the deplorable decision of the Zapatero government in Spain to accede to the terrorists' demand to withdraw from Iraq inspired al Qaeda to see whether they could achieve a comparable success in Britain. But in that respect, the resoluteness of the Blair government and the British people could well mean that July 7—despite the terrible cost in innocent lives—will turn out to be a setback for al Qaeda. Certainly we must do our best to help make it so.

"We will show through our spirit and dignity that our values will long outlast theirs," Tony Blair said Thursday. "The purpose of terrorism is just that—to terrorize people, and we will not be terrorized." This is the necessary, and admirable, first response. The second is to do everything it takes to crush the terrorists in Iraq, Afghanistan, Europe, and elsewhere; to deter or remove regimes that cooperate with terrorists; and to insist on practical change in nations whose dictatorial regimes provide a breeding ground for terror. Victory in this respect may never be final or complete. But victory remains nonetheless the indispensable aim for the civilized world, if it is to remain civilized. London reminds us that there really is, in this case, no substitute for victory.

David Cole and Jules Lobel

Why We're Losing the War on Terror

President George W. Bush is fond of reminding us that no terrorist attacks have occurred on domestic soil since 9/11. But has the Administration's "war on terror" actually made us safer? According to the July 2007 National Intelligence Estimate, Al Qaeda has fully reconstituted itself in Pakistan's northern border region. Terrorist attacks worldwide have grown dramatically in frequency and lethality since 2001. New terrorist groups, from Al Qaeda in Mesopotamia to the small groups of young men who bombed subways and buses in London and Madrid, have multiplied since 9/11. Meanwhile, despite the Bush Administration's boasts, the total number of people it has convicted of engaging in a terrorist act since 9/11 is one (Richard Reid, the shoe bomber).

Nonetheless, leading Democratic presidential candidate Hillary Clinton claims that we are safer. Republican candidate Rudy Giuliani warns that "the next election is about whether we go back on defense against terrorism . . . or are we going to go on offense." And Democrats largely respond by insisting that they, too, would "go on offense." Few have asked whether "going on offense" actually works as a counterterrorism strategy. It doesn't. The Bush strategy has been a colossal failure, not only in terms of constitutional principle but in terms of national security. It turns out that in fighting terrorism, the best defense is not a good offense but a smarter defense. . . .

In the name of the "preventive paradigm," thousands of Arab and Muslim immigrants have been singled out, essentially on the basis of their ethnicity or religion, for special treatment, including mandatory registration, FBI interviews and preventive detention. Businesses have been served with more than 100,000 "national security letters," which permit the FBI to demand records on customers without a court order or individualized basis for suspicion. We have all been subjected to unprecedented secrecy about what elected officials are doing in our name while simultaneously suffering unprecedented official intrusion into our private lives by increased video surveillance, warrantless wiretapping and data-mining. Most tragically, more than 3,700 Americans and more than 70,000 Iraqi civilians have given their lives for the "preventive paradigm," which was used to justify going to war against a country that had not attacked us and posed no imminent threat of attack. . . .

All other things being equal, preventing a terrorist act is, of course, preferable to responding after the fact—all the more so when the threats include weapons of mass destruction and our adversaries are difficult to detect, willing to kill themselves and seemingly unconstrained by any recognizable considerations of law, morality or human dignity. But there are plenty of preventive counterterrorism measures that conform to the rule of law, such as increased protections at borders and around vulnerable targets, institutional reforms designed to encourage better information sharing, even military force and military detention when employed in self-defense. The real problems arise when the state uses highly coercive measures—depriving people of their life, liberty or property, or going to war—based on speculation, without adhering to the laws long seen as critical to regulating and legitimizing such force.

Even if one were to accept as a moral or ethical matter the "ends justify the means" rationales advanced for the preventive paradigm, the paradigm fails its own test: There is little or no evidence that the Administration's coercive pre-emptive measures have made us safer, and substantial evidence that they have in fact exacerbated the dangers we face.

Consider the costliest example: the war in Iraq. Precisely because the preventive doctrine turns on speculation about non-imminent events, it permitted the Administration to turn its focus from Al Qaeda, the organization that attacked us on 9/11, to Iraq, a nation that did not. The Iraq War has by virtually all accounts made the United States, the Iraqi people, many of our allies and for that matter much of the world more vulnerable to terrorists. By targeting Iraq, the Bush Administration not only siphoned off much-needed resources from the struggle against Al Qaeda but also created a golden opportunity for Al Qaeda to inspire and recruit others to attack US and allied targets. And our invasion of Iraq has turned it into the world's premier terrorist training ground.

The preventive paradigm has been no more effective in other aspects of the "war on terror." According to US figures, international terrorist attacks increased by 300 percent between 2003 and 2004. In 2005 alone, there were 360 suicide bombings, resulting in 3,000 deaths, compared with an annual average of about ninety such attacks over the five preceding years. That hardly constitutes progress.

But what about the fact that, other than the anthrax mailings in 2001, there has not been another terrorist attack in the United States since 9/11? The real question, of course, is whether the Administration's coercive preventive measures can be credited for that. There were eight years between the first and second attacks on the World Trade Center. And when one looks at what the preventive paradigm has come up with in terms of concrete results, it's an astonishingly thin file. At Guantánamo, for example, once said to house "the worst of the worst," the Pentagon's Combatant Status Review Tribunals' own findings categorized only 8 percent of some 500 detainees held there in 2006 as fighters for Al Qaeda or the Taliban. More than half of the 775 Guantánamo detainees have now been released, suggesting that they may not have been "the worst of the worst" after all.

As for terror cells at home, the FBI admitted in February 2005 that it had yet to identify a single Al Qaeda sleeper cell in the entire United States. And it hasn't found any since—unless you count the Florida group arrested in 2006, whose principal step toward an alleged plot to blow up the Sears Tower was to order combat boots and whose only Al Qaeda "connection" was to a federal informant pretending to be Al Qaeda. . . .

Overall, the government's success rate in cases alleging terrorist charges since 9/11 is only 29 percent, compared with a 92 percent conviction rate for felonies. This is an astounding statistic, because presumably federal juries are not predisposed to sympathize with Arab or Muslim defendants accused of terrorism. But when one prosecutes prematurely, failure is often the result.

The government's "preventive" immigration initiatives have come up even more empty-handed. After 9/11 the Bush Administration called in 80,000 foreign nationals for fingerprinting, photographing and "special registration" simply because they came from predominantly Arab or Muslim countries; sought out another 8,000 young men from the same countries for FBI interviews; and placed more than 5,000 foreign nationals here in preventive detention. Yet as of September 2007, not one of these people stands convicted of a terrorist crime. The government's record, in what is surely the largest campaign of ethnic profiling since the Japanese internment of World War II, is 0 for 93,000.

These statistics offer solid evidence to support the overwhelming consensus that *Foreign Policy* found when it polled more than 100 foreign policy experts—evenly dispersed along the political spectrum—and found that 91 percent felt that the world is becoming more dangerous for the United States, and that 84 percent said we are not winning the "war on terror."

It is certainly possible that some of these preventive measures deterred would-be terrorists from attacking us or helped to uncover and foil terrorist plots before they could come to fruition. But if real plots had been foiled and real terrorists identified, one would expect some criminal convictions to follow. When FBI agents successfully foiled a plot by Sheik Omar Abdel Rahman (popularly known as "the blind sheik") and others to bomb bridges and tunnels around Manhattan in the 1990s, it also convicted the plotters and sent them to prison for life.

In October 2005 Bush claimed that the United States and its allies had foiled ten terrorist plots. But he couldn't point to a single convicted terrorist. Consider just one of Bush's ten "success" stories, the one about which he provided the most details: an alleged Al Qaeda plot to fly an airplane into the Library Tower, a skyscraper in Los Angeles. The perpetrators, described only as Southeast Asians, were said to have been captured in early 2002 in Asia. As far as we know, however, no one has ever been charged or tried for this alleged terror plot. Intelligence officials told the *Washington Post* that there was "deep disagreement within the intelligence community about . . . whether it was ever much more than talk." A senior FBI official said, "To take that and make it into a disrupted plot is just ludicrous." American officials claim to have learned about some of the plot's details by interrogating captured Al Qaeda leader Khalid Shaikh Mohammed, but he was captured in 2003, long after the perpetrators had been arrested. As the *Los Angeles Times* put it, "By the time anybody knew about it, the threat—if there had been one—had passed, federal counter-terrorism officials said." These facts—all omitted in Bush's retelling—suggest that such claims of success need to be viewed skeptically.

If the Bush strategy were merely ineffectual, that would be bad enough. But it's worse than that; the President's policy has actually made us significantly less secure. While the Administration has concentrated on swaggeringly aggressive coercive initiatives of dubious effect, it has neglected less dramatic but more effective preventive initiatives. In December 2005 the bipartisan 9/11 Commission gave the Administration failing or near-failing grades on many of the most basic domestic security measures, including assessing critical infrastructure vulnerabilities, securing weapons of mass destruction, screening airline passengers and cargo, sharing information between law enforcement and intelligence agencies, insuring that first responders have adequate communications and supporting secular education in Muslim countries. We spend more in a day in Iraq than we do annually on some of the most important defensive initiatives here at home.

The preventive paradigm has also made it more difficult to bring terrorists to justice, just as FBI Director Mueller warned on September 12. When the Administration chooses to disappear suspects into secret prisons and use waterboarding to encourage them to talk, it forfeits any possibility of bringing the suspects to justice for their alleged crimes, because evidence obtained coercively at a "black site" would never be admissible in a fair and legitimate trial. That's the real reason no one has yet been brought to trial at Guantánamo. There is debate about whether torture ever results in reliable intelligence—but there can be no debate that it radically curtails the government's ability to bring a terrorist to justice.

Assuming that the principal terrorist threat still comes from Al Qaeda or, more broadly, a violence-prone fundamentalist strain of Islam, and that the "enemies" in this struggle are a relatively small number of Arab and Muslim men, it is all the more critical that we develop close, positive ties with Arab and Muslim communities here and abroad. By alienating those whose help we need most, the preventive paradigm has had exactly the opposite effect.

At the same time, we have given Al Qaeda the best propaganda it could ever have hoped for. Then-Defense Secretary Donald Rumsfeld identified the critical question in an October 2003 internal Pentagon memo: "Are we capturing, killing or deterring and dissuading more terrorists every day than the madrassas and the radical clerics are recruiting, training and deploying against us?" While there is no precise metric for answering Rumsfeld's question, there can be little doubt that our preventive tactics have been a boon to terrorist recruitment throughout the world.

More broadly still, our actions have radically undermined our standing in the world. The damage to US prestige was perhaps most dramatically revealed when, after the report of CIA black sites surfaced in November 2005, Russia, among several other countries, promptly issued a press release claiming that it had nothing to do with the sites. When Russia feels the need to distance itself from the United States out of concern that its human rights image might be tarnished by association, we have fallen far.

In short, we have gone from being the object of the world's sympathy immediately after 9/11 to being the country most likely to be hated. Anti-Americanism is at an all-time high. In some countries, Osama bin Laden has a higher approval rating than the United States. And much of the anti-Americanism is tied to the perception that the United States has pursued its "war on terror" in an arrogant, unilateral fashion, defying the very values we once championed.

The Bush Administration just doesn't get it. Its *National Defense Strategy,* published by the Pentagon, warns that "our strength as a nation state will continue to be challenged by those who employ a strategy of the weak using international fora, judicial processes, and terrorism." The proposition that judicial processes and international accountability—the very essence of the rule of law—are to be dismissed as a strategy of the weak, aligned with terrorism itself, makes clear that the Administration has come to view the rule of law as an obstacle, not an asset, in its effort to protect us from terrorist attack.

Our long-term security turns not on "going on offense" by locking up thousands of "suspected terrorists" who turn out to have no connection to terrorism; nor on forcing suspects to bark like dogs, urinate and defecate on themselves, and endure sexual humiliation; nor on attacking countries that have not threatened to attack us. Security rests not on exceptionalism and double standards but on a commitment to fairness, justice and the rule of law. The rule of law in no way precludes a state from defending itself from terrorists but requires that it do so within constraints. And properly understood, those constraints are assets, not obstacles. Aharon Barak, who recently retired as president of Israel's Supreme Court, said it best in a case forbidding the use of "moderate physical pressure" in interrogating Palestinian terror suspects: "A democracy must sometimes fight terror with one hand tied behind its back. Even so, a democracy has the upper hand. The rule of law and the liberty of an individual constitute important components in its understanding of security. At the end of the day, they strengthen its spirit and this strength allows it to overcome its difficulties."

The preventive paradigm has compromised our spirit, strengthened our enemies and left us less free and less safe. If we are ready to learn from our mistakes, however, there is a better way to defend ourselves—through, rather than despite, a recommitment to the rule of law.

CHAPTER 9 CONFRONTING CHINA v. ENGAGING CHINA

Engaging China

Advocate: Zbigniew Brzezinski

Source: "Make Money, Not War," *Foreign Policy*, no. 146 (January/February 2005), pp. 46–47.

Confronting China

Advocate: John J. Mearsheimer

Source: "Better to Be Godzilla than Bambi," *Foreign Policy*, no. 146 (January/February 2005), pp. 47–48.

International relations experts agree that the next superpower will be China. To the untrained eye, such a proposition may seem startling. After all, in view of the unparalleled power of the United States, it is difficult to imagine that another country will come to rival its influence over international politics.

China's economic growth, nuclear weapons, and population resources are some of the factors that make it the best candidate to become the next superpower. At the same time, China has numerous weaknesses that might impede its rise, including a lack of energy resources, as well as the challenges associated with an aging population.

The rise of China will undoubtedly present a dilemma to the United States. As China's power grows, so will its interests. This brings up the question of how Washington should approach the new challenge: whether it should confront Beijing and attempt to stunt its power, or whether it should take a more conciliatory approach and try to accommodate China within the existing global order.

IN FAVOR OF ACCOMMODATION

China's transformation has been driven by its impressive economic growth during the past decade. The Chinese leadership, while remaining communist, has allowed economic liberalization that led to the country's rapid industrialization. As Zbigniew Brzezinski points out, the government is intent on sustaining this trend, and a confrontational foreign policy toward the United States would disrupt China's economic growth, considerably weakening the party's grip on power. Instead, he argues, China will continue to integrate itself into the global economy.

In addition, China's limited military capability and scarce resources make it very vulnerable to isolation imposed by the United States. Furthermore, if it were to adopt a confrontational approach, it would quickly face a powerful, nationalist Japan. That is to say, as Brzezinski maintains, the rational Chinese leadership will likely continue its assimilation into the international system, avoid a direct confrontation with the United States, and choose instead a strategy of slow expansion of influence.

IN FAVOR OF CONFRONTATION

The rise of one country's power inevitably leads to loss of power by another one—or so realists contend. In other words, China's rise will result in a loss of power by the United States. Many argue that the United States should confront China early on, in order to extend its primacy for a longer period of time. As John Mearsheimer maintains, China's rise cannot be accomplished peacefully and an intense security competition with the United States is in store.

As China's power grows, so will its interests, first in its backyard and then globally. Powerful China will not be willing to tolerate U.S. presence—and potential intervention against it—in Southeast Asia. As Mearsheimer argues, this will inevitably lead to a conflict between these two countries. Taking an offensive realist approach, Mearsheimer demonstrates that China will strive to become the regional hegemon in Asia, keeping the United States out and largely shaping the behavior of its main Asian competitors.

POINTS **TO PONDER**

1. Should the United States take preventive action in order to prevent or stall China's rise?
2. Will China's lack of energy resources and population dynamics halt its growing power?
3. How does Taiwan influence China's relationship with the United States?
4. What has been the impact of China's integration into the global economy?
5. Should the United States do more to improve the human rights situation in China?

Zbigniew Brzezinski
Make Money, Not War

Today in East Asia, China is rising—peacefully so far. For understandable reasons, China harbors resentment and even humiliation about some chapters of its history. Nationalism is an important force, and there are serious grievances regarding external issues, notably Taiwan. But conflict is not inevitable or even likely. China's leadership is not inclined to challenge the United States militarily, and its focus remains on economic development and winning acceptance as a great power.

China is preoccupied, and almost fascinated, with the trajectory of its own ascent. When I met with the top leadership not long ago, what struck me was the frequency with which I was asked for predictions about the next 15 or 20 years. Not long ago, the Chinese Politburo invited two distinguished, Western-trained professors to a special meeting. Their task was to analyze nine major powers since the 15th century to see why they rose and fell. It's an interesting exercise for the top leadership of a massive and complex country.

This focus on the experience of past great powers could lead to the conclusion that the iron laws of political theory and history point to some inevitable collision or conflict. But there are other political realities. In the next five years, China will host several events that will restrain the conduct of its foreign policy. The 2008 Olympic Games is the most important, of course. The scale of the economic and psychological investment in the Beijing games is staggering. My expectation is that they will be magnificently organized. And make no mistake, China intends to win at the Olympics. A second date is 2010, when China will hold the World Expo in Shanghai. Successfully organizing these international gatherings is important to China and suggests that a cautious foreign policy will prevail.

More broadly, China is determined to sustain its economic growth. A confrontational foreign policy could disrupt that growth, harm hundreds of millions of Chinese, and threaten the Communist Party's hold on power. China's leadership appears rational, calculating, and conscious not only of China's rise but also of its continued weakness.

There will be inevitable frictions as China's regional role increases and as a Chinese "sphere of influence" develops. U.S. power may recede gradually in the coming years, and the unavoidable decline in Japan's influence will heighten the sense of China's regional preeminence. But to have a real collision, China needs a military that is capable of going toe-to-toe with the

United States. At the strategic level, China maintains a posture of minimum deterrence. Forty years after acquiring nuclear-weapons technology, China has just 24 ballistic missiles capable of hitting the United States. Even beyond the realm of strategic warfare, a country must have the capacity to attain its political objectives before it will engage in limited war. It is hard to envisage how China could promote its objectives when it is acutely vulnerable to a blockade and isolation enforced by the United States. In a conflict, Chinese maritime trade would stop entirely. The flow of oil would cease, and the Chinese economy would be paralyzed.

I have the sense that the Chinese are cautious about Taiwan, their fierce talk notwithstanding. Last March, a Communist Party magazine noted that "we have basically contained the overt threat of Taiwanese independence since [President] Chen [Shuibian] took office, avoiding a worst-case scenario and maintaining the status of Taiwan as part of China." A public opinion poll taken in Beijing at the same time found that 58 percent thought military action was unnecessary. Only 15 percent supported military action to "liberate" Taiwan.

Of course, stability today does not ensure peace tomorrow. If China were to succumb to internal violence, for example, all bets are off. If sociopolitical tensions or social inequality becomes unmanageable, the leadership might be tempted to exploit nationalist passions. But the small possibility of this type of catastrophe does not weaken my belief that we can avoid the negative consequences that often accompany the rise of new powers. China is clearly assimilating into the international system. Its leadership appears to realize that attempting to dislodge the United States would be futile, and that the cautious spread of Chinese influence is the surest path to global preeminence.

John J. Mearsheimer

Better to Be Godzilla than Bambi

China cannot rise peacefully, and if it continues its dramatic economic growth over the next few decades, the United States and China are likely to engage in an intense security competition with considerable potential for war. Most of China's neighbors, including India, Japan, Singapore, South Korea, Russia, and Vietnam, will likely join with the United States to contain China's power.

To predict the future in Asia, one needs a theory that explains how rising powers are likely to act and how other states will react to them. My theory of international politics says that the mightiest states attempt to establish hegemony in their own region while making sure that no rival great power dominates another region. The ultimate goal of every great power is to maximize its share of world power and eventually dominate the system.

The international system has several defining characteristics. The main actors are states that operate in anarchy—which simply means that there is no higher authority above them. All great powers have some offensive military capability, which means that they can hurt each other. Finally, no state can know the future intentions of other states with certainty. The best way to survive in such a system is to be as powerful as possible, relative to potential rivals. The mightier a state is, the less likely it is that another state will attack it.

The great powers do not merely strive to be the strongest great power, although that is a welcome outcome. Their ultimate aim is to be the hegemon— the only great power in the system. But it is almost impossible for any state to achieve global hegemony in the modern world, because it is too hard to project and sustain power around the globe. Even the United States is a regional but not a global hegemon. The best outcome that a state can hope for is to dominate its own backyard.

States that gain regional hegemony have a further aim: to prevent other geographical areas from being dominated by other great powers. Regional hegemons, in other words, do not want peer competitors. Instead, they want to keep other regions divided among several great powers so that these states will compete with each other. In 1991, shortly after the Cold War ended, the first Bush administration boldly stated that the United States was now the most powerful state in the world and planned to remain so. That same message appeared in the famous National Security Strategy issued by the second Bush administration in September 2002. This document's stance on preemptive war generated harsh criticism, but hardly a word of protest greeted the assertion that the United States should check rising powers and maintain its commanding position in the global balance of power.

China is likely to try to dominate Asia the way the United States dominates the Western Hemisphere. Specifically, China will strive to maximize the power gap between itself and its neighbors, especially Japan and Russia, and to ensure that no state in Asia can threaten it. It is unlikely that China will go on a rampage and conquer other Asian countries. Instead, China will want to dictate the boundaries of acceptable behavior to neighboring countries, much the way the United States does in the Americas. An increasingly powerful China is also likely to try to push the United States out of Asia, much the way the United States pushed the European great powers out of the

Western Hemisphere. Not incidentally, gaining regional hegemony is probably the only way that China will get back Taiwan.

Why should we expect China to act differently than the United States? U.S. policymakers, after all, react harshly when other great powers send military forces into the Western Hemisphere. These foreign forces are invariably seen as a potential threat to American security. Are the Chinese more principled, more ethical, less nationalistic, or less concerned about their survival than Westerners? They are none of these things, which is why China is likely to imitate the United States and attempt to become a regional hegemon, China's leadership and people remember what happened in the last century, when Japan was powerful and China was weak. In the anarchic world of international politics, it is better to be Godzilla than Bambi.

It is clear from the historical record how American policymakers will react if China attempts to dominate Asia. The United States does not tolerate peer competitors. As it demonstrated in the 20th century, it is determined to remain the world's only regional hegemon. Therefore, the United States will seek to contain China and ultimately weaken it to the point where it is no longer capable of dominating Asia. In essence, the United States is likely to behave toward China much the way it behaved toward the Soviet Union during the Cold War.

CHAPTER 10 THE DANGER OF NUCLEAR WEAPONS *v.* THE NECESSITY OF NUCLEAR WEAPONS

The Dangers of Nuclear Weapons

Advocate: Robert S. McNamara

Source: "Apocalypse Soon," *Foreign Policy*, no. 148 (May/June 2005), pp. 28–35, excerpt.

The Necessity of Nuclear Weapons

Advocate: Kenneth N. Waltz

Source: "Peace, Stability, and Nuclear Weapons," *Institute on Global Conflict and Cooperation Publications*, 1995, excerpt.

The emergence and evolution of nuclear weapons in the twentieth century dramatically changed the nature of warfare. Because of their destructiveness, as exemplified by the bombings of Hiroshima and Nagasaki, the accumulation of nuclear weapons, the nuclear postures of the great powers, and attempts to curb proliferation continue to be the subject of debates. Although many policymakers and experts believe that nuclear weapons should either be eliminated or dramatically reduced in numbers, others vigorously argue they are necessary, even calling for continued proliferation. For instance, there is the widespread belief that the "long peace" of the Cold War was a result of the prospect of mutually assured destruction if nuclear weapons were used.

The mass demonstrations against nuclear armaments that were ubiquitous during the Cold War are only a fading memory now. However, the weapons continue to be a source of anxiety for many because of their potential to fall into the wrong hands—terrorist groups, hostile regimes—or because of the ease with which their launch could be authorized. While nuclear technology advances, the debates on the morality and usefulness of nuclear weapons continue.

IN FAVOR OF ELIMINATING NUCLEAR WEAPONS

While they were an everyday occurrence during the Cold War years, concerns with the growth of existing nuclear stockpiles are no longer front-page news. In an era when the security agenda is topped by fighting terrorism, we are more worried that terrorist organizations or rogue regimes might acquire nuclear weapons and inflict unspeakable damage to the targeted countries. The United States has chosen to negotiate with North Korea over that country's nuclear capabilities, while trying to coerce Iran to abandon its nuclear program, and has stepped up pressure on Pakistan and other states to ensure that weapons of mass destruction—including nuclear weapons—do not fall into the wrong hands.

Former Secretary of Defense Robert McNamara addresses the nuclear stance of the United States. His main argument is that the countries of the world should try to eliminate their nuclear arsenal because of the utter devastation these weapons can inflict on humanity. McNamara posits that the world is closer to nuclear detonation now than it has ever been. His sharpest criticism is pointed at U.S. nuclear policy which has not changed significantly since the Cold War, and which does not denounce first strike. Moreover, by intensifying its efforts in sustaining, modernizing, and improving its nuclear stockpile while refusing to ratify the Comprehensive Test Ban Treaty, the United States sends a message that it is not serious about nuclear non-proliferation. McNamara advocates a debate over the utility of these weapons, the risks of inadvertent use, the moral and ethical considerations involved in using or threatening to use nuclear weapons, and the impact of current U.S. policies on non-proliferation.

IN FAVOR OF NUCLEAR WEAPONS

Leading scholars of international relations and policymakers share in the belief that the sheer destructiveness of nuclear weapons prevents them from being used by friends and foes alike. The deterrent effect of nuclear weapons is rooted in their possession rather than in their use. Furthermore, being a nuclear power allows countries freedom to maneuver, making them less susceptible to coercion from other states.

Kenneth Waltz looks at the reasons why states seek to acquire nuclear weapons, and the risks and benefits these weapons bring. He argues that nuclear weapons make states cautious and less likely to engage in reckless behavior. Waltz discusses the problems associated with nuclear deterrence. He argues that while the enormous destructiveness of nuclear weapons makes them excellent weapons for defensive purposes—the weapons have no offensive rationale. Though Waltz does not advocate widespread nuclear proliferation, he does submit that nuclear weapons are great contributors to stability in the international system.

POINTS **TO PONDER**

1. The United States continues to work to make its nuclear weapons more effective. How does this affect its ability to persuade other countries to give up on their nuclear aspirations?

2. From what sources can terrorists obtain nuclear weapons?

3. How do nuclear weapons contribute to international stability?

Robert S. McNamara

Apocalypse Soon

It is time—well past time, in my view—for the United States to cease its Cold War-style reliance on nuclear weapons as a foreign-policy tool. At the risk of appearing simplistic and provocative, I would characterize current U.S. nuclear weapons policy as immoral, illegal, militarily unnecessary, and dreadfully dangerous. The risk of an accidental or inadvertent nuclear launch is unacceptably high. Far from reducing these risks, the Bush administration has signaled that it is committed to keeping the U.S. nuclear arsenal as a mainstay of its military power—a commitment that is simultaneously eroding the international norms that have limited the spread of nuclear weapons and fissile materials for 50 years. Much of the current U.S. nuclear policy has been in place since before I was secretary of defense, and it has only grown more dangerous and diplomatically destructive in the intervening years.

Today, the United States has deployed approximately 4,500 strategic, offensive nuclear warheads. Russia has roughly 3,800. The strategic forces of Britain, France, and China are considerably smaller, with 200–400 nuclear weapons in each state's arsenal. The new nuclear states of Pakistan and India have fewer than 100 weapons each. North Korea now claims to have developed nuclear weapons, and U.S. intelligence agencies estimate that Pyongyang has enough fissile material for 2–8 bombs.

How destructive are these weapons? The average U.S. warhead has a destructive power 20 times that of the Hiroshima bomb. Of the 8,000 active or operational U.S. warheads, 2,000 are on hair-trigger alert, ready to be launched on 15 minutes' warning. How are these weapons to be used? The United States has never endorsed the policy of "no first use," not during my seven years as secretary or since. We have been and remain prepared to initiate the use of nuclear weapons—by the decision of one person, the president—against either a nuclear or nonnuclear enemy whenever we believe it is in our interest to do so. For decades, U.S. nuclear forces have been sufficiently strong to absorb a first strike and then inflict "unacceptable" damage on an opponent. This has been and (so long as we face a nuclear-armed, potential adversary) must continue to be the foundation of our nuclear deterrent.

In my time as secretary of defense, the commander of the U.S. Strategic Air Command (SAC) carried with him a secure telephone, no matter where he went, 24 hours a day, seven days a week, 365 days a year. The telephone of the commander, whose headquarters were in Omaha, Nebraska, was linked to the underground command post of the North American Defense Command, deep inside Cheyenne Mountain, in Colorado, and to the U.S. president, wherever he happened to be. The president always had at hand nuclear release codes in the so-called football, a briefcase carried for the president at all times by a U.S. military officer.

The SAC commander's orders were to answer the telephone by no later than the end of the third ring. If it rang, and he was informed that a nuclear attack of enemy ballistic missiles appeared to be under way, he was allowed 2 to 3 minutes to decide whether the warning was valid (over the years, the United States has received many false warnings), and if so, how the United States should respond. He was then given approximately 10 minutes to determine what to recommend, to locate and advise the president, permit the president to discuss the situation with two or three close advisors (presumably the secretary of defense and the chairman of the Joint Chiefs of Staff), and to receive the president's decision and pass it immediately, along with the codes, to the launch sites. The president essentially had two options: He could decide to ride out the attack and defer until later any decision to launch a retaliatory strike. Or, he could order an immediate retaliatory strike, from a menu of options, thereby launching U.S. weapons that were targeted on the opponent's military-industrial assets. Our opponents in Moscow presumably had and have similar arrangements.

The whole situation seems so bizarre as to be beyond belief. On any given day, as we go about our business, the president is prepared to make a decision within 20 minutes that could launch one of the most devastating weapons in the world. To declare war requires an act of congress, but to launch a nuclear holocaust requires 20 minutes' deliberation by the president and his advisors. But that is what we have lived with for 40 years. With very few changes, this system remains largely intact, including the "football," the president's constant companion.

I was able to change some of these dangerous policies and procedures. My colleagues and I started arms control talks; we installed safeguards to reduce the risk of unauthorized launches; we added options to the nuclear war plans so that the president did not have to choose between an all-or-nothing response, and we eliminated the vulnerable and provocative nuclear missiles in Turkey. I wish I had done more, but we were in the midst of the Cold War, and our options were limited.

The United States and our NATO allies faced a strong Soviet and Warsaw Pact conventional threat. Many of the allies (and some in Washington as well) felt strongly that preserving the U.S. option of launching a first strike was necessary for the sake of keeping the Soviets at bay. What is shocking is that today, more than a decade after the end of the Cold War, the basic U.S. nuclear policy is unchanged. It has not adapted to the collapse of the Soviet Union. Plans and procedures have not been revised to make the United States or other countries less likely to push the button. At a minimum, we should remove all strategic nuclear weapons from "hair-trigger" alert, as others have recommended, including Gen. George Lee Butler, the last commander of SAC. That simple change would greatly reduce the risk of an accidental nuclear launch. It would also signal to other states that the United States is taking steps to end its reliance on nuclear weapons.

We pledged to work in good faith toward the eventual elimination of nuclear arsenals when we negotiated the Nuclear Non-Proliferation Treaty (NPT) in 1968. In May, diplomats from more than 180 nations are meeting in New York City to review the NPT and assess whether members are living up to the agreement. The United States is focused, for understandable reasons, on persuading North Korea to rejoin the treaty and on negotiating deeper constraints on Iran's nuclear ambitions. Those states must be convinced to keep the promises they made when they originally signed the NPT—that they would not build nuclear weapons in return for access to peaceful uses of nuclear energy. But the attention of many nations, including some potential new nuclear weapons states, is also on the United States. Keeping such large numbers of weapons, and maintaining them on hair-trigger alert, are potent signs that the United States is not seriously working toward the elimination of its arsenal and raises troubling questions as to why any other state should restrain its nuclear ambitions.

A Preview of the Apocalypse

The destructive power of nuclear weapons is well known, but given the United States' continued reliance on them, it's worth remembering the danger they present. A 2000 report by the International Physicians for the Prevention of Nuclear War describes the likely effects of a single 1 megaton weapon—dozens of which are contained in the Russian and U.S. inventories. At ground zero, the explosion creates a crater 300 feet deep and 1,200 feet in diameter. Within one second, the atmosphere itself ignites into a fireball more than a half-mile in diameter. The surface of the fire-ball radiates nearly three times the light and heat of a comparable area of the surface of the sun, extinguishing in seconds all life below and radiating outward at the speed of light, causing instantaneous severe burns to people within one to three miles. A blast wave of compressed air reaches a distance of three miles in about 12 seconds, flattening factories and commercial buildings. Debris carried by winds of 250 mph inflicts lethal injuries throughout the area. At least 50 percent of people in the area die immediately, prior to any injuries from radiation or the developing firestorm.

Of course, our knowledge of these effects is not entirely hypothetical. Nuclear weapons, with roughly one seventieth of the power of the 1 megaton bomb just described, were twice used by the United States in August 1945. One atomic bomb was dropped on Hiroshima. Around 80,000 people died immediately; approximately 200,000 died eventually. Later, a similar size bomb was dropped on Nagasaki. On Nov. 7, 1995, the mayor of Nagasaki recalled his memory of the attack in testimony to the International Court of Justice:

> Nagasaki became a city of death where not even the sound of insects could be heard. After a while, countless men, women and children began to gather for a drink of water at the banks of nearby Urakami River, their hair and clothing scorched and their burnt skin hanging off in sheets like rags. Begging for help they died one after another in the water or in heaps on the banks. . . . Four months after the atomic bombing, 74,000 people were dead, and 75,000 had suffered injuries, that is, two-thirds of the city population had fallen victim to this calamity that came upon Nagasaki like a preview of the Apocalypse.

Why did so many civilians have to die? Because the civilians, who made up nearly 100 percent of the victims of Hiroshima and Nagasaki, were unfortunately "co-located" with Japanese military and industrial targets. Their annihilation, though not the objective of those dropping the bombs, was an inevitable result of the choice of those targets. It is worth noting that during the Cold War, the United States reportedly had dozens of nuclear warheads targeted on Moscow alone, because it contained so many military targets and so much "industrial capacity." Presumably, the Soviets similarly targeted many U.S. cities. The statement that our nuclear weapons do not target populations per se was and remains totally misleading in the sense that the so-called collateral damage of large nuclear strikes would include tens of millions of innocent civilian dead.

This in a nutshell is what nuclear weapons do: They indiscriminately blast, burn, and irradiate with a speed and finality that are almost incomprehensible. This is exactly what countries like the United States and Russia, with nuclear weapons on hair-trigger alert, continue to threaten every minute of every day in this new 21st century.

No Way to Win

I have worked on issues relating to U.S. and NATO nuclear strategy and war plans for more than 40 years. During that time, I have never seen a piece of paper that outlined a plan for the United States or NATO to initiate the use of nuclear weapons with any benefit for the United States or NATO. I have made this statement in front of audiences, including NATO defense ministers and senior military leaders, many times. No one has ever refuted it. To launch weapons against a nuclear-equipped opponent would be suicidal. To do so against a nonnuclear enemy would be militarily unnecessary, morally repugnant, and politically indefensible. . . .

In articles and speeches, I criticized the fundamentally flawed assumption that nuclear weapons could be used in some limited way. There is no way to effectively contain a nuclear strike—to keep it from inflicting enormous destruction on civilian life and property, and there is no guarantee against unlimited escalation once the first nuclear strike occurs. We cannot avoid the serious and unacceptable risk of nuclear war until we recognize these facts and base our military plans and policies upon this recognition. I hold these views even more strongly today than I did when I first spoke out against the nuclear dangers our policies were creating. . . .

In addition to projecting the deployment of large numbers of strategic nuclear weapons far into the future, the Bush administration is planning an extensive and expensive series of programs to sustain and modernize the existing nuclear force and to begin studies for new launch vehicles, as well as new warheads for all of the launch platforms. Some members of the administration have called for new nuclear weapons that could be used as bunker busters against underground shelters (such as the shelters Saddam Hussein used in Baghdad). New production facilities for fissile materials would need to be built to support the expanded force. The plans provide for integrating a national ballistic missile defense into the new triad of offensive weapons to enhance the nation's ability to use its "power projection forces" by improving our ability to counterattack an enemy. The Bush administration also announced that it has no intention to ask congress to ratify the Comprehensive Test Ban Treaty (CTBT), and, though no decision to test has been made, the administration has ordered the national laboratories to begin research on new nuclear weapons designs and to prepare the underground test sites in Nevada for nuclear tests if necessary in the future. Clearly, the Bush administration assumes that nuclear weapons will be part of U.S. military forces for at least the next several decades.

Good faith participation in international negotiation on nuclear disarmament—including participation in the CTBT—is a legal and political obligation of all parties to the NPT that entered into force in 1970 and was extended indefinitely in 1995. The Bush administration's nuclear program, alongside its refusal to ratify the CTBT, will be viewed, with reason, by many nations as equivalent to a U.S. break from the treaty. It says to the nonnuclear weapons nations, "We, with the strongest conventional military force in the world, require nuclear weapons in perpetuity, but you, facing potentially well-armed opponents, are never to be allowed even one nuclear weapon."

If the United States continues its current nuclear stance, over time, substantial proliferation of nuclear weapons will almost surely follow. Some, or all, of such nations as Egypt, Japan, Saudi Arabia, Syria, and Taiwan will very likely initiate nuclear weapons programs, increasing both the risk of use of the weapons and the diversion of weapons and fissile materials into the hands of rogue states or terrorists. Diplomats and intelligence agencies believe Osama bin Laden has made several attempts to acquire nuclear weapons or fissile materials. It has been widely reported that Sultan Bashiruddin Mahmood, former director of Pakistan's nuclear reactor complex, met with bin Laden several times. Were al Qaeda to acquire fissile materials, especially enriched uranium, its ability to produce nuclear weapons would be great. The knowledge of how to construct a simple gun-type nuclear device, like the one we dropped on Hiroshima, is now widespread. Experts have little doubt that terrorists could construct such a primitive device if they acquired the requisite enriched uranium material. Indeed, just last summer, at a meeting of the National Academy of Sciences, former Secretary of Defense William J. Perry said, "I have never been more fearful of a nuclear detonation than now. . . . There is a greater than 50 percent probability of a nuclear strike on U.S. targets within a decade." I share his fears.

A Moment of Decision

We are at a critical moment in human history—perhaps not as dramatic as that of the Cuban Missile Crisis, but a moment no less crucial. Neither the Bush administration, the congress, the American people, nor the people of other nations have debated the merits of alternative, long-range nuclear weapons policies for their countries or the world. They have not examined the military utility of the weapons; the risk of inadvertent or accidental use; the moral and legal considerations relating to the use or threat of use of the weapons; or the impact of current policies on proliferation. Such debates are long overdue. If they are held, I believe they will conclude, as have I and an increasing number of senior military leaders, politicians, and civilian security experts: We must move promptly toward the elimination—or near elimination—of all nuclear weapons. For many, there is a strong temptation to cling to the strategies of the past 40 years. But to do so would be a serious mistake leading to unacceptable risks for all nations.

Kenneth N. Waltz

Peace, Stability, and Nuclear Weapons

> If proliferation does take place we may continue to complain about it, but we shall live with it. And leaders who now assert that nonproliferation is indispensable to our security will presumably find other subjects to dramatize.
> —*James R. Schlesinger, 1956*[1]

• • •

Why Countries Want Nuclear Weapons

In contemplating the likely future, we might first ask why countries want to have nuclear weapons. They want them for one or more of seven main reasons:

- First, great powers always counter the weapons of other great powers, usually by imitating those who have introduced new weapons. It was not surprising that the Soviet Union developed atomic and hydrogen bombs, but rather that we thought the Baruch–Lilienthal plan might persuade it not to.
- Second, a state may want nuclear weapons for fear that its great-power ally will not retaliate if another great power attacks. When it became a nuclear power, Britain thought of itself as being a great one, but its reasons for deciding to maintain a nuclear force arose from doubts that the United States could be counted on to retaliate in response to an attack by the Soviet Union on Europe and from Britain's consequent desire to place a finger on our nuclear trigger. As soon as the Soviet Union was capable of making nuclear strikes at American cities, West Europeans began to worry that America's nuclear umbrella no longer ensured that its allies would stay dry if it rained.
- Third, a country without nuclear allies will want nuclear weapons all the more if some of its adversaries have them. So China and then India became nuclear powers, and Pakistan naturally followed.
- Fourth, a country may want nuclear weapons because it lives in fear of its adversaries' present or future conventional strength. This was reason enough for Israel's nuclear weapons.
- Fifth, for some countries nuclear weapons are a cheaper and safer alternative to running economically ruinous and militarily dangerous conventional arms races. Nuclear weapons promise security and independence at an affordable price.

- Sixth, some countries are thought to want nuclear weapons for offensive purposes. This, however, is an unlikely motivation for reasons given below.
- Finally, by building nuclear weapons a country may hope to enhance its international standing. This is thought to be both a reason for and a consequence of developing nuclear weapons. One may enjoy the status that comes with nuclear weapons and even benefit from it. Thus, North Korea gained international attention by developing nuclear military capability. A yen for attention and prestige is, however, a minor motivation. Would-be nuclear states are not among the militarily most powerful ones. The security concerns of weaker states are too serious to permit them to accord much importance to the prestige that nuclear weapons may bring.

The Fear of Nuclear Weapons

Fears of what the further spread of nuclear weapons will do to the world boil down to five. First, new nuclear states may put their weapons to offensive use. Second, as more countries get the weapons, the chances of accidental use increase. Third, with limited resources and know-how, new nuclear states may find it difficult to deploy invulnerable, deterrent forces. Fourth, American military intervention in the affairs of lesser states will be impeded by their possession of nuclear weapons. Fifth, as nuclear weapons spread, terrorists may more easily get hold of nuclear materials. (In this chapter, I leave the fifth fear aside, partly because the likelihood of nuclear terror is low and partly because terrorists can presumably steal nuclear weapons or buy them on the black market whether or not a few more states go nuclear.)[2]

Offensive use

Despite the variety of nuclear motivations, an American consensus has formed on why some states want their own weapons—to help them pursue expansionist ends. "The basic division in the world on the subject of nuclear proliferation," we are authoritatively told, "is not between those with and without nuclear weapons. It is between almost all nations and the very few who currently seek weapons to reinforce their expansive ambition."[3] Just as we first feared that the Soviet Union and China would use nuclear weapons to extend their sway, so we now fear that the likes of Iraq, Iran, and Libya will do so. The fear has grown despite the fact that nuclear capability added little to the Soviet Union's or China's ability to pursue their ends abroad, whether by launching military attacks or practicing blackmail.

The fear that new nuclear states will use their weapons for aggressive purposes is as odd as it is pervasive. Rogue states, as we now call them, must be up to no good, else we would not call them rogues. Why would states such as Iraq, Iran, and North Korea want nuclear weapons if not to enable them to conquer, or at least to intimidate, others? The answer can be given in one word: fear. The behavior of their rulers is often brazen, but does their bluster convey confidence or fear? Even though they may hope to extend their domination over others, they first have to maintain it at home.

What states do conveys more than what they say. Idi Amin and Muammar el-Qaddafi were favorite examples of the kinds of rulers who could not be trusted to manage nuclear weapons responsibly. Despite wild rhetoric aimed at foreigners, however, both of these "irrational" rulers became cautious and modest when punitive actions against them seemed to threaten their continued ability to rule. Even though Amin lustily slaughtered members of tribes he disliked, he quickly stopped goading Britain when it seemed that it might intervene militarily. Qaddafi showed similar restraint. He and Anwar Sadat were openly hostile. In July 1977, both launched commando attacks and air raids, including two large air strikes by Egypt on Libya's el-Adem airbase. Neither side let the attacks get out of hand. Qaddafi showed himself to be forbearing and amenable to mediation by other Arab leaders. Shai Feldman used these and other examples to argue that Arab leaders are deterred from taking inordinate risks, not because they engage in intricate rational calculations but simply because they, like other rulers, are "sensitive to costs." Saddam Hussein further illustrated the point during, and even prior to, the war of 1991. He invaded Kuwait only after the United States gave many indications that it would acquiesce in his actions. During the war, he launched missiles against Israel, but they were so lightly armed that little risk was run of prompting attacks more punishing than Iraq was already suffering. Deterrence worked once again.

Many Westerners write fearfully about a future in which Third World countries have nuclear weapons. They seem to view Third World people in the old imperial manner as "lesser breeds without the law." As ever with ethnocentric views, speculation takes the place of evidence. How do we know that a nuclear-armed and newly-hostile Egypt, or a nuclear-armed and still-hostile Syria, would not strike to destroy Israel? Yet we have to ask whether either would do so at the risk of Israeli bombs falling on some of their cities? Almost a quarter of Egypt's people live in four cities: Cairo, Alexandria, El-Giza, and Shoubra el-Kheima. More than a quarter of Syria's live in three: Damascus, Aleppo, and Homs.[4] What government would risk sudden losses of such proportion, or indeed of much lesser proportion? Rulers want to have a country that they can continue to rule. Some Arab country may wish that some other Arab country would risk its own destruction for the sake of destroying Israel, but why would one think that any country would be willing to do so? Despite ample bitterness, Israelis and Arabs have limited their wars and accepted constraints placed on them by others. Arabs did not marshal their resources and make an all-out effort to destroy Israel in the years before Israel could strike back with nuclear warheads. We cannot expect countries to risk more in the presence of nuclear weapons than they did in their absence.

Second, many fear that states that are radical at home will recklessly use their nuclear weapons in pursuit of revolutionary ends abroad. States that are radical at home, however, may not be radical abroad. Few states have been radical in the conduct of their foreign policy, and fewer have remained so for long. Think of the Soviet Union and the People's Republic of China. States coexist in a competitive arena. The pressures of competition cause them to behave in ways that make the threats they face manageable, in ways that enable them to get along. States can remain radical in foreign policy only if they are overwhelmingly strong—as none of the new nuclear states will be— or if their acts fall short of damaging vital interests of other nuclear powers. States that acquire nuclear weapons are not regarded with indifference. States that want to be freewheelers have to stay out of the nuclear business. A nuclear Libya, for example, would have to show caution, even in rhetoric, lest it suffer retaliation in response to someone else's anonymous attack on a third state. That state, ignorant of who attacked, might claim that its intelligence agents had identified Libya as the culprit and take the opportunity to silence it by striking a heavy conventional blow. Nuclear weapons induce caution in any state, especially in weak ones.

Would not nuclear weapons nevertheless provide a cheap and decisive offensive force when used against a conventionally armed enemy? Some people once thought that South Korea, and earlier, the Shah's Iran, wanted nuclear weapons for offensive use. Yet one can neither say why South Korea would have used nuclear weapons against fellow Koreans while trying to reunite them nor how it could have used nuclear weapons against the North, knowing that China and the Soviet Union might have retaliated. And what goals might a conventionally strong Iran have entertained that would have tempted it to risk using nuclear weapons? A country that launches a strike has to fear a punishing blow from someone. Far from lowering the expected cost of aggression, a nuclear offense even against a non-nuclear state raises the possible costs of aggression to incalculable heights because the aggressor cannot be sure of the reaction of other states.

North Korea provides a good example of how the United States imputes doubtful motives to some of the states seeking nuclear weapons. Between 1989 and 1991, North Korea's world collapsed. The Soviet Union and South Korea established diplomatic relations; China and South

Korea opened trade offices in each other's capitols and now recognize each other. The fall of communist regimes in Eastern Europe, and the disintegration of the Soviet Union, stripped North Korea of outside support. The revolution in its international relations further weakened an already weak North Korea.

Like earlier nuclear states, North Korea wants the military capability because it feels weak and threatened.[5] The ratio of South Korea's to North Korea's GDP in 1993 was 15:1; of their populations, 2:1; of their defense budgets, 6:1.[6] North Korea does have twice as large an active army and twice as many tanks, but their quality is low, spare parts and fuel scarce, training limited, and communications and logistics dated. In addition, South Korea has the backing of the United States and the presence of American troops.

Despite North Korea's exposed position, Americans especially have worried that the North might invade the South and use nuclear weapons in doing so. How concerned should we be? No one has figured out how to use nuclear weapons except for deterrence. Is a small and weak state likely to be the first to do so? Countries that use nuclear weapons have to fear retaliation. Why would the North once again invade the South? It did so in 1950, but only after prominent American congressmen, military leaders, and other officials proclaimed that we would not fight in Korea. Any war on the peninsula would put North Korea at severe risk. Perhaps because South Koreans appreciate this fact more keenly than Americans do, relatively few of them seem to believe that North Korea will invade. Kim II Sung at times threatened war, but anyone who thinks that when a dictator threatens war we should believe him is lost wandering around somewhere in a bygone conventional world.[7] Kim II Sung was sometimes compared to Hitler and Stalin.[8] Despite similarities, it is foolish to forget that the capabilities of the North Korea he ruled in no way compared with those of Germany and the Soviet Union under Hitler and Stalin.

Nuclear weapons make states cautious, as the history of the nuclear age shows. "Rogue states," as the Soviet Union and China were once thought to be, have followed the pattern. The weaker and the more endangered a state is, the less likely it is to engage in reckless behavior. North Korea's external behavior has sometimes been ugly, but certainly not reckless. Its regime has shown no inclination to risk suicide. This is one good reason why surrounding states counseled patience. . . .

The control of nuclear weapons

Will new nuclear states, many of them technologically backward and with weapons lacking effective safety devices, be able to prevent the accidental or unauthorized use of their weapons and maintain control of them despite possible domestic upheavals?

"War is like love," the chaplain says in Bertolt Brecht's *Mother Courage*, "it always finds a way."[9] For half a century, *nuclear* war has not found a way. The old saying, "accidents will happen," is translated as Murphy's Law holding that anything that can go wrong will go wrong. Enough has gone wrong, and Scott Sagan has recorded many of the nuclear accidents that have, or have nearly, taken place.[10] Yet none of them has caused anybody to blow anybody else up. In a speech given to American scientists in 1960, C.P. Snow said this: "We know, with the certainty of statistical truth, that if enough of these weapons are made—by enough different states—some of them are going to blow up. Through accident, or folly, or madness—but the motives don't matter. What does matter is the nature of the statistical fact." In 1960, statistical fact told Snow that within, "at the most, ten years some of these bombs are going off." Statistical fact now tells us that we are twenty-five years overdue.[11] But the novelist and scientist overlooked the fact that there are no "statistical facts."

Half a century of nuclear peace has to be explained since divergence from historical experience is dramatic. Never in modern history, conventionally dated from 1648, have the great and major powers of the world enjoyed such a long period of peace.

Large numbers of weapons increase the possibility of accidental use or loss of control, but new nuclear states will have only small numbers of weapons to care for. Lesser nuclear states may deploy, say, ten to fifty weapons and a number of dummies, while permitting other countries to infer that numbers of real weapons are larger. An adversary need only believe that some warheads may survive its attack and be visited on it. That belief is not hard to create without making command and control unreliable. All nuclear countries live through a time when their forces are crudely designed. All countries have so far been able to control them. Relations between the United States and the Soviet Union, and later among the United States, the Soviet Union, and China, were at their bitterest just when their nuclear forces were in early stages of development and were unbalanced, crude, and presumably hard to control. Why should we expect new nuclear states to experience greater difficulties than the ones old nuclear states were able to cope with? Although some of the new nuclear states may be economically and technically backward, they will either have expert scientists and engineers or they will not be able to produce nuclear weapons. Even if they buy or steal the weapons, they will have to hire technicians to maintain and control them. We do not have to wonder whether they will take good care of their weapons. They have every incentive to do so. They will not want to risk retaliation because one or more of their warheads accidentally strike another country.

Deterrence is a considerable guarantee against accidents, since it causes countries to take good care of their weapons, and against anonymous use, since those firing the weapons can know neither that they will be undetected nor what punishment detection might bring. In life, uncertainties abound. In a conventional world, they more easily lead to war because less is at stake. Even so, it is difficult to think of conventional wars that were started by accident.[12] It is hard to believe that nuclear war may begin accidentally, when less frightening conventional wars have rarely done so.

Fear of accidents works against their occurring. This is illustrated by the Cuban Missile Crisis. Accidents happened during the crisis, and unplanned events took place. An American U-2 strayed over Siberia, and one flew over Cuba. The American Navy continued to play games at sea, such games as trying to force Soviet submarines to surface. In crises, political leaders want to control all relevant actions, while knowing that they cannot do so. Fear of losing control propelled Kennedy and Khrushchev to end the crisis quickly. In a conventional world, uncertainty may tempt a country to join battle. In a nuclear world, uncertainty has the opposite effect. What is not surely controllable is too dangerous to bear.

One must, however, consider the possibility that a nuclear state will one day experience uncertainty of succession, fierce struggles for power, and instability of regime. That such experiences led to the use of nuclear weapons neither during the Cultural Revolution in China nor during the dissolution of the Soviet Union is of some comfort. The possibility of one side in a civil war firing a nuclear warhead at its opponent's stronghold nevertheless remains. Such an act would produce a national tragedy, not an international one. This question then arises: Once the weapon is fired, what happens next? The domestic use of nuclear weapons is, of all the uses imaginable, least likely to lead to escalation and to regional or global tragedy.

Vulnerability of forces and problems of deterrence

The credibility of second strike forces has two faces. First, they have to be able to survive preemptive attacks. Second, they have to appear to be able to deliver a blow sufficient to deter.

The uneven development of the power of new nuclear states creates occasions that permit strikes and may invite them. Two stages of nuclear development should be distinguished. First, a country may be in an early stage of development and be obviously unable to make nuclear weapons. Second, a country may be in an advanced state of development and whether or not it has some nuclear weapons may not be surely known. All of the present nuclear countries went through both stages, yet until Israel struck Iraq's nuclear facility in June of 1981, no one had launched a preventive strike.

A number of causes combined may account for the reluctance of states to strike in order to prevent adversaries from developing nuclear forces. A preventive strike is most promising during the first stage of nuclear development. A state could strike without fearing that the country it attacked would be able to return a nuclear blow. But would one country strike so hard as to destroy another country's potential for future nuclear development? If it did not, the country struck could resume its nuclear career. If the blow struck is less than devastating, one must be prepared either to repeat it or to occupy and control the country. To do either would be forbiddingly difficult.

In striking Iraq, Israel showed that a preventive strike can be made, something that was not in doubt. Israel's act and its consequences, however, made clear that the likelihood of useful accomplishment is low. Israel's action increased the determination of Arabs to produce nuclear weapons. Israel's strike, far from foreclosing Iraq's nuclear career, gained Iraq support from some other Arab states to pursue it. Despite Prime Minister Menachem Begin's vow to strike as often as need be, the risks in doing so would have risen with each occasion.

A preemptive strike launched against a country that may have a small number of warheads is even less promising than a preventive strike during the first stage. If the country attacked has even a rudimentary nuclear capability, one's own severe punishment becomes possible. Nuclear forces are seldom delicate because no state wants delicate forces, and nuclear forces can easily be made sturdy. Nuclear warheads are fairly small and light; they are easy to hide and to move. Even the Model-T bombs dropped on Hiroshima and Nagasaki were small enough to be carried by a World War II bomber. Early in the nuclear age, people worried about atomic bombs being concealed in packing boxes and placed in the holds of ships to be exploded when a signal was given. Now more than ever, people worry about terrorists stealing nuclear warheads because various states have so many of them. Everybody seems to believe that terrorists are capable of hiding bombs.[13] Why should states be unable to do what terrorist gangs are thought to be capable of?

It was sometimes claimed that a small number of bombs in the hands of minor powers creates greater dangers than additional thousands in the hands of the United States or the Soviet Union. Such statements assume that preemption of a small force is easy. Acting on that assumption, someone may be tempted to strike; fearing this, the state with a small number of weapons may be tempted to use the few weapons it has rather than risk losing them. Such reasoning would confirm the thought that small nuclear forces create extreme dangers. But since protecting small forces by hiding and moving them is quite easy, the dangers evaporate.

Hiding nuclear weapons and being able to deliver them are tasks for which the ingenuity of numerous states is adequate. Means of delivery are neither difficult to devise nor hard to procure. Bombs can be driven in by trucks from neighboring countries. Ports can be torpedoed by small boats lying offshore. A thriving arms trade in ever more sophisticated military equipment provides ready access to what may be wanted, including planes and missiles suited to the delivery of nuclear warheads.

Lesser nuclear states can pursue deterrent strategies effectively. Deterrence requires the ability to inflict unacceptable damage on another country. "Unacceptable damage" to the Soviet Union was variously defined by former Secretary of Defense Robert S. McNamara as requiring the ability to destroy a fifth to a fourth of its population and a half to two-thirds of its industrial capacity. American estimates of what is required for deterrence were absurdly high. To deter, a country need not appear to be able to destroy a fourth or a half of another country, although in some cases that might be easily done. Would Libya try to destroy Israel's nuclear weapons at the risk of two bombs surviving to fall on Tripoli and Benghazi? And what would be left of Israel if Tel Aviv and Haifa were destroyed?

Survivable forces are seen to be readily deployed if one understands that the requirements of deterrence are low. Even the largest states recoil from taking adventurous steps if the price of failure is the possible loss of a city or two. An adversary is deterred if it cannot be sure that its preemptive strike will destroy all of another country's warheads. As Bernard Brodie put it, if a "small nation could threaten the Soviet Union with only a single thermonuclear bomb, which, however, it could and would certainly deliver on Moscow," the Soviet Union would be deterred.[14] I would change that sentence by substituting "might" for "would" and by adding that the threat of a fission bomb or two would also do the trick.

Once a country has a small number of deliverable warheads of uncertain location, it has a second-strike force. Belatedly, some Americans and Russians realized this.[15] McNamara wrote in 1985 that the United States and the Soviet Union could get along with 2,000 warheads between them instead of the 50,000 they may then have had.[16] Talking at the University of California, Berkeley, in the spring of 1992, he dropped the number the United States might need to sixty. Herbert York, speaking at the Lawrence Livermore National Laboratory, which he once directed, guessed that one hundred strategic warheads would be about the right number for us.[17] It does not take much to deter. To have second-strike forces, states do not need large numbers of weapons. Small numbers do quite nicely. Almost one-half of South Korea's population centers on Seoul. North Korea can deter South Korea by leading it to believe that it has a few well-hidden and deliverable weapons. The requirements of second-strike deterrence have been widely and wildly exaggerated. . . .

Stability

When he was Director of the CIA, James Woolsey said that he could "think of no example where the introduction of nuclear weapons into a region has enhanced that region's security or benefited the security interests of the United States."[18] But surely nuclear weapons helped to maintain stability during the Cold War and to preserve peace throughout the instability that came in its wake. Except for interventions by major powers in conflicts that for them are minor, peace has become the privilege of states having nuclear weapons, while wars are fought by those who lack them. Weak states cannot help noticing this. That is why states feeling threatened want their own nuclear weapons and why states that have them find it so hard to halt their spread.

At least some of the rulers of new and prospective nuclear states are thought to be ruthless, reckless, and war-prone. Ruthless, yes; war-prone, seldom; reckless, hardly. They have survived for many years, despite great internal and external dangers. They do not, as many seem to believe, have fixed images of the world and unbending aims within it. Instead they have to adjust constantly to a shifting configuration of forces around them. Our images of leaders of Third World states vary remarkably little, yet their agility is remarkable. Are hardy survivors in the Third World likely to run the greatest of all risks by drawing the wrath of the world down on them through aggressive use of their nuclear weapons?

Aside from the quality of national regimes and the identity of rulers, the behavior of nations is strongly conditioned by the world outside. With conventional weapons, a status-quo country must ask itself how much power it must harness to its policy in order to dissuade an aggressive state from striking. In conventional worlds, countries willing to run high risks are hard to dissuade. The characteristics of governments and the temperaments of leaders have to be carefully weighed. With nuclear weapons, any state will be deterred by another state's second-strike forces. One need not be preoccupied with the qualities of the state that is to be deterred or scrutinize its leaders.

America has long associated democracy with peace and authoritarianism with war, overlooking that weak authoritarian rulers often avoid war for fear of upsetting the balance of internal and external forces on which their power depends. Neither Italy nor Germany was able to persuade Franco's Spain to enter World War II. External pressures affect state behavior with a force that varies with conditions. Of all of the possible external forces, what could affect state behavior more strongly than nuclear weapons? Nobody but an idiot can fail to comprehend their destructive force. How can leaders miscalculate? For a country to strike first without certainty of success most of those who control a nation's nuclear weapons would have to go mad at the same time. Nuclear reality transcends political rhetoric. Did the Soviet Union's big words or our own prattling about nuclear war-fighting ever mean anything? Political, military, and academic hard-liners imagined conditions under which we would or should be willing to use nuclear weapons. None was of relevance. Nuclear weapons dominate strategy. Nothing can be done with them other than to use them for deterrence. The United States and the Soviet Union were both reluctant to accept the fact of deterrence. Weaker states find it easier to substitute deterrence for war-fighting, precisely because they are weak. The thought that a small number of nuclear weapons may tempt or enable weak countries to launch wars of conquest is the product of feverish imaginations.

States do what they can, to paraphrase Thucydides, and they suffer what they must. Nuclear weapons do not increase what states can do offensively; they do greatly increase what they may suffer should their actions prompt retaliation by others. Thus, far from contributing to instability in South Asia, Pakistan's nuclear military capability, along with India's, limits the provocative acts of both countries and provides a sense of security to them. Recalling Pakistan's recent history of military rule and the initiation of war, some have expected the opposite. For a more reasoned view we might listen to two of the participants. When asked recently why nuclear weapons are so popular in Pakistan, Prime Minister Benazir Bhutto answered: "It's our history. A history of three wars with a larger neighbor. India is five times larger than we are. Their military strength is five times larger. In 1971, our country was disintegrated. So the security issue for Pakistan is an issue of survival."[19] From the other side, Shankar Bajpai, former Indian Ambassador to Pakistan, China, and the United States, has said that "Pakistan's quest for a nuclear capability stems from its fear of its larger neighbor, removing that fear should open up immense possibilities"—possibilities for a less worried and more relaxed life.[20] Exactly. . . .

NOTES

1. James R. Schlesinger, "The Strategic Consequences of Nuclear Proliferation," *The Reporter,* 20 October 1956, pp. 35–8.
2. For a brief discussion, see Chapter 3 of Scott D. Sagan and Kenneth N. Waltz, *The Spread of Nuclear Weapons: A Debate* (New York: W. W. Norton, 1995).
3. McGeorge Bundy, William J. Crowe, Jr. and Sidney D. Drell, *Reducing Nuclear Danger* (New York: Council on Foreign Relations, 1994), p. 81.
4. *The Middle East and North Africa, 1994,* 40th ed. (London: Europa Publications, 1993), pp. 363, 810.

5. This section is based on Karen Ruth Adams and Kenneth N. Waltz, "Don't Worry Too Much About North Korean Nuclear Weapons," unpublished paper, April 1994.

6. International Institute for Strategic Studies, *The Military Balance 1994–1995* (London: Brassey's, 1994), pp. 178–181.

7. A.M. Rosenthal, "Always Believe Dictators," *New York Times*, 29 March 1994, p. A15.

8. R.W. Apple, "Facing Up to the Legacy Of An Unresolved War," *New York Times*, 12 June 1994, p. E-3.

9. Bertolt Brecht, *Mother Courage and her Children: a Chronicle of the Thirty Years' War*, trans. Eric Bentley (New York: Grove Press, 1966), p. 76.

10. Scott D. Sagan, "More Will Be Worse," in Sagan and Waltz, *Spread of Nuclear Weapons*, pp. 47–91.

11. C.P. Snow, "Excerpts from Snow's Speech to American Scientists," *New York Times*, December 28, 1960, p. 14.

12. Scott Sagan has managed to find three, not all of which are unambiguous. *The Limits of Safety: Organizations, Accidents and Nuclear Weapons* (Princeton: Princeton University Press, 1993), p. 263.

13. E.g., David M. Rosenbaum, "Nuclear Terror," *International Security* Vol. 1 (Winter 1977), p. 145.

14. Bernard Brodie, *Strategy in the Missile Age* (Princeton: Princeton University Press, 1959), p. 275.

15. Kenneth N. Waltz, "Nuclear Myths and Political Realities," *American Political Science Review*, 84:3 (September 1990).

16. Robert McNamara, "Reducing the Risk of Nuclear War: Is Star Wars the Answer?" *Millennium: Journal of International Studies* 15:2 (Summer 1986), p. 137.

17. Cited in Robert L. Gallucci, "Limiting U.S. Policy Options to Prevent Nuclear Weapons Proliferation: The Relevance of Minimum Deterrence," Center for Technical Studies on Security, Energy and Arms Control, Lawrence Livermore National Laboratory, 28 February 1991.

18. "Proliferation Threats of the 1990's," Hearing before the Committee on Governmental Affairs, U.S. Senate, 103rd Congress, 1st Session, February 24, 1993 (Washington DC: GPO, 1993), p. 134.

19. Claudia Dreyfus, "Benazir Bhutto," *New York Times Magazine*, 15 May 1994, p. 39.

20. Shankar, Bajpai, "Nuclear Exchange," *Far Eastern Economic Review*. 24 June 1993, p. 24.

CHAPTER 11 PREVENTING IRAN FROM ACQUIRING NUCLEAR WEAPONS v. ALLOWING IRAN TO ACQUIRE NUCLEAR WEAPONS

Preventing Iran from Acquiring Nuclear Weapons

Advocate: S. Enders Wimbush

Source: "The End of Deterrence: A Nuclear Iran Will Change Everything," *The Weekly Standard*, 11 January 2007.

Allowing Iran to Acquire Nuclear Weapons

Advocate: Barry Posen

Source: "We Can Live with a Nuclear Iran," *The New York Times*, 27 February 2006.

Iran's potential possession of nuclear weapons has been and is likely to remain an issue of great concern for the international community. This is for two main reasons: first, nuclear powers—and other countries—are unwilling to have the club expanded; second, Iran is perceived to be hostile toward the United States and denies Israel's right to exist.

Nuclear proliferation reduces the ability of the nuclear powers, including the United States, to effectively apply pressure on countries that defy their will. One way to prevent allies from acquiring nuclear weapons is through providing them with assurances of protection through the U.S. nuclear umbrella. For smaller countries that feel threatened, nuclear weapons can work as a deterrent as well as a bargaining chip with the great powers, as exemplified by North Korea's actions.

The international community led by the United States has been opposed to Iran's development of nuclear weapons. Despite Tehran's assertions that it is working on producing nuclear energy solely for peaceful, domestic purposes, the United States and other countries, mainly Israel, are determined to prevent it from continuing its efforts.

IN SUPPORT OF PREVENTING IRAN FROM BECOMING A NUCLEAR POWER

Possession of nuclear arsenal by any country greatly diminishes the ability of other countries to make credible threats, pursue sanctions, or contemplate military action against it. This is one of the main reasons for the nuclear powers' efforts to limit nuclear proliferation, especially in those that are perceived as hostile or undemocratic. With its history of antagonism toward the United States, key location as Iraq's neighbor, and challenger to Israel's right to exist, Iran is a prime example of a country that many states in the international community—led by the United States—have been unwilling to see armed with nuclear weapons.

S. Enders Wimbush argues that the United States must remain resolute in its determination to see Iran give up its nuclear program. Nuclear arms would solidify Iran's position as a military power in the Middle East and trigger nuclear proliferation in the region. In addition, Wimbush points out that a nuclear-armed Iran would be able to deter and diminish the ability of the United States to make credible threats, while allowing Iran to engage in coercive behavior that would enhance its influence.

IN SUPPORT OF ALLOWING IRAN TO BECOME A NUCLEAR POWER

U.S. policymakers have frequently vowed not to allow Iran to acquire nuclear weapons. The public debate in the United States has been dominated by politicians and pundits alike who have argued that the world could not afford a nuclear Iran, as it would make not only the Middle East but also the world as a whole more unstable. There are also those who believe that the world will be able to manage nuclear Iran, just as it has been able to accommodate a number of other countries that possess nuclear weapons.

Looking at the balance of power in the Middle East, Barry Posen argues that Iran's acquisition of nuclear weapons is unlikely to cause a nuclear proliferation in the region. Further, Posen examines the arguments that Iran might give nuclear weapons to terrorists, use them to coerce other states, or engage in aggression. He posits that these threats are either unlikely or manageable because both the United States and Israel have much larger and more effective nuclear arsenals. Accordingly, Iran is not likely to take actions that risk nuclear retaliation.

POINTS **TO PONDER**

1. Do nuclear weapons make states more or less likely to start a war?
2. How would Iran's acquisition of nuclear weapons affect the balance of power in the Middle East?
3. Does Iran, as a sovereign nation, have the right to develop nuclear weapons?

4. What causes Iran to develop nuclear weapons?
5. How can the United States and its allies prevent Iran from acquiring the bomb?
6. If Iran were to have nuclear weapons, would it attack Israel?

S. Enders Wimbush

The End of Deterrence: A Nuclear Iran Will Change Everything

If President Bush is persuaded by the Iraq Study Group to speak directly with Iran, he will be under strong pressure to cut a deal that makes Iran a significant partner in salvaging, at least temporarily, the mess in Iraq. For its quid pro quo in aiding America to come up with a face saving exit strategy, Iran will insist on a free hand to develop its "peaceful" nuclear power. One can almost hear the inevitable claims by those seeking to justify the president's giving ground on this issue. A nuclear Iran can be "managed" or deterred, we will hear; moreover, this is a good trade-off for extricating America from Iraq. President Bush should not be taken in. He must reject even the hint of compromise.

Iran is fast building its position as the Middle East's political and military hegemon, a position that will be largely unchallengeable once it acquires nuclear weapons. A nuclear Iran will change all of the critical strategic dynamics of this volatile region in ways that threaten the interests of virtually everyone else. The outlines of some of these negative trends are already visible, as other actors adjust their strategies to accommodate what increasingly appears to be the emerging reality of an unpredictable, unstable nuclear power. Iran needn't test a device to shift these dangerous dynamics into high gear; that is already happening. By the time Iran tests, the landscape will have changed dramatically because everyone will have seen it coming.

The opportunities nuclear weapons will afford Iran far exceed the prospect of using them to win a military conflict. Nuclear weapons will empower strategies of coercion, intimidation, and denial that go far beyond purely military considerations. Acquiring the bomb as an icon of state power will enhance the legitimacy of Iran's mullahs and make it harder for disgruntled Iranians to oust them. With nuclear weapons, Iran will have gained the ability to deter any direct American threats, as well as the leverage to keep the United States at a distance and to discourage it from helping Iran's regional opponents. Would the United States be in Iraq if Saddam had had a few nuclear weapons and the ability to deliver them on target to much of Europe and all of Israel? Would it even have gone to war in 1991 to liberate Kuwait from Iraqi aggression? Unlikely. Yet Iran is rapidly acquiring just such a capability. If it succeeds, a relatively small nuclear outcast will be able to deter a mature nuclear power. Iran will become a billboard advertising nuclear weapons as the logical asymmetric weapon of choice for nations that wish to confront the United States.

It should surprise no one that quiet discussions have already begun in Saudi Arabia, Egypt, Turkey, and elsewhere in the Middle East about the desirability of developing national nuclear capabilities to blunt Iran's anticipated advantage and to offset the perceived decline in America's protective power. This is just the beginning. We should anticipate that proliferation across Eurasia will be broad and swift, creating nightmarish challenges. The diffusion of nuclear know-how is on the verge of becoming impossible to impede. Advanced computation and simulation techniques will eventually make testing unnecessary for some actors, thereby expanding the possibilities for unwelcome surprises and rapid shifts in the security environment. Leakage of nuclear knowledge and technologies from weak states will become commonplace, and new covert supply networks will emerge to fill the gap left by the neutralization of Pakistani proliferator A. Q. Khan. Non-proliferation treaties, never effective in blocking the ambitions of rogues like Iran and North Korea, will be meaningless. Intentional proliferation to state and non-state actors is virtually certain, as newly capable states seek to empower their friends and sympathizers. Iran, with its well known support of Hezbollah, is a particularly good candidate to proliferate nuclear capabilities beyond the control of any state as a way to extend the coercive reach of its own nuclear politics.

Arsenals will be small, which sounds reassuring, but in fact it heightens the dangers and risk. New players with just a few weapons, including Iran, will be especially dangerous. Cold War deterrence was based on the belief that an initial strike by an attacker could not destroy all an opponent's nuclear weapons, leaving the adversary with the capacity to strike back in a devastating retaliatory blow. Because it is likely to appear easier to destroy them in a single blow, small arsenals will increase the incentive to strike first in a crisis. Small, emerging nuclear forces could also raise the risk of preventive war, as leaders are tempted to attack before enemy arsenals grow bigger and more secure.

Some of the new nuclear actors are less interested in deterrence than in using nuclear weapons to annihilate their enemies. Iran's leadership has spoken of its willingness—in their words—to "martyr" the entire Iranian nation, and it has even expressed the desirability of doing so as a way to accelerate an inevitable, apocalyptic collision between Islam and the West that will result in Islam's final worldwide triumph. Wiping Israel off the map—one of Iran's frequently expressed strategic objectives—even if it results in an Israeli nuclear strike on Iran, may be viewed as an acceptable trade-off. Ideological actors of this kind may be very different from today's nuclear powers who employ nuclear weapons as a deterrent to annihilation. Indeed, some of the new actors may seek to annihilate others and be annihilated, gloriously, in return.

What constitutes deterrence in this world? Proponents of new non-proliferation treaties and many European strategists speak of "managing" a nuclear Iran, as if Iran and the new nuclear actors that will emerge in Iran's wake can be easily deterred by getting them to sign documents and by talking nicely to them. This is a lethal naiveté. We have no idea how to deter ideological actors who may even welcome their own annihilation. We do not know what they hold dear enough to be deterred by the threat of its destruction. Our own nuclear arsenal is robust, but it may have no deterrent effect on a nuclear-armed ideological adversary.

This is the world Iran is dragging us into. Can they be talked out of it? Maybe. But it is getting very late to slow or reverse the momentum propelling us into this nuclear no-man's land. We should be under no illusion that talk alone—"engagement"—is a solution. Nuclear Iran will prompt the emergence of a world in which nuclear deterrence may evaporate, the likelihood of nuclear use will grow, and where deterrence, once broken, cannot be restored.

Barry Posen

We Can Live With a Nuclear Iran

The intense concern about Iran's nuclear energy program reflects the judgment that, should it turn to the production of weapons, an Iran with nuclear arms would gravely endanger the United States and the world. An Iranian nuclear arsenal, policymakers fear, could touch off a regional arms race while emboldening Tehran to undertake aggressive; even reckless, actions.

But these outcomes are not inevitable, nor are they beyond the capacity of the United States and its allies to defuse. Indeed, while it's seldom a positive thing when a new nuclear power emerges, there is reason to believe that we could readily manage a nuclear Iran.

A Middle Eastern arms race is a frightening thought, but it is improbable. If Iran acquires nuclear weapons, among its neighbors, only Israel, Egypt, Saudi Arabia and Turkey could conceivably muster the resources to follow suit.

Israel is already a nuclear power. Iranian weapons might coax the Israelis to go public with their arsenal and to draw up plans for the use of such weapons in the event of an Iranian military threat. And if Israel disclosed its nuclear status, Egypt might find it diplomatically difficult to forswear acquiring nuclear weapons, too. But Cairo depends on foreign assistance, which would make Egypt vulnerable to the enormous international pressure it would most likely face to refrain from joining an arms race:

Saudi Arabia, meanwhile, has the money to acquire nuclear weapons and technology on the black market, but possible suppliers are few and very closely watched. To develop the domestic scientific, engineering and industrial base necessary to build a self-sustaining nuclear program would take Saudi Arabia years. In the interim, the Saudis would need nuclear security guarantees from the United States or Europe, which would in turn apply intense pressure on Riyadh not to develop its own arms.

Finally, Turkey may have the resources to build a nuclear weapon, but as a member of the North Atlantic Treaty Organization, it relied on American nuclear guarantees against the mighty Soviet Union throughout the cold war. There's no obvious reason to presume that American guarantees would seem insufficient relative to Iran.

So it seems that while Iranian nuclear weapons might cause considerable disquiet among Iran's neighbors, the United States and other interested parties have many cards to play to limit regional proliferation. But what about the notion that such weapons will facilitate Iranian aggression?

Iranian nuclear weapons could be put to three dangerous purposes: Iran could give them to terrorists; it could use them to blackmail other states; or it could engage in other kinds of aggressive behavior on the assumption that no one, not even the United States, would accept the risk of trying to invade a nuclear state or to destroy it from the air. The first two threats are improbable and the third is manageable.

Would Iran give nuclear weapons to terrorists? We know that Tehran has given other kinds of weapons to terrorists and aligned itself with terrorist organizations, like Hezbollah in Lebanon. But to threaten, much less carry out, a nuclear attack on a nuclear power is to become a nuclear target.

Anyone who attacks the United States with nuclear weapons will be attacked with many, many more nuclear weapons. Israel almost certainly has the same policy. If a terrorist group used one of Iran's nuclear weapons, Iran would have to worry that the victim would discover the weapon's origin and visit a terrible revenge on Iran. No country is likely to turn the means to its own annihilation over to an uncontrolled entity.

Because many of Iran's neighbors lack nuclear weapons, it's possible that Iran could use a nuclear capacity to blackmail such states into meeting demands—for example, to raise oil prices, cut oil production or withhold cooperation with the United States. But many of Iran's neighbors are allies of the United States, which holds a strategic stake in their autonomy and is unlikely to sit by idly as Iran blackmails, say, Kuwait or Saudi Arabia. It is unlikely that these states would capitulate to a nuclear Iran rather than rely on an American deterrent threat. To give in to Iran once would leave them open to repeated extortion.

Some worry that Iran would be unconvinced by an American deterrent, choosing instead to gamble that the United States would not make good on its commitments to weak Middle Eastern states—but the consequences of losing a gamble against a vastly superior nuclear power like the United States are grave, and they do not require much imagination to grasp.

The final concern is that a nuclear Iran would simply feel less constrained from other kinds of adventurism, including subversion or outright conventional aggression. But the Gulf states can counter Iranian subversion, regardless of Iran's nuclear status, with domestic reforms and by improving their police and intelligence operations—measures these states are, or should be, undertaking in any case.

As for aggression, the fear is that Iran could rely on a diffuse threat of nuclear escalation to deter others from attacking it, even in response to Iranian belligerence. But while it's possible that Iranian leaders would think this way, it's equally possible that they would be more cautious. Tehran could not rule out the possibility that others with more and better nuclear weapons would strike Iran first, should it provoke a crisis or war. Judging from cold war history, if the Iranians so much as appeared to be readying their nuclear forces for use, the United States might consider a pre-emptive nuclear strike. Israel might adopt a similar doctrine in the face of an Iranian nuclear arsenal.

These are not developments to be wished for, but they are risks that a nuclear Iran must take into account. Nor are such calculations all that should counsel caution. Iran's military is large, but its conventional weapons are obsolete. Today the Iranian military could impose considerable costs on an American invasion or occupation force within Iran, but only with vast and extraordinarily expensive improvements could it defeat the American military if it were sent to defend the Gulf states from Iranian aggression.

Each time a new nuclear weapons state emerges, we rightly suspect that the world has grown more dangerous. The weapons are enormously destructive; humans are fallible, organizations can be incompetent and technology often fails us. But as we contemplate the actions, including war, that the United States and its allies might take to forestall a nuclear Iran, we need to coolly assess whether and how such a specter might be deterred and contained.

PART III
INTERNATIONAL POLITICAL ECONOMY

International political economy is a field that studies the intersection of politics and economics in international relations. It examines power and wealth and the ways in which these interact and reinforce one another. In addition to the relationship between economics and politics, central themes in international political economy include the nature and goals of economic activities, and key actors are states, non-state actors, such as multinational corporations (MNCs), and individuals.

Chapter 12 focuses on the concept of energy security, its strategic importance in the post-Cold War era, and strategies for ensuring reliable sources of energy for the foreseeable future. Daniel Yergin argues that the concept of energy security needs to be expanded to cope with the challenges of a globalized world. He points out that current events place energy security at the fore, and it remains a critical part of international relations. Yergin advocates diversification and new technologies, as well as the role of markets and secure infrastructure. Gawdat Bahgat examines the steps the European Union is taking in order to enhance its energy security. He argues that stability and predictability in energy markets are shared goals between producing regions and major consumers. European leaders are trying to diversify the continent's energy sources and strengthen their energy partnerships with Russia, the countries of the Caspian Sea, and the Middle East.

Chapter 13 discusses the benefits and potential harmful effects of free trade. While long a centerpiece of the international economic order and globalization, the debate on free trade has recently gained momentum. Its proponents, such as Gerald O'Driscoll and Sara Cooper, point to the benefits derived from free trade in terms of lifting countries out of poverty. They advocate the extension of free trade agreements so that they are global in scope, and cover sensitive sectors such as agriculture. On the other hand, opponents of free trade, such as Michael Parenti, focus on the erosion of democratic sovereignty, standards, social protections, and the growing poverty of millions in the Global South. Parenti's argument revolves around the loss of powers that were traditionally part of a state's domain to the ever-growing strength of transnational corporations.

Chapter 14 looks at the role of international financial institutions, specifically the International Monetary Fund (IMF). George Monbiot argues that the IMF disproportionately represents the interests of the United States and Western Europe, at the expense of rapidly expanding economies, such as China. The IMF is frequently criticized for not being democratic enough, lacking in transparency and accountability, and interfering deeply into the domestic politics of the loan recipient countries. Frequently, this leads to situations where global financial failures are not addressed, or the international arena is used for purposes that have little to do with addressing market failures. While agreeing with the need to reform the IMF, Kenneth Rogoff argues that the International Monetary Fund has implemented a number of successful programs in countries such as Brazil and Turkey, helping these countries regain financial stability. During the debt crisis in the late 1990s, the IMF helped orchestrate a global response, frequently supplying loans worth billions of dollars.

Chapter 15 explores possible solutions for global poverty, which remains the source of some of the most serious problems related to development, human rights, and even terrorism. The chapter looks at two alternative ways the United States can tackle this problem: by providing foreign aid or by creating conditions for free trade practices. Singham and Hrinak claim that the solution to poverty is free trade and open markets. While aid distorts markets in certain sectors, further economic liberalization with greater pro-competitive regulation within the developing countries is the key to economic growth. Jeffrey Sachs admits that there are significant problems with the impact of foreign aid, but maintains that there are areas—such as medical care and humanitarian aid—where foreign aid can make the difference between life and death for millions of people in the Global South.

CHAPTER 12

THE U.S. APPROACH TO ENERGY SECURITY *v.* THE EUROPEAN APPROACH TO ENERGY SECURITY

Comprehensive Energy Security in a Globalized World

Advocate: Daniel Yergin

Source: Committee on Foreign Affairs, U.S. House of Representatives, Hearing on "Foreign Policy and National Security Implications of Oil Dependence," March 22, 2007. Testimony by Daniel Yergin, Chairman, Cambridge Energy Research Associates, "The Fundamentals of Energy Security," excerpt.

Energy Security through Diversification of Energy Resources

Advocate: Gawdat Bahgat

Source: "Europe's Energy Security: Challenges and Opportunities," *International Affairs*, vol. 82, no. 5 (2006), pp. 961–975, excerpt.

Although a relatively new concept in international relations, energy security is a priority for almost all states. Energy security is the ability of countries to have access to sources of energy that will allow them uninterrupted economic growth. The issue has become important as a result of the rising prices of energy commodities and the related instability in the major energy-producing states.

Oil and natural gas are some of the most valuable natural resources and export commodities a country can have due to the finite nature of their reserves and the ever-growing demand. Vitally important for the economies as well as the national security of states, oil has been the most coveted of resources, even causing the outbreak of wars. The growing instability of the Middle East—one of the largest oil-producing regions in the world—has led to fears of disruption of the global oil supply. At the same time, growing energy demand in China, India, and other industrializing countries has put additional pressures on securing supply.

U.S. ENERGY SECURITY

The public and policy debate in the United States has centered around the issues of independence from foreign oil, diversification of sources, conservation, and investment in new technologies. Indeed, many have focused on the link between energy security and U.S. foreign policy, frequently arguing that energy independence can extricate the United States from turbulent regions of the world, such as the Middle East.

In contrast, Daniel Yergin focuses on the key principles of energy security for the United States: diversification, resilience, integration, and information. He argues that in order to meet future challenges, the United States has to diversify its sources of energy, continue with conservation, and invest in new research and technology development. Further, he emphasizes the need to integrate countries such as China and India into the global energy markets. In addition, securing the supply of oil and gas by protecting its infrastructure from terrorism or natural disasters, such as Hurricane Katrina, is a priority. Critically, the energy security of the United States is linked to stable, integrated energy markets, rather than to energy independence.

EUROPEAN ENERGY SECURITY

In 2009, the European continent was reminded of its dependence on foreign oil when Russia briefly discontinued its supply to Ukraine over a price disagreement. The incident also underlined the leverage that oil-producing countries can have in the conduct of foreign policy, and caused European states to work together toward a common energy policy.

Gawdat Bahgat examines Europe's growing dependence on oil and natural gas and the steps that have been taken to ensure the continent's energy security. He underlines the initiatives of the European Commission and the proposed solutions. His policy prescriptions for Europe's energy security mirror those of Daniel Yergin with respect to the obsolescence of self-sufficiency, the emphasis on global integrated markets, and importance of diversification of supply. He also advocates a role for governments and the European Union alike, particularly with respect to the conduct of energy policy toward Russia, the Caspian region, and the Middle East.

POINTS **TO PONDER**

1. Why are energy resources such valuable commodities?
2. Why is energy independence not the answer to energy security?
3. How vulnerable are European states to Russia's use of energy as a foreign policy instrument?
4. How vulnerable is the United States to Middle Eastern oil?
5. Should the United States seek to develop alternative energy sources?

Daniel Yergin

The Fundamentals of Energy Security

The Energy Security System

The current energy security system was created in response to the 1973 Arab oil embargo to ensure coordination among the industrialized countries in the event of a disruption in supply, encourage collaboration on energy policies, avoid bruising scrambles for supplies, and deter any future use of an "oil weapon" by exporters. Its key elements are the Paris-based International Energy Agency (IEA), whose members are the industrialized countries; strategic stockpiles of oil, including the U.S. Strategic Petroleum Reserve; continued monitoring and analysis of energy markets and policies; and energy conservation and coordinated emergency sharing of supplies in the event of a disruption. The emergency system was set up to offset major disruptions that threatened the global economy and stability. It was not established to manage prices and the commodity cycle.

Since the system's inception in the 1970s, a coordinated emergency drawdown of strategic stockpiles has occurred only twice: on the eve of the Gulf War in 1991 and in the autumn of 2005 after Hurricane Katrina. . . . We can be sure that the creators of the IEA emergency sharing system in the 1970s never for a moment considered that it might have to be activated to blunt the effects of a disruption in the United States—as happened in the immediate aftermath of the hurricanes.

Principles of Energy Security

Several principles underpin energy security. The first is what Winston Churchill urged more than 90 years ago: diversification of supply. On the eve of the First World War, Churchill—then the First Lord of the Admiralty—made the historic decision to shift the propulsion of the Royal Navy from coal to oil. "Safety and certainty in oil," he said, "lie in variety and variety alone."[1] Multiplying one's supply sources reduces the impact of a disruption in supply from one source by providing alternatives, serving the interests of both consumers and producers, for whom stable markets are a prime concern. But diversification is not enough. A second principle is resilience, a "security margin" in the energy supply system that provides a buffer against shocks and facilitates recovery after disruptions. Resilience can come from many factors, including sufficient spare production capacity, strategic reserves, backup supplies of equipment, adequate storage capacity along the supply chain, and the stockpiling of critical parts for electric power production and distribution, as well as carefully conceived plans for responding to disruptions that may affect large regions.

Hence the third principle: recognizing the reality of integration. There is only one oil market, a complex and worldwide system that moves and consumes about 86 million barrels of oil every day. For all consumers, security resides in the stability of this market. Secession is not an option.

A fourth principle is the importance of information. High-quality information underpins well-functioning markets. On an international level, the International Energy Agency has led the way in improving the flow of information about world markets and energy prospects. That work is being complemented by the new International Energy Forum, which will seek to integrate information from producers and consumers. . . .

As important as these principles are, recent years have highlighted the need to expand the concept of energy security in two critical dimensions: (1) the recognition of the globalization of the energy security system, which can be achieved especially by engaging China and India, and (2) the acknowledgment of the fact that the entire energy supply chain needs to be protected.

Bringing China and India "In"

Despite all the attention being paid to China's efforts to secure international petroleum reserves, for example, the entire amount that China currently produces per day outside of its own borders is equivalent to just a fraction of the daily production of one of the supermajor oil companies. If there were a serious controversy between the United States and China involving oil or gas, it would likely arise not because of a competition for the resources themselves, but rather because they had become part of larger foreign policy issues (such as a clash over a specific regime or over how to respond to Iran's nuclear program). Indeed, from the viewpoint of consumers in North America, Europe, and Japan, Chinese and Indian investment in the development of new energy supplies around the world is not a threat but something to be encouraged, because it means there will be more energy available for everyone in the years ahead as India's and China's demand grows.

It would be wiser—and indeed it is urgent—to engage these two giants in the global network of trade and investment rather than see them tilt toward a mercantilist, state-to-state approach. But, for that to happen, both countries need to be encouraged to see that their interests can be protected in global markets and that they will not be disadvantaged compared to other consumers. Engaging India and China will require understanding what energy security means for them. Both countries have already moved from self-sufficiency to integration into the world economy, which means they will grow increasingly dependent on global markets even as they are under tremendous pressure to deliver economic growth for their huge populations, which cope with energy shortages and blackouts on a daily basis. Thus, the primary concern for both China and India is to ensure that they have sufficient energy to support economic growth and prevent debilitating energy shortfalls that could trigger social and political turbulence. And so India and China, and other key countries such as Brazil, should be brought into coordination with the existing IEA energy security system to assure them that their interests will be protected in the event of turbulence and to ensure that the system works more effectively.

A strong continuing high-level dialogue with China on energy-related issues is a very high priority to allay suspicion and misunderstanding and to identify common interests and objectives, including on new technologies. There is much talk of a clash between the United States and China over oil. But there is nothing inevitable about it. Commercial competition need not turn into national rivalry. A fundamental reason for establishing the International Energy Agency in the 1970s was to modulate that mad scramble to preempt barrels. This contest threatened not only to rip apart the Western alliance, but also sent oil prices—after the Iranian Revolution—to what is still their highest level ever. The innovations of the 1970s transformed the scramble into more durable cooperation. That same kind of approach is needed now with the emergence of these two huge (and anxious) consumers, China and India, in the world market.

Securing Infrastructure and the Supply Chain

The current model of energy security, which was born of the 1973 crisis, focuses primarily on how to handle any disruption of oil supplies from producing countries. Today, the concept of energy security needs to be expanded to include the protection of the entire energy supply chain and infrastructure—an awesome task. In the United States alone, there are more than 150 refineries, 4,000 offshore platforms, 160,000 miles of oil pipelines, facilities to handle 15 million barrels of oil a day of imports and exports, 10,400 power plants, 160,000 miles of high-voltage electric power transmission lines and millions of miles of electric power distribution wires, 410 underground gas storage fields, and 1.4 million miles of natural gas pipelines. None of the world's complex, integrated supply chains were built with security, defined in this broad way, in mind. Hurricanes Katrina and Rita brought a new perspective to the security question by demonstrating how fundamental the electric grid is to everything else. After the storms, the Gulf Coast refineries and the big U.S. pipelines were unable to operate—not just because some were damaged, but also because they could not get electric power.

Energy interdependence and the growing scale of energy trade require continuing collaboration among both producers and consumers to ensure the security of the entire supply chain. Long-distance, cross-border pipelines are becoming an ever-larger fixture in the global energy trade. There are also many chokepoints along the transportation routes of seaborne oil and, in many cases, LNG that create particular vulnerabilities: the Strait of Hormuz, which lies at the entrance to the Persian Gulf; the Suez Canal, which connects the Red Sea and the Mediterranean; the Bab el Mandeb strait, which provides entrance to the Red Sea; the Bosporus strait, which is a major export channel for Russian and Caspian oil; and the Strait of Malacca, through which passes 80 percent of Japan's and South Korea's oil and about half of China's.

The challenge of energy security will grow more urgent in the years ahead, because the scale of the global trade in energy will grow substantially as world markets become more integrated. Currently, every day some 40 million barrels of oil cross oceans on tankers; by 2020, that number could jump to 67 million. The amount of natural gas crossing oceans as LNG could triple to 460 million tons by 2020. The United States will be an important part of that market. Assuring the security of global energy markets will require coordination on both an international and a national basis among companies and governments, including energy, environmental, military, law enforcement, and intelligence agencies. But in the United States, as in other countries, the lines of responsibility—and the sources of funding—for protecting critical infrastructures, such as energy, are far from clear. The private sector, the federal government, and state and local agencies need to take steps to better coordinate their activities. Maintaining the commitment to do so during periods of low or moderate prices will require discipline as well as vigilance. Both the public and private sectors need to invest in building a higher degree of security into the energy system—meaning that energy security will become part of both the price of energy and the cost of homeland security.

The Important Role of Markets

Let me address another element of energy security: markets *themselves* need to be recognized as a source of security. The energy security system was created when energy prices were regulated in the United States, energy trading was only just beginning, and futures markets were several years away. Today, large, flexible, and well-functioning energy markets provide security by absorbing shocks and allowing supply and demand to respond more quickly and with greater ingenuity than a controlled system could. Thus, governments do well to resist the temptation to respond to short-term political pressure and micromanage markets. Intervention and controls, however well meaning, can backfire, slowing and even preventing the movement of supplies to respond to disruptions. At least in the United States, any price spike or disruption evokes the images of the infamous gas lines of the 1970s. Yet those lines were to a considerable degree self-inflicted—the consequence of price controls and a heavy-handed allocation system that sent gasoline where it was not needed and denied its being sent where it was.

Contrast that to what happened immediately after Hurricane Katrina. A major disruption to the U.S. oil supply was compounded by reports of price gouging and of stations running out of gasoline, which together could have created new gas lines in the Southeast and along the East Coast. Yet the markets were back in balance much sooner, and prices came down more quickly, than had generally been expected. . . .

This experience highlights the need to incorporate regulatory and environmental flexibility—and a clear understanding of the impediments to adjustment—into the energy security machinery in order to cope as effectively as possible with disruptions and emergencies. Markets can more efficiently and effectively—and more quickly—resolve shortfalls and disruptions than controls can.

Efficiency, Investment, and New Technologies

The U.S. government and the private sector should also make a renewed commitment to energy efficiency and conservation. For the first time in many years, energy efficiency is once again a high priority. Although often underrated, the impact of conservation on the economy has been enormous over the past several decades. Over the past 30 years, the United States has doubled its energy efficiency—defined as the amount of energy needed to produce a unit of gross domestic product. We could aim to double efficiency once again.

The basic point remains: conservation has worked. Current and future advances in technology could permit very large additional gains, which would be highly beneficial not only for advanced economies such as that of the United States, but also for the economies of countries such as India and China. In fact, China has recently made conservation a priority. The potential growth highlighted earlier underlines the importance of moving on efficiency. This also is one of the most important things to do for climate change.

Finally, the investment climate itself must become a key concern in energy security and should be on the international energy agenda. There needs to be a continuous flow of investment and technology in order for new resources to be developed. Costs for energy development have been going up dramatically in recent years because of a shortage of people and equipment.

Our new IHS/CERA Upstream Capital Cost Index indicates that the cost for developing new oil and gas projects increased more than 50 percent over the last two years.[2] It is now estimated that as much as $20 trillion will be required for new energy development over the next 25 years. These capital flows will not materialize without reasonable and stable investment frameworks, timely decision-making by governments, and open markets. How to facilitate energy investment should be one of the questions for international discussions.

Inevitably, there will be shocks to energy markets in the future. Some of the possible causes may be foreseeable, such as coordinated attacks by terrorists, disruptions in the Middle East and Africa, or turmoil in Latin America. Other possible causes, however, may come as a surprise. The offshore oil industry has long built facilities to withstand a "hundred-year storm," but nobody anticipated that two such devastating storms would strike the energy complex in the Gulf of Mexico within a matter of weeks, requiring the activation of the IEA emergency sharing system to relieve a disruption in the United States.

Diversification will remain the fundamental starting principle of energy security for both oil and gas. Today, however, it will likely also require developing a new generation of nuclear power and "clean coal" technologies and encouraging a growing role for a variety of renewable energy sources as they become more competitive. It will also require investing in new technologies, ranging from near-term ones, such as the conversion of natural gas into a liquid fuel, to ones that are still in the lab, such as the biological engineering of energy supplies. Investment in technology all along the energy spectrum is surging today, and this will have a positive effect not only on the future energy picture but also on the environment and in meeting climate change objectives.

NOTES

1. Daniel Yergin, *The Prize: the Epic Quest for Oil, Money, and Power* (Simon and Schuster, 1991), p. 160.
2. *CERA Capital Costs Analysis Forum: A White Paper.*

Gawdat Bahgat

Europe's Energy Security: Challenges and Opportunities

Several geopolitical and economic developments in the first decade of the twenty-first century have heightened Europe's sense of vulnerability in respect of its energy supplies. On the supply side of the energy equation, the continuous fighting and rising ethnic and sectarian tension in Iraq, and the diplomatic confrontation over Iran's nuclear programme, have intensified concern over the stability of supplies from the Persian Gulf. On the demand side, China's and India's skyrocketing energy consumption and their efforts to secure supplies have intensified global competition over scarce hydrocarbon resources. These changes in the landscape of the global energy market, in conjunction with diminishing refinery capacity, shrinking spare capacity and a low level of investment, have driven oil and natural gas prices higher. Currently, the European Union's oil bill (for imported and domestically produced oil) stands at around €250 billion a year, or roughly 2.3 per cent of gross domestic product (GDP).[1] These soaring prices have exerted tremendous pressure on European economies and underscored the need for a common European energy policy.

The dispute between Russia and Ukraine over natural gas prices in January 2006 further highlighted the risks of dependence on a few energy suppliers. In early 2005 the Russian state monopoly, Gazprom, announced plans to start applying 'market rules' in its gas dealings with former Soviet republics. That meant that buyers would lose the heavily subsidized prices they had previously enjoyed and instead would have to pay similar prices to those charged to west European customers. It also meant that all bills would have to be settled in cash instead of through barter agreements. This new policy was largely seen as a punishment for the Ukrainian President Viktor Yushchenko, who had led the so-called Orange Revolution, defeated the Kremlin's favoured candidate in Ukraine's presidential election and pursued a pro-western foreign policy. In implementing it, Gazprom raised the price of gas sold to Ukraine from about $50 per 1,000 cubic metres in 2005 to approximately $230 per 1,000 cubic metres in 2006.

. . . Although there was no slowdown in the stream of Russian exports to Europe, the dispute raised doubts about Russia's reliability as a source of energy to Europe. Many European officials viewed the Russian action as an attempt to use gas as a political weapon to blackmail a neighbouring consumer state that depends heavily on Russian supplies of natural gas. . . .

Background and structure

On 8 March 2006 the European Commission issued a new Green Paper entitled *A European strategy for sustainable, competitive and secure energy*. At the Green Paper's launch, José Manuel Barroso, the President of the European Commission, highlighted the need for a common strategy for energy: 'We are in a new energy century. Demand is rising and Europe's reserves are declining. There is underinvestment and our climate is changing.[2] The Green Paper puts forward suggestions and options that could form the basis for the shape and direction of the EU's future energy policy. This important document was intensely debated by European heads of state and government in their spring summit in March and by various European institutions in the following months.

The Green Paper identifies six areas as priorities:

- completing the internal European electricity and gas markets;
- encouraging solidarity among member states;
- establishing a more sustainable, efficient and diverse energy mix;
- supporting an integrated approach to tackling climate change;
- encouraging a strategic energy technology plan;
- creating a coherent external energy policy.

Taking these proposed priority areas into consideration, it is important to identify the major characteristics of the EU's energy outlook and the projected changes.

Energy consumption in the EU has been growing more slowly than GDP. Energy intensity gives an indication of the effectiveness with which energy is being used to produce added value. It is defined as the ratio of gross consumption of energy to GDP. Thus a fall in energy intensity indicates an improvement in energy efficiency. The volatility of oil markets and prices in the mid-1970s led members of the then European Community to rethink their energy consumption patterns. As a result, measures were adopted to improve energy efficiency and break the link between growth in GDP and growth in energy demand. This was reflected in a structural shift in most European economies towards services and less energy-intensive industrial production. This commitment to improving energy intensity weakened in the 1990s, when oil prices were stable and relatively low, but has gained renewed force with the rising prices of the new century.

Europe's energy mix is strongly dominated by fossil fuels. In 2005 oil constituted approximately 37 per cent of the EU's energy consumption, natural gas 24 per cent, solid fuels 18 per cent[3] nuclear power 15 per cent and renewables 6 percent.[4] This heavy European dependence on fossil fuels reflects the pattern of global usage, which is unlikely to alter substantially. . . .

About half of the energy consumed in the EU is produced domestically, while the other half is imported. The underlying reason for this large and growing dependence on foreign supplies is Europe's limited indigenous energy production capacity. . . .

Under pressure from this combination of limited indigenous hydrocarbon resources and rising demand, the EU's dependence on foreign supplies is projected to grow from about 50 per cent in 2005 to approximately two-thirds in 2030, by which time the EU is expected to import 94 per cent of its oil needs, 84 per cent of natural gas consumption and 59 per cent of solid fuel used. These projections point to an undeniable fact: that EU energy security is fundamentally linked to the security of supply from the global fossil fuel markets.

Recognizing this inevitable and growing interdependence between the EU and major hydrocarbon-producing regions, the European Commission underscores specific measures that should be taken to improve the security of supply. These include:

- diversifying the EU's energy mix, with greater use of competitive indigenous and renewable energy, and diversifying sources and routes of supply of imported energy;
- creating the necessary framework to stimulate adequate investment to meet growing energy demand;
- better equipping the EU to cope with emergencies;
- improving the conditions for European companies seeking access to global resources;
- and ensuring that citizens and businesses have access to energy.[5]

To sum up, the EU's energy mix is dominated by fossil fuels and Europe is increasingly dependent on foreign supplies to meet growing demand. . . .

Energy security

Modern society has grown more dependent on energy in almost all human activities. Different forms of energy are essential in the residential, industrial and transportation sectors. Energy is also crucial in carrying out military operations. Indeed, the attempt to control oil resources was a major reason for the Second World War. In short, our increasing reliance on energy has heightened the importance of energy security. The first oil shock in the aftermath of the 1973 Arab–Israeli war put energy security, and more specifically security of supply, at the heart of the energy policy agenda of most industrialized nations.[6] Since then, policy-makers and analysts have sought to define the concept of 'energy security' and its implications.

. . . In short, energy security refers to sustainable and reliable supplies at reasonable prices. In this article, the concept of energy security is further refined by the following factors:

- Any definition of energy security should distinguish between geological and geopolitical threats. Most energy analysts agree that there are enough physical reserves to meet global demand for energy. The exploration, development and transportation of these resources, however, pose significant financial and political challenges that need to be addressed.

- In respect of price, security involves achieving a state where the risk of rapid and severe fluctuation of prices is reduced or eliminated. Oil prices vary from country to country depending on several factors, including the quality of crude product, destination, taxes, exchange rates and refining capacity, among others. It is important to emphasize that sustained high prices hurt both consuming and producing countries in the long term. True, in the short term higher prices mean higher profits for oil producers; but high oil prices tend to slow down global economic prosperity, encourage conservation and prompt switching to other fuels. In other words, from the producers' perspective supporting high prices would be like killing the goose that lays the golden eggs. Thus, consumers and producers share a common interest in ensuring stable supplies at 'reasonable' prices.

- Energy security depends on sufficient levels of investment in resource development, generation capacity and infrastructure to meet demand as it grows. The availability of funds for such investment is strongly linked to prices, but the flow of private and foreign investment depends to a great extent on political stability in the producing country.

- Spare capacity has traditionally played a significant role in temporary severe interruptions of oil supplies. A few OPEC producers, particularly Saudi Arabia, have deliberately maintained spare capacity to ensure stability in global markets. Global economic growth, particularly in Pacific Asia, has subjected the oil market to an unexpected demand shock that has practically eliminated spare capacity, taking the international oil industry into a period of fundamental change. In the mid-2000s spare capacity is at one of its lowest recorded levels.

- Security of supplies can be enhanced by an overall diversification of supply. To put this point differently, the development of several producing regions leads to more stability in international oil markets. Thus, increasing supplies from Russia, the Caspian Sea, West Africa and other regions would reduce the vulnerability associated with overdependence on any one single region. (The dispute between Russia and Ukraine in January 2006, referred to above, is a case in point.)

- From the producers' perspective, demand security also merits attention. Major resource-holders have voiced their concern regarding long-term security of demand for their oil.[7] This concern is based on two grounds: first, the cyclical growth patterns and policies that damp the demand for oil and favour other sources of energy; second, the failure of OPEC states to diversify their economies and their consequent continued heavy dependence on oil revenues. Thus they are anxious to secure markets for their major source of income. Rather than focusing solely on the dependence of consumers on producers, then, it is more instructive to talk about mutual dependence and to recognize that the degree of interdependence between energy producers and consumers will further increase in the future.[8]

To sum up, the globalization of the oil market suggests that rhetoric regarding the goal of self-sufficiency in energy is obsolete. Energy security is an international issue that necessarily entails growing interdependence between major producers and consumers. No country or region can alone achieve a state of energy security. Diversification of both energy mix and energy sources is the main route to energy security. Major industrialized countries should seek to enhance the reliability of those producing nations on which they are bound to depend for many years to come. . . .

Conclusion and policy implications

The analysis of Europe's efforts to ensure its energy security by diversifying both energy mix and energy sources suggests four conclusions.

- First, the potential for energy self-sufficiency within the EU is limited. Simply stated, Europe does not have the necessary energy resources to sustain its well-developed economies and high standard of living. For the foreseeable future Europe will continue to be dependent on foreign supplies.
- Second, despite efforts by the EU and individual member states to liberalize the energy sector, governments still have an important role to play. An active EU policy in Russia, the Caspian Sea, Iran and the rest of the Middle East opens the door for European oil companies to do business in these countries. European governments and various EU institutions have initiated dialogues with producing regions. These political initiatives have enhanced Europe's energy security.
- Third, diversification of sources has certainly enhanced Europe's energy security. Strong and growing relations with Russia and the Caspian Sea are important, but these two regions will not replace the Middle East. Given its geological advantages, the Middle East will always be a critical player in energy policy.
- Fourth, oil and, to a lesser extent, natural gas markets are global and well integrated. The source of one barrel of oil matters less than its availability. No country or region can alone protect itself from oil price swings or from the consequences of interruptions in oil production, wherever they occur.[9] Greater predictability in energy markets is increasingly seen as a goal shared by producers and consumers alike. It can facilitate global economic prosperity and political stability. It is a win-win opportunity.

. . . An effective and coherent energy policy would enable the EU to maintain its prominent position on the international scene. This energy policy must be based on a recognition that interdependence is the corner-stone of the energy landscape of the twenty-first century. Diplomatic and economic dialogues, not military confrontations, are likely to strengthen partnerships with producing regions and enhance Europe's energy security.

NOTES

1. Commission of the European Communities, 'Commission staff working document: annex to the Green Paper', http://europa.eu.int/comm/energy/index_en.html, accessed 8 March 2006.
2. Anthony Browne, 'Fearful EU aims to take energy policy from governments', *The Times*, www.thetimes.co.uk, accessed 9 March 2006.
3. Solid fuels include coal, lignite and peat.
4. Commission of the European Communities, 'Commission staff working document: annex to the Green Paper'.
5. Commission of the European Communities, *Green Paper: a European strategy for sustainable, competitive and secure energy*, http://europa.eu.int/comm/energy/index_en.html, accessed 8 March 2006.
6. Chantale LaCasse and André Plourde, 'On the renewal of concern for the security of oil supply', *Energy Journal* 16: 2, April 1995, pp. 1–23 at p. 1.
7. Adrian Lajous, 'Production management, security of demand and market stability', *Middle East Economic Survey* 47: 39, 27 Sept. 2004, www.mees.com, accessed 27 Sept. 2004.
8. For a thorough analysis of this mutual dependence of producers and consumers, see John Mitchell, 'Producer–consumer dialogue: what can energy ministers say to one another?', www.chathamhouse.org.uk, Nov. 2005, accessed 20 Jan. 2006.
9. John Gault, 'Energy as a security challenge for the EU', *Middle East Economic Survey* 47: 46, 15 Nov. 2004, on line at www.mees.com, accessed 15 Nov. 2004.

CHAPTER 13 THE BENEFITS OF FREE TRADE *v.* THE RISKS OF FREE TRADE

Free Trade and the Need for a Global Free Trade Agreement

Advocates: Gerald P. O'Driscoll Jr. and Sara F. Cooper

Source: "International Trade and Global Stability," *Economic Affairs*, vol. 25, no. 2 (June 2005), pp. 37–43, excerpt.

Free Trade and Its Risks

Advocate: Michael Parenti

Source: "Globalization and Democracy: Some Basics," CommonDreams.org. May 25, 2007, excerpt.

Free trade has been one of the hallmarks of the global economic order in the post-World War II era. The principles of open markets and free trade have been enshrined in the main international economic and financial institutions, and adherence to these principles is often required for economic assistance. The number of free trade agreements (FTAs) in the world has grown considerably, ranging in scope from bilateral, regional, or global.

Countries want to enter free trade agreements because of the benefits they bring to their economies. While it has been argued that all countries gain from free trade, it is the industrialized countries of the Global North that have reaped most of the benefits. Proponents of free trade continue to push for more agreements, even on a global scale. Many countries from the Global South, however, are beginning to look at agreements that are bilateral or regional in nature, which would allow them to escape the dominance of economic giants such as the United States.

Not all sectors of the economy, however, are subject to free trade. Agriculture is one such sector. In addition to imposing various non-tariff restrictions, most industrialized countries heavily subsidize their agricultural sectors, thus skewing trade to the detriment of the farmers in less developed countries. Hence, while some countries continue to press for further liberalization of trade in the agricultural sector, other countries that have experienced its devastating effects, mostly in the Global South, emphasize instead fair trade.

IN FAVOR OF GLOBAL FREE TRADE AREA

The benefits of free trade are considerable. They involve cheaper prices for the consumer, economic innovation and opportunities, and the promotion of values that are dear to the West: commitment to free trade, open investments, minimal market regulation and strong property rights. Hence, proponents of free trade, such as O'Driscoll and Cooper, forcefully maintain that both the United States and the European Union should advance free trade by any means possible: unilaterally, bilaterally, or multilaterally.

The World Trade Organization (WTO) is charged with enforcing the principle of free trade as well as arbitrating disputes between its members. In recent years, we have also seen the growth of bilateral and regional free trade and integration mechanisms. Critics claim that bilateral and regional agreements undermine the work of the WTO, but other supporters of free trade openly support this development.

Advocates propose an even more ambitious scheme of creating a global free trade area in the form of a Global Free Trade Association (GFTA). O'Driscoll and Cooper argue that such an association would include countries that have a proven record of commitment to free trade. Such a voluntary grouping of countries from around the globe would not compete with the WTO; instead, it would create more trade dynamism by providing incentives for those countries that would like to join, but do not qualify.

AGAINST FREE TRADE

The popularity of free trade as a solution to the problem of development has reached a new height since the 1990s. A fundamental aspect of the neoliberal international economic order, free trade has been seen by most countries around the world as a way to achieve prosperity. In recent years, however, the detractors of free trade have become more vocal, bringing attention to its negative aspects, including the growing gap between the countries of the Global North and South, and the perceived erosion of democratic sovereignty.

The central argument in Michael Parenti's article focuses on the democratic deficit in free trade. Parenti argues that free trade agreements and international institutions that facilitate their enforcement make decisions and laws that supersede those promulgated by national lawmakers. Further, Parenti argues, the mantra of free trade has helped enhance the role of transnational corporations vis-à-vis the state, thereby weakening environmental and labor standards, social protections, even the right to free speech. Free trade has also brought millions of people around the world below the poverty line. Parenti argues that free trade benefits the rich and harms the poor.

POINTS **TO PONDER**

1. Should the United States pursue free trade by all means possible?
2. Why are some sectors of the economy in the industrialized world, such as agriculture, protected from free trade?

3. Why do Latin American countries increasingly turn toward subregional organizations?

4. How do free trade agreements and regional organizations serve to maintain U.S. hegemony?

Gerald P. O'Driscoll, Jr. and Sara F. Cooper

International Trade and Global Stability[1]

While the Second World War was still being waged, the United States, Great Britain and their allies began to plan for the postwar global economy. They began crafting a set of international economic organisations that formed the institutional framework for the postwar economy. Their efforts culminated in the Bretton Woods conference of 1944. Initial efforts to create an International Trade Organization faltered at Bretton Woods. The efforts continued, however, culminating in the founding of the General Agreement on Tariffs and Trade (GATT) in 1947.[2]

The transatlantic allies intended to create a stable international economic order that would avoid the economic catastrophe of the interwar period, which included the Great Depression, a collapse in global capital flows, and a breakdown in the global trading system.[3] The advancement of global trade through GATT was seen as critical to establishing that economic order. The GATT and its successor, the World Trade Organization (WTO), would form the framework for multilateral trade negotiations.

A new global trading order did emerge and the postwar period, despite the Cold War and many other problems, was one of prosperity and growth. . . .

To ensure that continued progress, the transatlantic allies must be steadfast in their commitment to advancing global trade. We examine the prospects for further trade liberalisation, and analyse the chief impediments to achieving that goal.

Gerald P. O'Driscoll Jr., is Senior Fellow at the Cato Institute in Washington, DC. Sara F. Cooper is Research Fellow at the American Institute for Economic Research in Great Barrington, Massachusetts. When this paper was presented in 2003, Mrs. Sara Cooper was known as Sara Fitzgerald.

The benefits of free trade

. . . Since Adam Smith, economists have focused on the benefits of free trade for consumers. Policy-makers must grapple, however, with the sometimes conflicting interests of domestic producers. The political economy of trade policy must take account of producer benefits and losses from opening markets. . . .

The benefits of trade accrue to individuals both as lower prices for the goods they purchase, and higher incomes for those provided with more opportunities to seek higher-valued uses for their human and non-human capital. Open markets foster an economic dynamism as entrepreneurial individuals create new opportunities afforded by access to global markets. The International Monetary Fund (2002) cites empirical support for the proposition that the dynamic gains from trade greatly exceed the static gains (p. 86). We elaborate on the dynamic benefits of trade later in this article.

The trade debate all too often gets bogged down in 'job counting', i.e. does trade create or destroy jobs? In the long run, of course, trade neither creates nor destroys jobs: it raises incomes. Competitive labour markets ensure that everyone wanting to work at market wage rates can do so.[4] There are many factors determining labour force participation in a population, but tariff rates are not among them.

Trade liberalisation leads to the expansion of jobs in some sectors and contraction in others. All other things being equal, aggregate unemployment remains the same. As individuals in liberalising countries produce according to their comparative advantage, the resulting more efficient utilisation of resources leads to higher real incomes.

Free trade is the ideal. In trade agreements, a net increase in the freedom to trade is the attainable goal. What can we say about the benefits of recent trade agreements?

Benefits from the Uruguay Round

The achievements of the Uruguay Round make the case for future agreements at the bilateral, regional and multilateral levels. The benefits of expanded trade through the Uruguay Round have been especially important in developing countries. In its September 2002 *World Economic Outlook*, the IMF surveyed the literature on trade and growth. They found that 'many cross-country econometric studies have concluded that trade openness is a significant explanatory variable for the level or the growth rate of real GDP per capita'. . . .

Clearly, progress in the WTO negotiations has moved at a tortoise's pace. Additionally, the final deadline for the negotiations has been postponed and a new deadline has not been set. Without a deadline, there is little, if any, momentum to achieve a final agreement in the near future. The protectionist and interventionist policies of developed countries hinder agreement in the Doha Round. We examine this critical issue in the next section.

Agriculture

The United States is the world's largest agricultural exporter, exporting the crops from one out of every three acres. Agriculture is one of the few sectors in the US economy that consistently has a trade surplus. While the American farm lobby values the benefits of market access for its own goods, it continues to seek tariff and non-tariff barriers to hinder imports. This tale of hypocrisy is repeated around the world.

Patrick Messerlin (2003) of the World Bank notes, 'WTO negotiations in agriculture have embarked on a wild roller coaster'. Doha pledged to be a round for developing countries; yet, developed countries refuse to relinquish their tariffs and subsidies. Such a position was evidenced by European and Japanese reactions to the first draft proposal by the WTO's then agricultural chair, Stuart Harbinson, to cut tariffs and subsidies. While Tokyo hosted a mini-ministerial summit to discuss agriculture, Japan continues to embrace high tariffs and subsidies on farm products. Japan and the European Union (EU) want to hold onto protection for sensitive sectors and feel that the proposal goes too far whereas the United States and the Cairns Group are requesting deeper cuts.[5]. . .

The EU also introduced a WTO proposal in 2003 to liberalise agriculture and change the subsidy system that links payments to agricultural production. Meanwhile, the EU continues its Common Agricultural Policy (CAP), a programme that heavily subsidises farmers.

According to Oxfam,

> 'Member states have been allowed to protect their own interests. This CAP deal is a failure for the world's poor, member states have added a plethora of caveats and "get-out" clauses to this agreement, including completely sidestepping the serious problem of dairy dumping by the EU on poor countries.'[6]

In the US, the richest farmers receive the lion's share of subsidies. Special interests, not the small family farmer, stand to gain the most from support. . . .

WTO members have recently come to a preliminary agreement on agriculture. While much remains to be accomplished, the initial framework aims to eliminate export subsidies and make a 20% reduction in domestic subsidies. WTO members must make this happen. Yet, according to *The Economist* (2004), 'With few numbers or dates and no products specified, it is impossible to gauge how much reform this framework will deliver. Given the addiction of rich countries to coddling their farmers, anyone expecting rapid change will doubtless be disappointed.'

The gridlock in the Doha Round over agriculture has had deeper implications beyond agricultural reform. Until agriculture is dealt with, a host of other issues, including services and intellectual property rights, must be put on hold. Seattle's legacy should not become Doha's.

Regional and bilateral free trade agreements

In response to slow movement within the WTO, a spate of regional and bilateral free trade agreements (FTAs) have taken place. For instance, at the end of 2002, 'the WTO has been notified that roughly 250 bilateral and multilateral trade agreements had been approved, over half of them since 1995, and about 50 more are believed to be on the way', according to the *Far Eastern Economic Review* (Hiebert, 2003–04).

As Barfield (2004) observes, around the world countries are pursuing agreements outside the WTO. Singapore has free trade agreements with Japan, New Zealand, Australia, the European Free Trade Association (EFTA) and the Association of Southeast Asian Nations (ASEAN). If anything, the US is a latecomer to FTAs.

Critics claim that bilateral deals undermine the WTO. Such statements beg the question: 'Is the goal of international trade to promote the international trading system, or is the goal of the international trading system to promote international trade?' Clearly, the goal should be to promote international trade. So many countries are pursuing FTAs because they do not wish to wait for the cumbersome WTO process to run its course. . . .

. . . Bilateral and regional trade agreements establish a positive dynamic for further agreements, which, in principle, could constitute the framework for a multilateral agreement. They are complementary, not mutually exclusive strategies for advancing trade. . . .

If negotiating bilateral and regional free trade agreements adds wind to the sails of liberalisation, countries around the world should let the wind blow.

Global Free Trade Association

A Global Free Trade Association (GFTA) is an alternative approach to advancing trade, one that does not fit neatly into the multilateral, regional or bilateral models. It is a coalition of the willing in trade, a grouping of those countries already committed to open markets. Creating a GFTA would advance liberalisation by creating a voluntary grouping of those countries already committed to free trade, open investment, minimal regulation and strong property rights.[8]

The precise criteria would need to be agreed to in advance by those forming the association. New countries could then join voluntarily by showing they meet these criteria. GFTA would be a free trade club open to all meeting pre-specified criteria.

This association would only include those who have a proven track record, not those merely promising to do better. Such an association would advance trade while stirring competition to motivate those countries that are left behind. This association would not seek to replace the WTO; rather, it would complement the WTO by advancing free trade.

A GFTA would establish a positive trade dynamic: countries not qualifying would have an incentive to voluntarily adopt open markets. What is now accomplished through laborious negotiations and the 'stick' of WTO sanctions could be accomplished through the 'carrot' of membership of a global free trade club.

Under WTO rules, recalcitrant members can thwart a round of global trade liberalisation by blocking agreement. Consequently, trade liberalisers try to circumvent the protectionist blockade within the WTO by pursuing trade liberalisation through other means.

To permit countries to stay outside such trade agreements would be to give these countries a protectionist veto over trade agreements, which, while they may involve some trade diversion, are net trade enhancing. By its nature, the GFTA would be trade enhancing. A GFTA would provide incentives for countries *unilaterally* to move to free trade. Joining the GFTA would 'lock in' the unilateral opening. . . .

The trade policy of the United States and the European Union should be to achieve liberalisation by any means. A GFTA would add one more option to the trade toolbox.

Conclusion

In the years since the end of the Second World War, mankind has made unprecedented advances in virtually all measures of well-being: real income, health, education and life expectancy. Political and economic freedom, in decline through much of the century, once again expanded.[9] Greater trade and financial integration–globalisation–played a critical role in this progress. Those left behind were largely those not integrated in the global trading system.

Today, the world is at a crossroads as far as further trade liberalisation is concerned, at least through the traditional multilateral route afforded by WTO agreements. The Doha Round is threatened by gridlock over agriculture. Trade hypocrisy abounds. Developed countries have locked out agricultural exports of developing countries. And the developing countries often have high trade barriers against each other. Barriers harm, not help, these struggling countries.

The history of agricultural and trade liberalisation in Australia and New Zealand reveals both farmers and consumers benefit from more open trade in agriculture. The political leadership in each country overcame the rent-seeking opposition from entrenched interests. . . .

Trade creates economic opportunity, fosters innovation and enterprise, and lifts the incomes of the vast majority of citizens. Trade also promotes political values held dear in Western countries. There is a trade imperative for policy-makers on both sides of the Atlantic: advance trade by any means, multilaterally, regionally, bilaterally *and* unilaterally.

NOTES

1. This is a revision of a paper presented at the 78th annual meeting of the Western Economic Association International, 11–15 July 2003. For their comments on previous drafts, we thank Dan Griswold, Giancarlo lbarguen S., Lee Hoskins, Mary Anastasia O'Grady, Walker Todd, John Welch and anonymous readers of earlier drafts. We also thank Anthony Kim for his excellent research assistance.
2. Schaefer (2000, pp. 1 and 71–73).
3. Lindsey (2002) chronicles how countries turned to protectionist policies of higher tariffs–'beggar-thy-neighbour' polices–in self-defeating attempts to rekindle domestic prosperity in the aftermath of the First World War (pp. 80–83). These attempts culminated in the infamous Smoot–Hawley Tariff of 1930 in the United States, which Moore (2003) credits with contracting world trade by 26% and world industrial production by 32% (p. 27). The experience of the 1920s and 1930s is a telling counterfactual for those doubting the benefits of international trade.
4. On average, there will be a certain number of people unemployed in the process of moving between jobs. Economists designate such transitional unemployment as 'frictional'.
5. The Cairns Group was formed in 1986 and consists of 17 agricultural exporting countries.
6. www.oxfam.org/eng/pr030627_eu_cap_reform.htm.
7. Lavin (2000, p. 6).
8. See John H. Hulsman, Gerald P. O'Driscoll, Jr., and Denise H. Froning, 'The Free Trade Association: A Trade Agenda for the New Global Economy', in O'Driscoll, *et al.* (2001), Hulsman (2001), Froning and O'Driscoll (2001), Hulsman and Schavey (2001) and O'Driscoll (2003a).
9. O'Driscoll (2003b, pp. 5–6).

REFERENCES

Alston, R., J. R. Kearl and M. B. Vaughan (1992) 'Is There a Consensus Among Economists in the 1990s?', *American Economic Review*, 82, 2, 203–209.

Barfield, C. (2004) 'China, the United States and the Rise of Asian Regionalism', paper presented at the 79th annual meeting of the Western Economic Association international, 29 June to 3 July 2004.

Bhalla, S. S. (2002) *Imagine There's No Country: Poverty, Inequality, and Growth in the Era of Globalization*, Washington, DC: Institute for International Economics.

Chamberlin, B. (1996) *Farming and Subsidies: Debunking the Myths*, Wellington, New Zealand: Eurora Farms Ltd.

Dollar, D. and A. Kraay (2002) 'Growth is Good for the Poor', *Journal of Economic Growth,* 7, 195–225.

The Economist (2004) 'A Step Forward: World Trade Talks', 7 August.

Federated Farmers of New Zealand (1999) 'Life After Subsidies: The New Zealand Farming Experience, 15 Years Later'. Available at http://www.fedform.org.nz/issues/issues.htm/.

Fitzgerald, S. (2003) 'Liberalizing Agriculture: Why the US Should Look to New Zealand and Australia', Backgrounder No. 1624, The Heritage Foundation, Washington, DC.

Fitzgerald, S. J. and N. Gardiner (2003) 'The WTO Cancun Meeting: Why the US Should Question Europe's Orwellian Farm Reforms', WebMemo No. 321, The Heritage Foundation, Washington, DC.

Froning, D. and G. P. O'Driscoll, Jr. (2001) 'Free Trade: Why Think Local When You Can Go Global?', *The Wall Street Journal,* 19 April.

Gomory, R. E. and W. J. Baumol (2000) *Global Trade and Conflicting National Interests,* Cambridge: Cambridge University Press.

Griswold, D. T. (2002) 'Free-trade Agreements: Steppingstones to a More Open World', Center for Trade Policy Studies, No. 18, 10 July, Cato Institute, Washington, DC.

Hiebert, M. (2003–04) 'The Perils of Bilateral Deals', *Far Eastern Economic Review,* 25 December to 1 January, p. 19.

Hulsman, J. C. (2001) *The World Turned Rightside Up: A New Agenda for the Age of Globalisation,* Occasional Paper No. 114, London: Institute of Economic Affairs.

Hulsman, J. C. and A. Schavey (2001) 'The Global Free Trade Association: A New Trade Agenda', Backgrounder No. 141, 16 May, The Heritage Foundation, Washington, DC.

International Monetary Fund (2002) *World Economic Outlook,* September, Washington: IMF.

Irwin, D. (1996) *Against the Tide: An Intellectual History of Free Trade,* Princeton, NJ: Princeton University Press.

Kearl, J. R., C. L. Pope, G. C. Whiting and L. T. Wimmer (1979) 'A Confusion of Economists?', *American Economic Review,* 69, 2.

Krauss, M. (1997) *How Nations Grow Rich: The Case for Free Trade,* New York: Oxford University Press.

Lavin, F. L. (2000) 'Half a Loaf is Better Than None: The Case for Regional Free Trade Agreements', Economic Freedom Project Paper No. 00–02, The Heritage Foundation, Washington, DC.

Lindsey, B. (2001) 'Free Trade and Our National Security', *Washington Times,* 5 December.

Lindsey, B. (2002) *Against the Dead Hand: The Uncertain Struggle for Global Capitalism,* New York: John Wiley.

Meltzer, A. M. (2000) *Report of the International Financial Institutions Advisory Commission,* United States Department of the Treasury, Washington, DC.

Meltzer, A. M. (2003) 'Leadership and Progress', The Irving Kristol Lecture of the American Enterprise Institute, 26 February, Washington, DC.

Messerlin, P. (2003) 'Agriculture in the Doha Agenda', World Bank Policy Research Working Paper No. 3009, Washington, DC.

Moore, M. (2003) *A World Without Walls: Freedom, Development, Free Trade and Global Governance*, Cambridge: Cambridge University Press.

O'Driscoll, G. P., Jr. (2003a) 'Is a Global Free-trade Deal Best Way to Keep US Safe?', *Investors Business Daily*, 21 February.

O'Driscoll, G. P., Jr. (2003b) 'Economic Freedom: Do Governments Care?', paper presented at the regional meetings of the Mont Pelerin Society, September.

O'Driscoll, G. P., Jr. and S. F. Cooper (2004) 'Trade Policy in Theory and Practice', Authors' Note.

O'Driscoll, G. P., Jr., K. R. Holmes and M. Kirkpatrick (2001) *2001 Index of Economic Freedom*, Washington, DC: The Heritage Foundation and Dow Jones & Co., Inc.

Pruzin, D. (2004) 'EU Officials See No Threat to Farm Subsidies from WTO Ruling on Cotton', *BNA Daily Report for Executives*, No. 121, 24 June.

Rose, A. K. (2003) 'Do We Really Know that the WTO Increases Trade?', Working Paper, University of California, Berkeley, CA.

Schaefer, B. D. (2000) 'The Bretton Woods Institutions: History and Reform Proposal', Economic Freedom Project Paper No. 00–01, The Heritage Foundation, Washington, DC.

The Times (2002) 'New Zealand Thrives After Agony of Pruning', 28 August, London.

Tokarick, S. (2002) 'How Do Industrial Country Policies Affect Developing Countries?', International Monetary Fund, September, Washington, DC.

Welch, J. H. and W. C. Gruben (1991) 'Economic Liberalization in the Americas', *Federal Reserve Bank of Dallas 1991 Annual Report*, Dallas, TX.

World Trade Organization (2004) 'Agriculture Negotiations Backgrounder: Introduction', Geneva, 25 October. Available at http://www.wto.org/english/tratop_e/agric_e/negs_bkgrnd05_intro_e.htm#objective.

Michael Parenti

Globalization and Democracy: Some Basics

The goal of the transnational corporation is to become truly transnational, poised above the sovereign power of any particular nation, while being served by the sovereign powers of all nations. Cyril Siewert, chief financial officer of Colgate Palmolive Company, could have been speaking for all transnationals when he remarked, "The United States doesn't have an automatic call on our [corporation's] resources. There is no mindset that puts this country first."[1]

With international "free trade" agreements such as NAFTA, GATT, and FTAA, the giant transnationals have been elevated above the sovereign powers of nation states. These agreements endow anonymous international trade committees with the authority to prevent, overrule, or dilute any laws of any nation deemed to burden the investment and market prerogatives of transnational corporations. These trade committees–of which the World Trade Organization (WTO) is a prime example—set up panels composed of "trade specialists" who act as judges over economic issues, placing themselves above the rule and popular control of any nation, thereby insuring the supremacy of international finance capital. This process, called *globalization*, is treated as an inevitable natural "growth" development beneficial to all. It is in fact a global coup d'état by the giant business interests of the world.

Elected by no one and drawn from the corporate world, these panelists meet in secret and often have investment stakes in the very issues they adjudicate, being bound by no conflict-of-interest provisions. Not one of GATT's five hundred pages of rules and restrictions are directed against private corporations; all are against governments. Signatory governments must lower tariffs, end farm subsidies, treat foreign companies the same as domestic ones, honor all corporate patent claims, and obey the rulings of a permanent elite bureaucracy, the WTO. Should a country refuse to change its laws when a WTO panel so dictates, the WTO can impose fines or international trade sanctions, depriving the resistant country of needed markets and materials.[2]

Acting as the supreme global adjudicator, the WTO has ruled against laws deemed "barriers to free trade." It has forced Japan to accept greater pesticide residues in imported food. It has kept Guatemala from outlawing deceptive advertising of baby food. It has eliminated the ban in various countries on asbestos, and on fuel-economy and emission standards for motor vehicles. And it has ruled against marine-life protection laws and the ban on endangered-species products. The European Union's prohibition on the importation of hormone-ridden U.S. beef had overwhelming popular support throughout Europe, but a three-member WTO panel decided the ban was an illegal restraint on trade. The decision on beef put in jeopardy a host of other food import regulations based on health concerns. The WTO overturned a portion of the U.S. Clean Air Act banning certain additives in gasoline because it interfered with imports from foreign refineries. And the WTO overturned that portion of the U.S. Endangered Species Act forbidding the import of shrimp caught with nets that failed to protect sea turtles.[3]

Free trade is not fair trade; it benefits strong nations at the expense of weaker ones, and rich interests at the expense of the rest of us. Globalization means turning the clock back on many twentieth-century reforms: no freedom to boycott products, no prohibitions against child labor, no guaranteed living wage or benefits, no public services that might conceivably compete with private services, no health and safety protections that might cut into corporate profits.[4]

GATT and subsequent free trade agreements allow multinationals to impose monopoly property rights on indigenous and communal agriculture. In this way agribusiness can better penetrate locally self-sufficient communities and monopolize their resources. Ralph Nader gives the example of the neem tree, whose extracts contain natural pesticidal and medicinal properties. Cultivated for centuries in India, the tree attracted the attention of various pharmaceutical companies, who filed monopoly patents, causing mass protests by Indian farmers. As dictated by the WTO, the pharmaceuticals now have exclusive control over the marketing of neem tree products, a ruling that is being reluctantly enforced in India. Tens of thousands of erstwhile independent farmers must now work for the powerful pharmaceuticals on profit-gorging terms set by the companies.

A trade agreement between India and the United States, the Knowledge Initiative on Agriculture (KIA), backed by Monsanto and other transnational corporate giants, allows for the grab of India's seed sector by Monsanto, its trade sector by Archer Daniels Midland and Cargill, and its retail sector by Wal-Mart. (Wal-Mart announced plans to open 500 stores in India, starting in August 2007.) This amounts to a war against India's independent farmers and small businesses, and a threat to India's food security. Farmers are organizing to protect themselves against this economic invasion by maintaining traditional seed-banks and setting up systems of communal agrarian support. One farmer says, "We do not buy seeds from the market because we suspect they may be contaminated with genetically engineered or terminator seeds."[5]

In a similar vein, the WTO ruled that the U.S. corporation Rice Tec has the patent rights to all the many varieties of basmati rice, grown for centuries by India's farmers. It also ruled that a Japanese corporation had exclusive rights in the world to grow and produce curry powder. As these instances demonstrate, what is called "free trade" amounts to international corporate monopoly control. Such developments caused Malaysian prime minister Mahathir Mohamad to observe:

> We now have a situation where theft of genetic resources by western biotech TNCs [transnational corporations] enables them to make huge profits by producing patented genetic mutations of these same materials. What depths have we sunk to in the global marketplace when nature's gifts to the poor may not be protected but their modifications by the rich become exclusive property?

If the current behavior of the rich countries is anything to go by, globalization simply means the breaking down of the borders of countries so that those with the capital and the goods will be free to dominate the markets.[6]

Under free-trade agreements like General Agreements on Trade and Services (GATS) and Free Trade Area of the Americas (FTAA), all public services are put at risk. A public service can be charged with causing "lost market opportunities" for business, or creating an unfair subsidy. To offer one instance: the single-payer automobile insurance program proposed by the province of Ontario, Canada, was declared "unfair competition." Ontario could have its public auto insurance only if it paid U.S. insurance companies what they estimated would be their present and *future* losses in Ontario auto insurance sales, a prohibitive cost for the province. Thus the citizens of Ontario were not allowed to exercise their democratic sovereign right to institute an alternative not-for-profit auto insurance system. In another case, United Postal Service charged the Canadian Post Office for "lost market opportunities," which means that under free trade accords, the Canadian Post Office would have to compensate UPS for all the business that UPS thinks it would have had if there were no public postal service. The Canadian postal workers union has challenged the case in court, arguing that the agreement violates the Canadian Constitution.

Under NAFTA, the U.S.-based Ethyl Corporation sued the Canadian government for $250 million in "lost business opportunities" and "interference with trade" because Canada banned MMT, an Ethyl-produced gasoline additive considered carcinogenic by Canadian officials. Fearing they would lose the case, Canadian officials caved in, agreeing to lift the ban on MMT, pay Ethyl $10 million compensation, and issue a public statement calling MMT "safe," even though they had scientific findings showing otherwise. California also banned the unhealthy additive; this time a Canadian based Ethyl company sued California under NAFTA for placing an unfair burden on free trade.[7]

International free trade agreements like GATT and NAFTA have hastened the corporate acquisition of local markets, squeezing out smaller businesses and worker collectives. Under NAFTA better-paying U.S. jobs were lost as firms closed shop and contracted out to the cheaper Mexican labor market. At the same time thousands of Mexican small companies were forced out of business. Mexico was flooded with cheap, high-tech, mass produced corn and dairy products from giant U.S. agribusiness firms (themselves heavily subsidized by the U.S. government), driving small Mexican farmers and distributors into bankruptcy, displacing large numbers of poor peasants. The lately arrived U.S. companies in Mexico have offered extremely low-paying jobs, and unsafe work conditions. Generally free trade has brought a dramatic increase in poverty south of the border.[8]

We North Americans are told that to remain competitive in the new era of globalization, we will have to increase our output while reducing our labor and production costs, in other words, work harder for less. This in fact is happening as the work-week has lengthened by as much as twenty percent (from forty hours to forty-six and even forty-eight hours) and real wages have flattened or declined during the reign of George W. Bush. Less is being spent on social services, and we are enduring more wage concessions, more restructuring, deregulation, and privatization. Only with such "adjustments," one hears, can we hope to cope with the impersonal forces of globalization that are sweeping us along.

In fact, there is nothing impersonal about these forces. Free trade agreements, including new ones that have not yet been submitted to the U.S. Congress have been consciously planned by big business and its government minions over a period of years in pursuit of a deregulated world economy that undermines all democratic checks upon business practices. The people of any one province, state, or nation are now finding it increasingly difficult to get their governments to impose protective regulations or develop new forms of public sector production out of fear of being overruled by some self-appointed international free-trade panel.[9]

Usually it is large nations demanding that poorer smaller ones relinquish the protections and subsidies they provide for their local producers. But occasionally things may take a different turn. Thus in late 2006 Canada launched a dispute at the World Trade Organization over the use of "trade-distorting" agricultural subsidies by the United States, specifically the enormous sums dished out by the federal government to U.S. agribusiness corn farmers. The case also challenged the entire multibillion-dollar structure of U.S. agricultural subsidies. It followed the landmark WTO ruling of 2005 which condemned "trade-distorting" aid to U.S. cotton farmers. A report by Oxfam International revealed that at least thirty-eight developing countries were suffering severely as a result of trade distorting subsidies by both the United States and the European Union. Meanwhile, the U.S. government was maneuvering to insert a special clause into trade negotiations that would place its illegal use of farm subsidies above challenge by WTO member countries and make the subsidies immune from adjudication through the WTO dispute settlement process.[10] . . .

What is being undermined is not only a lot of good laws dealing with environment, public services, labor standards, and consumer protection, but also *the very right to legislate such laws.* Our democratic sovereignty itself is being surrendered to a secretive plutocratic trade organization that presumes to exercise a power greater than that of the people and their courts and legislatures. What we have is an international coup d'état by big capital over the nations of the world.

Globalization is a logical extension of imperialism, a victory of empire over republic, international finance capital over local productivity and nation-state democracy (such as it is). In recent times however, given popular protests, several multilateral trade agreements have been stalled or voted down. In 1999, militant protests against free trade took place in forty-one nations from Britain and France to Thailand and India.[11] In 2000–01, there were demonstrations in Seattle, Washington, Sydney, Prague, Genoa, and various other locales. In 2003–04 we saw the poorer nations catching wise to the free trade scams and refusing to sign away what shreds of sovereignty they still had. Along with the popular resistance, more national leaders are thinking twice before signing on to new trade agreements. . . .

. . . It is not only *national* sovereignty that is at stake, it is *democratic* sovereignty. Millions, of people all over the world have taken to the streets to protest free trade agreements. Among them are farmers, workers, students and intellectuals (including many Marxists who see things more clearly than the aforementioned ones), all of whom are keenly aware that something new is afoot and they want no part of it. As used today, the term *globalization* refers to a new stage of international expropriation, designed not to put an end to the nation-state but to undermine whatever democratic right exists to protect the social wage and restrain the power of transnational corporations.

The free trade agreements, in effect, make unlawful all statutes and regulations that restrict private capital in any way. Carried to full realization, this means the end of whatever imperfect democratic protections the populace has been able to muster after generations of struggle in the realm of public policy. Under the free trade agreements any and all public services can be ruled out of existence because they cause "lost market opportunities" for private capital. So too public hospitals can be charged with taking away markets from private hospitals; and public water supply systems, public schools, public libraries, public housing and public transportation are guilty of depriving their private counterparts of market opportunities, likewise public health insurance, public mail delivery, and public auto insurance systems. Laws that try to protect the environment or labor standards or consumer health already have been overthrown for "creating barriers" to free trade.

What also is overthrown is the *right* to have such laws. This is the most important point of all and the one most frequently overlooked by persons from across the political spectrum. Under the free trade accords, property rights have been elevated to international supremacy, able to take precedent over all other rights, including the right to a clean livable environment, the right to affordable public services, and the right to any morsel of economic democracy. Instead a new right has been accorded absolutist status, the right to corporate private profit. It has been used to stifle the voice of working people and their ability to develop a public sector that serves their interests.

Free speech itself is undermined as when "product disparagement" is treated as an interference with free trade. And nature itself is being monopolized and privatized by transnational corporations.

So the fight against free trade is a fight for the right to politico-economic democracy, public services, and a social wage, the right not to be completely at the mercy of big capital. It is a new and drastic phase of the class struggle that some Marxists–so immersed in classical theory and so ill-informed about present-day public policy–seem to have missed. As embodied in the free trade accords, globalization has little to do with trade and is anything but free. It benefits the rich nations over poor ones, and the rich classes within all nations at the expense of ordinary citizens. It is the new specter that haunts the same old world.

NOTES

1. Quoted in *New York Times*, May 21, 1989.
2. See Lori Wallach and Michelle Sforza, *The WTO* (New York: Seven Stories Press, 2000); and John R. MacArthur, *The Selling of Free Trade: Nafta, Washington, and the Subversion of American Democracy* (New York: Hill and Wang, 2000).
3. *New York Times*, April 30, 1996 and May 9, 1997; *Washington Post*, October 13, 1998.
4. See the report by the United Nations Development Program referenced in *New York Times*, July 13, 1999.
5. Project Censored, "Real News," April 2007; also Arun Shrivastava, "Genetically Modified Seeds: Women in India take on Monsanto," *Global Research*, October 9, 2006.
6. Quoted in *People's Weekly World*, December 7, 1996.
7. John R. MacArthur, *The Selling of "Free Trade": NAFTA, Washington, and the Subversion of American* Democracy (New York: Hill & Wang, 2000; and Sarah Anderson and John Cavanagh, "Nafta's Unhappy Anniversary," *New York Times*, February 7, 1995.
8. John Ross, "Tortilla Wars," *Progressive*, June 1999.
9. For a concise but thorough treatment, see Steven Shrybman, *A Citizen's Guide to the World Trade Organization* (Ottawa/Toronto: Canadian Center for Policy Alternatives and James Lorimer & Co., 1999).
10. "US seeks "get-out clause" for illegal farm payments" Oxfam, June 29, 2006, http://www.oxfam.org/en/news/pressreleases2006/pr060629_wto_geneva
11. *San Francisco Chronicle*, June 19, 1999.

CHAPTER 14 THE BENEFITS OF INTERNATIONAL FINANCIAL INSTITUTIONS *v.* THE NEED FOR REFORM

Benefiting from the IMF

Advocate: Kenneth Rogoff

Source: "The World Still Needs the IMF," *Newsweek International,*
September 25, 2006.

Reforming the IMF

Advocate: George Monbiot

Source: "Don't Be Fooled by This Reform: The IMF Is Still the Rich World's Viceroy,"
The Guardian, Tuesday September 5, 2006.

International financial institutions—the International Monetary Fund (IMF), World Bank, and the World Trade Organization (WTO)—are elements of the international economic and financial regimes created to uphold the principles of neoliberal economic order supported by most countries in the world.

These international regimes trace their beginnings to 1944. Following the devastation of World War II, the United States and its allies met at Bretton Woods and agreed on the basic rules needed to maintain the smooth functioning of trade and financial markets. The main purpose of the IMF is to ensure stable exchange rates and help countries with their balance of payment problems. The World Bank provides loans to countries that experience decline in economic growth but also to promote development. The World Trade Organization works to promote and ensure the conduct of free trade around the world, and settles trade disputes among its members.

The activities of the international financial institutions have come under increasing scrutiny over the past decade. The main issues under debate are their transparency and accountability, the extent of their conditionality, and the inequitable representation of developing countries in their decision-making structures.

IN FAVOR OF THE IMF

The international economic institutions play a very important role in international politics. They help to provide stability in international markets and to maintain the neoliberal economic order that was created in the aftermath of World War II. The IMF and the World Bank are also lenders of last resort to countries that experience economic declines. The IMF provides loans when a country has a balance of payment problems. Over the years, it has also developed lending instruments intended to reduce poverty and provide humanitarian assistance. The funds that it provides are not given freely; indeed, in order for a country to receive a loan it needs to implement strict conditions set by the IMF.

Kenneth Rogoff, a former chief economist at the IMF, admits that the IMF is in urgent need of reforms, such as ending the European prerogative of choosing its managing director and reallocating voting shares. He argues, however, that the world does need a newly empowered IMF that would be able to meet the challenges of the global economy and maintain financial stability. While not all of the IMF's lending programs have been successful, the loans that it has provided to emerging markets on the brink of bankruptcy have averted many fiscal crises with global repercussions.

IN FAVOR OF REFORMING THE IMF

There are three main criticisms of the IMF. These include the institution's questionable lending practices, lack of transparency and accountability, and inequitable representation of the Global South. Many experts, including IMF insiders, question whether the emphasis on neoliberal reforms does the recipient countries more good than harm, and whether the insistence on political reforms infringes on their sovereignty. The record of success in the IMF's lending programs and the opacity of its decision-making procedures have also been questioned.

In his article, George Monbiot argues that, despite the limited reforms introduced by the IMF, it remains an instrument of the wealthy countries of the world. Through the conditionality of its loans, the IMF is able to exert tremendous influence on the economies of the recipient countries and maintain the dominance of the West. Monbiot claims that this discrepancy has led the countries of the Global South and their supporters in the Global North to clamor for the democratization of the IMF.

POINTS **TO PONDER**

1. What was the outcome of the Bretton Woods conference?
2. What are the incentives of the G-7 countries to democratize the IMF?

3. How does the IMF help maintain the dominance of the West in the global economy?
4. What is the role of the international financial institutions in the domestic political governance of the recipient countries?

Kenneth Rogoff

The World Still Needs the IMF

As the International Monetary Fund holds its big fall meetings in Singapore this week, it faces a financial world that has been turned on its head. Traditionally, the Fund has helped out bankrupt emerging-market governments using loan money collected mainly from Western nations. But now, the Fund is being asked, in effect, to play a much broader role in helping maintain financial stability in a world where the lenders and creditors are trading places. With the United States borrowing two thirds of global net savings and Euro-zone countries like Italy, Greece and Portugal struggling to control their government finances—while emerging markets sit on mounting foreign-exchange reserves—many worry that ground zero for the next big global financial crisis could be somewhere in the wealthy West. Given that Asia now accounts for almost 40 percent of global income, and an even larger share of its surpluses, it makes no sense that IMF voting rights and leadership posts are still dominated by the United States and Europe.

At immediate issue in Singapore is a relatively modest proposal by the Fund's managing director, Spaniard Rodrigo Rato, that would give slightly more voting power to China, South Korea, Turkey and Mexico. But this proposal is just a stalking horse for a larger reshuffling that would acknowledge the seismic shifts in global income that have taken place since the International Monetary Fund was founded after World War II. For an institution that pretends to reflect countries' relative economic influence, it is simply untenable to have China, with 15 percent of global income, own only 2.9 percent of the Fund's voting shares.

But attempts to reallocate power in global financial governance are meeting stiff resistance. True, the all-important United States stands firmly on the side of change, perhaps hoping that a more empowered Asia will feel obliged to take a less nationalistic approach to economic policy. Europe, however, is resisting fiercely, especially small, rich nations such as Belgium, the Netherlands, and the Nordic countries. They see their outsize role in the Fund—each controls more votes than China—as a key affirmation of their continuing relevance in a growing world. Curiously Asia, which ought to see the enhancement of its Fund voting shares as a milestone, is deeply ambivalent.

Many Asians, fueled by polemicists who seek to blame the Fund for the region's late 1990s financial crisis, remain deeply hostile to the IMF. Rather than seek deeper involvement in the organization, some Asian leaders are arguing for a regional alternative that would pool the trillions of dollars their economies have accumulated over the past ten years by running massive trade surpluses with the rest of the world.

Perhaps the biggest obstacle to reform are those who simply do not see the importance or urgency of revamping the IMF. Four years of rapid global growth have lulled many into thinking that the Fund is an anachronism, that nothing will ever go wrong. Sovereign debt markets, in particular, seem to have forgotten the spate of spectacular global debt crises that raced across the developing world only a short while ago. These include Mexico in 1994, South Korea, Indonesia and Thailand in 1997, Russia in 1998, and Brazil, Argentina and Turkey in the early 2000s. Each time, global financial stability stood on the brink, and each time the Fund helped orchestrate a global response, often pouring in billions of dollars in bridge loans out of its own resources.

Consider, for example, the Fund's risky and creative lending package to Brazil in August 2002, when markets were terrified that the impending election of leftist President Luiz Inácio Lula da Silva would induce Brazil to cast aside its newly stable macroeconomic policies. With market access suddenly freezing up and the country on the brink of default, the Fund stepped in with $30 billion. The Fund's loan arguably helped avert a meltdown that would have slammed global markets from Manila to Istanbul, and forestalled the benign period that emerging market economies have enjoyed the past few years.

Of course, not all of the Fund's programs have proved so successful. The most notable failure was Argentina in 2001, when the Fund was too slow to pull the plug even after it became obvious that the country was not willing to reform its finances in a way needed to avert default. In between these two diverse performances is the Asian crisis, where Fund intervention helped stave off default but not a deep recession. True, the root cause of the crisis was the Asian governments' attempts to rigidly peg their currencies to the dollar, even as they opened up their capital market to massive speculative flows. This was a recipe for catastrophe that I and a few other academic economists had been warning about for several years prior. The Fund, however, was too weak and inconsistent in its efforts to convince national authorities in Asia of the urgent need to adopt more sustainable policies.

For the Panglossians, who seem to hold sway now in sovereign debt markets where interest spreads are at or near record lows, all this is ancient history. Many investors have come to believe that today's newly prudent governments, backed up by newly improved monetary policies, will indeed ensure the world of at least a couple decades of financial-crisis-free living. Perhaps they are right.

Maybe the world will one day look back on the sovereign debt crises of the 1980s and 1990s as mere growing pains on the path to global financial nirvana. Perhaps even today's massive U.S. current-account deficit of more than $800 billion per year will prove a nonissue—just a reallocation of global assets, soon to be dwarfed by ever-expanding global capital markets.

If so, the rest of us may be losing sleep over prospective financial crises for nothing. But just in case, wouldn't it be a good idea to keep trying to improve the IMF, rather than to eviscerate it? Perhaps the biggest question facing the Fund today is how to assert greater influence over the big players like the United States and China, whose massive borrowing and lending activities pose risks no one can easily assess. Indeed, the Fund has already become quite outspoken in questioning China's rigid exchange-rate regime and budget deficits in the United States. But in Singapore, the finance ministers and central bankers who oversee the Fund must decide how far they are willing to go in assigning the Fund an enhanced role in surveillance of these economies, not to mention Europe's.

Speaking of Europe, one desperately needed reform is an immediate end to Europe's prerogative of choosing the Fund's leader. Although Europe's candidates have generally compared favorably with their counterparts at other international economic organizations, the practice is still a horrible anachronism. Even as the Fund board struggles over voting shares, it should immediately agree that the next managing director should be the best and most qualified candidate, regardless of nationality.

Will the Fund's leaders make any progress in Singapore on the institutions' governance and future direction? Let's hope so. In a world where global capital markets are now 10 times the size of the U.S. economy, we need a fully empowered multilateral financial institution, ready to mitigate the risk of future global financial crises, even if there is no way to completely avoid them.

George Monbiot

Don't Be Fooled by This Reform: The IMF Is Still the Rich World's Viceroy

The glacier has begun to creak. In the world's most powerful dictatorship we detect the merest hint of a thaw. I am not talking about China or Uzbekistan, Burma or North Korea. This state runs no torture chambers or labour camps. No one is executed, though plenty starve to death as a result of its policies. The unhurried perestroika is taking place in Washington, in the offices of the International Monetary Fund.

Like most concessions made by dictatorial regimes, the reforms seem designed not to catalyse further change, but to prevent it. By slightly increasing the shares (and therefore the voting powers) of China, South Korea, Mexico and Turkey, the regime hopes to buy off the most powerful rebel warlords, while keeping the mob at bay. It has even thrown a few coppers from the balcony, for the great unwashed to scuffle over. But no one—except the leaders of the rich nations and the leader writers of just about every newspaper in the rich world—could regard this as an adequate response to its problems.

The fund is a body with 184 members. It is run by seven of them—the US, Japan, Germany, the UK, France, Canada and Italy. These happen to be the seven countries that (with Russia) promised to save the world at the G8 meeting in 2005. The junta sustains its control by insisting that each dollar buys a vote. The bigger a country's financial quota, the more say it has over the running of the IMF. This means that it is run by the countries that are least affected by its policies.

A major decision requires 85% of the vote, which ensures that the US, with 17%, has a veto over the fund's substantial business. The UK, Germany, France and Japan have 22% between them, and each has a permanent seat on the board. By a weird arrangement permitting rich nations to speak on behalf of the poor, Canada and Italy have effective control over a further 8%. The other European countries are also remarkably powerful: Belgium, for example, has a direct entitlement to 2.1% of the vote and indirect control over 5.1%—more than twice the allocation of India or Brazil. Europe, Japan, Canada and the US wield a total of 63%. The 80 poorest countries, by contrast, have 10% between them.

These quotas no longer even reflect real financial contributions to the running of the IMF: it now obtains much of its capital from loan repayments by its vassal states. But the G7 nations still behave as if it belongs to them. They decide who runs it (the managing director is always a European and his deputy always an American) and how the money is spent. You begin to wonder why the developing countries bother to turn up.

In principle, this power is supposed to be balanced by something called the "basic vote"—250 shares (entitling them to $25m worth of votes) are allocated to every member. But while the value of the rich countries' quotas has risen since the IMF was founded in 1944, the value of the basic votes has not. It has fallen from 11.3% of the total allocation to 2.1%. The leaked paper passed to me by an excellent organisation called the Bretton Woods Project (everything we know about the IMF has to be leaked) shows that the fund intends to democratise itself by "at least doubling" the basic vote. That sorts it all out, then—the 80 poorest countries will be able to claim, between them, another 0.9%. Even this pathetic concession was granted only after the African members took a political risk by publicly opposing the fund's proposals. Doubtless the US government is currently reviewing their trading status.

All this is compounded by an internal political process that looks as if it was contrived in North Korea, not Washington. There are no formal votes, just a "consensus process" controlled by the Dear Leaders of the G7. The decisions taken by each member state cannot be revealed to the public. Nor can the transcripts of the board's meetings and the "working papers" on which it bases its internal reforms. Even reports by the IMF's ombudsman—the "independent evaluation office"—are censored by the management, and their conclusions are changed to shift the blame for the fund's failures to its client states. Needless to say, the IMF insists that the states it lends to must commit themselves to "good governance" and "transparency" if they are to receive its money.

None of this would matter so much if it had stuck to its original mandate of stabilising the international monetary system. But after the collapse of the Bretton Woods agreement in 1971 the IMF more or less lost its mission to maintain exchange rates, and began to look for a new role. As a paper by the law professor Daniel Bradlow shows, when it amended its articles of association in 1978 they were so loosely drafted as to grant the IMF permission to interfere in almost any aspect of a country's governance. It lost its influence over the economic policies of the G7 and became instead the rich world's viceroy, controlling the poorer nations at its behest. It began to micromanage their economies without reference to the people or even their governments. Since then, no rich country has required its services, and few poor countries have been able to shake it off.

This casts an interesting light on the decision—to be endorsed at the IMF's meeting in Singapore next week—to enhance the quota for the four middle-income countries. After the fund "helped" the struggling economies of east and south-east Asia in 1997, by laying waste to them on behalf of US hedge funds and investment companies, the nations of that region decided that they would never allow themselves to fall prey to it again.

They began indemnifying themselves against the fund's tender loving care by building up their own reserves of capital. Now, just as China and South Korea have ensured that they will never again require the IMF's services, they have been granted more power to decide how it operates. In other words, they are deemed fit to govern when—like the G7—they can exercise power without reaping the consequences. The smaller your stake in the outcome, the greater your vote.

None of this seems to cause any difficulties to the gatekeepers of mainstream opinion. On Saturday a leading article in the *Washington Post* observed that "to be legitimate, multilateral institutions must reflect the global distribution of power as it is now, not as it was when these institutions were set up more than half a century ago". What a fascinating definition that is, and how wrong we must have been to imagine that legitimacy requires democracy. Hurrah for corporatism—it didn't die with Mussolini after all.

I am among those who believe that the IMF is, and always will be, the wrong body—inherently flawed and constitutionally unjust. But if its leaders and supporters are to persuade us that it might, one day, have a legitimate role in running the world's financial systems, they will have to do a hell of a lot better than this.

CHAPTER 15 ALLEVIATING POVERTY THROUGH AID *v.* ALLEVIATING POVERTY THROUGH FREE TRADE

Free Trade and Open Markets as the Solution to Poverty

Advocate: Shanker Singham and Donna Hrinak

Source: "Poverty and Globalization," *The National Interest*, no. 82 (Winter 2005/2006), pp. 117–123, excerpt.

Developmental Aid Helps Alleviate Poverty

Advocate: Jeffrey D. Sachs

Source: "Letter: How Aid Can Work," *The New York Review of Books*, vol. 53, no. 20 (December 21, 2006).

Poverty in the Global South has been an important topic in international relations for decades. In the age of globalization, however, it has become abundantly clear that the stability and prosperity of the industrialized world are inextricably linked to the economic growth and political development of developing countries. Whether it is for reasons of migration, terrorism, or public health concerns, in today's interconnected world the wealthy countries of the Global North can scarcely afford to remain aloof to the plight of the poor in the Global South.

Solutions to this problem have included debt restructuring or forgiveness, provision of foreign aid, and attempts to accelerate the incorporation of the developing world in the international economic system. Each path has met with uneven success. A handful of countries have benefited, but the majority continue to struggle. With some notable exceptions, primarily countries in Southeast Asia, the gap between the Global North and Global South has widened in recent decades in terms of income as well as human development. Hence, addressing the challenge of poverty is likely to remain on the global agenda for years to come, although perhaps not with the urgency that it deserves.

IN FAVOR OF FREE TRADE

In an era dominated by the logic of economic liberalism, it is hardly surprising that free trade has found a following in the area of development. Many economists

214

argue that foreign aid distorts certain economic sectors of the developing countries, and instead call for market openness and deregulation.

Singham and Hrinak claim that aid can distort the economy and that the solution to poverty is free trade and open markets. They advocate economic liberalism and posit that truly free trade can lift countries out of poverty. They argue that failures have resulted not from free trade, but from the fact that trade is rarely free: even those countries that espouse its mantra frequently put forward the interests of producers before those of consumers. Singham and Hrinak claim that consumer welfare-driven free trade can be the solution to poverty. They submit that further economic liberalization with greater pro-competitive regulation within the developing countries is the key to economic growth.

IN FAVOR OF AID

In recent years, conservative politicians and adherents of neoliberal economics alike have questioned the benefits of foreign aid. Many of them have argued that foreign aid does not contribute to economic growth in the developing world, and the money spent on it is, in fact, money wasted. Challenging this view, other experts have argued that aid can indeed be beneficial when there is good governance, and is irreplaceable when it comes to saving lives in the least-developed countries.

Along similar lines, Jeffrey Sachs, a prominent economist, argues that some countries in the world are trapped in a cycle of poverty, and foreign aid is indispensable if they are to extricate themselves from it. He forcefully argues that foreign aid can be a matter of life and death when it comes to disease prevention, healthcare, humanitarian aid, or education. The amount of aid that the United States provides pales in comparison to the war spending in Iraq or Afghanistan—while its results can have far-reaching and long-term benefits.

POINTS **TO PONDER**

1. How can free trade help address poverty in the developing world?
2. Which countries have benefited the most from the philosophy of economic liberalism?
3. What is the role of interest groups in obstructing free trade?
4. How does aid alleviate poverty?

Shanker Singham and Donna Hrinak
Poverty and Globalization

Most of the world's people live in countries where markets do not work properly and resources are not efficiently allocated. The notion that liberal economics has "failed" misses the point that in many areas of the world it has not really been tried.

Poverty—often cast as the fault of multinational corporations or "imperialist governments"—is the most virulent killer on our planet. Many continue to believe that increased government regulation and control, particularly when it comes to international trade, is the best way to combat poverty, ignoring the fact that real liberalization—truly free and competitive markets—is in fact the agenda of the world's poor.

It is therefore ironic that efforts to ensure that markets are competitive often fall on the sword of "national interest." Alleged threats to sovereignty are often cited by countries as reason not to negotiate on matters that touch domestic regulation and policies. In practice, this means that they reserve the right to maintain the status quo in which local producer interests trump consumer welfare. Allowing such notions of sovereignty to dominate over economic empowerment of people is to consign the vast majority of citizens to poverty.

It is remarkable that one of the most effective vehicles for empowering individual citizens—global trade negotiations—has largely disregarded this pivotal element of its work. Trade discussions have long centered on enhancing the welfare of producers, rather than on empowering consumers, despite the fact that the fundamental principles on which trade agreements are based are consumer-welfare enhancing ones. Today, the divide between those who would adopt a more consumer-led approach to market-opening and economic growth and those who maintain a producer-led focus represents a major factor opposing free trade and contributes notably to the stagnation of the international trade agenda.

One of the main problems is that governments and elites have refused to recognize the most basic fact of economic life: We are all consumers. Even businesses are also consumers of raw materials or finished or unfinished products. Yet trade negotiations are conducted with a strong bias toward mercantilism. It is quite revealing that in trade talks negotiators continue to refer to tariff cuts as concessions, as if lowering a tariff requires a "payment" by one's trading partner. This mercantilist logic is now applied to a whole raft of rules-based negotiations. Countries that employ this approach are really saying that they reserve the right to harm their consumers so that producers may receive a benefit in some unrelated area. This is irrational and destructive economics, which if not rooted out will perpetuate misery for billions of people. . . .

Because so little attention was paid to consumer welfare, the unprecedented amount of trade liberalization that occurred in the 1990s did not lead to the competitive markets as had been predicted. At first this lag went unnoticed by trade negotiators from major developed countries, such as the United States and the EU countries, where competitive markets were much more the norm. The assumption was that removing trade barriers would inevitably lead to competitive markets inside the border.

But these negotiators failed to factor in the decades of state control and import-substitution economics that had pervaded most of the world's markets. In this context, removal of at-the-border barriers, which were often accompanied by significant privatization programs, often only enriched the gatekeepers, who initially invested in the privatizations at the expense of new entrants. Consumers in countries with low levels of competition were not always empowered by an opening to trade because the prices they paid for products were determined not by tariffs but by levels of competition in the market, which had not changed. The result was an increase in the perceived—and actual—disparity of wealth between the gatekeepers and consumers while poverty persisted. So instead of reacting by advocating more competitive markets and greater pro-competitive regulation inside borders, consumers questioned the entire process of liberalization itself.

Reform Fatigue in Latin America

In Latin America, the reaction has been so pervasive that one would be hard pressed to find anyone in the region who would not agree that the privatizations and liberalization of the 1990s had been a costly failure. Few would identify that failure with a lack of competitive markets, but they are linked. In many cases, public monopolies with regulation were simply converted into private monopolies without regulation. In other situations, laws were left on the statute books that not only tolerated but actually mandated anti-competitive conduct by private parties, such as laws that prevented foreign suppliers from severing relationships with failed distributors or taxes that discriminated against new market entrants, especially through foreign investment.

Today, the economic environment in many countries in Latin America and the Caribbean is dominated by two conditions: fatigue and fear. We talk about societies inflicted with "reform fatigue": They are tired of dealing with economic reforms that fail to fulfill their promise of growth and development. And we lament studies that show many Latin Americans and citizens throughout the Caribbean, some of whom lived under authoritarian rule and military dictatorships just twenty years ago, are today also tired of democracy—tired of a system of government that guarantees free and fair elections at regular intervals but that brings no concrete benefits in between.

It's easy to see why many societies in our region are experiencing reform fatigue. Today in our hemisphere, after over a decade of supposed free market economics and democratic government, there are still eighty million people who live on less than $2 per day. For these eighty million people, all the political and economic reforms have been largely meaningless.

This fatigue with reforms is dangerous, because when countries, peoples and societies are tired, they often opt for the easy way out. Today, there is a new wave of populist leaders—from Hugo Chavez in Venezuela to Nestor Kirchner in Argentina to potential leaders like Evo Morales in Bolivia—prepared to offer that alternative. Their rhetoric varies somewhat from country to country, of course, but the message at its core is that those who are poor find themselves in that circumstance because others are rich—because the pie of prosperity is only so big and someone has taken your piece. And the only way to change the status quo is to cut the pie a different way, to take your piece back. That view also figures in the populists' foreign policy, which holds that the developed world has grown rich only through the exploitation of other countries and that the emerging world is poor because of that abuse.

While overly simplistic, these claims deserve serious examination, because they contain a kernel of truth. They accurately describe the zero-sum game that has too long distorted reform initiatives and liberalization. Too often there have been cozy arrangements between the political and business elites that have ignored the welfare of the majority of the people. One example of this is the much-studied Mexican telecommunications sector, which has recently been the subject of a WTO case for anti-competitive post-privatization practices. Another example is the plethora of dealer-protection laws around the hemisphere, where it is almost impossible for foreign suppliers to terminate their local distributors, because the laws effectively mandate that supplier-distributor relationships go on forever. This chokes off competition at the distribution level and leads to rent-seeking behavior by the gatekeepers of the economy, in this case the local distributors. As a result of such laws, the prices of some basic products are kept artificially high. In the case of medicines in some countries, local distributors have been able to maintain 100 percent profit margins. Indeed, there are examples of local distributors refusing to allow suppliers to make charitable donations, claiming that such an act would effectively terminate the agreement between them and trigger the very high termination indemnities under these laws. . . .

The oft-quoted remark that there are winners and losers in free trade unfortunately reinforces the idea of a zero-sum environment by suggesting that if someone is winning, someone else is losing. Positing the idea that someone must end up on the zero side of the free trade ledger engenders fear. The fearful believe that, in this new world, they will not be able to compete. A good example of this is the resistance in some Latin American countries, notably Ecuador and the Dominican Republic, to a competition law. Viewed through the lens of producers only, local producers do not want to face competition in their markets and do not want to change their customary practices, however damaging those practices are to consumers. But competition can benefit local producers also. Viewed through a consumer-welfare lens, even small businesses, which often buy raw materials for their productive processes, would benefit enormously from more competitive practices at this level.

Strengthening Competition

In the current discourse, we have tended to classify countries into those that espouse free market economics with all its implications, and those that favor central control or greater government interference. In weighing their policy options, few countries look at microeconomic policy through a consumer lens.

The current model for trade negotiations is for all partners to defend their producer interests, which almost inevitably clash, leading to an impasse in the talks or, as in the case of negotiations to create the Free Trade Area of the Americas (FTAA), to such a limited set of objectives that the goal of free trade is virtually set aside. In the case of the FTAA, before negotiation stalled completely, some countries, led by the Mercosur trade bloc, resisted the notion that the trade agreement should cover more than traditional border measures and reach into the domestic regulatory measures in states. Attempts to introduce a consumer-welfare-oriented competition policy or to protect intellectual property rights were sacrificed to national sovereignty, as countries maintained that they reserved the right to have whatever domestic policies they chose. But this is a canard. International trade rules have already impacted domestic policy: A country's tariff law is itself a national law. What is really being said, in effect, is that they reserve the right to harm their own consumers or not to protect property rights. If this is indeed the claim, their own people should be aware of it.

To express more clearly the central importance of consumers, competition policy should be brought into the mainstream of trade negotiations. Competition policy must move from being merely an add-on to driving trade talks. Issues that affect the business climate in the target market—such as a country's rules on standards or the way it enforces intellectual property rights—are increasingly cited as legitimate topics for trade negotiators. It is also essential to ensure that the level of competition in the market is not itself a barrier to entry that would undermine the real goal of free trade. The principal benefactors of this approach will be consumers, who will have access to a greater variety of higher quality goods and services at lower prices and, not coincidentally, efficient producers capable of competing on a level playing field. . . .

What Will It Take?

At present, one cannot point to any country in the world that has fully embraced the cause of consumer welfare in its trade negotiations. It is often too difficult to ask trade ministries to see beyond the forces that their producer constituencies are exerting on them. Countries or specific economic sectors (since frequently countries are two-faced on these issues depending on which sector you are analyzing) often move back and forth between measures that protect producers and those that would empower consumers. While embracing certain aspects of free market norms, countries will advocate for old-style industrial policy in the building of national champions through government subventions. This occurs even in developed countries, such as France, where the government recently decided to list certain companies that are deemed strategically important and are therefore protected from foreign takeover. Recently, certain EU member states rejected the process of service liberalization within the European Union. . . . What we see is countries trying to have their cake and eat it, too—good old-fashioned mercantilism—seeking better market access for their producers while resisting competition for their own markets. . . .

What we are witnessing now is the teasing out of these differences at the global level. China provides us a very good example of this—where the guiding economic principle is the "socialist market economy." Here, China is moving to a competitive market, complete with a competition authority, while at the same time operating in an environment with a large number of state-owned companies and corporate welfare. However, examples of this kind of picking of options from both sides of the consumer-producer ledger are certainly not confined to China and exist in many countries and many sectors. This is not a developed-versus-developing-world dichotomy, but rather a problem that plagues both developing and developed countries alike.

Clearly, open trade and competitive markets are just two of the factors required if the world economy is to grow and develop and to ensure that growth and development are sustainable and broad-based. . . .

Jeffrey D. Sachs
How Aid Can Work

In a very different era, President John Kennedy declared

> to those peoples in the huts and villages across the globe strug-
> gling to break the bonds of mass misery, we pledge our best
> efforts to help them help themselves, for whatever period is
> required—not because the Communists may be doing it, not
> because we seek their votes, but because it is right. If a free soci-
> ety cannot help the many who are poor, it cannot save the few
> who are rich.

It is difficult to imagine President Bush making a similar pledge today, but he is far from alone in Washington. The idea that the US should commit its best efforts to help the world's poor is an idea shared by Bill Gates, Warren Buffett, and Jimmy Carter, but it has been almost nowhere to be found in our capital. American philanthropists and nonprofit groups have stepped forward while our government has largely disappeared from the scene.

There are various reasons for this retreat. Most importantly, our policy-makers in both parties simply have not attached much importance to this "soft" stuff, although their "hard" stuff is surely not working and the lack of aid is contributing to a cascade of instability and security threats in impoverished countries such as Somalia. We are spending $550 billion per year on the military, against just $4 billion for Africa. Our African aid, incredibly, is less than three days of Pentagon spending, a mere $13 per American per year, and the equivalent of just 3 cents per $100 of US national income! The neglect has been bipartisan. The Clinton administration allowed aid to Africa to languish at less than $2 billion per year throughout the 1990s.

A second reason for the retreat is the widespread belief that aid is simply wasted, money down the rat hole. That has surely been true of some aid, such as the "reconstruction" funding for Iraq and the cold war–era payouts to thugs such as Mobutu Sese Seko of Zaire. But these notorious cases obscure the critical fact that development assistance based on proven tech-nologies and directed at measurable and practical needs—increased food production, disease control, safe water and sanitation, schoolrooms and clin-ics, roads, power grids, Internet connectivity, and the like—has a distin-guished record of success.

The successful record of well-targeted aid is grudgingly acknowledged even by a prominent academic critic of aid, Professor Bill Easterly. Buried in his "Bah, Humbug" attack on foreign aid, *The White Man's Burden,*[1] Mr. Easterly allows . . . that

> foreign aid likely contributed to some notable successes on a global scale, such as dramatic improvement in health and education indicators in poor countries. Life expectancy in the typical poor country has risen from forty-eight years to sixty-eight years over the past four decades. Forty years ago, 131 out of every 1,000 babies born in poor countries died before reaching their first birthday. Today, 36 out of every 1,000 babies die before their first birthday.

Two hundred pages later Mr. Easterly writes that we should

> put the focus back where it belongs: get the poorest people in the world such obvious goods as the vaccines, the antibiotics, the food supplements, the improved seeds, the fertilizer, the roads, the boreholes, the water pipes, the textbooks, and the nurses. This is not making the poor dependent on handouts; it is giving the poorest people the health, nutrition, education, and other inputs that raise the payoff to their own efforts to better their lives.

These things could indeed be done, if American officials weren't so consistently neglectful of development issues and with many too cynical to learn about the constructive uses of development assistance. They would learn that just as American subsidies of fertilizers and high-yield seed varieties for India in the late 1960s helped create a "Green Revolution" that set that vast country on a path out of famine and on to long-term development, similar support for high-yield seeds, fertilizer, and small-scale water technologies for Africa could lift that continent out of its current hunger-disease-poverty trap. They would discover that the Gates and Rockefeller Foundations have put up $150 million in the new Alliance for a Green Revolution in Africa to support the development and uptake of high-yield seed varieties there, an effort that the US government should now join and help carry out throughout sub-Saharan Africa.

They would also discover that the American Red Cross has learned—and successfully demonstrated—how to mass-distribute antimalaria bed nets to impoverished rural populations in Africa, with such success and at such low cost that the prospect of protecting all of Africa's children from that mass killer is now actually within reach. Yet they'd also learn that the Red Cross lacks the requisite funding to provide bed nets to all who need them. They would learn that a significant number of other crippling and killing diseases, including African river blindness, schistosomiasis, trauchoma, lymphatic filariasis, hookworm, ascariasis, and trichuriasis, could be brought under control for well under $2 per American citizen per year, and perhaps just $1 per American citizen!

They would note, moreover, that the number of HIV-infected Africans on donor-supported antiretroviral therapy has climbed from zero in 2000 to 800,000 at the end of 2005, and likely to well over one million today. They would learn that small amounts of funding to help countries send children to school have proved successful in a number of African countries, so much so that the continent-wide goal of universal attendance in primary education is utterly within reach if financial support is provided.

As chairman of the Commission on Macroeconomics and Health of the World Health Organization (2000–2001) and director of the UN Millennium Project (2002–2006), I have led efforts that have canvassed the world's leading practitioners in disease control, food production, infrastructure development, water and sanitation, Internet connectivity, and the like, to identify practical, proven, low-cost, and scalable strategies for the world's poorest people such as those mentioned above.

Such life-saving and poverty-reducing measures raise the productivity of the poor so that they can earn and invest their way out of extreme poverty, and these measures do so at an amazingly low cost. To extend these proven technologies throughout the poorest parts of Africa would require around $75 billion per year from all donors, of which the US share would be around $30 billion per year, or roughly 25 cents per every $100 of US national income.

When we overlook the success that is possible, we become our own worst enemies. We stand by as millions die each year because they are too poor to stay alive. The inattention and neglect of our policy leaders lull us to believe casually that nothing more can be done. Meanwhile we spend hundreds of billions of dollars per year on military interventions doomed to fail, overlooking the fact that a small fraction of that money, if it were directed at development approaches, could save millions of lives and set entire regions on a path of economic growth. It is no wonder that global attitudes toward America have reached the lowest ebb in history. It is time for a new approach.

NOTE

1. Penguin, 2006.

PART IV
INTERNATIONAL ORGANIZATION

The days when international relations were only about interstate relations are long gone. Non-state actors play an ever-growing role in all areas of international politics. Their importance is evident in the growing number of intergovernmental as well as non-governmental organizations, especially since the end of the Cold War. In areas such as human rights, the environment, and development, international organizations bring about awareness and help place issues on the agenda, monitor governmental activities, and mobilize public opinion and action.

Chapter 16 centers on the role of the state in the age of globalization. The advances in communications and technology have made state borders more porous and eroded state control over many human and economic activities. Globalization has also facilitated the proliferation of non-governmental organizations and enhanced their ability to monitor the activities of actors such as governments, corporations, and international institutions. Contrary to the many scholars' vision, Linda Weiss argues that globalization reinforces, and in some respects augments, the state's role in social and economic development. While admitting that globalization does produce some constraining effects, she contends that it strengthens domestic institutions, as well as centralizes political authority that can provide policy responses. P. J. Simmons, on the other hand, describes the growing impact of NGOs in domestic and international politics, their participation in the policy process, and influence on state and other non-state actors.

Chapter 17 looks at one of the most contentious issues facing the European Union: possible membership for Turkey. The importance of the topic stems from the transformative impact Turkish accession would have on the EU and the example it could set for relations with the Arab world, which is seen as especially important in the fight against terrorism. Hans Arnold discusses why Turkey should not become a member: it is not a European country, its political realities are different than those of other European states, and its foreign policy will at times counteract that of the EU. Most importantly, Turkey's membership will prevent Europe's unification. Adam Hug, on the other hand, sees future Turkish membership as central for the evolution of the European Union. Arguing that not letting Turkey in would be a grand strategic failure, he urges Europe's business community to take the lead in educating the public about the benefits of Turkish accession.

Chapter 18 discusses the importance of the International Criminal Court (ICC) and the United States' absence from its membership. The ICC was created in 1998 with the intent to prosecute individuals suspected of committing crimes of genocide, crimes of war, crimes against humanity, and crimes of a particularly heinous nature. Its emergence was seen as progress in upholding human rights, signaling to the world that no one who had committed such crimes—whether head of state, high-ranking military personnel, or paramilitary officials—would go unpunished. The United States' stance against the ICC dealt a serious blow to the effectiveness and legitimacy of the Court. Washington's decision was based on the assumption that its military and civilian personnel, as well as private U.S. citizens working abroad could become targets for prosecution. Hence, acting on the principle of self-interest, the United States denounced the ICC.

Chapter 19 examines the moral, legal, and practical reasons in support for and against humanitarian intervention. This issue came into the spotlight in the 1990s, especially with the international community's intervention in Kosovo to stop the ethnic cleansing conducted by the Serbian government. Many in the West saw this as progress in upholding human rights. The reasons against this development are focused on the principles of international law, specifically state sovereignty, national interest, selectivity of intervention, and the imposition of Western standards of human rights and state duties.

Chapter 20 discusses the current issue of climate change and the challenges it causes in international relations. Specifically, the chapter looks at the debate over the economic impact of emissions cuts versus the need for collective action to mitigate the effects of global climate change. To illustrate the division that has emerged between some developed and developing countries, it discusses the position of the United States and China on the issue. The United States has a substantial demand for fossil fuels as the world's largest economy, but it has not ratified the Kyoto Protocol. Instead, Washington emphasizes continued economic growth and insists that developing countries must do their share by implementing mandatory emissions cuts. China, a developing country with a sizeable part of its population living below or near the poverty line, is the largest overall emitter of carbon dioxide and is vulnerable to the effects of climate change, but it has ratified the Kyoto Protocol.

CHAPTER 16 NGOS *v.* STATES IN THE AGE OF GLOBALIZATION

Globalization and the Strengthening Role of the State

Advocate: Linda Weiss

Source: "State-Augmenting Effects of Globalisation," *New Political Economy*, vol. 10, no. 3 (2005), pp. 345–353.

NGOs, Accountability, and the Weakening of the State

Advocate: P. J. Simmons

Source: "Learning to Live with NGOs," *Foreign Policy*, no. 112 (Fall 1998), pp. 82–95, excerpt.

It is difficult to imagine modern day international relations without the presence of non-governmental organizations (NGOs). The post-Cold War era saw the proliferation of NGOs that are engaged in all aspects of life and that perform valuable roles, such as monitoring government activity, providing information, and proposing alternative solutions.

It is often said that NGOs have contributed to the erosion of state sovereignty in the age of globalization. As the development of information technology and communications has led to the increased interconnectedness of state and non-state actors, many have argued that the Westphalian nation-state may be fading away. Other scholars have disagreed, pointing out that becoming part of integrated international structures has actually served to strengthen the role of the state. While the debate continues, NGOs and states frequently work together to solve many of the world's most pressing problems.

IN FAVOR OF STRENGTHENING THE ROLE OF THE STATE

In the era of globalization, states have had to share the international spotlight with non-state actors such as international organizations, multinational corporations, and, increasingly, terrorist groups. The march toward economic liberalism has meant that activities and policies that were exclusively under state control are now performed, at least in part, by other actors. This has led to the pronouncement of the "death" of the state.

Linda Weiss looks at the impact of globalization on the role of states. Contrary to most scholars, she argues that globalization makes indispensable certain services that states provide. These include managing welfare states, facilitating multilateral trade regimes, fostering economic sectors, and setting priorities. The state-reinforcing impact of globalization is also visible in the structuring role of domestic institutions, where market-oriented economies retain much of their distinctive national characteristics in areas from electoral systems to labor-business relations.

IN FAVOR OF NGOS

In the aftermath of the Cold War, the number of NGOs around the world grew dramatically as new issues came to dominate the agenda. Specifically, in the euphoria brought by the triumph of liberal democracy, issues such as human rights, the environment, and globalization came to the fore, bringing with them a plethora of new and old organizations that purported to act as watchdogs, activists, and alternative sources of information. With their access to the media and savvy communication abilities, NGOs have long become a mainstay in the public discourse and important players in international politics.

P. J. Simmons discusses the importance of NGOs and the roles they play. He stresses that NGOs can have an impact on all levels of government, as well as on non-state actors such as national and multinational corporations. Simmons notes that NGOs can play a powerful role in the policy process by setting agendas, negotiating outcomes, conferring legitimacy, and implementing solutions.

POINTS **TO PONDER**

1. How has globalization eroded state sovereignty?
2. How effective are NGOs in holding states accountable?
3. Why did NGOs flourish in the post-Cold War era?

Linda Weiss

The State-Augmenting
Effects of Globalisation

Global integration raises many questions about the state of the state. Its policy capacities, its institutional integrity and, not least, its political powers have been dramatically altered, so many pundits claim, by the spread of social relations across the globe. Although debate on these issues continues unabated, the ground has recently shifted. Nowadays, political analysts talk less of the *decline* of the state, and even less of its continuing potency, than of its *transformation.* Tightly constrained by exposure to global capital markets, the exit power of multinationals, participation in the multilateral trade regime and, in specific cases, European integration, the transformed state appears to be 'straitjacketed' rather than 'in retreat'. In this updated vision, global integration acts as a force that constrains states and reshapes institutions, severely restricting the room for manoeuvre, standardising domestic institutions and dispersing decision-making authority downwards, upwards and sideways to other power actors. In the new global drama of multilayered governance, states are metamorphosing not into minor figures, but into supporting players in a cast led by ever new protagonists. This is the influential 'constraints' view of state transformation. It is the story being told about globalisation's impact on the domestic capacities of the world's most advanced political institutions—those that prevail in the developed world. It is these that are the focus of discussion here.

There is, of course, a strong kernel of truth to the 'constraints' view of state transformation. Nevertheless, it suffers from two major limitations. One is an overwhelming concentration on the *constraining* effects of globalisation, which ignores its *enabling* consequences. The constraints can certainly seem convincing when examined in their own right, but when set within the larger context of state behaviour, the picture alters. Using two eyes rather than one, we find that some policy constraints are real (such as the difficulty in controlling interest and exchange rates), but that these become less important when set against the existence of ample room for action in key policy areas (such as social welfare, trade and industrial development); that important challenges for domestic adjustment do arise from the pressures of economic integration, but that these are neutralised, moderated

Linda Weiss, Government and International Relations, HO4, School of Economics and Political Science, University of Sydney, Sydney NSW, 2006, Australia.

or heightened by the domestic institutional context; and that pressures for policy and institutional conformity can at times be strong, but that this interpretation is less compelling than the general finding that states are doing similar things differently from one another. So we need to step back from the constraints to see them in the larger context of what state authorities are actually doing.

The second limitation of the 'constraints' view is a preoccupation with *power shift*—the dispersion and transfer of state power—while overlooking its *entwinement* with other power networks, especially at the transnational and supranational levels. The idea that we have some sort of power contest and power displacement going on between the national and the global—the idea that the state is either winning or losing out to the transnational—is deeply entrenched in the debate. And our newspapers supply us with ready anecdotes, along such lines as 'the WTO [World Trade Organization] rules against the EU [European Union] in the banana dispute' or 'the EU Commission directs France to rein in its budget deficit'.

But the metaphor of entwinement, rather than of winning and losing, seems a more useful image for our times. In this connection, Michael Mann has made the striking observation that, in the long run, 'transnational and national economic interaction have surged together, not one at the expense of the other'.[1] We need to build on that observation. Indeed, there is strong evidence that in the contemporary period the growth of the state has gone hand-in-hand with the rise of global corporations and multilateral institutions, and that these contemporary global networks remain intimately entwined with the domestic structures of nation-states. As national networks have grown, so too have transnational ones. This is a story of structural and political entwinement, of mutual reinforcement, rather than of power displacement. If we combine both long-run and contemporary trends, it is difficult to avoid the conclusion that globalisation is *reinforcing* and, in some important respects, *augmenting* the role of territorially-based institutions.

Drawing these points together, I offer three sets of arguments as to why the state will remain a central actor in economic and social development rather than become a residual authority under globalisation, and why economic integration has both state-reinforcing and state-augmenting effects.

The state-enabling effects of economic integration

The constraints that global integration places on policy autonomy—via financial markets and multilateral trade rules—have been amply rehearsed: currency and interest rates are more difficult to control; large budget deficits financed by government borrowing are susceptible to capital flight as investors anticipate inflation; and the use of certain policy instruments such as tariffs and subsidies, once favoured by wealthy countries in their climb up the ladder of development, is now heavily disciplined under international trade agreements. Consequently, when reduced to the logic of constraint, globalisation is associated with welfare retrenchment, tax cuts and the demise of trade and industrial governance. Yet the reality is rather different. The common view of withering welfare states, dwindling tax revenues and the demise of strategic trade policy sits well with ideological fashion and global market norms, but it fits poorly with the evidence. That evidence shows that, in the context of growing economic integration, states are on the whole either maintaining or moderately expanding (and indeed centralising) state expenditure and taxation, as well as strengthening the national infrastructure for producers and exporters in response to increased vulnerability. In this light, we need to recognise that globalisation has two logics, not just one. As well as a constraining impact, it produces a strong enabling dynamic that operates along parallel lines.

While the constraining aspect of globalisation is often explained by the economic logic of capital exit, the enabling aspect has more to do with the political logic of voice—that is, with the demand for coping solutions to ease adjustment pressures. The enabling logic of globalisation derives from a need to manage the increased vulnerability that economic integration brings. The more countries become integrated into the global economy, the more exposed certain social sectors become to the risks and uncertainties of market fluctuations, and consequently the more vulnerable to economic and social dislocation.[2] In this respect, globalisation is enlisting governments in multi-faceted efforts to cope with increased economic vulnerability.

Consider the welfare state. Although widely perceived as one of globalisation's victims, social spending patterns tell a story of the state's *increased* importance under globalisation, as well as the scope for political choice within *domestic* constraints. Three general trends support that conclusion. First, the welfare effort has not withered in spite of huge and ever-growing demands on the public purse. Average social spending in the Organisation for Economic Cooperation and Development (OECD) over the past 20 years has actually increased, not declined, as a share of national income; and the pressure has stemmed predominantly from changes in domestic structures, not global markets. These pressures have originated from changing social patterns, such as the ageing population and increases in the number of single-parent households, coupled with the rising cost of child care, pensions and health care. Even so, restructuring rather than outright retrenchment has been the main response, as governments everywhere trim some programmes in favour of maintaining or expanding others. Second, in spite of similar pressures, nation-states have generally approached welfare reform in systematically different ways. Third, and most tellingly, nowhere has such spending been maintained at higher levels than in countries with the highest levels of trade integration.

In a nutshell, trade openness continues to be associated with maintenance or growth in social spending, rather than with its contraction.

The trend of welfare maintenance and expansion across Europe contrasts with that of welfare retrenchment more typical of Anglo-Saxon countries, the club of so-called liberal welfare states in the United Kingdom, Ireland, the United States and Canada. Yet, here too the 'declines' in social spending have been modest and have fluctuated over several decades, rather than exhibiting clear downward trends. The institutional resilience reflected in the different patterns of restructuring is, of course, at odds with the standard expectation of generalised welfare retrenchment.

In order to pay for these services, the overall tax burden has been increased in the period of growing economic integration and, again, the increases have been most significant in the most 'globalised' settings. Between 1965 and 1999 governments throughout the OECD have generally *increased* tax yields (from direct much more than indirect taxes, and especially from personal taxes at middle-income levels). Average tax burdens grew by 20 per cent and government expenditure by 23 per cent. The increases were most pronounced where integration went furthest: in the European Union, tax and expenditure burdens grew by 25 per cent and 28 per cent respectively. Notwithstanding increased capital mobility, corporate income taxes as a share of gross domestic product (GDP)—that is, effective tax *burdens*, not nominal rates—have also increased significantly. Compared with the start of this period (1965–9), the corporate tax burdens imposed by all levels of government in 23 OECD countries were 35 per cent *higher* for the 1995–7 period (and 40 per cent higher at central government level for 1995–9). And, once again, in the most globalised settings—referring this time to countries with very high dependence on inflows of foreign direct investment (FDI)—the 1995–9 burdens compared with those of 1980–4 were on average much higher than the OECD average (by 32 per cent and 17 per cent respectively).[3] It must be acknowledged that *nominal* corporate rates (as opposed to effective tax burdens) have been *lowered* in many countries as governments put in place new tax structures from the mid 1980s onwards. However, governments have found scope to protect (and increase) their revenue by broadening the base, and simultaneously reducing tax concessions. Of course, the opposite pattern of higher nominal rates and concessions has also been seen in the higher-taxing, more highly integrated economies.

A similar relationship between increasing openness and state augmentation can be seen in the approach to trade and industrial promotion under the new multilateral trade regime. Here, too, expectations that the WTO would act to crush policy capacity have not been met. Although states are now heavily disciplined in the use of old-style tariffs and subsidies to promote domestic industries (agriculture being a major exception), new WTO rules offer significant room to pursue national objectives. Under the banner of science and technology policy, on one hand, and export facilitation, on the other, governments across the OECD are interacting with the private sector in much more complex and proactive ways than was required under an earlier regime of tariff protection and industrial rescue. Nowadays, national authorities are co-sponsoring the venture-capital funding of high-tech start-ups, financing pre-commercial technologies and product development, transferring intellectual property from public agencies to the private sector, engaging in strategic screening of FDI, offering concessional finance and other sweeteners to assist home-country multinationals win foreign procurement contracts, and providing financial and infrastructural support for export promotion.[4] Similarly, states have restructured and scaled up their export promotion infrastructure in the face of declining export subsidies.

Despite the pervasive ideology of competitive liberalism, the new multilateral discipline has produced a more proactive and strategically oriented approach to industrial governance, manifested not only in state authorities setting priorities and designating preferred sectors or technologies for support, but also in designing results-based incentive schemes that stipulate performance outcomes. Thus, while it is generally true that industrial (though not agricultural) subsidies have diminished, this is because governments have curbed the use of 'industrial welfare' policy (rescues of ailing firms, often in so-called 'sunset' industries) in favour of putting their limited resources into 'sunrise' sectors—the industries of growing importance in international trade. These are located increasingly in science-based, knowledge- and information-intensive sectors, which, over the 1990s, increased from 18 per cent to 25 per cent of world manufacturing trade.

Indeed, WTO law is currently most restrictive for sectors that are now least technologically important for the developed nations, and potentially most important for developing countries. This means that, at least for the more established economies, the global trade rules offer ample room to move where it matters most. However, while WTO rules allow rich countries enough scope to promote new industry through science and technology programmes, for those countries still climbing the ladder of development the WTO agreements on Trade-Related Investment Measures (TRIMS) and Trade-Related Aspects of Intellectual Property Rights (TRIPS) reduce the developmental space that the General Agreement on Tariffs and Trade (GATT) formerly allowed.

For all this activism, national policy-makers prefer to use the free-market language of 'levelling the playing field' or even the geopolitical language of 'defending national security' to justify their interventions, rarely owning up to pursuing 'national economic objectives' as this goes against the new globalist ethos. Nevertheless, many states are choosing where and how to target resources, often in collaboration with the private sector. The implication is that, far from confining governments to providing a business-friendly investment environment for companies of whatever national origin, the lifting of tariff barriers has provided the stimulus for an increasing number of states (noted more for industrial rescues and tariff protection than industrial promotion and upgrading) to take a more proactive approach in order to meet the challenges of openness.

The structuring role of domestic institutions

We can see the state-reinforcing effects of globalisation particularly clearly in the structuring role of domestic, territorially-based institutions. Domestic institutions are the normative and organisational structures which shape policy preferences and structure opportunities for public–private collaboration, as well as opportunities for the representation of interests hurt or harmed by globalisation. As comparative studies of policy reform in sectors ranging from financial regulation to social welfare have shown, domestic institutions not only shape the ability of key constituencies affected by globalisation to make their interests count politically, but also structure the political values and incentives that encourage governments to respond in particular ways.[5]

The centrality of domestic institutions is illustrated by the varying forms of welfare reform observed above. Institutional configurations are significant not only because they structure opportunities for representation of those who are harmed by market integration, but also because they shape the values that underlie policy preferences. For example, the domestic structures of liberal market economies like Britain and the US are identified as those most likely to promote retrenchment. By contrast, in coordinated market economies like Germany, states are embedded in extensive social infrastructures and face potentially strong resistance to retrenchment. In these settings, domestic structures are more likely to encourage policy adjustments that blunt the pressures of openness.[6] This cross-national variation in welfare commitment, in turn, attests to the reinforcement of the state's infrastructural powers—the ability to access and redistribute territorially-generated resources in line with socially negotiated objectives.

For many, European integration offers several clues about the likely effects of globalisation more generally. Proponents of globalisation claim that institutions lose their distinctive structuring influence as integration brings more standardisation and convergence in economic practices. They expect that, under the twin pressures of regionalisation and global competition, the countries of Europe will grow ever more alike as they move towards a standard, market model of capitalism. Yet, despite the pressures of European integration, and notwithstanding certain modifications, the three major varieties of capitalism—exemplified by market capitalist Britain, coordinated or managed capitalist Germany and state-guided capitalist France—continue to co-exist and shape economic policy and practice. Evidence of national pathways of adjustment spanning finance, production and the role of the state indicates that, although liberalising reforms have made European member states more market-oriented, their institutional structures of government, business and labour relations nonetheless remain distinctive.[7] The general trend of nationally distinctive adaptation to the forces of globalisation has been described by some analysts of Europeanisation as 'domestic adaptation with national colors'.[8] This is exemplified by the process of policy adjustment to European directives.

States sit astride the domestic institutions which configure interest group and electoral arrangements, shape programmatic norms and policy preferences, structure relations within and between government and business, and even inform the operational and adjustment strategies of globally oriented business. As the normative and organisational complexes which aggregate and represent interests in the political arena, domestic institutions are perhaps most fruitfully understood as the filters through which states mediate and respond to globalisation pressures. What this implies is that, in an age when borders are less significant in delimiting networks of interaction and, consequently, when territory appears less decisive as a power resource, domestic institutions have become more rather than less important in structuring social space.

The entwinement of national and global power networks

Many note that state authority is being pooled, delegated, transferred or redistributed to new sites of decision making that create multilayered structures of governance. While some argue that the shift of power upwards to supranational actors and institutions extends territorial reach, enabling states to achieve their goals, others see it as a curb on autonomy that transforms the state into a residual authority. Ultimately, many of these disputes are conceptual—disagreements over the nature of power—rather than substantive. More headway with our opening question can be made by sidestepping these disputes and turning to the third way in which global integration can be seen to reinforce the state. The most significant change to the transformed state is not the dispersion of national authority, but rather its *entwinement* with global and supranational networks and institutions of governance. This is nowhere more powerfully illustrated than in the national foundations of European integration and the political foundations of the WTO.

While some argue that European integration represents an era of post-statehood, there is little agreement over the nature of the EU or its impact on national governance. In order to maintain legitimacy and member compliance, European institutions have been designed to safeguard national differences and to accommodate and preserve state interests. These characteristics make European institutions inherently ambiguous insofar as they result in the fragmentation of power, the creation of rules open to interpretation, and decision-making practices which offer 'escape routes' from common undertakings in order to cope with unwillingness to relinquish sovereignty and disagreement over how the EU should evolve; and, above all, to secure compliance and legitimacy for European institutions.[9] While policy expansion in everything from environment, telecommunications and consumer protection is enormous, this is often framed in a very general way that allows member states considerable latitude over the details of implementation, a point amply supported by research showing substantial divergence in policy outcomes.[10] The most striking feature of Europeanisation has been not the transfer or parcelling out of powers from one level to another, but rather their entwinement in a system of reciprocal consent.

Political entwinement of global and national networks is perhaps more striking in the basic operation of the world trade regime. In the case of the WTO, the argument is often made that power and interest politics in international relations are being supplanted by legalism, embodied in the role of the Appellate Body in dispute settlement. Recent research throws that idea into question. It demonstrates a consistent pattern of behaviour among the major actors—the WTO, EU and US. The process of dispute resolution underscores the strategic nature of interaction before, during and after dispute resolution and, more generally, the political limits of the WTO's legitimacy. The pattern of interaction demonstrates a kind of political calculus, where the major power actors calculate the likely impact of their actions on the legitimacy of the WTO system and adjust their actions accordingly.[11] This again illustrates how firmly an ostensibly global system of legal rules is bound up with the strategic interactions of territorial political networks.

Political entwinement is a fundamental feature of both global and supranational systems of governance, which depend heavily on the institutional resources of the nation-state to legitimate their continued operation and to execute their goals. But it is not confined to these networks. Entwinement remains significant even in that most globalised of markets, the government bond market. While much has been made of the power of the bond markets to constrain government policy, the other side to the story is the dependence of bond markets on government debt. Should governments go too far in their zeal to be debt free, the bond market would simply disappear. The first to protest such a move would, of course, be investors and traders!

All this suggests that pure globalism is an impossibility and that robust nation-states are essential for its progress (though states, robust or otherwise, can frustrate its progress too). Unlike early globalisation which preceded the formation of nation-states, integration today takes place in a system already constituted by territorially centralised powers. They are not just important drivers of globalisation; they are also its normative and organisational supports. This makes contemporary globalisation intrinsically *also* 'national' in its construction.

Conclusion

The argument I have put forward suggests that deepening integration has a state-augmenting effect, emphasising the state's centrality to social life. If there is a significant constraint from globalisation, it is not in the direction expected. Generally speaking, states have increased direct tax yields, maintained or expanded social spending, and devised more complex systems of trade and industrial governance in order to cope with deepening integration. Moreover, the significant relationship between strong trade integration and high social expenditure discovered more than two decades ago appears no less valid today. There is good evidence that economic integration is strongly linked with the centralisation of public expenditure and taxation, as fiscal resources have generally shifted into the hands of national governments (even while subnational officials may find their political autonomy enhanced).[12] Territorially-based institutions continue to structure responses to the adjustment pressures of integration, which in turn reinforces distinctive varieties of political economy, welfare capitalism and even transnational firm behaviour. Even the smooth operation and evolution of the most seemingly transnational networks of governance—the EU and WTO—are inextricably tied to the organisational and normative resources of constituent states. Much has changed in the international economic environment, but the enabling effects of economic integration and the entwinement of global and national structures ensure that states command a central place in the unfolding drama.

The conclusion is thus not simply that globalisation's effects are complex and contingent or that the state has both lost and gained, trading some powers for others. It is that, in the larger scheme of things, globalisation reinforces and augments the state's centrality to social life. Given that nation-states are the pivots of the global political economy, it would be not only misleading but also unwise to give credence to the ideas that national authorities now have less capacity, scope and responsibility, or that states are becoming superannuated, residual powers in a world of multilayered governance.

NOTES

An earlier version was presented as a keynote paper at the 'State of the World' inaugural conference of the Princeton Institute for International & Regional Studies, 13–14 February 2004, Princeton University. I wish to acknowledge the support of an Australian Research Council Discovery Grant for the larger research project on which this paper draws.

1. Michael Mann, *Globalisation and Modernity*, unpublished manuscript, Department of Sociology, UCLA, 2000, p. 44.

2. For the more detailed argument concerning globalisation's enabling logic, see Linda Weiss, 'Bringing domestic institutions back in', in: Linda Weiss (ed.), *States in the Global Economy: Bringing Domestic Institutions Back In* (Cambridge University Press, 2003), pp. 1–36.

3. John M. Hobson, 'Disappearing taxes or the "race to the middle"? Fiscal policy in the OECD', in: Weiss, *States in the Global Economy*, pp. 46–50.

4. This and the following material on industrial governance is drawn from Linda Weiss, 'Global Governance, National Strategies: How Industrialized States Make Room to Move Under the WTO', *Review of International Political Economy*, forthcoming 2005.

5. On regulatory reform, see Steven Vogel, *Freer Markets, More Rules* (Cornell University Press, 1996); on welfare restructuring, see Duane Swank, 'Withering welfare? Globalisation, political economic institutions, and contemporary welfare states', in: Weiss, *States in the Global Economy*, pp. 58–82.

6. See Swank, 'Withering welfare?'.

7. On the main varieties of capitalism in Europe, see Vivien A. Schmidt, *The Futures of European Capitalism* (Oxford University Press, 2002); and Peter A. Hall & David Soskice (eds), *Varieties of Capitalism: The Institutional Foundations of Comparative Advantage* (Oxford University Press, 2001).

8. Maria Green Cowles, James Caporaso & Thomas Risse (eds), *Transforming Europe: Europeanization and Domestic Change* (Cornell University Press, 2000).

9. Adrienne Héritier, *Policy-Making and Diversity in Europe* (Cambridge University Press, 1999); and Andrew Moravcsik, 'Federalism in the European Union: rhetoric and reality', in: K. Nicolaidis & R. Howse (eds), *The Federal Vision* (Oxford University Press, 2001), pp. 161–87.

10. Adrienne Héritier & Christopher Knill, 'Differential responses to European policies: a comparison', in: Adrienne Héritier (ed.), *Differential Europe: New Opportunities and Restrictions for Member-State Policies* (Rowman & Littlefield, 2001), pp. 257–94.

11. Geoffrey Garrett & James McCall Smith, 'The Politics of WTO Dispute Settlement', unpublished manuscript, UCLA and George Washington University, 2002.

12. Geoffrey Garrett & Jonathan Rodden, 'Globalisation and fiscal decentralization', in: Miles Kahler & David A. Lake (eds), *Governance in a Global Economy: Political Authority in Transition* (Princeton University Press, 2003), pp. 87–109.

P. J. Simmons

Learning to Live with NGOs

In the summer of 1994, U.S. environmental advocacy groups were getting ready to celebrate. The United States was about to join almost 90 other nations in ratifying the Convention on Biodiversity, which enjoyed broad support from U.S. environmentalists, agro-business groups, and the biotechnology sector. After hearings characterized in the press as a "love fest," members of the Senate Foreign Relations Committee were almost unanimously prepared to back the treaty. Then a group of agricultural and trade nongovernmental organizations (NGOs) previously uninvolved in the debate weighed in, warning that ratification could, in effect, destroy U.S. agriculture. As the *Chicago Tribune* reported in September 1994, evidence later surfaced that some of this opposition was based on a virulent misinformation campaign claiming, among other things, that treaty advocates were all foes of farming, logging, and fishing. But by then, the biodiversity treaty had been relegated to the back of a long line of treaties competing for congressional attention.

At a time when NGOs are celebrating their remarkable success in achieving a ban on landmines and creating an International Criminal Court (ICC), it may seem churlish to recall a four-year-old episode that many would likely regard as a defeat. But amid the breathless accounts about the growing power of NGOs, the failure of the biodiversity treaty is a useful reminder of the complexity of the role that these groups now play in international affairs. Embracing a bewildering array of beliefs, interests, and agendas, they have the potential to do as much harm as good. Hailed as the exemplars of grassroots democracy in action, many NGOs are, in fact, decidedly undemocratic and unaccountable to the people they claim to represent. Dedicated to promoting more openness and participation in decision making, they can instead lapse into old-fashioned interest group politics that produces gridlock on a global scale.

The question facing national governments, multilateral institutions, and national and multinational corporations is not whether to include NGOs in their deliberations and activities. Although many traditional centers of power are fighting a rear-guard action against these new players, there is no real way to keep them out. Instead, the real challenge is figuring out how to incorporate NGOs into the international system in a way that takes account of their diversity and scope, their various strengths and weaknesses, and their capacity to disrupt as well as to create.

Why NGOs Matter

Defining NGOs is not an exercise for the intellectually squeamish. A 1994 United Nations document, for example, describes an NGO as a

> non-profit entity whose members are citizens or associations of citizens of one or more countries and whose activities are determined by the collective will of its members in response to the needs of the members of one or more communities with which the NGO cooperates.

This formulation embraces just about every kind of group except for private businesses, revolutionary or terrorist groups, and political parties. Other popular substitutes for the term NGO (private voluntary organizations, civil society organizations, and the independent sector) are likewise almost terminally vague. A better approach to understanding NGOs and what they are would focus on their respective goals, membership, funding sources, and other such factors. . . .

Yet although there may be no universal agreement on what NGOs are exactly, there is widespread agreement that their numbers, influence, and reach are at unprecedented levels. . . . In 1948, for example, the UN listed 41 consultative groups that were formally accredited to cooperate and consult with the UN Economic and Social Council (ECOSOC); in 1998, there were more than 1,500 with varying degrees of participation and access. Until recently, NGOs clustered in developed and democratic nations; now groups sprout up from Lima to Beijing. They are changing societal norms, challenging national governments, and linking up with counterparts in powerful transnational alliances. And they are muscling their way into areas of high politics, such as arms control, banking, and trade, that were previously dominated by the state.

In general terms, NGOs affect national governments, multilateral institutions, and national and multinational corporations in four ways: setting agendas, negotiating outcomes, conferring legitimacy, and implementing solutions.

Setting Agendas

NGOs have long played a key role in forcing leaders and policymakers to pay attention. In the early 1800s, U.S. and European bodies such as the British and Foreign Anti-Slavery Society were driving forces behind government action on the slave trade; by the turn of the century, groups such as the Anglo-Oriental Society for the Suppression of the Opium Trade were leading an influential antidrug movement that culminated in the 1912 Hague Opium Convention. In 1945, NGOs were largely responsible for inserting human-rights language in the UN Charter and have since put almost every major human-rights issue on the international agenda. Likewise, NGO activism since the 1960s and 1970s successfully raised the profile of global environmental and population issues.

Instead of holding marches or hanging banners off buildings, NGO members now use computers and cell phones to launch global public-relations blitzes that can force issues to the top of policymakers' "to do" lists. Consider the 1997 Nobel Prize–winning campaign by NGOs to conclude a treaty banning landmines over the objections of the United States. The self-described "full working partnership" between the Canadian government and a loose coalition of more than 350 humanitarian and arms-control NGOs from 23 countries was key to the negotiations' success. But what seized the attention of the public and policymakers was the coalition's innovative media campaign using the World Wide Web, faxes, e-mail, newsletters, and even *Superman* and *Batman* comic books. Treaty supporters won the signatures of 122 nations in 14 months. When several coalition members announced plans for a follow-on campaign against small arms, the U.S. government sprang into action, meeting with 20 other countries in July 1998 to launch official talks on a possible treaty. . . .

Negotiating Outcomes

NGOs can be essential in designing multilateral treaties that work. Chemical manufacturing associations from around the world helped set up an effective verification regime for the 1997 Chemical Weapons Convention that could be supported by industries and militaries. Throughout the various sessions of negotiations on climate change, groups such as the Environmental Defense Fund and the World Business Council for Sustainable Development have helped craft compromise proposals that attempt to reconcile environmental and commercial interests; meanwhile, NGOs have been instrumental in helping government negotiators understand the science behind the issues that they seek to address.

NGOs can also build trust and break deadlocks when negotiations have reached an impasse. In 1990, a sole Italian NGO, the Comunità di Sant'Egidio, started the informal meetings between the warring parties in Mozambique that eventually led to a peace settlement. During talks in 1995 to extend the Treaty on the Non-Proliferation of Nuclear Weapons, NGOs from several countries working with the South African government delegation helped forge a compromise that led to the treaty's permanent extension.

Conferring Legitimacy

NGO judgments can be decisive in promoting or withholding public and political support. The World Bank learned this lesson in the early 1990s, albeit the hard way. After decades of watching the bank do business with only a handful of NGOs and brush off demands for change, more than 150 public-interest NGOs took part in a sustained campaign to spur greater openness and accountability and to encourage debt reduction and development strategies that were more equitable and less destructive to the environment. Today, partly as a result of this high-profile pressure, about half of the bank's lending projects have provisions for NGO involvement—up from an average of only 6 percent between 1973 and 1988. The bank has even included NGOs such as Oxfam International in once sacrosanct multilateral debt relief discussions—against the wishes of many World Bank and International Monetary Fund (IMF) officials. Even the IMF is beginning to change its tune. In June 1998, the IMF Board of Directors met with several NGO leaders to discuss their proposals to increase the fund's transparency.

Making Solutions Work

NGOs on the ground often make the impossible possible by doing what governments cannot or will not. Some humanitarian and development NGOs have a natural advantage because of their perceived neutrality and experience. The International Committee of the Red Cross, for example, is able to deliver health care to political prisoners in exchange for silence about any human-rights violations that its members witness. Other groups such as Oxfam International provide rapid relief during and after complex humanitarian disasters—with and without UN partners. Moreover, as governments downsize and new challenges crowd the international agenda, NGOs increasingly fill the breach. Willy nilly, the UN and nation-states are depending more on NGOs to get things done. Total assistance by and through international NGOs to the developing world amounted to about $8 billion in 1992—accounting for 13 percent of all development assistance and more than the entire amount transferred by the UN system.

International NGOs also play critical roles in translating international agreements and norms into domestic realities. Where governments have turned a blind eye, groups such as Amnesty International and the Committee to Protect Journalists call attention to violations of the UN Declaration on Human Rights. Environmental NGOs police agreements such as the Convention on International Trade in Endangered Species, uncovering more accurate data on compliance than that provided by member nations. Perhaps one of the most vital but overlooked NGO roles is to promote the societal changes needed to make international agreements work. Signatories of the Organization for Economic Cooperation and Development's 1997 Bribery Convention, for example, are counting on the more than 80 chapters of Transparency International to help change the way their societies view bribery and corruption.

Increasingly, however, NGOs operate outside existing formal frame-works, moving independently to meet their goals and establishing new stan-dards that governments, institutions, and corporations are themselves compelled to follow through force of public opinion. The UN moratorium on driftnet fishing in 1992 and the U.S. International Dolphin Conservation Act of 1994, for example, largely codified changes in fishing practices that NGOs had already succeeded in promoting and then winning from commer-cial fisheries. More recently, even as governments and multilateral institu-tions slowly begin to consider measures to promote the sustainable use of forests, the environmental NGO Greenpeace led a European consumer boy-cott that persuaded a leading Canadian logging company to announce that it would change the way that it harvests trees. . . .

CHAPTER 17

TURKEY AND THE EUROPEAN UNION: EXCLUSION v. MEMBERSHIP

Turkey as a Privileged Partner of the European Union

Advocate: Hans Arnold

Source: "Political Arguments Against Turkey's Accession to the European Union," *International Politics and Society*, no. 3 (2007), pp. 101–113, excerpt.

Turkey as a Member of the European Union

Advocate: Adam Hug

Source: "Turkey: Europe's Future," *guardian.co.uk.* Nov. 10, 2008.

In October 2005, the European Union and Turkey started accession negotiations, which was the culmination of more than 40 years of institutionalized relationship between the two parties. Unlike all other previous and ongoing negotiations, however, the talks with Turkey had the distinction of not having accession as their explicitly stated goal. This stipulation revealed the deep divide among the EU's member states on Turkey's candidacy. Led by the current governments of France and Germany, some member states see some form of "privileged partnership"—which would mean Turkey is excluded from participation in EU institutions—as the most Turkey could be offered. Other members warn of dramatic consequences should the EU offer Turkey anything but membership. Turkey also firmly rejects "privileged partnership" or any other institutionalized arrangement that falls short of full membership.

The negotiations have been difficult and the process promises to be arduous and lengthy at best. Turkish officials readily admit that their country must undertake further political and economic reforms in order to be ready for EU membership. While Turkey must do more to meet European standards, in the end all it can do is become suitable to be included in the club. Turkey's membership will be decided by the 27 members of the EU, each one acting in accordance with its interests and its vision of the future of European integration. Whether a democratic country with an overwhelmingly Muslim population can be accepted as an equal among some of the most affluent liberal democracies of the world is a topic of utmost importance for the future of the EU, as well as the coexistence of two great civilizations: Islam and Christianity.

IN FAVOR OF PRIVILEGED PARTNERSHIP

Opposition to Turkey's membership in the EU rests on geographical, economic, political, and cultural factors. Turkey's geographical location—the vast majority of the country lies in Asia—along with its history and religion as well as political development prompt many opponents of membership to claim that it is not European, and therefore, has no place in the EU. The populist fear of millions of Muslim Turks immigrating to Europe following accession is another major source of opposition, especially among the public. Finally, the presupposed financial costs for the EU and the very real institutional consequences of the accession of such a large country also play a role in the calculations of its opponents.

Hans Arnold begins his argument by pointing out that admitting Turkey into the club would be in gross violation of EU treaties simply because Turkey is not a European country and its people are not European. In addition, he questions the impact of the influx of Turkish immigrants on European societies and their ability to integrate. Finally, Arnold makes the case that possible Turkish accession would have negative consequences for EU's foreign policy and contests the notion that Turkey can be a "bridge" between Europe and the Arab world. Turkey's membership, he posits, is advocated only by those who do not want to see a unified Europe, including the United States.

IN FAVOR OF MEMBERSHIP FOR TURKEY

Turkey is a democratic country founded on secular principles with a predominantly Muslim population that is often considered to be a model for countries in the Middle East. It has a rapidly expanding economy and a dynamic young population. It has been a reliable member of NATO and all other multilateral organizations in Europe. These reasons make up the cornerstone of support for Turkey's membership in the EU.

Adam Hug makes the case for Turkey's membership in the European Union. He points to the strategic importance of the country, which served the NATO alliance well during the Cold War and which today makes it a key player in three of the most important geopolitical regions of the world: the Middle East, the Caucasus, and Central Asia. The Turkish economy has been steadily growing and is already deeply intertwined with the European Union. Most importantly, Hug argues that Europe's choice over Turkey's membership will define what kind of an organization the EU becomes. While the road to membership is challenging and long, he posits that the EU, European businesses, and trade unions should take the lead in making Turkish membership a reality.

POINTS **TO PONDER**

1. What is the United States' position on Turkey's candidacy for membership in the European Union?
2. Are Islam and democracy inherently incompatible?
3. How would Turkey's membership in the EU affect its other member states?

———————

Hans Arnold

Political Arguments Against Turkey's Accession to the European Union

The Limits on EU Accession

The original six western European states founded the European Community for Coal and Steel in 1952, followed by the European Economic Community (EEC) in 1957 (what is now the EU). In the preamble of the EEC treaty they inserted the solemn declaration that they had made this treaty "determined to lay the foundations of an ever closer union among the peoples of Europe." Article 237 of the same treaty stipulates accordingly: "Each European state can apply to become a member of the Community."

Since then this aim and this provision have been integral parts of the legal and political basis of the EU and its basic policy to unify Europe. They can be found again in the Treaty on the European Union (EU) of 1993 (the so-called Maastricht Treaty that contained the whole of the EEC treaty) and most recently they can be found in the project for a Treaty on a Constitution for Europe signed by the EU member states on October 29, 2004. . . .

These contractual provisions are thus part of the common law established by the European treaties. They bind the member states and the institutions of the EU. The member states could change them but with regard to the legal provisions for accession to the EU so far this has not been considered an option. Therefore, there is no doubt that according to the basic and legal principles of the EU only European states and peoples can become members. And there is no doubt either that Turkey is not a European state and that its citizens are not a European people. Turkish accession to the EU would thus be a gross violation of the European treaties. If the EU member states decided otherwise some would say that it would be a kind of suicide on the part of the EU. . . .

European Uncertainties

Against this background it is certainly regrettable that the member states of the EU, despite their clear treaties, have not been able to develop a common position with regard to the Turkish application for EU membership. Instead they have produced uncertainties which ever since have governed every discourse or discussion on the issue. On the other hand, it cannot be ignored that the current situation is the result not only of a common decision by the member states or just a reaction of them, but also of continuous political pressure exerted over a long period by the United States, both on the EU as a whole and on individual member states to start up negotiations with Turkey. The European uncertainties of today have their origin more in transatlantic than in European–Turkish relations. And they are the result of the inability of the EU states to develop an adequate joint response to US pressure. . . .

In addition to the legal and political limitations on EU extension there is the purely political problem of the inability of EU member states to define what the EU should ultimately be. Should it become an integrated legal and political entity—this idea governed European policy until the end of the Cold War—or should it be no more than a fully developed common market with a few political, social and cultural decorations? Most Europeans appear to want to take the first route, but there are forces that want to take European policy in the other direction. The Turkish application for EU membership is thus not only another case of EU extension. Judging by the way this issue is being handled by the EU it is rather a decisive test of which future the EU is going to choose.

Turkish Uncertainties

. . .Today Turkey presents itself to Europe as a country in which radical nationalism and religious fundamentalism are decisive political forces, and where much depends on military rule, and democratic procedures, independent jurisdiction, and the protection of human and civil rights are below the standards of all new member states at the time of accession. The problems connected with the Armenians and Kurds create strong and lasting doubts in Europe concerning whether satisfactory standards will be reached in the foreseeable future.

Certainly, there have been improvements in recent years. But a number of the changes claimed by Turkey seem to exist only on paper and the will for further improvements seems to have waned. The list of shortcomings is long, including in areas of great importance to the EU and its citizens. For example, while in Europe it is an official offense to deny the Holocaust, in Turkey it is an official offense to acknowledge the massacre of the Armenians. While in the EU Gaelic, the Irish language, was recently declared an official language, minorities in Turkey still have difficulties using their own languages. Furthermore, in the EU Muslims have more rights than Christians in Turkey, while the Turkish offense of insulting the Turkish state looks rather exotic in European eyes, to say the least. Apart from all that, the necessary changes concern matters which are deeply rooted in history, political culture and religious belief and so will be extremely difficult to handle. Further, there seems to be no power in Turkey strong enough to do the job. The military community backs secularism against religious fundamentalism, but is equally enthusiastic for extreme nationalism, including suppression of the liberties of ethnic and cultural minorities (to force them to become really "Turkish Turks"). . . .

Effects of Turkish EU Membership

The possible effects of Turkey's accession to the EU cannot be predicted with precision. But it can be assumed that there would be three kinds of problem: first, problems within the existing EU states related to the harmonization of specific elements and structures of Turkish civilization and society with European civilization and society; second, problems within the EU caused by the entry of a nation state of the size of Turkey; and third, the international effects of Turkish EU membership.

One problem would be how Turks came to settle in other EU states, once they were granted full freedom of movement: primarily in groupings or individually, spread out all over the country of residence? Immigrants living in closed communities usually have more social, cultural and political difficulties living in harmony with the native citizens of their host country. The question is, would Turkish EU citizens living in other EU states rather become citizens of their host country or would they form parallel societies of their own? This question gains additional weight as Europeans are witnessing efforts made by Turkish political, social and cultural institutions to target Turkish immigrants in EU countries to manipulate them for nationalistic and other purposes. Ultimately the nature of such influence would depend on the Turkish uncertainties already mentioned, though they may change over time. Given the general freedom of movement within the EU internal instability in Turkey could increase migration flows to other parts of the EU. This, certainly, would be in full compliance with the European treaties, European policy and European normality, but it could be considered a threat by the countries receiving the migration flows.

None of this has anything to do with real or assumed differences between Islam and Christianity nor with ethnic considerations. Widespread European concerns rather have to do with social and political questions concerning Turkey after EU accession, above all the three basic questions: first, what role can basic European values play in future Turkish society and in particular in the communities living in other EU states? Second, would such values be fully consolidated within Turkish society? And third, would they be respected by Turkish institutions? These questions arise primarily because the cultural and national identities of European peoples and states are rooted in the common European cultural ground in which they have grown for nearly two thousand years. The non-European ground in which Turkish society is rooted is obviously of another kind. Therefore the question is whether social, cultural and political harmonization equal or similar to that existing between current EU states would be possible between the EU and Turkey. Or would Turkey's accession to the EU perhaps only be possible if either the Europeans or the Turks were ready to give up essential parts of their cultural identity? And if this were necessary, could it really be Europe's task to force such harmonization or standardization on Turks and Europeans for the sake of a political project?. . .

Apart from the internal Turkish and European–Turkish problems the EU itself, after its extension from 12 to 27 members, is in a fragile condition. It is in real danger of overstretch, with the risk of damaging its cohesion. Taking everything together, the experiment of including Turkey in the EU would be a tremendous and incalculable risk for the Union and there is not the slightest advantage for the EU that could justify such a risk. From the point of view of European interests the inclusion of Turkey in the EU would be irresponsible.

In this context it is no coincidence that exactly those Europeans and European governments who are striving for a more loosely conceived common-market EU also argue for Turkish EU membership. Among other things they reason that an ever larger EU would have an ever growing weight and influence in world affairs. This reasoning, however, is simply wrong. Experience inside the EU provides evidence that international organizations become weaker the more members they have. Today's EU lacks cohesion, something which is particularly visible in relation to the EU's position in international relations.

The EU's ability to act in world affairs as a single entity is still limited. The effects of Turkish EU membership on this could only be negative. The EU would have common borders with Georgia, Armenia, Iran, Iraq, and Syria. Politically it would thus automatically be part of the Middle East and its political problems, including above all the situation in and around Iraq and the Israeli–Palestinian conflict. The common European policy towards and within that region would quite naturally be strongly influenced by the interests and policy of its large member Turkey, which as an EU member would be neighbor and part of that region at the same time. . . .

Furthermore, after Turkey's EU accession an application from Israel for EU membership could be expected with certainty. Israel considers itself as a European state situated geographically in the Middle East. The idea of Israeli EU membership is already being discussed in political circles in Israel and the USA. It is a fair guess that pressure from the USA in favor of Israeli EU membership would certainly not be weaker than the pressure in favor of Turkey. There can be few doubts concerning how the EU, taking into account history and with—by then—over 100 million Muslim EU citizens would react to such an application. With Israel as an EU member the EU among other things would be an integral part of the Israeli–Palestinian conflict and would have to find an answer to the question of whether the Palestinians, too, should become EU members. . . .

Another particular problem would be created by Turkish EU membership in view of the EU's neighbors east of Europe. If non-European Turkey, which has only a very short common border with the EU, were to become a member of the Union, how could membership be refused to Belarus, Ukraine and Moldavia, which have long common borders with the EU and which believe strongly that they belong to Europe? Turkish EU membership would mean the end of Europe as an actor in world affairs, the end of a closely unified Europe and the beginning of all kinds of negative uncertainties for European cooperation. . . .

Adam Hug

Turkey, Europe's Future

Drowned out by the acclamation for the Obama victory last week, the European commission quietly released its progress report on Turkish accession to the EU. While it welcomed Turkey's economic performance and the progress it had made strengthening its legal system, the commission's message was that there was a lot done but a lot still to do.

The road towards Turkish membership is long and rocky but I believe that Turkey is central to the future development of the EU. The eventual decision to accept or reject Turkey will have significant ramifications for the type of organisation it will become.

Put crudely, Turkish membership will signify a choice for Europe between becoming an outward-looking union at peace with its internal diversity that prioritises the economic and security needs of its members, or an insular, almost parochial grouping, searching for an imagined cultural homogeneity. This is why the Foreign Policy Centre has released a new pamphlet to coincide with the report arguing that we have to clearly lay out the practical case that both the EU and Turkey would be more prosperous and secure if accession is successful.

Turkish membership is often described as a "win-win" situation for the EU and Turkey but it is clear that victory will be hard fought. The majority of European public opinion opposes Turkish membership and leading politicians in member states including France, Germany and Austria have publicly stated that they do not see Turkey as a future member and have pushed for a nebulous "privileged partnership". Turkish support for membership has also waned in recent years due to the sluggish progress of the accession process and the opposition of some EU leaders.

The challenge set before advocates of Turkish membership then, is to transform a climate of cynicism and opposition to ensure membership is granted once Turkey meets the strict criteria required for entry. Prosperity and security form the twin pillars of the case for Turkish membership. Turkey has been at the bedrock of European security since the cold war, joining NATO in 1952 and guarding Europe's south-eastern flank against the former Soviet Union. Today it sits at the gateway to the Middle East, the Caucasus and central Asia, a key strategic player in all three regions. Turkey can play a critical role in our energy security, where it is the key alternative transit route to Russia for Caspian oil and gas and the swiftest route for Iraqi crude.

The key dynamics of the economic relationship between Turkey and the EU are clear. The EU is the market for 56% of Turkish exports, ten times that of any other export destination, while Turkey is the EU's fifth largest export market. European firms annually invest over €3bn in Turkey. After economic setbacks in 1994 and at the turn of the millennium, Turkey has grown at an average annual rate of 6.8%. According to the World Bank, eventual Turkish membership should boost its GDP per capita growth by 1.5% per year, and allow it to expand as a market for European goods.

There remain significant political challenges that Turkey must face up to if it is to be ready for membership. This summer prosecutors in Ankara came within a whisker of removing the current Justice and Development (AKP) government on charges of undermining the secular state that included the decision to allow women to wear the hijab in universities. Had it succeeded, it would have dealt a hammer-blow to hopes of Turkish membership in the foreseeable future. Other outstanding issues include restrictions on freedom of speech, the future of Cyprus and the challenges faced by the Kurdish community over language rights and identity. These issues must be fully resolved prior to Turkish membership, but in these and the other main challenges Turkey faces, the rigorous criteria provided by the EU accession process act as an immense force for change.

At its core, the argument must be that if Turkey succeeds in fully implementing the EU's accession criteria, the toughest given to any candidate country, it will have earned the right to join the EU. If Turkey has undergone the massive economic, political, social and legal transformation required, the denial of its right to join would be an affront to the principles of fairness that must underpin the EU and could lead a spurned Turkey to re-orientate itself away from the West, forming new alliances in the Middle East and central Asia to the detriment of Europe.

Although Turkey has already benefited from economic and political reforms necessary for accession to take place, the pace of change needs to increase, improving the quality of life in Turkey, and strengthening support for membership, both among Turks and EU citizens. Turkey must also reach out to EU citizens with effective public diplomacy, busting myths and raising awareness of Turkey as a modern European society with deep roots in the continent's history. These steps must be reciprocated within the EU through cultural exchange and the use of economic links to break down barriers. The European business community has an important role to play in standing up for Turkey and this must include leadership at the European level.

European companies operating in Turkey should take the lead in educating their workforces about the country and show the benefits that closer co-operation with it can bring. Similarly Europe's trade unions can play a proactive role in informing their members and dampening fears over Turkish migration damaging employment opportunities.

Failure to grant Turkish accession would be one of the greatest strategic mistakes the EU could inflict upon itself, one that would be hugely harmful to business and undermine European prosperity and security. The path to accession is challenging for both the EU and Turkey, but advocates of an open and progressive Europe need to stand up and make the case that it is a challenge that we must not fail to meet.

CHAPTER 18

SUPPORT FOR THE INTERNATIONAL CRIMINAL COURT (ICC) *v.* OPPOSITION TO THE ICC

The International Criminal Court and the Benefits of U.S. Non-Participation

Advocate: John Bolton

Source: "American Justice and the International Criminal Court," *Remarks at the American Enterprise Institute*, Washington, D.C., November 3, 2003.

The International Criminal Court and the Consequences of U.S. Non-Participation

Advocate: Steve Crawshaw

Source: "Why the US Needs This Court," Human Rights Watch Commentary, *The Observer*, June 15, 2003.

The International Criminal Court (ICC) was created in 1998 with the signing of the Rome Statute and became operational in 2002 when 60 countries from around the world ratified it. It is intended to bring to justice individuals accused of war crimes, crimes against humanity, genocide, and other crimes. The creation of the ICC was considered a major step forward in the promotion of human rights worldwide, and advancement of international law. It meant that heads of state and government, members of the military from all ranks, as well as other individuals who could not—or would not—be tried in their home countries would be held accountable for their crimes.

The non-participation of the United States and other major countries significantly undermines the effectiveness and legitimacy of the ICC. The issues that surround the ratification of the ICC call attention to the debates over national interests, state sovereignty, international law, international organizations, and human rights.

OPPOSING THE INTERNATIONAL CRIMINAL COURT

The United States has steadfastly refused to become a party to the ICC. In fact, in an unprecedented step, the Bush Administration "unsigned" the statute—a clear sign of the administration's hostility toward the ICC. The absence of the most powerful country in the world, and a key player in a number of international security crises, has clearly led to some loss of relevancy of the ICC.

John Bolton, former U.S. ambassador to the UN, lays out the most salient arguments as to why the United States should not become a signatory of the ICC. He makes the case that the ICC affects the national interests and security of the United States and its allies. Hence, the United States concluded a number of bilateral agreements designed to prevent U.S. citizens from being turned over to the ICC. Bolton argues that U.S. personnel should be subject to only the laws and courts of the United States. In turn, being exempt from the ICC would allow the United States to retain its flexibility in world affairs without being concerned that its troops and government officials would be subject to international justice.

IN FAVOR OF THE INTERNATIONAL CRIMINAL COURT

For most proponents of international law and human rights around the world, the creation of the ICC signified a significant step forward. It signaled that no one who committed crimes against humanity, war crimes, or genocide would escape accountability, regardless of his or her rank and status.

For some countries, however, the ICC presented a challenge to their sovereignty. As such, France, and particularly the United States, sought exemption for their citizens from the ICC's prosecution.

Steve Crawshaw illustrates how U.S. non-participation severely weakens the ICC. He points out that the annual renewal of U.S. peacekeepers' immunity from the ICC's jurisdiction is a blow to its legitimacy because it shows that there are different standards for different countries. Crawshaw argues that the United States has nothing to fear from the ICC because it is a court of last instance and it is hardly likely that Washington will ever perpetrate egregious crimes on a mass scale and thus warrant the attention of the ICC.

POINTS **TO PONDER**

1. What crimes fall under the jurisdiction of the International Criminal Court?
2. What risks does the International Criminal Court pose to U.S. citizens, including the U.S. military?
3. Should U.S. military personnel be subjected to different standards of justice than those of other countries?
4. Is the International Criminal Court a key step toward world order?

John Bolton

American Justice and the International Criminal Court

There has been considerable debate in the United States about the International Criminal Court (ICC), much of it in this very room. Rather than rehearse many of those arguments, however, I thought it might be helpful to give you a report from the front, describing current efforts by the United States to protect its citizens from the illegitimate assertion of authority over them. As President Bush has argued as far back as the 2000 campaign, the problems inherent in the ICC are more than abstract legal issues; they are matters that touch directly on our national interests and security, and therefore also affect the security of our friends and allies world-wide. As a result, the United States is engaged in a global campaign to conclude bilateral agreements that will ensure U.S. persons are not subjected to the ICC's jurisdiction.

For numerous reasons, the United States decided that the ICC had unacceptable consequences for our national sovereignty. Specifically, the ICC is an organization that runs contrary to fundamental American precepts and basic Constitutional principles of popular sovereignty, checks and balances, and national independence.

U.S. military forces and civilian personnel and private citizens are currently active in peacekeeping and humanitarian missions in almost 100 countries at any given time. It is essential that we remain steadfast in preserving the independence and flexibility that America needs to defend our national interests around the world. As President Bush said: The United States cooperates with many other nations to keep the peace, but we will not submit American troops to prosecutors and judges whose jurisdiction we do not accept. Every person who serves under the American flag will answer to his or her own superiors and to military law, not to the rulings of an unaccountable International Criminal Court.

Accordingly, in order to protect all of our citizens, the United States is engaged in a worldwide effort to conclude legally binding, bilateral agreements that would prohibit the surrender of U.S. persons to the Court. These Article 98 agreements, so named because they are specifically contemplated under Article 98 of the Rome Statute that created the ICC, provide U.S. persons with essential protection against the Court's purported jurisdictional claims, and allow us to remain engaged internationally with our friends and allies.

Thus far, the United States has concluded and signed Article 98 agreements with 70 countries all over the globe, representing over 40 percent of the world's population. Each Article 98 agreement meets our key objective—ensuring that all U.S. persons are covered by the terms of the agreement. This broad scope of coverage is essential to ensuring that the ICC will not become an impediment to U.S. activities around the world. We must guarantee the necessary protection to our media, delegations of public and private individuals traveling to international meetings, private individuals accompanying official personnel, contractors working alongside official personnel (particularly in the military context), participants in exchange programs, former government officials, arms control inspectors, people engaged in commerce and business abroad, students in government sponsored programs, to name just a few categories of persons. The orderly conduct of news reporting, diplomatic relations, economic activity, tourism, military operations, humanitarian programs, cultural and education exchanges, and other contacts between peoples around the world depend upon rules that are fair, well understood, and subject to appropriate due process.

Article 98 agreements serve to ensure that U.S. persons will have appropriate protection from politically motivated criminal accusations, investigations, and prosecutions. These straightforward agreements require that our partners agree, either reciprocally or non-reciprocally, not to surrender U.S. persons to the International Criminal Court, not to retransfer persons extradited to a country for prosecution, and not to assist other parties in their efforts to send U.S. persons to the ICC. We have worked hard to find mechanisms and formulations in these agreements that meet our requirement of blanket coverage while also responding to the needs of our bilateral partners. . . .

Increasingly, Article 98 agreements play an important role in U.S. bilateral relationships regardless of whether a State is a Party to the Rome Statute. Of importance here is the decision by the Congress to ensure that these agreements are a foundation for military cooperation relationships around the world. The American Servicemembers Protection Act, which was enacted with strong bipartisan support by both houses of the Congress, prohibits military assistance to countries that have ratified the Rome Statute but not entered into Article 98 agreements with the United States. Additionally, there are strong reasons for entering into these agreements with States that are not Party to the Rome Statute. First, a State not currently a Party to the Rome Statute may become one at any time. Second, the ICC may request that a non-Party arrest and surrender to the Court a U.S. person on its territory. The Rome Statute contains no requirement for the State to notify the United States, or receive our consent, before such a surrender. Concluding an Article 98 agreement is thus important to future cooperation on a range of diplomatic, military, and security initiatives. It also sends an important political signal that American concerns are widely shared around the world.

It is a misconception that the United States wants to use these agreements to undermine the ICC. To the contrary, we are determined to be proper in our relations with the Court, proceeding in a manner specifically contemplated by the Rome Statute itself. Moreover, in each agreement, the United States makes clear its intention to bring to justice those who commit genocide, crimes against humanity and war crimes. This is the stated goal of ICC supporters, and a goal that the United States has and will maintain.

Proponents of the ICC refuse to concede that the Court poses any problems for the United States. One of the principal arguments of the ICC's supporters has been that it will function, in effect, as a court of last resort. For countries that have functioning judicial systems, they contend, there is no reason to question the legitimacy of those countries investigating and prosecuting their own nationals accused of crimes covered by the Rome Statute. Indeed, this concept, given the name complementarity, was touted in the debates leading up to the Rome Statute, and in the lobbying campaign in the United States after the signing of the Statute, as perhaps the main reason the United States had nothing to fear from the ICC. . . .

What the United States is basically seeking, through Article 98 agreements, is nothing more than what States Parties to the Rome Statute claim they already have. If someone were to assert that the American judicial system was corrupt, incompetent or tolerant of war crimes and crimes against humanity, and therefore amounted to the kind of failed state for whose judicial system the ICC was intended to substitute, that would be one thing. We would, I can assure you, certainly be prepared to contest those assertions. Not surprisingly, however, no one seriously makes this argument. No one contends, openly at least, that the American judicial system would not, properly and diligently, perform its function in appropriate circumstances. Nor could they. As Secretary Powell has said: We have the highest standards of accountability of any nation on the face of the earth.

Of course, since the United States is not even a party to the Rome Statute, there is even less reason why we should be treated more harshly than States Parties. It is neither reasonable nor fair that the crimes laid out in the Rome Statute should apply to a greater extent to States that have not agreed to its terms than to those that have. This aspect of the Rome Statute is, among other things, a fundamentally unfair and highly dangerous break from the long-established premise of the International Court of Justice that there is no jurisdiction without the consent of States Parties.

But let us return to the fundamental point that complementarity, one of the supposed bedrocks of the ICC, is being denied the United States by those countries that do not accept Article 98 agreements. Here, we can only conclude that another agenda is at work, namely the continued determination of some ICC supporters who hope to cajole the United States into adhering to the Rome Statute, ironically under the rubric of better protecting its own citizens. This is an interesting approach, and one that is doomed to failure. We will not join the ICC, and we will continue to press for Article 98 agreements.

Subjecting U.S. persons to this treaty, with its unaccountable Prosecutor and its unchecked judicial power, is clearly inconsistent with American standards of constitutionalism. This is a macro-constitutional issue for us, not simply a narrow, technical point of law. Our concerns about politically motivated charges against U.S. persons are not just hypothetical. Recently in Belgium, allegations of war crimes were brought against the President, the Vice President, the Secretaries of State and Defense, and former President Bush under that country's notorious and far-reaching universal competence statute. That problem was brought closer to home when senior Belgian officials themselves were charged under the statute, and the law was subsequently amended to limit its scope. Without sufficient protection against such frivolous charges, responsible officials may be deterred from carrying out a wide range of legitimate functions across the spectrum, from actions integral to our national defense to peacekeeping missions or interventions in humanitarian crises or civil wars, such as in Liberia. Simply launching criminal investigations has an enormous political impact. Although subsequent indictments and convictions are unquestionably more serious, a zealous independent Prosecutor can make dramatic news just by calling witnesses and gathering documents, without ever bringing formal charges.

Accumulated experience strongly favors a case-by-case approach to resolving serious political and military disputes, rather than the inevitable resort to adjudication. One alternative to the ICC is the kind of Truth and Reconciliation Commission created in South Africa. This approach was intended to make public more of the truth of the apartheid regime in the most credible fashion, to elicit admissions of guilt, and then to permit society to move ahead without the prolonged opening of old wounds that trials, appeals, and endless recriminations might bring.

Another alternative, of course, is for the parties themselves to try their own alleged war criminals, as the doctrine of complementarity supposedly contemplates. In fact, the fullest cathartic effect of the prosecutorial approach to war crimes occurs when the responsible population itself comes to grips with its past and administers appropriate justice. The international effort should encourage warring parties to resolve questions of criminality within national judicial systems, as part of a comprehensive solution to their disagreements. Removing key elements of the dispute to a distant forum, especially the emotional and contentious issues of war crimes and crimes against humanity, undercuts the very progress that these peoples, victims and perpetrators alike, must make if they are ever to live peacefully together.

We strongly support states fulfilling their sovereign responsibility to hold perpetrators of war crimes accountable rather than abdicating that responsibility to the international community. For this reason, the United States has been a major proponent of the special court in Sierra Leone because it is grounded in sovereign consent, combines domestic and international participation in a manner that will generate a lasting benefit to the rule of law within Sierra Leone and its regional environs, and interfaces with the truth and reconciliation commission of that country to address accountability for a wide range of perpetrators.

In the past, the United States has supported the establishment of ad hoc tribunals, such as those for Yugoslavia and Rwanda, which, unlike the ICC, are created and overseen by the U.N. Security Council, under a U.N. Charter to which virtually all nations have agreed. But we are now moving beyond that. The international community can help equip local governments to try cases domestically in a credible manner. We are doing this in the Balkans and in Rwanda. On October 30, the United States pledged $10 million at a donors conference in The Hague to support domestic war crimes trials in Bosnia and Herzegovina. We are supporting preparations for war crimes trials in Croatia and Serbia and Montenegro, something that would have been unthinkable a few years ago. We are also supporting such efforts in Rwanda. Now, the Security Council tribunals are beginning to look at transferring cases under their jurisdictions to domestic courts.

In matters of international justice, the United States has many foreign policy instruments to utilize that are fully consistent with our values and interests. We will continue to play a worldwide leadership role in strengthening domestic judicial systems and promoting freedom, transparency and the rule of law. We seek no immunity for our citizens, but only a simple, non-surrender agreement as contemplated in the Rome Statute. We fully commit ourselves, where appropriate, to investigate and prosecute serious, credible accusations of war crimes, crimes against humanity and genocide that have been made against any of our people.

We respect the decision of states to become parties to the Rome Statute, but they in turn must respect our decision not to be bound by jurisdictional claims to which we have not consented. As President Bush stated in his National Security Strategy, we will take the actions necessary to ensure that our efforts to meet our global security commitments and protect Americans are not impaired by the potential for investigations, inquiry, or prosecution by the International Criminal Court, whose jurisdiction does not extend to Americans and which we do not accept. States Parties to the Rome Statute have created an ICC to their liking, and they should live with it. The United States did not agree to be bound, and must not be held to its terms.

Steve Crawshaw

Why the US Needs This Court

First, the good news, which deserves to be savored for a moment. The inauguration in the Hague tomorrow of the first chief prosecutor of the International Criminal Court marks a remarkable moment in history. Dictators and tyrants around the world can be brought to book, by a single court. It is an astonishing achievement—and one that seemed, until just a few years ago, quite unimaginable.

Even after the signing in 1998 of the Rome Treaty, which laid the foundations for the new court, many believed that the ICC would never become real. They were wrong. Last year, the number of countries ratifying the treaty reached 60, thus allowing the court itself to be created.

The prosecutor and judges have been selected. Now, to crown that process, the inauguration tomorrow of Luis Moreno Ocampo—a former prosecutor of the Argentine junta—means that the ICC show is well and truly on the road. Last July, when the court was constituted as a formal entity, it remained without practical power. From tomorrow, its power will be tangible. The court will be authorized to prosecute some of the horrific crimes now being committed around the world—for example, in the Democratic Republic of Congo, which may provide the first cases.

Ninety countries, including almost all the world's major democracies, have now ratified the treaty. But not the United States—which is where the problems begin. Those problems are increasing by the month and by the day. The US administration, not content with refusing to ratify, and then 'unsigning' the treaty (a murky legal concept, at best), seeks to prevent this crucial instrument of international justice from building up the strength it needs to do its work successfully. It is, in short, doing its level best to kill the court. (The 'Hague invasion clause', signed into law by President Bush last year, allows him to use 'all means necessary and appropriate' to free US servicemen detained by the ICC.)

In recent days, there have been small glimmers of light. A vote in the Security Council last Thursday was 12-0 in favor of a renewal of a special one-year deal that was agreed last July, allowing US peacekeepers immunity from prosecution. That sounds like another victory for the US hawks. But equally significant were the diplomatic dogs that refused to bark: France and Germany both withheld their vote, because they were so unhappy at the US pressures. Nor was this just the same old post-Iraq rift. Kofi Annan himself warned that the court—and the Security Council—would be undermined, if such renewals became an annual routine. Many countries—from Switzerland to South Africa—spoke out against the idea that the Security Council should start rewriting international treaties.

The US pressures at the United Nations have been only part of the story. The bully tactics against countries which defy America by refusing to weaken their commitment to the court have become blatant in recent months, as private (and much-denied) arm-twisting has given way to public threats. Countries vulnerable to American pressure—these days, the list of such countries is long—are told that unless they offer the Americans the desired immunity from prosecution, punishment will be swift and severe. Thus, the US ambassador to Zagreb recently published an open letter warning that Croatia would lose $19 million in military assistance if it failed to sign. Other countries have received similar threats; some—like the Bosnians, who, one might think, had already suffered more than their fair share of threats and ultimatums in recent years—have reluctantly surrendered.

The irony is obvious that Washington simultaneously demands complete co-operation with international justice at the Yugoslav war crimes tribunal (or else), and complete non-co-operation with international justice at the ICC (or else). Elsewhere, Caribbean countries have been told that they will no longer be eligible for hurricane assistance unless they give the Americans what they want, right now. Like every practiced bully, Washington has given an early date for the implementation of its threats. For many countries, the proclaimed deadline for kowtowing to the US pressures runs out on 1 July, the first anniversary of the court itself.

The American view of the court, described by the deputy US ambassador to the UN as 'a fatally flawed institution', is that the court will act as a giant conspiracy against America. Accordingly, Americans will be unfairly targeted. But this misunderstands the essence of the court. The ICC is a court of last resort, which prosecutes only the most serious war crimes and crimes against humanity, and comes into play only where domestic courts have shown themselves unwilling or unable to prosecute. Despite the depressing and dangerous insouciance about international law shown by America at Guantanamo and elsewhere, one would assume that US politicians and commanders are not eager to commit atrocities on a grand scale, à la Saddam or Milosevic, which could bring them before the ICC.

As Kofi Annan pointed out, no UN peacekeeper of any nationality has been accused of a crime 'anywhere near the crimes that fall under the jurisdiction of the ICC'. The Americans may be right to fear that there will be attempts to bring politically motivated cases. But the court has a solid panoply of safeguards, which make it difficult to imagine that malicious and frivolous cases could get past judicial first base.

Britain, which played a key role during the negotiations of the Rome treaty five years ago, has in recent months played a less dignified role—constantly eager to tweak the European diplomatic language in order (unsuccessfully) to appease the US loathing of the court. The UK has been depressingly reluctant to confront Washington's bully tactics, confining itself instead to occasional hand wringing expressions of regret. And yet, almost no issue can be of greater importance. The strength of the ICC—which does not have retrospective jurisdiction beyond July 2002—can become an international guarantor of stability in the years to come.

American contempt for the court—and its determination to bring the court's supporters to heel—sends a disastrous message worldwide. It suggests that there is one standard of justice for Americans and another for everybody else. Such haughty foolishness makes the world a less safe place—for Americans too.

CHAPTER 19 HUMANITARIAN INTERVENTION v. RESPECT FOR STATE BOUNDARIES

Humanitarian Intervention as a Moral Obligation in the Post-9/11 Era

Advocate: Amitai Etzioni

Source: "Genocide Prevention in the New Global Architecture," *British Journal of Politics and International Relations*, vol. 7 (2005), pp. 469–484, excerpt.

Humanitarian Intervention as a Threat to Order in the International System of States

Advocate: Mohammed Ayoob

Source: "Humanitarian Intervention and State Sovereignty," *The International Journal of Human Rights*, vol. 6, no. 1 (2002), pp. 81–102.

The concept of humanitarian intervention came to the fore in the 1990s when conflicts from Somalia to the former Yugoslavia and Rwanda claimed hundreds of thousands of lives. As the governments of various countries failed to protect their citizens from gross violations of human rights or became accomplices in a range of atrocities perpetrated against them, the international community saw it fit to intervene on behalf of the defenseless.

Humanitarian intervention, while not a new concept, became the subject of heated debates revolving around fundamentals such as state sovereignty, international law, and human rights. Freed from the superpower rivalry of the Cold War, in an era when liberal democracy and globalization seemed to have triumphed, many in the international community held human rights above the principle of state sovereignty. They urged countries to intervene in conflicts even when no national interest was involved. In contrast, others defend the inviolability of state sovereignty.

IN FAVOR OF HUMANITARIAN INTERVENTION

When the United States led NATO into air strikes on Serbia in 1999, experts and jurists were divided on the legality of this action. While dissenters were concerned with the implications of such an action on state sovereignty, supporters of humanitarian intervention frequently looked at moral principles and ethical obligations to justify the need for such action.

Amitai Etzioni forcefully makes the case for humanitarian intervention by debunking the most frequently expressed criticisms of this concept. He argues that decision-making rarely involves only one set of considerations, hence, the argument that there might be other motives than simply humanitarian impulses should not prevent other states from undertaking humanitarian missions. Furthermore, the value placed on saving human lives overrides all other considerations. He also discusses whether a state is required to engage in nation-building following a humanitarian intervention. He finds that no such obligation exists.

IN FAVOR OF STATE SOVEREIGNTY

Humanitarian intervention, while laudable as a concept, remains a major challenge to state sovereignty. As Mohammed Ayoob argues, humanitarian intervention redefines the Westphalian idea of sovereignty if it includes human rights as a responsibility of the state, and greatly weakens the standard that each state is equal to the others before international law if a "standard of civilization" is introduced. An even more important question is who speaks in the name of the international community and makes these determinations.

Another set of challenges, according to Ayoob, has to do with national interests. It is inevitable that the presence (or lack thereof) of a national interest will determine whether or not a state will participate in a humanitarian intervention. The historical record indeed shows that countries have followed their strategic interests. This inevitably leads to inconsistency in the application of humanitarian intervention, revealing the double standard, and ultimately de-legitimizing it as a legal as well as a morally based action.

POINTS **TO PONDER**

1. What are some of the conditions that make successful humanitarian intervention possible?
2. When should the United States conduct humanitarian interventions?
3. From the perspective of non-Western countries, what are the dangers and risks that accompany a U.S. humanitarian intervention?

Amitai Etzioni

Genocide Prevention in the New Global Architecture

• • •

Humanitarian intervention as the continuation of foreign policy by other means: Scholars and policy-makers often define humanitarian interventions as if they all involve arms. For instance, J. L. Holzgrefe defines humanitarian intervention as:

> the threat or use of force across state borders by a state (or group of states) aimed at preventing or ending widespread and grave violations of the fundamental human rights of individuals other than its own citizens, without the permission of the state within whose territory force is applied (Holzgrefe 2003, 18).

Fernando R. Tesón defines 'permissible' humanitarian intervention as the 'proportionate international use or threat of military force, undertaken in principle by a liberal government or alliance, aimed at ending tyranny or anarchy, welcomed by the victims, and consistent with the doctrine of double effect' (Tesón 2003, 94). In contrast, J. L. Holzgrefe offers a much wider definition that includes 'threat or use of economic, diplomatic, or other sanctions' (Holzgrefe 2003, 94). It hence makes sense to distinguish between humanitarian interventions in general and armed ones, as well as between those that seek to stop (or prevent) a genocide and those that seek merely to prevent smaller-scale atrocities or human suffering. It follows that one might best view genocide prevention as a sub-category of armed humanitarian interventions and view these as a sub-category of humanitarian interventions of all kinds. Each category raises separate sets of issues concerning who will decide that the time to intervene has come, who will do the intervening and so on.

Obviously, armed interventions deserve much closer and stricter scrutiny than 'softer' interventions. However, for many purposes it is best to treat armed humanitarian intervention, to paraphrase Clausewitz, as a continuation of genocide prevention efforts by other means. To approach a brewing genocide as an either/or proposition (either one ignores the threatening developments or sends troops marching in) blinds one to the fact that in most circumstances it is best first to employ other preventive means, ranging from diplomacy and formal condemnations by various nations and the UN to threats to bring the leaders of the threatening group before the International Criminal Court (ICC) and so on.

These softer measures, though, will benefit if it is crystal clear that if these nonviolent measures are not effective, armed action will follow. In the recent emphasis on the importance of soft power, one tends to overlook the old adage 'speak softly but carry a big stick' (or at least have it hanging within easy reach on a nearby wall).

Moreover, many of the arguments made against armed humanitarian interventions are also made against the 'softer' acts, such as moral condemnation and economic sanctions, and hence it is best to respond to them in unison. For instance, those who oppose armed humanitarian interventions on the grounds that they impose a Western conception of rights (Frank 2001) also oppose moral censure on the same grounds of cultural relativism. Responding to such untenable claims is essential for justifying the prevention of mass and systematic murder, by whatever means are to be employed.

Mixed motives do not undermine legitimacy: Critics have no case when they reveal that humanitarian interventions draw on a variety of motives and that not all of them are noble or altruistic ones, as the term 'humanitarian' implies. The same is true of most, if not all, human actions, from donating organs to saving Jews from Nazis (Brown 2003). There is no reason to deny that humanitarian interventions take place for a variety of reasons, including fear of a refugee crisis if law and order is not restored in a given country, because members of some of the ethnic groups involved have a sizable representation in the intervening country (e.g. Croats in Germany) or because the intervening nations are keen to maintain their self-image as big powers (e.g. Russia and France). So long as intervening forces help to prevent or at least stop genocides once they have started, their actions are highly legitimate in terms of what most people value highly—a life free from the threat of displacement, annihilation, torture and rape.

Inconsistency is not a barrier: Other critics have argued that humanitarian interventions cannot claim the moral high ground—and hence help legitimate those who provide them—as they are inconsistently applied. For instance, Edward Luttwak asks, 'What does it mean for the morality of a supposedly moral rule when it is applied arbitrarily, against some but not others?' (*Times Literary Supplement*, 14 July 2000). Two responses are called for. First, foreign policy is never driven by merely one consideration or to maximise the realisation of one principle. Humanitarian interventions (just like democratisation) must be squared with other concerns, including narrowly defined national interests. One cannot expect a nation to give up, say, access to fuels on which its economy depends in order to be 'consistent,' for instance in dealing with Saudi Arabia. It does not follow however that other nations, without such concerns, cannot step up to the plate or that the same nation cannot discharge its humanitarian duty in other situations. After all, we cannot prevent all crimes at home either, but this does not mean we ought to give up on law and order. Moreover, the argument against inconsistent application is as much a case for more consistent application than it is for no application at all. The more consistently humanitarian interventions are employed, the less they will need to be employed.

Chris Brown puts it well in his defence of inconsistent humanitarianism. While acknowledging that 'it does actually seem widely believed that morality is about rule-following . . . and thus that there is something wrong with the idea that moral behaviour could be arbitrary or inconsistent' (Brown 2003, 40), he concludes, 'there is no viable universal moral rule that can tell statespersons what is the right thing to do in response to particular circumstances' (ibid., 47). He advises not letting perfection become the enemy of good while advocating the use of sound judgement and pragmatic calculation by statesmen.

Limited scope essential: One of the most damaging critiques of humanitarian intervention is based on the so-called 'Pottery Barn rule,' which states, 'you break it, you own it.' (*New York Times* writer Thomas L. Friedman popularised this phrase in a series of articles, which also was common in pre-invasion discussions in the Bush administration, especially in the State Department.) That is, once a nation interferes in the internal affairs of another, it 'must' engage in nation building. As nation building turns out to be at best very onerous and often fails, critics—including George W. Bush during his first election campaign—have argued that one should not go down this road in the first place.

However, it has been pointed out before that pottery barns have no such rules (*The Washington Post*, 28 April 2004). The moral precept that if nation X saves population Y from being wiped out in country Z, the intervening nation 'owes' the country in which the genocide was taking place anything (other than a gracious acceptance of thanks) is hard to follow. Practically, it might be necessary to engage in some peacekeeping for a limited period of time to prevent the genocidal tendencies from reasserting themselves. However, there is no moral obligation or even pragmatic reason I recognise that a country, once 'invaded,' has to be economically developed and democratised. Both may well be desirable but are often very difficult to achieve and are not necessarily preconditions for avoiding the reactivation of latent genocidal tendencies. Moreover, the resulting differences, not from armed humanitarian intervention but from the nation building that follows, often themselves become a source of new tensions and stresses. Armed humanitarian intervention should not be discouraged in order to avoid the obligation to engage in nation building, as no such obligation exists.

I already mentioned in passing the critique that those intervening for ostensibly humanitarian purposes are out to impose Western values on the world (Pollis and Schwab 1979a, xiii). Such critics argue that each nation should be free to follow its own values (Pollis and Schwab 1979b, 4), that people must themselves decide from within when they can no longer abide by the abuses of their regime, rather than such a determination coming from without (Walzer 1977) and that humanitarian interventions are called for only if the majority of the people in a given country calls for them. Michael Walzer, in *Just and Unjust War*, offers a caveat to the rights of sovereign states when it comes to humanitarian protections, arguing that ultimate power rests in the people to enforce human rights and the rule of law: 'when a government turns savagely upon its own people, we must doubt the very existence of a political community to which the idea of self-determination must apply' (Walzer 1977, 101). It is useful in this context to distinguish between what might be called vital human rights (those that directly concern life) and all others (including many legal and political rights and not just socioeconomic rights). These vital rights are quite widely respected, not just in the West. Where they are not universally respected, those who champion these rights have a strong moral claim on the grounds that they are 'self-evident' moral truths—rights to which all human beings are entitled. Adding that if there are some people who in their blind hatred for others would rather kill and even be killed than respect the right to live by those of different racial, ethnic or religious affiliation, we ought to treat them as morally uninformed rather than accord them a veto power on genocide prevention. However, it also follows that one must beware of vague definitions of what constitutes human rights for which armed humanitarian interventions are justified. . . .

BIBLIOGRAPHY

Brown, C. (2003) 'Selective humanitarianism: In defence of inconsistency', in D. K. Chaterjee and D. E. Scheid (eds), *Ethics and Foreign Intervention* (Cambridge: Cambridge University Press), 31–50.

Bull, H. (1977) *Anarchical Society: A Study of Order in World Politics* (New York, NY: Columbia University Press).

Clark, W. (2003a) 'America's virtual empire', *Washington Monthly* (November).

Clark, W. (2003b) *Winning Modern Wars: Iraq, Terrorism, and the American Empire* (New York, NY: Public Affairs).

Cronin, B. (2002) 'The two faces of the United Nations: The tension between intergovernmentalism and transnationalism', *Global Governance*, 8, 52–71.

Etzioni, A. (2003) *My Brother's Keeper: A Memoir and a Message* (Lanham, MD: Rowman & Littlefield).

Etzioni, A. (2004a) *From Empire to Community* (New York, NY: Palgrave Macmillan), 75–80.

Etzioni, A. (2004b) 'A self-restrained approach to nation-building by foreign powers', *International Affairs*, 80:1, 1–17.

European Parliament Temporary Committee on the EHELON Interception System (2001) *Report on the Existence of a Global System for the Interception of Private and Commercial Communications* (A5-0264/2001 PARI), 11 June, 133. Available at: http://www.europarl.eu.int/tempcom/echelon/pdf/rapport_echelon_en.pdf.

Frank, T. (2001) 'Are human rights universal?', *Foreign Affairs*, 80:1, 191–204.

Gallup International (2002) *Voice of the People Public Opinion Poll*, 29 August, available at: http://www.voice-of-the-people.net/ContentFiles/docs/VOP_Environmental_Results.pdf.

Harbour, F. (1995) 'Basic moral values: A shared core', *Ethics and International Affairs*, 9, 155–170.

Holzgrefe, J. L. (2003) 'The humanitarian intervention debate', in J. L. Holzgrefe and R. O. Keohane (eds), *Humanitarian Intervention: Ethical, Legal, and Political Dilemmas* (Cambridge: Cambridge University Press), 15–52.

Ikenberry, G. J. (2001) *After Victory: Institutions, Strategic Restraint, and the Rebuilding of Order After Major Wars* (Princeton, NJ: Princeton University Press).

Jackson, R. (1995) 'International community beyond the cold war', in G. Lyons and M. Mastanduno (eds), *Beyond Westphalia: State Sovereignty and International Intervention* (Baltimore, MD: Johns Hopkins University Press).

Johnson, C. (2004) *The Sorrows of Empire: Militarism, Secrecy, and the End of the Republic* (New York, NY: Metropolitan Books).

Kaplan, R. (2002) 'US military bases and empire', *Monthly Review*, 35:10, 1–14.

Kaplan, R. (2003) 'Supremacy by stealth: Ten rules for managing the world', *The Atlantic Monthly*, 292:1, 66–83.

Keefe, P. R. (2005) *Chatter: Dispatches from the Secret World of Global Eavesdropping* (New York, NY: Random House).

Mautner, T. (1996) 'Deontology', in *A Dictionary of Philosophy* (Cambridge, MA: Blackwell Publishers), 99.

Mayer, J. (2005) 'Outsourcing torture', *The New Yorker*, 14–21 February, 106–123.

Merriam-Webster (1994) 'Legitimacy', in *Merriam-Webster's Collegiate Dictionary* (Springfield, MA: Merriam-Webster, Inc.), 665.

Meyer, J. (1987) 'The world polity and the authority of the nation-state', in G. M. Thomas, J. W. Meyer, F. O. Ramirez and J. Boli (eds), *Institutional Structure: Constituting the State, Society, and the Individual* (Newbury Park, CA: Sage), 41.

Nye, J. (2004) *Soft Power: The Means to Success in World Politics* (New York: Public Affairs).

Pew Research Center for the People and the Press (2002) *2002 Global Attitudes Survey*, 4 December, available at: http://peoplepress.org/reports/pdf/165topline.pdf. Question 15d, T-21; Question 64, T-51.

Pollis, A. and Schwab, P. (1979a) 'Introduction', in A. Pollis and P. Schwab (eds), *Human Rights: Cultural and Ideological Perspectives* (New York, NY: Praeger Publishers).

Pollis, A. and Schwab, P. (1979b) 'Human rights: A western construct with limited applicability', in A. Pollis and P. Schwab (eds), *Human Rights: Cultural and Ideological Perspectives* (New York, NY: Praeger Publishers).

Power, S. (2002) *A Problem from Hell: America and the Age of Genocide* (New York, NY: Perennial).

Program on International Policy Attitudes (PIPA) (2003) *World Public Opinion Says World Not Going in Right Direction*, 4 June, available at: http://www.pipa.org/OnlineReports/Global_Issues/globescan_press_06_04.pdf.

Pugh, M. and Sidhu, W. P. S. (eds) (2003) *The United Nations and Regional Security* (Boulder, CO: Lynne Rienner).

Schwarz, S. and Bardi, A. (2000) 'Moral dialogues across cultures: An empirical perspective', in E. W. Lehmann (ed), *Autonomy and Order: A Communitarian Anthology* (Lanham, MD: Rowman & Littlefield), 155–179.

Slaughter, A. M. (2004) *A New World Order* (Princeton, NJ: Princeton University Press).

Tesón, F. (2003) 'The liberal case for humanitarian intervention', in J. L. Holzgrefe and R. O. Keohane (eds), *Humanitarian Intervention: Ethical, Legal, and Political Dilemmas* (Cambridge: Cambridge University Press).

Tuck, C. (2000) 'Every Car or Moving Object Gone: The ECOMOG intervention in Liberia', *African Studies Quarterly*, 4:1, 5.

United Nations (UN) Panel on Peace Operations (2000) *Executive Summary*, 21 August. Available at: http://www.un.org/peace/reports/peace_operations.

United Nations Security Council (UNSC) (2001a) Security Council Resolution 1368, 12 September.

United Nations Security Council (UNSC) (2001b) Security Council Resolution 1373, 28 September.

US Department of State (USDOS) (2005) 'Proliferation Security Initiative Frequently Asked Questions' Fact Sheet, Bureau of NonProliferation, 11 January. Available at: http://www.state.gov/t/np/rls/fs/32725.htm.

Walt, S. (2005) 'In the national interest', *Boston Review*, Feb/Mar, 6.

Walzer, M. (1977) *Just and Unjust War* (New York, NY: Basic Books).

Walzer, M. (1994) *Thick and Thin: Moral Argument at Home and Abroad* (Notre Dame, IN: University of Notre Dame Press).

The White House (2003) 'Fact Sheet: The President's Emergency Plan for AIDS Relief', Office of the Press Secretary. Available at http://www.whitehouse.gov/news/releases/2003/01/print/20030129-1.html

The White House (2005) 'The Millennium Challenge Account', available at: http//www.whitehouse.gov/infocus/developingnations/millennium.html

Williams, M. (2004) 'Why ideas matter in international relations: Hans Morgenthau, Classical Realism, and the moral construction of power politics', *International Organization*, 58:4, 633–655.

Mohammed Ayoob

Humanitarian Intervention and State Sovereignty

It is increasingly apparent that the greatest challenge to the notion of international society comes from the new found proclivity on the part of major powers as well as international and regional organisations to intervene in the domestic affairs of juridically sovereign states for ostensibly humanitarian purposes.[1] The concept of international society privileges the state as the sole repository of sovereign authority and is based on the assumption that international order can be best maintained if states respect each other's sovereignty by adhering to the norms of non-intervention in the internal affairs of other states. This has been the fundamental premise on whose basis the rules and institutions governing international society, including international law, diplomacy, and international organisations, have been traditionally established.[2] Respect for state sovereignty, therefore, forms the cornerstone of what Robert Jackson has termed the 'global covenant' which, in turn, acts as the foundation for international order. Respect for this covenant is all the more important in the contemporary context where membership of the international system has expanded exponentially and the notion of a common (European) culture undergirding international order has been dramatically eroded.[3]

In contrast to this global covenant which emphasises sovereignty and nonintervention, the proclaimed goal of humanitarian intervention, undertaken with increasing frequency during the last decade, is to protect the citizens of the target state from flagrant violations of their fundamental human rights usually by agents of the state. These rights are defined as being vested in individuals as members of the human race. They exist independent of their status as citizens of particular states. While this may be true at one level, it does not provide the complete picture. For, as David Forsythe has pointed out, 'Even if human rights are thought to be inalienable, a moral attribute of persons that the state cannot contravene, rights still have to be identified—that is, constructed—by human beings and codified in legal systems.'[4] Therefore, the question of agency—who constructs and codifies human rights—becomes important. This, as we will see later, has an important bearing on the issue of humanitarian intervention because those who define human rights and decree that they have been violated also decide when and where intervention to protect such rights should and must take place.

Mohammed Ayoob, James Madison College, Michigan State University

Humanitarian interventions have also been conducted in some cases where existing institutions of the state, for one reason or another, have been rendered incapable of providing even the minimum degree of security and order to their populations. Their citizens' lives, in terms of Hobbes's classic formulation, have therefore become 'poor, nasty, brutish and short.' In other words, these are instances where the state has failed or collapsed and the social contract binding the subject to the sovereign ceases to operate.[5] In such cases sovereignty ceases to exist and, therefore, the rules of international society that privilege state sovereignty are no longer relevant. External intervention, therefore, does not derogate from state sovereignty for none exists. This is a very different argument from the one that decries the use of sovereignty as a tool used by the agents of the state to violate the human rights of citizens with impunity. It will be addressed briefly at the end of the article separate from, but connected to, the main body of the argument.

Sovereignty as Authority

In order to analyse the problem of intervention and state sovereignty, it will be appropriate first to define the term sovereignty itself. Sovereignty is often defined in terms of internal control and external autonomy. However, since both control and autonomy wax and wane in the real world of politics, it is better to define sovereignty as authority (the right to rule over a delimited territory and the population residing within it).[6] Such a definition accepts that sovereignty has both internal and external dimensions. However, it has certain advantages in comparison to definitions based on control and autonomy since it is a normative construct used to signify the standard of behaviour among members of international society. International norms, including those of sovereignty, are expected to hold despite variations, including violations, which occur in particular cases. Degrees of control and autonomy can vary as they always do in particular instances, but the right to rule remains the constant ingredient of sovereignty even when control is diminished and autonomy diluted.

Sovereignty is thus not only an internal attribute of states. It is based in substantial part on recognition by the community of peers (states) and is as much constituted by external recognition as by internal acquiescence. Such recognition and constitution of sovereignty by international norms are important in an international system in which power is distributed in a highly unequal fashion. This is the case because, as Benedict Kingsbury has pointed out, 'The normative inhibitions associated with sovereignty moderate existing inequalities of power between states, and provide a shield for weak states and weak institutions. These inequalities will become more pronounced if the universal normative understandings associated with sovereignty are to be discarded.'[7] The capacity of sovereignty to act as a normative barrier to unwanted external intervention should not be underrated. International society is based on a set of normative structures, with sovereignty being the foremost among them. If these structures are undermined, it may lead to either unadulterated anarchy or unmitigated hegemony or a combination of the two—anarchy within and hegemony without.

Human Rights and Sovereignty

How does this conception of sovereignty square with the concern for human rights (and more particularly their violation) that has been demonstrated by members of international society increasingly during the past few decades? This concern acquired much greater intensity and seriousness of purpose during the 1990s. It has, in fact, become fashionable these days to dismiss the notion of sovereignty as an anachronism or to dilute it so greatly as to make its operation ineffectual when it suits major powers or important international constituencies. Both the current UN Secretary General, Kofi Annan, and his predecessor, Boutros Boutros-Ghali, have gone on record to declare that state sovereignty is not absolute and exclusive and can be circumscribed, even overridden, in special circumstances.

These statements as well as actions authorised by the UN Security Council and undertaken by multinational coalitions, including organisations like NATO, during the past decade demonstrate an inherent tension between international concern increasingly translated into intervention for humanitarian purposes and the notion of sovereignty. Non-intervention in the domestic affairs of states is an essential corollary of sovereignty. It acts as a 'no trespassing' sign protecting the exclusive territorial domain of states.'[8] This sign has not prevented all external intervention into the affairs of states because signs by themselves are never able to keep off all trespassers. Strong states have routinely intervened, even forcibly, in the affairs of weaker ones. Nevertheless, during the past 50 years, following the emergence of postcolonial states in large numbers, the notion of sovereignty and its corollary of non-intervention had forced the strong to make at least mildly credible cases for intervention into the affairs of the weak. Sovereignty had thus acted as a restraint on the former's interventionary instincts.

The New Interventionism

During the past ten years, however, the notion of intervention has been given a qualitatively new and different thrust. This has been done in two ways. First, intervention is increasingly defined in terms of purposes or goals which are radically different from the traditional objectives that intervention was expected to achieve before the 1990s. These new goals are supposed to be humanitarian and universal in character rather than political and strategic and, therefore, specific in nature.

Second, intervention is sought to be projected as being undertaken by, or on behalf of, the 'international community' rather than by a state or a coalition of states for its/their own ends. States that undertake intervention portray themselves as acting as agents of the 'international community.' In short such intervention is represented as 'international' intervention that is undertaken to achieve 'humanitarian' objectives. It is further argued that these objectives are intrinsically far too valuable to be held hostage to the norm of state sovereignty and, therefore, ought to override that norm.[9] In other words, 'sovereignty is no longer sacrosanct.'[10] This is a radical departure from the Cold War era when intervention was undertaken unabashedly to promote strategic ends, and justifications were provided within the framework of sovereignty (often that such intervention bolstered the sovereignty of the target states and the stability of their regimes) rather than in contravention of that norm.

Sovereignty as Responsibility

Simultaneously, there has been a concerted attempt beginning in the 1990s to redefine sovereignty to include the notion of responsibility as well as authority.[11] This has meant adding 'respect for a minimal standard of human rights' as an essential attribute of sovereignty. Such responsibility, according to this line of reasoning, is owed by the state both to its people and to the international community and those of its institutions that have come to be seen as the guardians of international norms of civilised behaviour. In other words, the state has to act toward its citizens in ways that meet not only with the approval of the latter but also of other states and certain crucial international organisations.

Without denying the considerable moral force of the 'sovereignty as responsibility' approach, one cannot help but notice echoes of the 'standard of civilisation' argument in this proposition.[12] According to this latter thesis, which was the prevailing political wisdom in Europe until the end of the nineteenth century, only those countries that had reached a certain standard of civilised behaviour had the right to attain sovereign status and interact with each other on the basis of mutual recognition of sovereignty. The others, being barbarians if not savages, were to remain subject to, or under the tutelage of, sovereign (European) powers. Where they could not be subjugated, as was the case with the Ottoman Empire, rules of European international law that enjoined reciprocity in interstate interactions did not apply to them. This denied them the protection of norms that had been developed in Europe to govern interstate relations, the chief among them being the principle of non-intervention in the internal affairs of states.

It is interesting to note in this context that 'capitulations' were originally extended by the Ottomans as 'extraterritorial jurisdiction to European "infidels" who could not be expected to understand the religious codes which regulated the daily lives of the Sublime Porte's other subjects'. However, 'as the standard of "civilisation" emerged as an explicit legal concept, the capitulations became a symbol in European eyes of Ottoman inability to uphold "civilised" standards.'[13] Voluntary, even magnanimous, concessions were transformed into instruments of discrimination that then became justifications for further discriminatory treatment.

The resurrection of the 'standard of civilisation' assumptions in the late twentieth century, and their application under the guise of 'sovereignty as responsibility' thesis, once again raises the spectre of a return to colonial habits and practices on the part of major Western powers. It also has the potential to divide the world once again into zones of civilised and uncivilised states and legitimise predatory actions by the former against the latter. As Benedict Kingsbury points out 'The theory of liberal and non-liberal zones proposes differential treatment where the boundaries of the liberal zone are crossed, conferring privileges based on membership in the liberal zone, and setting high barriers to entry . . . [T]he outcome seems likely to be the maintenance of a classificatory system which is itself both an explanation and a justification for those at the margins remaining there for generations.'[14] This is likely to erode the legitimacy of an international society that for the first time has become truly global in character.

Humanitarian Concerns and National Interests

In addition to bifurcating international society into civilised and uncivilised zones, the concept of humanitarian intervention raises a number of additional questions. A major problem emerges from the fact that the new interventionary logic 'presupposes the existence of a meaningful international community in whose name intervention may be carried out.'[15] This assumption raises a host of important issues that need to be addressed. The most fundamental of these relates to the mechanism through which the will of the international community to intervene is determined. In other words, as Lyons and Mastanduno put it, 'The important question is, who determines that a state has not met its sovereign obligations and that the consequences are such that intervention to force compliance is justified.'[16]

However, one cannot even begin to address this issue without noting the fact that we operate in an international system in which the most important political and military decisions are taken not at the international but national level. It is, therefore, impossible to prevent considerations of national interest from intruding upon decisions regarding international intervention for ostensibly humanitarian purposes. This immediately complicates the problem of deciphering international will, for one is never sure whether decisions taken on behalf of the international community are truly the result of altruistic motives or are driven by the national interests of states that have a stake in intervening in particular crises or locales.

On the question of the link between national interest and humanitarian intervention, advocates of intervention are caught between a rock and a hard place for two reasons.[17] First, as past practice demonstrates, most states will not be inclined to undertake humanitarian intervention unless their national interests are directly or indirectly involved. Even if they commit themselves to intervene for altruistic and humanitarian reasons, in the absence of pressing national interest concerns they will normally not be in a position to sustain such a commitment when faced by human and material costs that their publics most likely will not be willing to pay. Past experience, above all the case of the U.S. intervention in Somalia in 1992–93, demonstrates that the threshold of pain for states undertaking humanitarian intervention in which their national interests are not substantially involved will be low. Second, as long as decisions to undertake such interventions are primarily taken at the national level, national interest considerations, under one guise or another, are likely to determine states' decisions to intervene or desist from such intervention. Despite Stanley Hoffmann's exhortation that 'The concept of "national interest" . . . should be widened to incorporate ethical concerns,'[18] decisions to intervene when taken by national decision-making bodies make humanitarian interventions immediately suspect. When one adds to this the fact that such interventions are undertaken on a selective basis and the same criteria are not applied uniformly and universally in every case, such interventions lose legitimacy and credibility in the eyes of many, if not most, members of the international system.[19] Even as interventionist a UN Secretary-General as Kofi Annan has been forced to concede that 'If the new commitment to intervention in the face of extreme suffering is to retain the support of the world's peoples, it must be—and must be seen to be—fairly and consistently applied, irrespective of region or nation.'[20]

However, selectivity in humanitarian interventions seems to be inevitable. As staunch an advocate of humanitarian intervention as Thomas G. Weiss has been compelled to admit that as far as such interventions are concerned, 'there can be no universal imperative. States will pick and choose.'[21] It may be possible, as MacFarlane and Weiss assert, that as a result of humanitarian political activity the construction of national interest, especially in the case of liberal democracies, comes to include humanitarian concerns.[22] However, there is the distinct possibility that such a humanitarian construction of national interest may run headlong at some point into the narrower and realpolitik construction of national interest. When this happens; more often than not the latter construction is likely to prevail for domestic political and economic reasons. Decisions to intervene, not to intervene, or to withdraw, will be made (as they have been made in the past) largely on the basis of strategic and economic considerations that may have little to do with humanitarian concerns even if they are justified with reference to such ideals.

The impossibility of determining the predominance of humanitarian concerns in a state's decision to intervene was responsible in large measure for the international condemnation of the Indian intervention in the former East Pakistan in 1971 and the Vietnamese intervention in Cambodia in 1979. A large majority of states had strong reservations about these interventions despite the fact that in the former instance at least 300,000 civilians had been killed and 10 million refugees had crossed the border into India as a result of the reign of terror let loose by the Pakistan army in what was then East Pakistan. In the latter case, Pol Pot had killed over one million of his countrymen and women in order to create a Cambodia of his dreams. However, it was clear in both cases that Indian and Vietnamese strategic interests were involved in these interventions because of existing hostile relations between India and Pakistan and between Vietnam and the Cambodian regime, respectively.[23] The opposition to these two interventions among members of international society was, therefore, quite strong despite the fact that the violations of human rights, including large-scale killings, in these two cases were of such an order that northern Iraq, Bosnia, Kosovo and Haiti pale into insignificance before them.

Humanitarian Interventions and Double Standards

International society turned out to be more receptive to arguments in favour of humanitarian intervention during the early and middle 1990s. This happened to be the case even when obviously interested parties carried out such intervention for reasons whose connection with humanitarian concerns was rather dubious. This can be explained to a substantial extent by the unusual circumstances surrounding the fundamental transformation of the balance of global power that took place during the early part of that decade. Few states could muster the courage in the first half of the 1990s to point out to the lone superpower and the coalition it led that the altruism of their actions was suspect and that they were often guilty of double standards.[24]

Such double standards were particularly glaring in the case of the Middle East. They were most obvious in the case of the intervention in northern Iraq and the imposition of no-fly zones in northern and southern Iraq. The treatment of Kurds in Turkey was hardly better than that meted out to their cousins in Iraq. However, no humanitarian intervention was ever contemplated in the case of Turkey, a NATO member and a key player in enforcing economic and military sanctions against Iraq. Moreover, as MacFarlane and Weiss have pointed out,

> This intervention [in northern Iraq] reflected the connection of NATO to Turkey and American antipathy to Iran dating from the overthrow of the Shah and the hostage crisis of 1979. The effects of these strategic impulses were evident in that the Kurds on the Turkish border were the primary focus of the intervention, although the majority of displaced Kurds were found not on the Turkish but on the Iranian border. These latter were receiving only 10 per cent of their assessed needs in April 1991. Although the crisis in Iran was 2–3 times as severe as that in Turkey, international assistance to Turkey was substantially higher.[25]

The impression that the national interests of major powers determine decisions regarding humanitarian interventions is strengthened by the fact that

> Military operations under chapter VII [undertaken for humanitarian purposes] are agreed largely on the basis of a calculus of shared interests or of tradeoffs among the five permanent members of the Security Council. In June 1994, for example, disparate interests resulted in separate council decisions to authorise interventions by the French in Rwanda, the Americans in Haiti, and the Russians in Georgia. Each of the three permanent members traded its vote for the favored intervention of the other in return for support of its own favored operation.[26]

In other words, decisions to intervene even when taken for ostensibly humanitarian purposes and within the framework of the UN Security Council were subject to bargaining among the major powers that engaged in quid pro quo to enhance their respective strategic and economic interests in their spheres of influence.

Determining International Will

Since humanitarian interventions are supposedly undertaken in order to enforce the will of the international community, such bargaining and selectivity led to the strong suspicion that the concept of 'international will' is being used as a fig leaf to hide motivations based on national interest. These misgivings cannot be allayed unless one addresses the issue as to how international will is defined and deciphered. It is clear that the definition of such will cannot be left to major powers or a dominant coalition of major powers especially when they may have special reasons to carry out particular interventions to suit their own political and strategic objectives. A mechanism that not merely is, but is also seen to be, transparent, fair, and broadly participatory must be established to determine international will. Such a mechanism is not present at the current time.

Recourse to the UN Security Council for authorisation or endorsement is inadequate as a measure for determining international political will. This is the case primarily because of the lopsided composition of that body and the seemingly firm resolve of its permanent members to block the expansion of its permanent membership and prevent the distribution of permanent seats more equitably in geographic and demographic terms.[27] The veto power wielded by its permanent members makes the Security Council even more suspect in terms of its ability to apply uniform criteria for intervention to all humanitarian crises that may arise in the future. This is so because it excludes the possibility of international intervention against the veto-wielding powers and their friends and allies. In short, since the veto power of the P-5 can be exercised to deny humanitarian relief and to prevent humanitarian intervention, it creates a visibly discriminatory system that brings into question the legitimacy of all humanitarian interventions sanctioned by the Security Council.[28]

Furthermore, even if one accepts for argument's sake that the UN Security Council is the proper agency for authorising humanitarian interventions, this does not resolve the legitimacy problem for such authorised interventions. A major concern arises from the lack of control by the Security Council over interventions authorised by it and undertaken in its name. Many of these operations have been subcontracted to groups of states that set the military, and often political, objectives of such interventions thus raising doubts about their legitimacy if not their legality.

Iraq and Haiti

The decisions to intervene in northern Iraq and Haiti clearly raised qualms in many people's minds that it was the UN Security Council to which a role had been allotted by the intervening powers rather than the other way around. In the case of northern Iraq it could be argued plausibly that UN Security Council Resolution 688, which was used to justify forcible intervention by the United States, Britain and France, 'did not specifically authorize the use of force, and the Secretary-General did not request it, although he did in the end acquiesce in the intervention'.[29] That resolution, one could reason, was essentially hijacked by the intervening powers to punish Iraq and destabilise the Iraqi regime in the aftermath of the Gulf War. It was thus utilised as a substitute for the Allies' unwillingness to use force during that war to over-throw Saddam Hussein.

In the case of Haiti, the UN Security Council Resolution 940 of July 1994 authorised member states 'to form a multinational force [and] . . . to use all necessary means to facilitate the departure from Haiti of the military dictator-ship'. This was a more unambiguous authorisation of the use of force than in the case of northern Iraq. However, the fact that the U.S. had a very strong motive in intervening in Haiti to stop the flow of Haitian refugees into the country raised doubts in the minds of many observers regarding the legitimacy of such intervention.[30] These suspicions were reinforced by the fact that

> segments of the American foreign policy establishment [had] provided moderate to strong support to the de facto [military] government. For instance it has been credibly alleged that US intelligence personnel were involved in the formation and train-ing of the FRAPH, a paramilitary group that was accused of some of the worst human rights violations under the Cedras regime.[31]

It was only when the flow of refugees into the United States became intolera-ble that Washington took the lead in putting pressure upon the UN to sanc-tion intervention in Haiti.

Rwanda

The feeling that the U.S. was using double standards in the case of Haiti was strengthened by the realisation that refugee movements of a much higher order from Rwanda during the same year did not evoke a similarly strong interventionary response from the Security Council. This inaction was attrib-uted to the fact that the U.S. was disinclined to support intervention in Africa in the aftermath of the debacle in Somalia. In short, in this view the successful intervention in Haiti and the humanitarian disaster in Rwanda were both related to the presence or absence of U.S. national interest concerns.

The International Panel of Eminent Personalities set up by the Organisation of African Unity (OAU) in 1998 to investigate the 1994 geno-cide in Rwanda endorsed this view. The panel came to the conclusion that

> Once the genocide began, the US repeatedly and deliberately un-dermined all attempts to strengthen the UN military presence in Rwanda . . . [W]ith the genocide taking tens of thousands of lives daily, the Security Council . . . chose to cut the UN forces in half at the exact moment they needed massive reinforcement. As the horrors accelerated, the Council did authorise a stronger mission . . . but once again the US did all in its power to undermine its

effectiveness. In the end, not one single additional soldier or piece of military hardware reached the country before the genocide ended.[32]

The panel also concluded that the performance of other powers, especially France, was even worse.

Bosnia

The treatment meted out by the major powers, and by extension by the United Nations Security Council, to the recognised government of Bosnia during the early phase of the Bosnian crisis also created grave misgivings about the legality of several actions authorised by the Security Council in that country in the name of humanitarian intervention. In this particular case, the UN Security Council's attempt initially to maintain impartiality between the Bosnian state and the Serb insurgents in that country clearly violated international law and the norm of state sovereignty once Bosnia had been admitted to UN membership. As a leading commentator pointed out,

> The Bosnian government . . . expected, because Bosnia was a recognised member state, that the UN should protect its sovereignty against the Bosnian Serbs. Many Bosnians and Bosnian supporters believed that the principle of neutrality was totally inappropriate because it assumed a legal, military, and moral equality between them and the heavily armed Bosnian Serbs . . . Simple logic told them that the UN's neutrality meant it was in fact siding with the Serbs.[33]

The treatment of the Bosnian government more or less on par with the Serbian-supported Bosnian Serb insurgents continued until the massacre of Bosnian Muslims in the UN protected 'safe haven' of Srebrenica in the summer of 1995 forced the UN and the major powers to change track. A great deal of bloodshed in Bosnia could have been avoided had the Security Council acted on the basis of established norms and practices of international law and provided the much needed help to the Bosnian government under attack by rebels backed by Serbia instead of imposing an arms embargo on it. The embargo left the Bosnian state in a position of acute disadvantage against Serb forces equipped by Serbia, especially since the latter was in control of most of the equipment belonging to the Yugoslav army before the disintegration of the federation. As the involvement of Serbia in the Bosnian conflict, both in terms of the transfer of arms and military personnel, had been clearly established, the Security Council could have treated this case from the very beginning as one of aggression from outside Bosnia's borders.

International assistance to Bosnia could then have been rendered under the ambit of Chapter VII of the UN Charter. It would have also prevented the human tragedy of Bosnia epitomised by the Srebrenica massacre.[34]

Circumventing the Security Council

While controversy continues to surround UN-sanctioned interventions, the legitimacy of humanitarian interventions becomes even more suspect when they are undertaken without the authorisation of the Security Council. Kosovo is the primary case in point. The UN Security Council had voted unanimously in September 1998 to demand a halt to indiscriminate attacks against the civilian population in Kosovo. However, afraid that Russia and China would prevent the Security Council from authorising a military intervention in Kosovo to enforce this demand, NATO took the decision in October 1998 to intervene unilaterally and began its air operation against Yugoslavia in March 1999. As for NATO's right to act without explicit UN authorisation, [NATO Secretary General] Solana argued that 'it [NATO] is a serious organization that takes a decision by consensus among serious countries with democratic governments,' implying this fact alone conferred sufficient legitimacy on the contemplated action.[35]

Despite the existence of a strong moral case for intervention in Kosovo, the lack of authorisation by the UN Security Council immediately made it suspect in the eyes of a large number of states in the international system. The Security Council, even if a flawed instrument, at least gave some degree of legitimacy to actions taken on behalf of the society of states. The Kosovo intervention not only ignored the Security Council, but its proponents and executors added insult to injury by continuing to proclaim that it had been undertaken on behalf of the international community.[36] If generalised, this type of justification for intervention, either by a single power or by a multinational coalition, undertaken without proper authorisation and oversight by the Security Council, is likely not merely to confuse the discussion about humanitarian intervention but to discredit the very idea itself. It is likely to do so because such intervention is based on the unilateral arrogation by a state or a coalition of states of the right to speak and act on behalf of the international community and to represent international will when this is patently not the case.

When such arrogation takes place as the preliminary but crucial step toward violating the fundamental organising principle of international political life—state sovereignty—it raises serious concerns in the minds of policy makers and analysts around the world. When it has the potential to be used as a precedent to justify other similar actions it clearly undermines international order. As Bruno Simma has argued, '[T]he decisive point is that we should not change the rules simply to follow our humanitarian impulses; we should not set new standards only to do the right thing in a single case. The legal issues presented by the Kosovo crisis are particularly impressive proof that hard cases make bad law.'[37]

The concept of sovereignty and the degree to which it can be exercised today may be contested. However, one cannot deny the fact that not merely the UN Charter but also the accumulated norms of international society create a distinct predisposition towards accepting sovereignty claims unless a very strong case can be made that these claims need to be overridden. In order to disregard the legal claims of sovereignty, there must be a clear and demonstrated consensus on the part of a very large majority of states that such exceptional circumstances exist in a particular instance that they demand violation of the sovereignty norm. It must also be demonstrated that such violation is not being committed for ulterior motives by intervening states. Furthermore, it must be established clearly that the same yardstick will apply to all cases similar to the one in which intervention is sanctioned for humanitarian reasons. If the Kosovo case proves anything it is that the criteria for intervention must be very stringent, restrictive, and non-discriminatory for such interventions to be considered legitimate.

Potential for Abuse

The foregoing analysis brings up some very fundamental concerns that I harbour about humanitarian intervention in a world composed of sovereign states but where power is unequally distributed among them. First, given the disparity in power among states, humanitarian intervention has the strong potential of becoming a tool for the interference by the strong in the affairs of the weak, with humanitarian considerations providing a veneer to justify such intervention. This would be a throwback to a hyper-realist world that will no longer be undergirded by the norms of international society. This outcome must be avoided at all costs for it will be extremely derogatory to international order and is likely to create a Hobbesian 'state of nature' in the interactions of states with each other. In other words, the international system will revert to the state where it is merely a 'system' but no longer a 'society'.[38]

Second, and equally important, the selective derogation of state sovereignty by the use or misuse of humanitarian intervention may end up detracting from the most essential instrument, the principle of sovereignty, that has been used for the maintenance of international order during the past four centuries.[39] The principle of sovereignty has also contributed to international justice, even if modestly, by acting as a normative barrier against the predatory instincts of the more powerful states. Sovereignty has underwritten international order primarily by enshrining the doctrine of non-intervention in the internal affairs of states as an essential ingredient of international society.

While this may not have prevented interventions in the past, it has acted quite effectively as a normative requirement by forcing potential or actual interveners to justify their actions before their sovereign, and legally equal, peers. Changing the normative yardsticks governing intervention (which have traditionally had a pronounced bias toward non-intervention) may end up doing more harm than good to international order in the long run.

My third concern, and one very inadequately addressed in the debate about humanitarian intervention, is that state sovereignty, as a legal and normative concept, acts as the cornerstone for the only institutional architecture capable of providing order within territorially defined political communities. It goes without saying that the preservation of domestic order is essential for the maintenance of international order. But preserving domestic order is also essential for the attainment of other values, including human rights, that most people hold dear. By eroding the legal basis of sovereign authority, humanitarian intervention, especially as practised during the past decade, may be opening the floodgates for domestic disorder. This, in turn, could negatively affect international order as well as the individuals' most basic requirements for civilised existence. In the absence of domestic order one does not experience freedom but anarchy where the weak and the vulnerable (both within states and among them) are at the greatest disadvantage.

One has only to have a passing acquaintance with Thomas Hobbes's writings to realise the verity of this assertion.[40] Furthermore, as recent experience has demonstrated, there is no institution other than the state that has the will or the ability to provide domestic order to societies. International organisations, NCOs, as well as external powers have all tried their hand at providing political order but have failed to do so. They have eventually been forced to re-establish institutions of state to perform this most fundamental task. The UN Transitional Authority in Cambodia (UNTAC) had to hand over the reins of power to a Cambodian government although the latter's legitimacy was less than completely established and its effectiveness was in question.[41] In East Timor, the UN continues to face a conundrum because of the unwillingness or inability of the UN Transitional Administration in East Timor (UNTAET) to hand over the substance of power to local authorities. As a result, it is increasingly alienating the local population and may find a revolt on its hands.[42] In the absence of feasible alternatives, eroding the legitimacy and capacity of the state as an institution to provide order, even if it does so at times by the use of excessive force, usually turns out to be counter-productive.

State Making and Violence

Finally, given the past record, it would appear that the likely targets of humanitarian intervention in the future would be new and weak states struggling to establish themselves as full-fledged members of the international system. It would be unrealistic to assume that they will be able to do so without the exercise of some violence. Such violence is, and will be, unavoidable, in light of the fact that new states, meaning those that have emerged since the end of World War II and form a majority of members of the international system, will continue to suffer for quite some time from the twin problems of incomplete state making and inadequate nation formation.[43] Consequently, the coercive forces of the state may be frequently pitted against recalcitrant elements that refuse to accept the authority of the emerging state that is attempting to centralise power in its hands. Viewed through this prism it becomes clear that Kosovo was not so much an exception to the rule as a part of a historical trajectory that goes back several centuries to the founding of modern sovereign states in Western Europe.

Those familiar with the history of Europe (or, indeed of the United States) will immediately recognise such violence as belonging to the same category of state making wars that Western and Central Europe experienced from the sixteenth to the nineteenth centuries and the United States did in the Civil War of the 1860s and in its campaigns against native Americans. Such intrastate and interstate conflicts were then considered essential instruments for the imposition, maintenance, and legitimisation of political order. They serve much the same purpose now.[44] Using such outbursts of violent conflict as justification for humanitarian intervention not merely defies the historical trajectory of state making but is likely to have major negative impact on the endeavour to impose and maintain domestic order. This is a subject that is under-explored in the literature on humanitarian intervention but deserves closer and fuller scrutiny.

The bottom line is that a degree of violence is bound to accompany the state making and nation building process. Such violence is inescapable in light of the fact that political entities that emerged after World War II and, again, in the early 1990s after the demise of the Soviet Union and the disintegration of Yugoslavia have had no other option but to emulate the established states in terms of acquiring control over populations and territories. Where they have not been able to acquire such control, as in parts of sub-Saharan Africa and Central Asia, they have remained the butt of international ridicule and suffer from permanent marginalisation in international affairs.

Established international norms demand effective statehood from new states in a drastically shortened time frame compared to their European predecessors. At the same time, these states are subjected to a contradictory set of normative demands emanating from the international system, viz., that of civilised behaviour toward their populations, including those within their boundaries who oppose the dominant state making project. One wonders if West European and North American states would have successfully completed their state building endeavours and eventually emerged as liberal, democratic states, if they had the UN Human Rights Commission, Amnesty International and now the UN Security Council breathing down their necks during the crucial early phases of their state making endeavours.

It is true, however, that international sensibility regarding human rights and their violations have changed quite radically during the past 50 years and this reality cannot be ignored. Therefore, a moral case can certainly be made regarding the need for humanitarian intervention and the violation of sovereignty that such intervention may necessarily entail. As one author has suggested, '[I]t would be extreme to suggest that sovereignty is absolute to the point of protecting the right of a state to carry out genocide, massive human rights violations, and generally terrorizing the population.'[45] But, even in this changed normative context, one cannot neglect totally the imperatives of the state making process, especially since states continue to be the only providers of domestic order. Balancing the two demands, therefore, means that not only should the decision to intervene not be taken lightly, but also that there must be a transparent and legitimate mechanism through which such decisions are made on an impartial basis not affected by the national interest concerns of the intervening powers. For, once the latter is seen to happen the moral force of the humanitarian intervention argument will dissipate very quickly.

Humanitarian Intervention and Chapter VII

In an attempt, however partial, to address this crucial issue of reconciling the demands of state sovereignty with the need for humanitarian intervention where there is irrefutable evidence of sustained and systematic violation of human rights, I would like to make the following two suggestions. First, I would like to argue strongly that humanitarian interventions should not be undertaken under the provisions of Chapter VII of the UN Charter because the circumstances that lead to such interventions usually do not fall within the ambit of threats to international peace and security as defined in that chapter. Much of the violence that usually prompts such intervention is intrastate in character. Even where there are cross border implications of such violence, usually in the form of refugees spilling over into neighbouring states, these do not normally fall in the category of interstate conflict or aggression by one state against another. It was certainly not the intent of the framers of the Charter to use Chapter VII provisions for purposes of intervention within the domestic jurisdiction of states. Chapter VII was intended to augment the sovereignty of states and protect them from external aggression and unwanted intervention, not to intervene in their domestic affairs. As such, humanitarian interventions subvert the very purpose for which the Chapter was written.

Paradoxically, the use of Chapter VII has precluded the use of the UN as an instrument of intervention in certain cases where such action was likely to have been vetoed by one or more of the permanent members of the Security Council. Kosovo was the prime example of this type of intervention undertaken without the authorisation of the UN because of the inadequacy of Chapter VII in reconciling the P-5's right to veto with the ostensibly altruistic intent of humanitarian intervention. Consequently, even a document as sympathetic to humanitarian intervention as the report by the Independent International Commission on Kosovo was forced to admit that 'The intervention laid bare the inadequate state of international law. The intervention was not legal because it contravened the Charter prohibitions on the unauthorized use of force.'[46]

Need for a New Mechanism

In light of these deficiencies it is clear that Chapter VII is not the proper mechanism for authorising humanitarian intervention. It is clear that in order to provide for such intervention the Charter must be amended and new articles included carefully listing the conditions under which humanitarian intervention can be considered permissible and the mechanism through which such intervention must be conducted. This means, above all that decisions regarding such interventions must be removed from the jurisdiction of the Security Council. A new more broadly based body, call it the Humanitarian Council if you will, must be created with adequate representation from all regions and with rotating membership reflecting the diverse composition of the United Nations. It should consist of at least 50 members, approximately a quarter of the total membership of the UN. Decisions to intervene for humanitarian purposes must require at least a three-quarters majority of the membership of the proposed Council with no state having the right to veto such a decision. It must also be vested with oversight functions in regard to every intervention sanctioned by it. This oversight function should be exercised through the UN Secretary General who must report periodically to the proposed body.

It is essential that the authority for undertaking humanitarian intervention be removed from the Security Council and vested in a larger and more representative body in order to provide the much needed legitimacy and credibility to such intervention. This becomes imperative because there is no sign that the P-5 will be willing to suspend their veto powers when it comes to dealing with humanitarian crises or to act with consistency regarding similar crises no matter where they develop around the world. Such a major amendment of the UN Charter may appear impossible to many advocates of humanitarian intervention who would consider it unrealistic and not adequately sensitive to the realpolitik considerations driving the policies of major powers. This, however, would demonstrate the internal inconsistency of their logic. For, decisions to intervene for humanitarian purposes are not supposed to be subject to the logic of realpolitik. If they are, then such interventions are not humanitarian in character. Eroding the normative basis of international society in order to provide major powers the facility to intervene selectively in the domestic affairs of weaker states should not be a part of the logic of humanitarian intervention.

Complex Political Emergencies

A transparent and participatory process will also allow the international community to clearly distinguish human rights violations by institutions of the state from 'complex political emergencies' that result primarily from state failure.[47] In the former case, state elites use disproportionate force in order to promote their state and/or nation building project and bring dissent to a quick if violent end. In the process they violate the human rights of groups and individuals that are opposed to their state and nation building goals. A quick and definitive outcome, even if not always achieved, is clearly envisaged by the state elites perpetrating violence and violating human rights.

In the case of 'complex political emergencies', state collapse leads, among other things, to the emergence of 'conflict entrepreneurs' who benefit from internal chaos and war and thus possess a vested interest in their indefinite, or at least prolonged, continuation.[48] Their goal is, therefore, to perpetuate conflict rather than bring it to an end. This has led David Keen to point out that

> [I]nternal conflicts have persisted not so much *despite* the intentions of rational people, as *because* of them. The apparent "chaos" of civil war can be used to further local and short-term interests. These are frequently *economic*: to paraphrase Carl von Clausewitz, war has increasingly become the continuation of economics by other means. War is not simply a breakdown in a particular system, but a way of creating an alternative system of profit, power and even protection.[49]

A major reason for state collapse and the emergence of conflict entrepreneurs is related to the end of the Cold War. The superpowers lost interest in a large number of peripheral states, especially in Africa, that no longer served their strategic purpose. During the Cold War, client regimes had been supplied with external assistance by the superpowers to help them stay in power by buying off and/or suppressing domestic opponents. With the withdrawal of external support these regimes were confronted by strong-men whom they could neither purchase nor control. Consequently, as William Reno has made clear with regard to civil wars in Liberia and Sierra Leone, such conflicts, which often lead to state collapse, are 'an outgrowth of the struggle between once dominant regimes and increasingly enterpris-ing strongmen to control markets, both internally and externally, and con-vert that control into political authority.'[50] In many cases, this results in the collapse of the state with various contenders fighting over its carcass prima-rily in order to attain external legitimacy that donning the mantle of the state provides to them.

Liberia, Somalia, Sierra Leone, Congo/Zaire, among others, fall within this category of complex political emergencies that accompany state failure. Northern Iraq, Haiti and Kosovo certainly did not. It is interesting, however, that Great Power interest in intervening in the latter cases was of a much higher order than in the former. It also explains why ECOWAS's interven-tion in Liberia and the UN mission in Somalia were far less controversial than the Security Council's decision to authorise intervention in northern Iraq and the NATO intervention in Kosovo. The profusion of state collapse, or its likelihood, in sub-Saharan Africa explains to a considerable degree the greater acceptance of outside intervention in Africa as compared to other regions.[51] Simultaneously, the low priority of that region in the strategic cal-culations of the dominant coalition as compared to Europe or the Middle East explains the relative indifference of the 'international community' to humanitarian crises in Africa.

From the perspective of international society it is clear that the interven-tion in the two sets of cases distinguished above must be crafted in very differ-ent ways from each other, with the complex political emergencies deserving greater attention and more intense military involvement. Moral suasion, eco-nomic sanctions, and the equivalent of an international social boycott must be the instruments of first choice when dealing with states that routinely violate the human rights of their citizens. These tools are unlikely to work in the cases defined as complex political emergencies where states have collapsed or are about to do so. In the latter case, forcible, primarily military, intervention may be the only means available to provide essential goods and services to suffering populations as well as to bring the multiple perpetrators of terror to book. Humanitarian emergencies accompanying state failure are unlikely to pose the normative constraints on international intervention that the former would pose. In the absence of a recognisable sovereign authority, the question of vio-lating state sovereignty becomes largely redundant. Therefore, the legal barri-ers for international action are drastically lowered.

These two ideal types of conflict do not exhaust all the scenarios in which international intervention may be demanded and/or considered. In fact, most concrete cases are likely to fall somewhere between the two ideal types and to possess characteristics that straddle the divide between them. Political leaders may attempt to use the state-making justification for purely predatory purposes à la Mobutu of Zaire. Alternatively, the use of excessive violence for state-making purposes may itself prompt state collapse, as for example in East Pakistan in 1970–71.

The likely prevalence of cases that combine the characteristics of state-making violence with those accompanying state failure makes it more imperative that decisions to intervene be taken by a body that is perceived to be genuinely representative of the international community and is considered to be largely impartial. Unlike the Security Council as it is currently constituted, such a body will be able to deliberate about complex cases transparently without being unduly influenced by the national interest considerations of major powers. Ad hoc decisions that lead to selective intervention and that are viewed as being linked to the national interests of major powers are likely to eventually discredit the very notion of humanitarian intervention as well as introduce greater disorder into international society.

The future of international order may well hinge on the way we are able to resolve the tension between 'international intervention' and 'state sovereignty'. In some cases, as those of state failure, such intervention may become a necessity. In others, a more prudent as well as non-discriminatory approach will be required. The demands for humanitarian activism and respect for state sovereignty can be credibly balanced only when decisions to intervene are taken by an institution that is representative and through a process that is transparent. These qualities are essential to provide international legitimacy for decisions to intervene in the internal affairs of states when such decisions are supposedly taken on behalf of the international community. In their absence suspicions will persist that it is the national interests of the powerful that dictate such decisions rather than the collective interests of the society of states.

Order versus Justice

Underlying the debate over humanitarian intervention and state sovereignty is the perennial problem of order versus justice in the international system. However, in this case the debate intertwines two levels of the order–justice problem. At one level, the demand for human rights, which usually provides the context and often the pretext for humanitarian intervention, can be seen as the claim of individuals and substate groups for justice pitted against the state's claim that order comes prior to justice. The corollary of the latter claim is that as the sole dispenser of domestic order the state has the right to tailor the need for justice to the requirements of order.

At another level, the defence of state sovereignty against the undue excesses of humanitarian intervention can be seen as the demand for justice by the weaker states against the stronger states' proclivity to impose their preferred view of international order on the weak in the name of justice within states. Moral and normative claims can and will be advanced in the name of justice at both levels. The trick is to balance these claims carefully so as not to detract severely either from fragile domestic orders or from an international order that itself continues to remain in uneasy equilibrium.

The tension between state sovereignty and humanitarian intervention also brings to the fore the fundamental tensions between the Northern and Southern perspectives on order and justice in the international system. This tension can be summarised, with some risk of oversimplification, in the following manner: While the North is primarily interested in justice within states and order among them, the South is basically committed to order within states and justice among them. This divergence in the Northern and Southern perceptions of order and justice and the different realms to which they apply is intimately related to where the two groups are generally located in terms of their state-making odyssey and the technological, military and economic capabilities at their disposal. States at an earlier stage of state making and inferior in terms of capabilities are likely to defend their sovereignty zealously. Those states that are well established, i.e. possess unconditional legitimacy in the eyes of their populations, and more powerful are, on the other hand, likely to be more interventionist in their inclinations. They can be presumed to be more inclined to overrule the claims of state sovereignty, especially since they know that their own sovereign claims are unlikely to be challenged from within or superseded from without.

The tension analysed in this article is, therefore, likely to remain with us for a long time to come. It will be resolved only when the newcomers to the international system succeed in establishing effective and legitimate states as well as in narrowing the power gap between them and the established states of the global North. In the meantime, the society of states will have to continuously grapple with this issue and balance the demands of the two sides in such a fashion that neither side's basic commitment to the fundamental rules governing international society is eroded and the 'global covenant' endangered. Ignoring the power and perceptual gaps between the North and the South and working on the misleading assumption that a community of interests exists within the society of states as regards humanitarian intervention is likely to put international order at considerable risk. Both sides should remember that while order must be tempered by justice for it to attain legitimacy, the demand for justice when oblivious to the need for order can easily lead to anarchy. They should also realise that this applies to the condition within states as well as among them.

NOTES

1. In my view the concept of international society is by definition pluralist in character. Take away the pluralism and the society no longer remains 'inter-national.' For an elegantly presented contrary view that advances a solidarist notion of international society, albeit acknowledging pluralist restraints on international solidarism, see Nicholas J. Wheeler, *Saving Strangers: Humanitarian Intervention in International Society* (New York: Oxford University Press, 2000). I would argue the opposite: that international society at the beginning of the twenty-first century continues to be essentially pluralist although there may be certain solidarist restraints imposed on its basic pluralist character.

2. For a discussion of the fundamental characteristics of international society as well as the rules and norms governing it, see Hedley Bull. *The Anarchical Society: A Study of Order in World Politics* (New York: Columbia University Press, 1977).

3. According to Robert Jackson, 'The global covenant is the first attempt in world history to construct a society of states that operates with a doctrine of recognition and non-intervention that bridges different civilizations and cultures around the world.' Robert Jackson, *The Global Covenant: Human Conduct in a World of States* (New York: Oxford University Press, 2000), p. 13.

4. David P. Forsythe, *Human Rights in International Relations* (New York: Cambridge University Press, 2000), p. 3.

5. For a discussion of state failure and collapse, see 1. William Zartman (ed.), *Collapsed States: The Disintegration and Restoration of Legitimate Authority* (Boulder, CO: Lynne Rienner, 1995), especially chs. 1 and 17.

6. For a powerful rendering of this argument, see Janice E. Thomson, 'State Sovereignty in International Relations: Bridging the Gap Between Theory and Empirical Research,' *International Studies Quarterly*, Vol. 39, No. 2 (June 1995), pp. 213–33.

7. Bendedier Kingsbury, 'Sovereignty and Inequality,' in Andrew Hurrell and Ngaire Woods (eds.), *Inequality, Globalization, and World Politics* (New York: Oxford University Press, 1999), p. 86.

8. See, R.J. Vincent, *Nonintervention and International Order* (Princeton, NJ: Princeton University Press, 1974), p. 331.

9. For one authoritative expression of such sentiment, see the text of Kofi Annan's statement to the UN General Assembly on 20 September 1999. The text is published under the title 'Human Security and Intervention' in *Vital Speeches of the Day*, New York, 15 October 1999.

10. Jarat Chopra and Thomas G. Weiss, 'Sovereignty is No Longer Sacrosanct: Codifying Humanitarian Intervention,' *Ethics and International Affairs*, Vol. 6 (1992), pp. 95–118.

11. For example, see Francis M. Deng *et al., Sovereignty as Responsibility* (Washington, D.C.: The Brookings Institution, 1996).

12. For details, see Gerritt W. Gong, *The Standard of 'Civilization' in International Society* (Oxford: Clarendon Press, 1984).

13. Ibid., p. 107.

14. Kingsbury (note 7), pp. 90–91.

15. Gene M. Lyons and Michael Mastanduno, 'Introduction' in Gene M. Lyons and Michael Mastanduno (eds.), *Beyond Westphalia? State Sovereignty and International Intervention* (Baltimore, MI): Johns I Jopkins University Press, 1995), p. 13.

16. Lyons and Mastanduna, 'Introduction' in Lyons and Mastanduno (ibid.), p. 8.

17. I do not intend to enter into the controversy in this article about how national interests themselves are defined, who defines them, etc. For the purposes of this article it will be assumed that national interests are those objectives articulated as such by authoritative spokesmen for the states on the basis of widely reflected consensus among the foreign policy and security communities within those states.

18. Stanley Hoffmann, 'The Politics and Ethics of Military Intervention,' *Survival*, Vol. 37, No. 4 (Winter 1995–96), p. 29.

19. Adam Roberts, 'The Road to Hell . . .: A Critique of Humanitarian Intervention', *Harvard International Review*, Vol. 16, No. 1 (Fall 1993).

20. See Kofi Annan, 'Human Security and Intervention' in *Vital Speeches of the Day* (New York: 15 October 1999.

21. Thomas G. Weiss, 'The Politics of Humanitarian Ideas,' *Security Dialogue*, Vol. 31, No. 1 (March 2000), p. 20.

22. S. Neil MacFarlane and Thomas Weiss, 'Political Interest and Humanitarian Action,' *Security Studies*, Vol. 10, No. 1 (Autumn 2000), pp. 120–52.

23. For details of the two interventions and events preceding and following them, see Richard Sisson and Leo and E. Rose, *War and Secession: Pakistan, India, and the Creation of Bangladesh*, Berkeley: University of California Press, 1990; and Nayan Chanda, *Brother Enemy: The War After the War*, San Diego: Harcourt Brace Jovanovich, 1986.

24. This point has also been made in connection with the selective use of the collective security argument. See Mohammed Ayoob, 'Squaring the Circle: Collective Security in a System of States', in Thomas G. Weiss (ed.), *Collective Security in a Changing World* (Boulder, CO: Lynne Rienner, 1993), pp. 45–62.

25. MacFarlane and Weiss (note 22), p. 136.

26. MacFarlane and Weiss (ibid.), p. 137.

27. The Independent International Commission on Kosovo 'concluded that additional UN reforms could address the growing gap between legality and legitimacy that always arises in cases of humanitarian intervention. The global credibility of the UN is undermined by the lack of representivity of the current structure of the UN Security Council. Expansion of the UNSC and of the permanent members will be an essential step toward regaining the credibility to maintain an effective role as guardian of world security.' Independent International Commission on Kosovo, *The Kosovo Report* (Oxford University Press, 2000), p. 291.

28. Richard Falk has summed up these reservations regarding the legitimacy of actions authorised by the Security Council in the following words: 'Particularly confusing is the uncertainty regarding whether a Security Council decision involves a genuinely collective and community interventionary judgement guided predominantly by considerations of public good. Uncertainty clouds the

degree to which such a decision is little more than a legitimating rationale for use of force that would otherwise be more widely viewed as "illegal" if undertaken by a state on its own or in coalition with other states.' Richard Falk, 'The Complexities of Humanitarian Intervention: A New World Order Challenge', *Michigan Journal of International Law*, Vol. 17 (Winter 1996), pp. 492–3.

29. Francis Kofi Abiew, *The Evolution of the Doctrine and Practice of Humanitarian Intervention*, Kluwer Law International, Cambridge, MA, 1999, p. 153.

30. See, for example, Cynthia Weber, 'Dissimulating Intervention: A Reading of the US-Led Intervention in Haiti', *Alternatives*, Vol. 20, No. 3 (1995), pp. 265–78.

31. Chetan Kumat and Elizabeth M. Cousens, *Policy Briefing: Peacebuilding in Haiti*, New York: International Peace Academy, 1996), p. 4. Accessed on the internet at http://www.ipacademy.org/Publications/Reports/Research/PublRepoReseHaitPrint

32. OAU International Panel of Eminent Personalities to Investigate the 1994 Genocide in Rwanda and the Surrounding Events, *Special Report*, 7 July 2000, Executive Summary, p. 7. Accessed on the internet at: http://www.oau-oua.org/Document/ipep/report/rwanda-e/EN-II-EX

33. Susan L. Woodward, *Balkan Tragedy: Chaos and Dissolution After the Cold War* (Washington, D.C.: Brookings Institution, 1995), p. 320.

34. For a powerful indictment of the UN's imposition of an arms embargo on Bosnia and its policy of evenhandedness between the Bosnian government and Serbian insurgents, who perpetrated most of the human rights violations in Bosnia, see Haris Silajdzic, 'Since the UN Can't Protect Us, Lift the Arms Embargo', *New Perspectives Quarterly*, Vol. 12 (Summer 1995), pp. 38–9. The author was the Prime Minister of Bosnia when this article was published.

35. Ivo H. Daalder, 'NATO, the UN, and the Use of Force', paper prepared for UNA-USA, March 1999, p. 10. Accessed on the internet at: http://www.unausa.org/issues/sc/daalder

36. For a perceptive discussion of the controversies surrounding the Kosovo intervention, see Nicholas J. Wheeler, 'Reflections on the Legality and Legitimacy of NATO's Intervention in Kosovo', *International Journal of Human Rights*, Vol. 4, Nos. 3/4, 2000, pp. 145–63.

37. Bruno Simma, 'NATO, the UN and the Use of Force: Legal Aspects', *European Journal of International Law*, Vol. 10, No. 1 (1999), accessed on the internet at: www.ejil.org/journal/Vol10/No1/ab1-2.

38. For an authoritative discussion of the difference between a hyperrealist world which is confined to being a 'system' and one governed by norms and rules that establish, as well as symbolise, a 'society' of states or international society, see Hedley Bull, *The Anarchical Society: A Study of Order in World Politics*, New York: Columbia University Press (1977), ch. 1.

39. See Alan James, 'The Practice of Sovereign Statehood in Contemporary International Society', in Robert Jackson (ed.), *Sovereignty at the Millennium* (Malden, MA: Blackwell, 1999), pp. 35–51.

40. For one perceptive interpretation of Hobbes as a theorist of domestic order, see Michael Williams, 'Hobbes and International Relations: Reconsideration'. *International Organization*, Vol. 50, No. 2 (1996).

41. For an evaluation of UNTAC's achievements and failures, see Trevor Findlay, *Cambodia: The Legacy and Lessons of UNTAC*, SIPRI Research Report No. 9 (New York: Oxford University Press, 1995).

42. For a stringent critique of the UNTAET's policies and actions by an insider, see Jarat Chopra. 'The UN's Kingdom of East Timor', *Survival*, Vol. 42, No. 3 (Autumn 2000), pp. 27–39.

43. This assertion is based on the premise, borne out by historical analysis, that most cases of successful nation formation have been those where the state has been able to fashion the nation through the exercise of coercion as well as persuasion but, above all, by the very existence and resilience of state institutions within roughly the same boundaries over a considerable period of time. For a concise yet perceptive account, see Cornelia Navari, 'The Origins of the Nation-State', in Leonard Tivey (ed.), *The Nation-State: The Formation of Modern Politics* (Oxford: Martin Robertson, 1981), pp. 13–36.

44. For details of this argument, see Mohammed Ayoob, 'State Making, State Failure and the Revolution in Military Affairs', in Gwyn Prins and Hylke Tromp (eds.), *The Future of War* (Boston: Kluwer Law International, 2000), pp. 147–66.

45. Frederick J. Petersen, 'The Façade of Humanitarian Intervention for Human Rights in a Community of Sovereign States', *Arizona Journal of International and Comparative Law*, Vol. 15, No. 3 (1998), p. 882.

46. Independent International Commission on Kosovo (note 27), p. 290.

47. For a review of the literature on state failure and interventions to reverse this process, see Tonya Langford, 'Things Fall Apart: State Failure and the Politics of Intervention', *International Studies Review*, Vol. 1, No. 1 (Spring 1999), pp. 59–79.

48. Jonathan Goodhand and David Hulme, 'From Wars to Complex Political Emergencies: Understanding Conflict and Peace-Building in the New World Disorder', *Third World Quarterly*, Vol. 20, No. 1 (February 1999), p. 19.

49. David Keen, *The Economic Functions of Violence in Civil Wars*, Adelphi Paper 320 (Oxford: Oxford University Press, for the International Institute for Strategic Studies, London, 1998), p. 11.

50. William Reno, *Humanitarian Emergencies and Warlord Economies in Liberia and Sierra Leone*, Working Paper No. 140 (UNU World Institute for Development Economics Research, 1997), p. 2.

51. According to one author, 'During the same period [1990–96] when membership of the UN shot up by 16 per cent, primarily due to the dissolution of the Soviet Empire, over one-third of the total number of states in Africa alone have collapsed or are at risk . . .' Karin von Hippel, *Democracy by Force: US Military Intervention in the Post-Cold War World* (New York: Cambridge University Press, 2000), p. 2.

CHAPTER 20 DEVELOPED v. DEVELOPING COUNTRIES AND THE CHALLENGE OF CLIMATE CHANGE

The United States and Global Climate Change

Advocates: Julianne Smith and Derek Mix

Source: "The Transatlantic Climate Change Challenge," *The Washington Quarterly,* vol. 31, no. 1 (2007), pp. 139–154.

China and Global Climate Challenge

Advocate: Kelly Sims Gallagher

Source: "China Needs Help with Climate Change," *Current History,* (November 2007), pp. 389–394, excerpt.

Climate change has received significant attention in the media. It is a transnational issue that affects us all, and its solution will require the commitment of countries from across the globe. While the scientific evidence on climate change and its effects has accumulated, there is still considerable discord on the appropriate policy responses to this impending problem. Mitigating the effects of climate change means that countries will have to adopt measures that may have repercussions for their economies and security.

A divide exists in the responses of the rich and poor countries. Countries in the Global North, and the United States in particular, insist that the developing countries must take their share of responsibility and reduce their emissions. America would like to see countries, such as China and India, curb their emissions as a precondition for its own participation in this environmental regime, which would otherwise hurt the U.S. economy. Most developing countries, on the other hand, point out that the majority of carbon dioxide released in the atmosphere is from the developed countries, and thus, those countries should bear the burden of reductions. At the UN Climate Change Conference in Bali in December 2007, the United States lifted its objections and agreed to new negotiations, cutting emissions and technology transfers, while the developing countries agreed to take actions on climate change.

IN FAVOR OF DEVELOPING COUNTRY PARTICIPATION

For a long time the position of the United States was one that emphasized the economic repercussions of cutting emissions and insisted that developing countries, such as China and India, must commit to cuts as well. Although the Clinton Administration signed the Kyoto Protocol, the U.S. Senate made it clear that ratification was not possible. The Bush Administration long held the view that there was not sufficient scientific basis for the human causes of climate change. Citing possible negative economic effects of emissions cuts, it did not participate in multilateral frameworks for addressing climate change concerns. It also made China and India's assent to mandatory cuts a precondition for its own adoption of such standards.

The participation and leadership of the United States in this area are indispensable for any meaningful solutions to climate change, considering that the United States is responsible for 20 percent of the total global emissions. As Smith and Mix argue, in recent years there has been a shift in the perception of climate change among the public. A number of states and cities around the country have voluntarily adopted emissions curbs that are equivalent or deeper than those mandated by the Kyoto Protocol. The Obama Administration and Congress are more likely to ratify international instruments committing the United States to cooperation in this area. However, a number of obstacles remain to U.S. participation in any international regime addressing climate change, which, as Smith and Mix claim, would be futile without the United States.

IN FAVOR OF DEVELOPMENT

The argument that emissions cuts may adversely affect a country's economic growth is particularly salient in the Global South. Although the emissions by countries such as India and China—which recently surpassed the United States as the largest net emitter—are rapidly increasing, the developing countries account for less than one-fifth of emissions per capita compared to the developed world. With a sizeable portion of their populations still living in poverty, these countries emphasize their need for development and the industrialized world's historic responsibility for climate change. It is also the case that the impact of climate change will first be felt in the developing countries. Nevertheless, although the Kyoto Protocol did not require countries to commit to cuts, many in the Global South have, in fact, voluntarily adopted limits on their emissions.

China is the largest overall emitter of greenhouse gases in the world. The size of its population and growing economy suggests that its emission will continue to increase. As a developing country, where hundreds of millions of people live below or just above the poverty line, China has a tremendous incentive to prioritize development. Kelly Sims Gallagher argues that China is also very vulnerable to the effects of climate change, including its water supply, agriculture, and sea levels. In contrast to the United States, China has ratified the Kyoto Protocol, but much work remains to be done in reducing emissions. Gallagher urges the U.S. government to form a partnership with China to search for innovative low-carbon technologies, wider markets for energy technologies, and investment opportunities. Catastrophic climate change may be avoided only if the two countries reduce their emissions.

POINTS **TO PONDER**

1. Should the developing nations be allowed to have only voluntary cuts on their greenhouse emissions?

2. Are emissions cuts going to weaken the U.S. economy?

3. Why is U.S. leadership essential for the success of international environmental regimes?

4. What role has Europe played in the drive to reduce emissions? Contrast the role of Europe to the role of the United States.

5. Why is the United States seen as the global laggard in reducing emissions? Is this perception a fair one?

Julianne Smith and Derek Mix

The Transatlantic Climate Change Challenge

The U.S.-European relationship has evolved into a partnership that stretches well beyond the Atlantic area to address global challenges such as the proliferation of weapons of mass destruction, radical extremism, the rise of China, global poverty, and health issues. Climate change is becoming a part of that list as well, although this phenomenon is fairly new. The difficulty in forging transatlantic cooperation on this issue is that Europe and the United States are addressing it at different speeds and in different ways.

Europe is often portrayed as the global leader that has placed its faith in national and international regulation. By contrast, the United States has assumed the image of the global laggard unwilling to make sacrifices and much more interested in supporting technological solutions than regulatory ones. Although elements of these stereotypes ring true, the transatlantic landscape on this issue is changing, with an increasing recognition on both sides of the Atlantic that cooperation in this area is possible and critical. The question is, can it come together quickly enough to help forge a framework to replace the Kyoto Protocol before the agreement expires in 2012?

Europe's Track Record on Climate Change

Europe is rightly perceived as a global leader when it comes to climate change policy. The European Union was a central actor in the formulation and adoption of the UN Framework Convention on Climate Change (UNFCCC), the first intergovernmental framework for addressing the issue, from 1992 to 1994. Over the next three years, the EU again played a crucial role in negotiating the Kyoto Protocol.

Having come into force in 2005, the Kyoto Protocol sets mandatory and legally binding targets for participating industrialized countries to reduce their greenhouse gas emissions by an overall total of five percent from 1990 levels by 2012. The protocol incorporates a number of flexibility mechanisms to allow countries to meet their emissions reduction goals. These include national or regional emissions trading schemes and credits for sponsoring clean development projects or increasing carbon sinks, such as forests, either at home or in developing countries. By the time the Kyoto Protocol came into effect in early 2005, an internal EU Emissions Trading Scheme (ETS), the first international carbon-trading system, had already been set up. The ETS was established in October 2003 and came into operation in January 2005.[1]

The new Energy Policy for Europe (EPE), presented by the European Commission in January 2007 and approved by the European Council in the spring of 2007, makes it clear that addressing climate change is a top EU priority. The EPE commits the EU to independently reducing its greenhouse gas emissions by 20 percent by 2020 (compared to 1990), with a pledge for a 30 percent reduction, should other developed countries follow suit.[2] The Action Plan for the EPE calls for the EU, already the global pacesetter in renewable energy with, for example, nearly two-thirds of the world's wind energy market, to triple its use of renewable energy sources by 2020 to provide for 20 percent of overall consumption. The plan additionally sets out, albeit in general terms, new regulatory measures to improve energy efficiency, including by leveraging the internal European energy market while pointing out the importance of the use and development of energy-saving and low-carbon technologies.[3]

The awareness and concern of European policymakers regarding climate change are reinforced by European public opinion, with more than four-fifths of respondents to a Gallup poll released in March 2007 "aware that the way they consume and produce energy in their country has a negative impact on climate" and 87 percent either "very much concerned" or "to some degree concerned" about the effects of climate change and global warming.[4]

Within the overall goal of a 5 percent reduction in emissions by 2012, commitments under the Kyoto Protocol by individual countries vary. The then-15 EU member states and eight of the 10 central and eastern European states that joined the EU in 2004 and 2007 committed to the greatest reduction (8 percent) of any Kyoto protocol participants. In deciding how the overall 8 percent reduction could be achieved, the EU-15 states in turn distributed widely varying targets among themselves. On one end, Germany and Denmark each committed to a 21 percent decrease in greenhouse gas emissions, while Greece and Portugal have ceilings under which emissions may increase no more than 25 percent and 27 percent, respectively.[5]

At the National Level

Although the European continent deserves kudos for its ability to match its rhetoric on climate change to tangible action, not all European countries perceive the challenge in the same way. There are differences within Europe on how countries have chosen to address the challenge. The size and composition of national industrial and transportation sectors, for example, make for greenhouse gas emissions–level differences in the type and level of adjustments a national economy can tolerate in the name of protecting the environment.

Similarly, individual countries have their own unique mixture of energy dependencies, in terms of what their core sources are and where they come from. Thus, although an EU-wide consensus on the issue of climate change and the need to address it does indeed exist, there are also 27 underlying national perspectives, not to mention those of non-EU members such as Norway, on the importance of and best solution to the problem.

Germany is an important leader of the European charge on climate change policy and shoulders a substantial part of the burden. As Europe's largest economy, Germany's planned 21 percent reduction of carbon dioxide (CO_2) emissions by 2012 under the Kyoto Protocol accounts for nearly three-quarters of the overall 8 percent EU reduction. With the ambitious commitments of the EPE, Europe is faced with the challenge of achieving a further 12 percent reduction between 2012 and 2020, and with its weighted portion factored in, Germany is looking at a total 40 percent reduction in CO_2 generation over a 15-year period.

Achieving such an ambitious goal requires a nearly holistic approach, linking a gradual overhaul of the way German industry operates and a society-wide commitment to changes in everyday lifestyle. This philosophy means a strong emphasis on energy efficiency from the industrial level all the way down to household electrical appliances, including lamps and light bulbs. A nation-wide switch to such products, combined with greater use of renewable energy sources and possibly such controversial measures as a 130-kilometers-per-hour speed limit on the autobahn, which in some stretches has no limit at all, have the potential to drastically reduce German CO_2 emissions even beyond Kyoto Protocol targets, as research on new technologies for environmentally friendly CO_2-free power plants and fuels continues.[6]

Supplementing its own national vision, Germany has put considerable effort into garnering more international support for climate change initiatives at a regional and global level. Following the first-ever European government to include a Green party, the grand coalition government of Chancellor Angela Merkel opted to push climate change and environmental issues as a key part of its agenda during its 2007 presidencies of the EU and the Group of Eight (G-8). The focus, as witnessed during the G-8 summit in Heiligendamm, has been on turning global concern into action. In Merkel's eyes, recognizing the severity of the problem is only the first step. The next step, which she continues to pursue with great enthusiasm, is getting international actors, including the United States, China, and India, to agree to binding targets.

Under Prime Minister Tony Blair, the United Kingdom set about achieving its Kyoto Protocol commitment of a 12.5 percent emissions reduction by raising emissions standards for automakers, introducing a graduated auto tax based on fuel efficiency, and aiming to increase national use of bio-fuels. In March 2007, Blair also set a long-term national goal of a 60 percent CO_2 emissions reduction by 2050, which will be implemented through a series of five-year "carbon budgets."[7] Although it is debatable whether the United Kingdom is currently on pace to meet the target for 2050, it is on track to fulfill its Kyoto Protocol commitment.

Yet, the tactics of British climate change policy do split along party lines. The Labour Party stance emphasizes the importance of international agreements and the role of positive incentives to change behavior, such as lower taxes for environmentally friendly vehicles and buildings. The Conservatives, however, advocate managing the issue through higher national taxation on emissions-causing behavior, such as emissions taxes on airline passengers and airplane fuel. Although a consensus on the need to address climate change thus exists across the British political community, the governing party has a firm grasp on the reins of policy implementation in the British parliamentary system. Thus, Labour is free for the time being to work for emissions reduction within the strategy that the party has laid out. The opposition Conservatives, however, can be expected to continue to present alternative visions of how to combat climate change as they seek to differentiate their policies from those of Labour ahead of the general election expected in the spring of 2009.

In general, the French government and public are in line with the European consensus regarding the importance of countering climate change. Initially, however, France did oppose the EPE because its nuclear power industry, which provides for more than three-fourths of France's power needs, was excluded from national calculations of emissions responsibility. Once the EU agreed to take the French nuclear sector fully into account as a low-carbon energy source, France threw its complete political backing behind the EPE.

Today, France can boast that its emissions have actually slightly decreased even though the French assignment under the Kyoto Protocol was simply to maintain emissions at 1990 levels. France is expected to play an even larger role in Europe's climate policy with the arrival of President Nicolas Sarkozy, who has already made a number of pledges to strengthen his country's commitment to combating global warming. In his acceptance speech, Sarkozy also urged the United States to show more leadership on tackling global warming.[8]

Shortcomings and Divisions

Despite Europe's laudable focus on climate change at the regional and national levels, fruitful action has not always followed the rhetoric. Countries such as France, Sweden, and the United Kingdom are on track to meet or even exceed their Kyoto Protocol targets for CO_2 emissions reduction; others, such as Spain, Portugal, and Ireland, are badly off pace.[9]

Although the ETS carries real symbolic importance, the first phase (2005–2007) has witnessed a number of serious shortcomings. At the start of the ETS, many targets for major emitters were set too high, and the allocation of carbon credits was conducted far too generously. As a result, many large polluters were not required to reduce emissions, nor did they ever have to purchase credits because many were already sitting on a surplus. When news of the credit hoards became public in the spring of 2006, the ETS market price for carbon credits collapsed.

Furthermore, under the Kyoto Clean Development Mechanism, European companies can trade credits outside of Europe, paying large sums to cash-hungry polluters in the developing world, especially China and India, for their carbon credits. This influx of cash spurs expansion and new operations in the developing world, generating new emissions. Critics also argue that the money spent in the global emissions trading market—$30 billion in 2006—would have made a much greater difference had it instead been invested in emissions-reducing technologies.

In fact, the very existence of the market acts as a disincentive to many companies to change their polluting ways and move away from fossil fuels toward renewable energy sources and new technologies. With this first phase of the ETS admittedly a learning phase, the EU will need to apply its lessons vigorously to the second phase in 2008–2012, including setting stricter emissions limits and auctioning credits off, rather than handing them out.[10]

Beyond emissions trading, it is widely expected that Europe will continue to be a global leader in climate change policy. Yet, internal divisions on the continent do pose a number of potential problems. Intra-European east-west tensions flared during the European Council negotiations of the EPE. The economies of the new member states of central and eastern Europe are generally far more dependent on coal, gas, and CO_2-generating manufacturing than their western counterparts. Poland, for example, derives 90 percent of its energy from coal.[11]

These countries also have a much lower portion of renewable sources in their energy mix. Estonia's renewable energy sources account for 1 percent of energy sources, whereas Austria's account for 60 percent. These facts led the Czech Republic, Hungary, and Poland to oppose the EPE. They felt that the potential economic burdens of emissions reduction would be too great and the difficulty of meeting the renewable energy targets too extreme. In the resulting compromise, the implementation of the EPE will mean more permissive emissions targets for the new members and possibly west-to-east subsidies of technology and energy supply.[12]

Intriguingly, diversification of energy supply through the development of renewable, alternative energy sources would be of greatest benefit to the central and eastern EU members because of their current energy dependence on Russia. With many of these states highly dependent on Russian oil and gas for their energy needs, they find the affordability and availability of their energy sources increasingly vulnerable to the political aims of a Kremlin that boldly wields energy as an instrument of foreign policy. Thus, those countries with the least realistic capacity to diversify their energy and where economics still outweigh environmental concerns ironically have arguably the greatest political rationale for seeking alternative sources.

Energy dependence is also an issue for western Europe, with the EU-15 accounting for nearly 90 percent of an EU-25 gas market that relies on Russia for 24 percent of its supply.[13] In addition, western Europe stands at the end of a pipeline infrastructure that runs out of Russia through eastern Europe, making it subject to disruptions anywhere along the way. Yet, the western European countries are seemingly more inclined to diversify out of environmental rather than political concerns. One can only hope for the gradual evolution of a state of affairs wherein all member states find it in their interest to pursue the same ends of emissions reduction and energy diversification seriously, even if it would be for widely differing reasons.

The desirability and acceptability of nuclear power as a carbon-free energy source is another persistent topic of passionate debate in Europe. This issue has led to the creation of unlikely coalitions of interest, with pro–nuclear energy countries such as the Czech Republic, Finland, France, and Slovakia on one side and countries with broadly antinuclear publics, such as Austria, Denmark, and Ireland, on the other. Despite its appeal, some countries have already taken dramatic steps to reduce their reliance on nuclear energy. In a decision made under the Red-Green government of Chancellor Gerhard Schroeder, Germany plans to do away with its nuclear plants, which currently provide one-third of the country's power, by 2020. This power supply will have to be replaced mainly by coal, which already accounts for more than one-half of Germany's electricity.

Finally, business leaders have predictably expressed concern that the EPE will hurt competitiveness and that it is unclear how the targets can be met. In January 2007, the heads of BMW, DaimlerChrysler, and Volkswagen sent a joint letter to the European Commission complaining that the EPE would unduly burden and harm the German auto industry. Although German car-makers have introduced some new technologies that reduce auto emissions and are gradually introducing hybrid vehicles, the very foundation of German auto engineering and profit remains power and luxury. Manufacturers often argue that significantly lower emissions limits simply cannot be met by most of the car models currently made by companies such as Audi, BMW, Mercedes, and Porsche.

Europe's Pivotal Role

The many shortcomings of the Kyoto Protocol are well known. As is the nature of international agreements, there is no real enforcement mechanism to make the targets truly legally binding. Moreover, with the Kyoto Protocol limited to countries that are defined as industrialized, key developing countries are not covered. This factor led the United States, the world's largest generator of CO_2, to refuse to ratify the agreement. Whereas the EU appears likely to meet its emissions reduction targets by 2012, growth in greenhouse gas emissions remains strong among Brazil, Canada, China, India, and the United States.

The future of managing climate change nevertheless rests with the next round of international agreement. With the Kyoto Protocol set to expire in 2012, the details of a regime to replace and build on it remain unclear. Many look to the EPE as setting the bar for a new international accord on climate change, which means European credibility is now on the line. Even if Europe achieves its internal goals on greenhouse gas emissions, which it may very well do, it will only address a small portion of the problem.

With Europe's share of global pollution and energy consumption set to decline significantly over the next 30 years, the vision of the EU must now turn outward. In scenarios projecting decades ahead, the effects of climate change in Africa, the Middle East, South Asia, and elsewhere will radically impact Europe at home. As a result, European policymakers need to set a broad international negotiating strategy and get started on the far-ranging diplomacy needed to bring an aggressive post–Kyoto Protocol treaty into being. This means engaging the United States and focusing on developing an understanding with China and India to bring these key players into the fold. Europe must embrace its pivotal role and maintain its will to play it.

The U.S. Track Record

The global perception of the United States vis-à-vis climate change is that of a laggard. Given its size and large contribution to global emissions, many countries around the world believe the United States could and should be doing more to combat climate change. Data from the Pew 2007 Global Attitudes project show that, in 34 of the 37 countries surveyed, the United States is named by a majority or a clear plurality as the country "hurting the world's environment the most."[14] That sentiment is shared by many Americans as well, with one-third of those surveyed rating their own country as the world's biggest polluter. For almost three decades, small groups of Americans have worked to promote climate policies; but to date, the United States has shown very little leadership on this global challenge.

U.S. awareness of the potential problem of climate change first became widespread in the late 1980s. In 1986–1987, climate expert James Hansen began expounding the view that global warming due to the greenhouse effect was to become a serious issue over the next 20 years.[15] Hansen's congressional testimony on the topic in the summer of 1988—a summer featuring severe droughts and heat waves—catalyzed the attention of the media, environmental groups, and the scientific community.

Hansen's efforts, however, were countered in 1989 when corporations from big industry, notably petroleum and automobile companies, founded the Global Climate Coalition. The sole purpose of this coalition was to refute any suggestion that action against the greenhouse effect was needed. The coalition's views on the subject found a largely receptive audience within the administration of George H. W. Bush. Yet, just before leaving office, Bush did sign on to the UNFCCC to counter his bad environmental reputation. Of course, the UNFCCC was not binding in any way, which made it easier for groups such as the Global Climate Coalition to accept.

From the release of the first Intergovernmental Panel on Climate Change (IPCC) report in 1990 to the second report in 1995, international consensus on the severity of global warming gradually solidified and gained strength, particularly within the scientific community. Spearheaded by Vice President Al Gore, the Clinton administration pushed strongly for the Kyoto Protocol in 1997. Ironically, the United States fought to have a cap-and-trade system, something the United States first developed as part of the 1990 Clean Air Act, inserted into the protocol. In the face of mounting congressional opposition, however, the Clinton administration refused to sign it.

The conservative-led Congress, fueled by groups such as the Global Climate Coalition, argued that adherence to the Kyoto Protocol would raise U.S. energy and gas prices and give other countries, such as India and China, an unfair economic advantage. Following a Senate declaration passed 95–0 that Congress would not ratify the Kyoto Protocol unless developing countries were included, the Clinton administration did not bother submitting the treaty for ratification. Subsequently, the administration of George W. Bush has been pointedly skeptical on climate change, introducing no legislation to address it.[16] In advance of the G-8 summit in June 2007, during some tense negotiations on whether or not the summit communiqués would include binding targets, Bush did invite the top 15 emitters to attend a climate conference in Washington in late September 2007, following a UN meeting in New York on the same issue earlier that week.

The Washington meeting represented a significant breakthrough in the U.S. approach, as Bush acknowledged the importance of the issue, calling for the world's leading emissions producers to work together and set long-term emissions reduction goals in the context of a Kyoto Protocol successor treaty for 2012. Yet, the presentations made by Bush and Secretary of State Condoleezza Rice also served to reillustrate the wide gap between the thinking of policymakers in the United States and much of the rest of the international community, with the United States continuing to oppose binding international treaties that contain minimum requirements and penalties for noncompliance. Rather, without suggesting concrete numbers, the administration proposed that each country should determine its own goals, to be pursued voluntarily, and that developing countries bear as much responsibility as developed ones. From the perspective of European policymakers, this episode represents an important shift in a positive direction for the United States, while demonstrating that U.S. policy on climate change remains largely isolated and out of step with the worldview of Europe.[17]

Signs of Progress

Although the U.S. government has been dragging its feet on addressing climate change, there have been some positive shifts in U.S. policy in recent months. As one U.S. climate expert put it, "[T]he United States is lacing up its running shoes and preparing to join the race."[18] Scientific evidence, support from businesses and industry, the promotion of climate-friendly policies as an element of faith, state and local initiatives, and the Democratic majority in Congress are enabling progress on this contentious issue.

First, the science has become both stronger and more visible. The Third Assessment Report of the IPCC, published in 2001, provided the media, policymakers, the general public, and academics with much stronger evidence of a warming Earth, even though parts of the report were strongly contested. It also highlighted the role of greenhouse gas emissions. Perhaps most striking was the observable evidence, often through satellite imaging, that the report provided on the impacts of warming on the biosphere and on human societies. The Fourth Assessment Report in 2007 had an even greater impact, confirming with near certainty that carbon dioxide and other greenhouse gases from human activity are the main cause of global warming. Various extreme climate incidents, ranging from the European heat wave of 2003 to destructive storms such as Hurricane Katrina in 2005 to severe droughts and dwindling water resources in eastern Australia, have also provided skeptics in the United States and elsewhere with troubling firsthand accounts of the impact of warming on their societies.

Second, increasing numbers of business leaders have gradually come to consider action on global warming as imperative for the sake of energy security, economic growth and trade, and U.S. global leadership. Industry has also discovered that "going green," however vaguely defined, has considerable appeal among the public. Furthermore, businesses now see economic opportunities in new "green" technologies. Therefore, as the science of climate change advanced and grew in scope in the 1990s and the indirect and direct benefits of becoming environmentally friendly became more apparent, corporations began pulling out of the Global Climate Coalition, reducing the threat of the business veto on U.S. government action. In fact, many U.S. corporations are now serving as agents of change on this issue through efforts such as the U.S. Climate Action Partnership, which is a joint endeavor among large corporations such as Alcoa, BP America, Caterpillar, Duke Energy, DuPont, and GE and environmental groups to press for urgent action.

Third, many evangelical Christian groups have come to view combating climate change to be an obligation of faith. At first, these groups promoted individual responsibility to conserve.[19] Some prominent church leaders have recently taken their cause to Washington, however, urging the federal government to take a more aggressive stance in addressing the problem. In early 2006, for example, a coalition of evangelical leaders issued "An Evangelical Call to Action," asking Congress and the Bush administration to restrict CO_2 emissions.[20] That call triggered some fierce debates inside the evangelical community, but the increased attention on this issue among evangelicals and a wide array of other religious groups, including Roman Catholics and

Jews, has heightened awareness among the general public and caught the ears of Republican leaders in Congress and the administration.

Fourth, absent federal-level participation in the Kyoto Protocol, the United States has witnessed a number of innovative approaches at the local and state levels. The best known model is California, which has established a state Climate Action Team to devise greenhouse gas emissions-reduction strategies based on technology and regulation. Numerous businesses in California, including DuPont and IBM, have voluntarily agreed to state emissions-reduction targets. The state's motor vehicle plan aims to reduce car emissions, the greatest source of greenhouse gas emissions, by 30 percent by 2016. If the entire United States reduced its per capita emissions to California's level, U.S. pollution would be significantly lower than that outlined in the Kyoto Protocol.[21]

California is not the only state in the union showing muscle on this issue. Twelve other states have adopted caps on auto emissions, and 435 U.S. mayors, Republicans and Democrats alike, have signed the U.S. Mayors Climate Protection Agreement, committing their cities to meeting Kyoto Protocol emissions targets.[22] In another sign that climate change is no longer associated with those on the Left, Jon Huntsman Jr. (R), the governor of conservative Utah, has become a cap-and-trade advocate and committed himself to working with California on reducing carbon emissions. Dan Schnur, a Republican political analyst, called that shift "the energy equivalent of Nixon going to China."[23]

Finally, the Democratic takeover of Congress in 2006 has also advanced climate change debates in Washington. According to a recent Zogby International postelection survey, one-half of Americans who voted in the 2006 midterm elections said concern about global warming made a difference in whom they supported.[24] A handful of global warming skeptics lost influential posts in that political transition, including the chairman of the Senate Environment and Public Works Committee, James Inhofe (R-Okla.), who has called global warming "the greatest hoax ever perpetrated on the American people."[25] He was replaced as committee chair by Senator Barbara Boxer (D-Calif.), an outspoken critic of the Bush administration, particularly on climate issues.

To date, however, concrete progress in Congress on climate change has been slow. Mandates for more energy efficiency in federal buildings and a $2 million program to measure greenhouse gas emissions better have been approved, but major climate legislation has yet to surface. Democrats blame the White House and continuing opposition from industry but claim that they will push for a major bill in late 2007 to reduce emissions.

Many Democrats and some Republicans, including Senators John Warner (Va.) and John McCain (Ariz.), now support a cap-and-trade system that would allow those industries that fall under a mandated emissions cap to trade credits to those that do not.[26] Some hope that as Bush looks to build a legacy that reaches beyond Iraq and the war on terrorism, he will become increasingly accommodating on adopting mandatory controls. Environmentalists are also hopeful that the 2008 presidential election will bring increased attention to climate issues, as many of the presidential candidates appear to be making climate a core part of their political platforms.

Evolving Public Opinion

These scientific, business, political, and religious shifts have been accompanied by shifts in public opinion. According to a survey conducted in February 2007, the percentage of Americans who say global warming is a serious problem has risen to 83 percent from 70 percent in 2004.[27] Some argue that the success of Al Gore's *An Inconvenient Truth*, which won the Oscar award for best documentary in 2007, has also heightened awareness of the dangers of climate change.

A number of skeptics, however, continue to question the science and oppose policy changes regarding climate change. Some claim that climate change is not taking place at all and that warming is simply a natural cycle of change that is not due to human activity. If Hurricane Katrina forced some skeptics to rethink their assumptions about the severity of the threat, the unusually cold winter in 2006–2007 was cited as further evidence of the uncertainty of the problem. A sizeable portion of the U.S. population continues to believe that changing human behavior will have no effect on the process whatsoever. Instead, humans must simply adapt to changing circumstances.

Caught between climate change advocates and the skeptics are those that admit that warming is occurring but oppose any initiative that might hurt the U.S. economy. These individuals, recognizing that the United States is the world's largest per-capita source of greenhouse gases, argue that the United States will pay the highest price for change. If the United States were to put in place a cap-and-trade system, for example, operating costs for U.S. firms would rise, making imported goods, especially from India and China, even more competitive and possibly driving U.S. companies out of business. Any solution must therefore include China and India.

Bridging the Gap

The challenge for the United States in the coming years will be to find a way to bridge the gaps between those that support mandatory cap-and-trade programs and those advocating alternative solutions, such as voluntary targets, while persuading as many skeptics as possible to alter their views on the science. This will be difficult for many reasons. First, time is short. With the Kyoto Protocol expiring in 2012, the United States and the broader international community do not have much time to begin the arduous task of reaching a global consensus on a post–Kyoto Protocol agreement. Many believe that, at the very latest, negotiations would need to start in 2009 as a new U.S. president will be coming into office. Yet, climate experts also often concede that the United States is unlikely to sign an international treaty before domestic legislation is in place, which will certainly take more time than the pending Kyoto Protocol deadline provides.

Second, although U.S. public concern about this issue appears to be growing, Americans, even those that support the science, simply do not feel the same sense of urgency as others around the world. A common but false assumption is that the impact of climate change will spare the industrialized world, especially the United States, Europe, and Australia.[28] This makes building and maintaining the required momentum on this issue perhaps more challenging on U.S. soil than in other corners of the world.

In reality, a U.S. commitment to future climate change regimes will be essential to the regimes' success. As the world's greatest producer of greenhouse gases and the world's largest consumer of energy, any solution to this challenge must include the United States. Without it, any hope of bringing China and India on board is futile.

Crafting a Transatlantic Agenda

Transatlantic cooperation on the issue of climate change over the last two decades and outside the climate community has been quite limited. It would be unfair, however, to assume that no progress has been made. Small-scale but ambitious initiatives, often stemming from city-to-city or state-to-state partnerships, are spreading across Europe and the United States at a fairly rapid pace.[29] Both sides of the Atlantic appear to be moving away from their disparate steadfast convictions on the best means to address climate change. Political elites are increasingly promoting a hybrid approach that will draw on technological advances and some international regulation. Despite such achievements, Europe and the United States have much more to do in and out of government to tackle the problem, especially if they have hopes of launching a major effort for an effective successor to the Kyoto Protocol in any form.

First and foremost, Europeans will need to accept that the most viable post–Kyoto Protocol regime in the eyes of Americans will probably be the one that resembles the protocol the least. Americans might be warming up to the idea of caps, but binding international limits are unlikely to attract the support of the U.S. government, regardless of which presidential candidate wins the next election. William Pizer, a senior fellow at Resources for the Future, outlines five characteristics of a future climate regime that would win the support of a wide variety of policymakers, especially those in the United States: it must defer to domestic interests, need not focus on all countries, must include technology development, must engage the developing countries, and must stress evaluating action after the fact.[30]

On the other side of the Atlantic, Americans need to find ways to capitalize on the momentum that is starting to build on this issue. One of the unique ways to do this is to pull non–climate change communities into the debate to make this challenge a key component of U.S. foreign policy. To date, a handful of studies have worked to bridge the gap between the national security and climate change communities so that global warming receives the same attention that other global challenges receive. Climate change will have major ramifications for migration, force posturing, failed states, and federal resource allocation. The sooner national governments treat climate change as a national security issue, the faster it will receive the intellectual and financial resources it merits.

The two sides of the Atlantic must also jointly examine the economic implications of a failure to act. Most American skeptics argue that the United States will risk economic damage by cutting its carbon emissions, particularly if others do not follow suit. Others, such as Sir Nicholas Stern, author of the infamous "Stern Review on the Economics of Climate Change," make the exact opposite point, that the economic costs of acting on global warming are far lower than the cost of inaction.[31] Although Stern's report has been criticized for its methodology (using an incorrect discount rate in its calculations), its overarching thesis merits more discussion and research, particularly if Europeans have hopes of shrinking the pool of U.S. skeptics.

Any viable solution to the challenge of climate change rests on the ability of Europe and the United States to combine their strengths, experiences, and positions into a post–Kyoto Protocol framework. Ultimately, the United States will eventually need to agree to some form of emissions caps. Because that appears unlikely in the remaining months of the Bush administration, Europeans will need to focus on short- and medium-term strategies. In the coming months, Europeans and Americans should work to increase the tempo of their dialogue, bring in new communities, continue to dissuade the skeptics, and capitalize on the fact that public opinion is primed for action. In the medium term, Europeans should be preparing to engage the next U.S. president on this issue, with the hope of putting it at the top of the transatlantic agenda within the first 100 days in office.

NOTES

1. Peter Goldmark and Ernst von Weizsäcker, "The Decarbonization Challenge: U.S. and European Perspectives on Climate Change," *Bertelsmann Stiftung Transatlantic Thinkers Paper Series*, pt. 2 (March 7, 2007), p. 6.

2. "Brussels European Council, 8/9 March 2007: Presidency Conclusions," 7224/1/07 Rev. 1, May 2, 2007, p. 12, http://www.consilium.europa.eu/ueDocs/cms_Data/docs/pressData/en/ec/93135.pdf.

3. European Commission, "Energy for a Changing World," March 2007, http://ec.europa.eu/dgs/energy_transport/index_en.html.

4. Gallup Organization, "Attitudes on Issues Related to EU Energy Policy," *Flash Eurobarometer*, no. 206a (March 2007), http://ec.europa.eu/public_opinion/flash/fl206a_en.pdf.

5. "Countries Included in Annex B to the Kyoto Protocol and Their Emissions Targets," UN Framework Convention on Climate Change (UNFCCC), http://unfccc.int/kyoto_protocol/background/items/3145.php; "A Summary of the Kyoto Protocol," UNFCCC, http://unfccc.int/kyoto_protocol/background/items/2879.php.

6. "Europa muss eine vorreiterrolle haben" [Europe must play a pioneering role], *Sueddeutsche Zeitung*, March 5, 2007, http://www.sueddeutsche.de/deutschland/artikel/331/104227/; "Der Klimawandel sollte Thema in UN-Sicherheitsrat werden" [Politics is avoiding the argument with industry], *Sueddeutsche Zeitung*, March 3, 2007, http://www.sueddeutsche.de/wissen/artikel/246/104142.

7. George Monbiot, "Just a Lot of Hot Air," *Guardian*, March 5, 2007, http://www.guardian.co.uk/g2/story/0,,2026711,00.html.

8. For text, see http://worldnews.about.com/od/presidentialelection/a/sarkozy_speech.htm.

9. "From Free Trade to Deep Integration," *EU Monitor*, no. 45 (April 18, 2007), p. 31, http://www.dbresearch.com/PROD/DBR_INTERNET_EN-PROD/PROD0000000000209719.pdf.

10. Goldmark and Weizsäcker, "Decarbonization Challenge"; Emily Flynn Vencat, "The Carbon Folly," *Newsweek*, March 12, 2007, http://www.msnbc.msn.com/id/17435875/site/newsweek/.

11. Dan Bilefsky, "EU Drafts Compromise to Fight Climate Change," *International Herald Tribune*, March 10, 2007, http://www.iht.com/articles/2007/03/09/news/eu.php.

12. Ibid.; "Green Grind," *Times* (London), March 10, 2007, http://www.timesonline.co.uk/tol/comment/leading_article/article1494964.ece.

13. "Statistics 2005," *Eurogas*, http://www.eurogas.org/uploaded/statistics%202005.pdf.

14. Pew Research Center, "34 Nations Call U.S. Biggest Threat to Environment," *Daily Number*, http://pewresearch.org/databank/dailynumber/?NumberID=343.

15. Spencer Weart, "The Public and Climate Change," July 2007, http://www.aip.org/history/climate/public2.htm.

16. Spencer Weart, "The Discovery of Global Warming," July 2007, http://www.aip.org/history/climate/index.html.

17. "Warming to the Environment," *Economist*, September 28, 2007, http://www.economist.com/daily/news/displaystory.cfm?story_id=9890672&top_story=1; Fiona Harvey and Andrew Ward, "Bush Calls for Fresh Global Approach to Climate Change," *Financial Times*, September 29, 2007, http://www.ft.com/cms/s/0/34a19ce6-6e64-11dc-b818-0000779fd2ac.html.

18. Peter Goldmark, "Time to Act Together: How Europe and the United States Can Collaborate on Climate Change and Energy Independence" (presentation, German Marshall Fund, Washington, D.C., May 24, 2007).

19. Karen Breslau and Martha Brant, "God's Green Soldiers," *Newsweek*, February 13, 2006, http://www.msnbc.msn.com/id/11179145/site/newsweek.

20. Ibid.

21. "California's Program to Reduce the Impacts of Global Warming: Questions and Answers," http://www.climatechange.ca.gov/climate_action_team/factsheets/2005-06_CAT_Q+A.PDF (fact sheet).

22. Anne Underwood, "Mayors Take the Lead," *Newsweek*, April 16, 2007, http://www.msnbc.msn.com/id/17996836/site/newsweek/.

23. Michael Gardner, "Governor Acquires Unlikely Ally in Regional Global Warming Fight," Copley News Service, May 20, 2007, http://www.signonsandiego.com/news/politics/20070520-9999-ln20utah.html.

24. Zogby International, "Zogby Post-Election Poll: Dems Gained From Global Warming Debate," November 16, 2006, http://www.zogby.com/news/ReadNews.dbm?ID=1194.

25. "Climate Change Update—Senate Floor Statement by U.S. Sen. James M. Inhofe (R-Okla.)," January 4, 2005, http://inhofe.senate.gov/pressreleases/climateupdate.htm.

26. Frank Davies, "Congress Stymied on Global Warming Bills," *San Jose Mercury News*, July 23, 2007, http://www.mercurynews.com/lifestyle/ci_6441203.

27. Global Strategy Group, "2007 Environment Survey: Key Findings," March 5, 2007, http://www.loe.org/images/070316/yalepole.doc.

28. See Jay Gulledge, "Three Plausible Scenarios of Future Climate Change for Security Risk Assessment" (working paper, CSIS Climate Security Project, July 12, 2007), pp. 4–5.

29. See "Partnership on Global Climate Change Action Between the Federal Republic of Germany and the State of Florida," http://theclimategroup.org/assets/resources/partnership_germany.pdf.

30. William A. Pizer, "A U.S. Perspective on Future Climate Regimes," *Resources for the Future Discussion Paper*, no. RFF DP 0704 (February 2007), http://www.rff.org/Documents/RFF-DP-07-04.pdf.

31. "Time for Global Action on Climate Change," *Financial Times*, December 29, 2006. http://www.ft.com/cms/s/a3b0b376-96e0-11db-8ba1-0000779e2340,_i_email=y.html.

Kelly Sims Gallagher

China Needs Help with Climate Change

This year, China will have become the largest aggregate emitter of greenhouse gases in the world, surpassing the United States for the first time since records have been kept. America will be the largest per-capita emitter and the second-largest aggregate emitter. These two countries have the unique ability to make or break the global climate change problem.

While it has long been recognized that China would be a pivotal nation in terms of dealing with climate change, the rate of growth of greenhouse gas emissions in China has been breathtaking, even to the Chinese themselves. At a minimum, it is now imperative to find incentives and mechanisms to induce China to reduce the growth of its emissions in the near term and, ultimately, to significantly reduce emissions below current levels.

It is also imperative to assist China in this endeavor. Indeed, increased cooperation between Washington and Beijing is probably necessary if the climate change threat is to be effectively addressed. This will require that the two countries stop using each other as an excuse for inaction and instead form a partnership to ameliorate global warming.

Based on China and America's shared challenges of reducing greenhouse gas emissions and their economies' reliance on coal, a climate partnership should include high-level policy coordination and the establishment of a fund to provide low-cost financing for low-carbon projects in both countries. It should include capacity-building measures to help enhance the effectiveness of China's institutions, policies, and enforcement measures to reduce emissions. And it should include a joint innovation initiative to promote precommercial research, development, and demonstration of low-carbon technologies, particularly focused on carbon capture and storage, renewable energy, and energy efficiency technologies.

A Big-Time Emitter

China's contribution to the gases that are warming the world by trapping heat in the atmosphere is a direct result of the country's astonishingly rapid economic growth and rising demand for energy. Along with the United States, China is now one of the world's two largest energy producers and consumers. In terms of oil and electricity consumption, the People's Republic remains somewhat behind the United States. It consumes two-thirds as much commercial energy as

America does, consumes one-third as much oil, imports one-third as much petroleum (although China's oil import growth rate has been much faster in recent years), and uses two-thirds as much electricity.

But when it comes to coal, the picture is different. China consumes twice as much coal as does the United States, though it has only 13 percent of the world's coal reserves, compared with 27 percent for the United States. Coal absolutely dominates the energy picture in China, accounting for 70 percent of its commercial energy supply. In 2006, China reportedly consumed 2.8 billion metric tons of coal, mostly for power plants and industry. By comparison, the United States consumed 1.3 billion metric tons, nearly all of which was used by power plants. In the United States, coal accounts for one-third of the total energy supply and half the country's electricity generation.

The growth in China's power sector has been almost unbelievably fast. Between 2005 and 2006, for example, electricity capacity increased by about 20 percent, from 517 gigawatts (GW) to 622 GW, nearly all of which was coal-fired. At this growth rate, China's total power sector capacity increased by double every three and a half years.

The transportation sector at this point is a relatively small consumer of energy in China, accounting for less than 10 percent of overall consumption. China has adopted new fuel-efficiency standards for passenger cars and tax policies for fuel consumption that should help to avoid a big increase in oil consumption. But the potential market for automobiles in China is huge. Fuel efficiency standards will need to be further strengthened and complementary measures introduced to reduce demand for cars if China is to avoid becoming the biggest oil-consuming country in the world.

As a result of all this industrial development, the growth in China's greenhouse emissions has been considerable. According to the latest official data from America's Oak Ridge National Laboratory, China in 2004 accounted for approximately 18 percent of the world's total carbon dioxide emissions from fossil fuel–burning and cement production, as compared with 22 percent for the United States. As of 2007, we now know that China has caught up to the United States. (China's per-capita emissions, on the other hand, are only one-fifth those of the United States.)

Both countries have signed and ratified the United Nations Framework Convention on Climate Change. Both have also signed the Kyoto Protocol, but only China has ratified it. At the central government level, neither country has binding policies aimed specifically at reducing greenhouse gas emissions, although both have efficiency-oriented policies that have the benefit of reducing carbon emissions.

In June, the Chinese government for the first time issued a specific package of voluntary measures aimed at cutting greenhouse gas emissions;

several sets of voluntary policies have been promoted as well by the past three presidential administrations in the United States. At the state and local levels, many US governmental entities have passed regulations to reduce carbon dioxide emissions. This is not true of China's provinces and localities, where many local governmental bodies ignore or flout even the most basic energy-efficiency policies.

Energy Challenges

China's energy-related challenges are many. They include the country's need for energy to sustain economic growth, its increasing dependency on foreign oil and gas, its aspiration to provide modern forms of energy to the poor, its increasingly severe urban air pollution, and its already massive acid deposition (dispersed in rain or deposited on surfaces). This is not to dismiss growing domestic and international concerns about global climate change or the need for affordable, advanced energy technologies to address all of these challenges. However, as China begins to consider how to address global warming, it will be simultaneously weighing the competing energy-related challenges, all of which are seen as more pressing by the Chinese government today.

Economically, China's growing energy consumption presents both challenges and opportunities. One concern is that as China imports greater amounts of energy, prices of these commodities could rise until supply catches up, and price spikes will be especially likely during supply disruptions. At the same time, there is a pressing need simply to supply enough energy, especially in the form of electricity, to meet the very high demand created by Chinese industry. The power sector has been through several boom-and-bust cycles because, when electricity shortages emerge, the power industry responds by adding huge quantities of new capacity as fast as it can. This causes oversupply for a time until the economy catches up and a new shortage emerges. The shortages have been harmful to the Chinese economy intermittently, whenever electricity has been rationed and factories have been forced to shut down.

On the opportunity side, the Chinese energy sector is already large and is growing rapidly, so it represents a remarkable market opportunity for both Chinese and foreign energy services companies. In 2006 alone, China installed 101 GW of new power capacity, 90 GW of which was coal-fired. To put this astounding number in perspective, India's entire electricity system, as of 2004, was 131 GW.

Despite the perception that China has become an industrial powerhouse, 135 million Chinese still live in absolute poverty (on less than $1 a day) and millions more remain just above that arbitrary poverty divide, so there is a tremendous imperative to foster economic development and high growth rates. In addition, the need to provide better energy services to the poor—to improve the quality of life for those still reliant on traditional forms of energy such as charcoal, crop wastes, and dung—remains very much a preoccupation of the Chinese government. Because of the country's gigantic population, China's total energy consumption and greenhouse gas emissions would still be large even if everyone consumed a very small amount of energy.

Since the beginning of the twenty-first century, China has emerged as a major consumer of oil, and there is strong potential for China to become a major natural gas consumer as well, especially when it gets serious about reducing its greenhouse gas emissions. China became a net importer of oil in the mid-1990s. It is now the world's second-largest consumer of oil, and the third-largest oil importer.

About half of China's oil imports come from the Middle East. However, Angola became its largest supplier in 2006, and China has invested heavily in energy resources in Africa. Although there have been several new oil discoveries in China recently, reserves there are on the decline. China has relatively few natural gas reserves, and therefore uses virtually no natural gas in its power sector. It is trying to increase production of coal-bed methane. If China decides to increase its use of natural gas, it will likely import it through liquid natural gas import terminals on the coast or by overland pipeline from Central Asia or Russia. In any event, China's long-term energy security depends not only on its having sufficient supplies of energy to sustain its rapid economic growth, but also on its ability to manage the growth in energy demand. Unmanaged demand, it is becoming clear, will cause intolerable environmental damage.

Coal is at the heart of many of China's environmental woes. Particulate matter from coal is a major air pollutant. Sulfur dioxide emissions from coal combustion, the source of most acid deposition, rose 27 percent between 2001 and 2005. Coal is also the most carbon-intensive of the fossil fuels, and it is China's main source of energy. It accounts for four-fifths of China's CO_2 emissions, most of which come from the industrial and electricity sectors. As of 2000, electricity accounted for 52 percent of China's CO_2 emissions (and 75 percent of China's electricity is consumed by industry), while cement production accounted for 28 percent, iron and steel production for 9 percent, and transportation for 8 percent. Already today, annual emissions from Chinese coal are three times as great as US emissions from transportation, although US transportation emissions are 17 times higher than Chinese transportation emissions.

The possible impact of climate change on China itself has not been studied as well as the possible impact on the United States, but it is clear that we could see very adverse effects on China's water supply, agriculture, and sea levels. Between 1956 and 2000, precipitation decreased 50–120 millimeters per year along the northern Yellow River, an already arid region. During the same period, precipitation increased 60–130 millimeters per year along the southern Yangtze River, an area that has long been plagued by heavy flooding. The mountain glaciers on the Tibetan plateau are receding rapidly, which carries major implications for fresh water supply in already water-stressed northern China. The glacier in the Tianshan Mountains that is the source of the Urumqi River, for example, shrank 11.3 percent between 1962 and 2001. Meanwhile, a sea level rise of 30 centimeters would cause massive coastal inundation. Chinese analysts have estimated this would cause the equivalent of $7.5 billion in economic losses to the Pearl River Delta area, $1.3 billion for the Yangtze Delta area, and $6.9 billion for the Yellow River Delta (including the Bohai Sea).

The Chinese Approach

China has already taken important steps toward moderating future growth in greenhouse gas emissions, largely through energy efficiency and renewable energy measures. Energy intensity (the amount of energy used to generate economic activity, usually calculated as total energy consumption divided by GDP) dramatically declined in China from 1980 to 2004. This means that China's overall energy efficiency improved and that significant growth in greenhouse gas emissions was avoided. Despite this improvement, however, China's overall energy efficiency remains considerably lower than most industrialized countries' and, unfortunately, it appears to have worsened in the past two years.

The central government has set forth some aggressive policies and targets for energy efficiency for the coming years. Because so much of China's energy is derived from coal, efficiency measures that reduce coal combustion will greatly help to reduce greenhouse gas emissions. China's 11th Five-Year Plan (2006–2010) called for a 20 percent reduction in energy intensity by 2010. This goal is already proving hard to achieve—last year's efficiency improvements fell short of the plan's objective, and in 2005 China's energy intensity actually *increased* slightly. Even so, the energy intensity target was at the heart of the climate change plan that the Chinese government announced in June 2007 in advance of the Group of Eight summit. By improving thermal efficiency, Beijing estimated that it could reduce China's carbon dioxide emissions by a total of 110 million tons by 2010.

The Chinese government issued its first fuel efficiency standards for passenger cars in 2005, and they will be strengthened in 2008. China also has implemented vehicle excise taxes so that the purchase of a car or sport utility vehicle with a big engine requires a much higher tax payment than does the purchase of a car with a small, energy-efficient engine. In the case of both fuel efficiency standards and excise taxes, China's policies are more stringent than comparable ones in the United States. And Beijing has adopted strong efficiency standards for appliances as well. The China Energy Group at Lawrence Berkeley National Laboratory estimates that, by 2010, those standards will have reduced carbon dioxide emissions in China by 40 million tons. By comparison, the US appliance standards will have saved 50 million tons of CO_2 by 2010.

The Chinese government has also aggressively promoted low-carbon energy supply options, especially renewable energy, hydropower, and nuclear energy. If you exclude large hydropower but include small hydropower, China has twice as much installed renewable power capacity as the United States. In fact, as of 2005, China led the world in total installed renewable energy capacity at 42 GW, compared to 23 GW in the United States. China accounts for 63 percent of the solar hot water capacity in the world, and as of 2005 it had installed 1.3 GW of wind capacity.

China in 2005 enacted a Renewable Energy Law that requires grid operators to purchase electricity from renewable generators. It sets a target of 10 percent of electric power generation capacity coming from renewable energy sources by 2010 (not including large hydro). By expanding bioenergy, solar, wind, geothermal, and tidal energy sources, the government estimates it can reduce CO_2 emissions another 90 million tons by 2010. The government has exploited its large hydropower resources at some social and ecological cost, such as forced relocations of communities, loss of ecosystems, and decreased river flow, but it believes it has substantial scope for increasing hydropower further still. In fact, it estimated this year that it could achieve a reduction of 500 million tons of carbon dioxide by 2010 with increased hydropower.

Compared with coal and hydro, China has scarcely begun its expansion of nuclear power. By 2020, the government plans to have built 40 GW of new nuclear power plants. But even if Beijing meets that goal, the 40 GW would only account for about 4 percent of the total electric capacity anticipated to exist by then.

The Chinese government is also devoting a substantial portion of its R&D dollars to the research, development, and demonstration of advanced energy technologies. During the period covered by the 11th Five-Year Plan, the Ministry of Science and Technology's budget for energy research, development, and demonstration is about 3.5 billion yuan (about $466 million). The budget for advanced coal technology is about 700 million yuan (about $93 million). Five coal co-production and gasification demonstration projects are planned for the next five years, in collaboration with Chinese industry. If all are actually built, there will be more coal gasification and co-production plants in China than in the United States.

Powered by Coal

Despite all of the Chinese government's laudable efforts to improve energy efficiency and expand the use of low-carbon energy sources such as renewable energy, nuclear power, and hydroelectric power, China's carbon dioxide emissions grew at the worrying rate of 9 percent per year from 1999 to 2004. At this rate, the Chinese will double emissions by 2009. The main drivers of this growth are heavy reliance on coal using conventional technologies, the still relatively poor efficiency of most power-plant technologies, and the weakness of government institutions when it comes to implementing and enforcing policies. . . .

Moral and Practical

Chinese leaders increasingly are expressing concern about the effects of global warming on China itself, while also worrying about the general deterioration of China's air and water quality. As international pressure builds because of China's new status as the largest overall emitter, and as scientific evidence accumulates regarding China's own vulnerability to climate change, the government in Beijing likely will be looking for help and ideas for how to reduce emissions. As a matter of morality, the United States would do well to acknowledge that it put the largest portion of greenhouse gases into the atmosphere during the twentieth century, just as China will be the dominant emitter during the twenty-first century, and so it has an obligation to help China, still very much a developing country, confront this challenge.

Similarly, the pragmatic response would be to acknowledge that, since the two countries are the world's biggest emitters, the United States might as well form a partnership with China to develop creative ideas, technologies, and policies for preventing dangerous climate change in ways that are designed to produce mutual benefits. Such a partnership could help produce innovative low-carbon technologies for public and private benefit, wider and more open markets for advanced energy technologies, investment opportunities for Wall Street, and a more effective governance system in China. Catastrophic climate change might still be avoided if, but only if, the United States and China both act in time to reduce their emissions.

Credits